The Art of Thinking

A Guide to Critical and Creative Thought

NINTH EDITION

Vincent Ryan Ruggiero

SUNY Delhi College (Emeritus)

Longman
New York   San Francisco   Boston
London   Toronto   Sydney   Tokyo   Singapore   Madrid
Mexico City   Munich   Paris   Cape Town   Hong Kong   Montreal

To all my children, with a love that transcends time
and trouble

Senior Sponsoring Editor: Virginia L. Blanford
Senior Marketing Manager: Sandra McGuire
Production Manager: Kathy Sleys
Creative Director: Jayne Conte
Cover Design: Bruce Kenselaar
Cover Illustration/Photo: Getty Images
Full-Service Project Management/Composition: Yasmeen Neelofar/GGS Book Services PMG
Printer/Binder: R.R. Donnelley & Sons, Inc.

For permission to use copyrighted material, grateful acknowledgment is made
to the copyright holders on pp. 273–277, which are hereby made part of this
copyright page.

Library of Congress Cataloging-in-Publication Data
Ruggiero, Vincent Ryan.
    The art of thinking : a guide to critical and creative thought / Vincent Ryan
Ruggiero. — 9th ed.
        p. cm.
    Includes index.
    ISBN-13: 978-0-205-66833-5
    ISBN-10: 0-205-66833-X
    1. Critical thinking.   2. Creative thinking.   3. Thought and thinking—
Problems, exercises, etc. I. Title.
    BF441.R84 2009
    153.4'2—dc22   2008032714

ISBN 13: 978-0-205-66833-5
ISBN 10:   0-205-66833-X

    5 6 7 8 9 10—DOH—11 10

Longman
is an imprint of

www.pearsonhighered.com

Brief Contents

PART I   BE AWARE 1

1   Developing Your Thinking: An Overview 3

2   Establish a Foundation 25

3   Broaden Your Perspective 50

4   Be a Critical Reader, Listener, and Viewer 67

PART II   BE CREATIVE 95

5   The Creative Process 97

6   Search for Challenges 112

7   Express the Problem or Issue 127

8   Investigate the Problem or Issue 140

9   Produce Ideas 164

PART III   BE CRITICAL 183

10   The Role of Criticism 185

11   Refine Your Solution to the Problem 197

12   Evaluate Your Argument on the Issue 210

13   Refine Your Resolution of the Issue 228

PART IV   COMMUNICATE YOUR IDEAS 237

14   Persuading Others 239

15   Writing and Speaking Effectively 252

Thinking is an art, with its own purposes, standards, principles, rules, strategies, and precautions. And it is an art well worth learning, for every important thing we do is affected by our habits of mind.

Contents

To the Instructor Xiii

PART I **BE AWARE 1**

1 Developing Your Thinking: An Overview 3
What Is Thinking? 4
The Importance of Thinking 5
Brain and Mind at Work 6
   The Production Phase 7   *The Judgment Phase 7*
Good Thinking Is a Habit 8
The Structure of This Book 8
Getting the Most from Your Efforts 9
Using Feelings to Advantage 10
Learning to Concentrate 11
Coping with Frustration 11
Making Discussion Meaningful 12
   Whenever Possible, Prepare in Advance 13
   Set Reasonable Expectations 13
   Leave Egotism and Personal Agendas at the Door 13
   Contribute But Don't Dominate 13
   Avoid Distracting Speech Mannerisms 13
   Listen Actively 14   *Judge Ideas Responsibly 14*
   Resist the Urge to Shout or Interrupt 14
Preliminary Thinking Strategies 14
Sample Exercises and Responses 17
 Warm-Up Exercises 18

Applications 19
Issue for Extended Analysis 21

2   Establish a Foundation   25

Free Will versus Determinism 26
What Is Truth? 27
What Is Knowing? 28
Ways of Knowing 30
   Experience 30   *Observation 31*
   Report 31
The Problem of Remembering 32
What Are Opinions? 34
   Expressions of Taste 34   *Expressions of Judgment 34*
Understanding Cause and Effect 35
Debating Moral Questions 40
The Basis of Moral Judgment 41
Dealing with Dilemmas 44
   Warm-Up Exercises 44
   Applications 45
   Issue for Extended Analysis 47

3   Broaden Your Perspective   50

Becoming an Individual 52
Habits That Hinder Thinking 54
   The Mine-Is-Better Habit 54   *Face Saving 55*
   Resistance to Change 56   *Conformity 58*
   Stereotyping 59   *Self-Deception 60*
Overcoming Bad Habits 61
   Warm-Up Exercises 62
   Applications 62
   Issue for Extended Analysis 64

4   Be a Critical Reader, Listener, and Viewer   67

Critical Evaluation Defined 68
Making Important Distinctions 69
   The Distinction Between the Person and the Idea 69
   *The Distinction Between Matters of Taste and Matters of
   Judgment 69*

The Distinction Between Fact and Interpretation 70

The Distinction Between Literal and Ironic Statements 71

The Distinction Between an Idea's Validity and the Quality of Its Expression 72

The Distinction Between Language and Reality 72

A Strategy for Critical Reading 73

Step 1: Skim the Work 73

Step 2: Reflect on Your Views 74

Step 3: Read the Work 74

Step 4: Evaluate What You Read 75

Step 5: Express Your Judgment 76

A Sample Evaluation and Judgment 77

A Strategy for Critical Listening 79

Step 1: Set Aside Preconceptions 80

Step 2: Focus on the Message 80

Step 3: Identify Key Assertions and Supporting Information 81

Steps 4 and 5: Evaluate the Message and Express Your Judgment 81

A Strategy for Critical Viewing 81

Warm-Up Exercises 83

Applications 83

Issue for Extended Analysis 91

PART II **BE CREATIVE 95**

5 **The Creative Process 97**

Key Facts About Creativity 98

Characteristics of Creative People 100

Applying Creativity to Problems and Issues 102

Taking a Novel Approach 102

Devising or Modifying a Process or System 102

Inventing a New Product or Service 103

Finding New Uses for Existing Things 103

Improving Things 104

Inventing or Redefining a Concept 104

Stages in the Creative Process 105

    The First Stage: Searching for Challenges 105

    The Second Stage: Expressing the Problem or Issue 105

    The Third Stage: Investigating the Problem or Issue 106

    The Fourth Stage: Producing Ideas 106

  Warm-Up Exercises 107

  Applications 107

  Issue for Extended Analysis 108

6 Search for Challenges 112

The Importance of Curiosity 113

How Curiosity Is Lost 115

Regaining Your Curiosity 115

Six Helpful Techniques 116

    Be Observant 116

    Look for the Imperfections in Things 118

    Note Your Own and Others' Dissatisfactions 118

    Search for Causes 119

    Be Sensitive to Implications 120

    Recognize the Opportunity in Controversy 120

Warm-Up Exercises 121

Applications 122

Issue for Extended Analysis 123

7 Express the Problem or Issue 127

Distinguishing Problems from Issues 128

Expressing Problems 128

Expressing Issues 129

When Problems Become Issues 130

Guidelines for Expressing Problems and Issues 131

Benefits of Careful Expression 131

    It Helps You Move Beyond the Familiar and Habitual 131

    It Keeps Your Thinking Flexible 131

    It Opens Many Lines of Thought 132

A Sample Problem 133

A Sample Issue 134

  Warm-Up Exercises 135

Applications 136
Issue for Extended Analysis 137

8 Investigate the Problem or Issue 140

What to Look For 141

Eyewitness Testimony 141   *Unpublished Report 142*

Published Report 142   *Expert Opinion 142*

Experiment 143   *Statistics 143*

Survey 144   *Observational Study 144*

Research Review 144   *Your Personal Experience 145*

The Experiences of People You Know 146

Using the Library 146

Using the Internet 148

Maintaining a Questioning Perspective 151

Managing an Interview 152

Avoiding Plagiarism 153

Conducting Your Own Research 157

Consider Doing a Survey 157

Consider Doing an Observational Study 157

Keeping Creativity Alive 158

Warm-Up Exercises 158

Applications 159

Issue for Extended Analysis 161

9 Produce Ideas 164

Stimulating Your Imagination 165

Force Uncommon Responses 166

Use Free Association 166   *Use Analogy 166*

Look for Unusual Combinations 167

Visualize the Solution 167

Construct Pro and Con Arguments 167

Construct Relevant Scenarios 168

Aiming for Originality 169

Withholding Judgment 170

Overcoming Obstacles 170

Thinker's Block 170   *Vagueness and Confusion 171*

Inflexibility 172

How Insight Occurs 172

A Sample Problem 173

A Sample Issue 175

  Warm-Up Exercises 177

  Applications 177

  Issue for Extended Analysis 178

PART III   **BE CRITICAL 183**

  10   The Role of Criticism 185

Why Criticism Is Necessary 185

Focus on *Your* Ideas 186

Overcoming Obstacles to Critical Thinking 187

Applying Curiosity 187

Avoiding Assumptions 188

Refining Your Solutions to Problems 189

A Sample Problem 189

Refining Your Positions on Issues 190

A Sample Issue 191

  Taking Action on the Issue 192

  Warm-Up Exercises 193

  Applications 193

  Issue for Extended Analysis 194

  11   Refine Your Solution to the Problem 197

Three Steps in Refining 198

  Step 1: Working Out the Details 198

  Step 2: Finding Imperfections and Complications 199

  Step 3: Making Improvements 200

Two Sample Problems 202

  The First Problem 202   *The Second Problem 203*

  Warm-Up Exercises 205

  Applications 205

  Issue for Extended Analysis 206

  12   Evaluate Your Argument on the Issue 210

Errors Affecting Truth 210

  Either/Or Thinking 211   *Avoiding the Issue 211*

  Overgeneralizing 211   *Oversimplifying 212*

Double Standard 213

Shifting the Burden of Proof 213

Irrational Appeal 214

Errors Affecting Validity 214

A Special Problem: The Hidden Premise 216

Recognizing Complex Arguments 218

Steps in Evaluating an Argument 219

The Case of Parents Protesting TV Programs 220

The Case of the Mentally Impaired Girls 221

Warm-Up Exercises 222

Applications 222

Issue for Extended Analysis 225

13 Refine Your Resolution of the Issue 228

Step 1: Deciding What Action Should Be Taken 229

Step 2: Recognizing and Overcoming Difficulties 229

Should Children Pledge Allegiance? 230

Should the Miranda Rule Be Abolished? 231

Warm-Up Exercises 233

Applications 233

Issue for Extended Analysis 234

PART IV COMMUNICATE YOUR IDEAS 237

14 Persuading Others 239

Understanding Why People Reject Ideas 240

Knowing Your Audience 241

Anticipating Your Audience's Objections 243

The Brainstorming Technique 243

The Imaginary-Dialogue Technique 243

Presenting Your Ideas to Advantage 245

Respect Your Audience 245

Begin with the Familiar 246

Select the Most Appropriate Tone 246

Emphasize the Evidence for Your View 247

Answer All Significant Objections 247

The Importance of Timing 247

Warm-Up Exercises 248

Applications 249
Issue for Extended Analysis 249

15 Writing and Speaking Effectively 252
Characteristics of Effective Writing 253
A Step-by-Step Approach to Composition 254
  Planning 254   Drafting 256
  Revising 256   Editing 257
Developing a Readable Style 257
A Sample Composition 259
The Challenge of Effective Speaking 260
Types of Speeches 261
Organizing Your Material 261
Sample Outline and Speech 263
Practicing the Delivery 265
  Warm-Up Exercises 266
  Applications 266
  Issue for Extended Analysis 268

Solutions to Sample Problems 271
  The Three Glasses Problem 271
  The Young Girl/Old Woman Problem 271
  The Vase and Faces Problem 272

Notes 273
Index 279

To the Instructor

Throughout the last century, many educators felt that thinking was learned automatically when certain subjects (notably science and math) were studied and that therefore it need not be formally taught. Others believed that thinking could not be learned, at least not by the average student. As a result, schools did not generally offer formal instruction in thinking, and colleges confined their offerings to formal logic courses inaccessible to students outside the discipline of philosophy.

This situation has never gone unchallenged. There have always been dissenters, here and abroad, who urged that systematic training in thinking be offered to all students. But when they were heard at all, such people were either misunderstood or dutifully applauded—and then ignored.

Now, thanks to the persistence of those prophets and that of the small but determined number of educators who continued to press for the reforms those prophets championed, a new era has dawned. Many prestigious studies, beginning with the one released by the U.S. Department of Education in November 1981, call attention to the lack of critical thinking and problem-solving skills in today's students. Support for thinking instruction has been registered by numerous respected organizations, including the National Council of Teachers of English, the Presidential Commission on Excellence in Education, the College Board, the Carnegie Foundation for the Advancement of Teaching, the American Federation of Teachers, the Association of American Colleges, the National Institute of Education, the U.S. Department of Education, the Association for Supervision and Curriculum Development, and the University/Urban Schools National Task Force. Numerous colleges and universities now require students to complete one or more courses in thinking.

THIS BOOK'S PREMISES

This book has been designed both for existing courses in thinking and for those that are being instituted in various departments: philosophy, humanities, social science, and English. As the title *The Art of Thinking* suggests, this book is more comprehensive than most texts on thinking. The following four premises underlie its content and organization.

1. *The emphasis in a textbook on thinking should be more on what to* do *than on what to* avoid *doing.* Thinking is not an ivory tower enterprise. It is a

practical matter. Moreover, it is active and dynamic, not reactive and static. Effective thinkers do not merely sit back and criticize others' efforts; they solve problems, make decisions, and take stands on issues. For this reason, textbooks focusing on fallacies are no more successful than music books that focus on avoiding the wrong notes or keyboarding manuals that focus on avoiding all possible misstrokes.

2. *A textbook on thinking should introduce students to the principles and techniques of* creative *thinking.* The considerable literature that has been published on thinking in the past three decades demonstrates that the creative process and the critical process are intertwined: first, we produce ideas (more or less creatively); then we judge them. It is not enough to give students *already formed* problems and issues; they must be taught how to generate problems and issues of their own.

3. *A text on thinking should teach students how to evaluate their own ideas, as well as the ideas of others.* Human beings have a great capacity for self-deception. Accordingly, it is much more difficult for students to see their own blind spots, prejudices, and errors than it is for them to see other people's. Yet it is their own weaknesses and mistakes that pose the greatest obstacle to their effective thinking.

4. *A text on thinking should teach students how to persuade others.* Many brilliant ideas have never been put into practice simply because the originators assumed that others would recognize their excellence without assistance. Students need to learn how to anticipate objections to their ideas before they occur and how to overcome them.

SPECIAL FEATURES RETAINED FROM PREVIOUS EDITIONS

- Wherever possible, the chapters are presented in the sequence that occurs in actual problem solving and issue analysis. For example, expressing the problem (Chapter 7) is followed by investigating the problem (Chapter 8), producing ideas (Chapter 9), and refining the solution (Chapter 11).
- Part II, "Be Creative," offers direct answers to the questions that most baffle students and prevent their progress in thinking. These are questions such as "How can I be more imaginative, more original in my solutions to problems?," "What should I do when I experience 'thinker's block,' when I get confused, or when I get in the rut of producing the same kinds of solutions?," and "How does insight occur, and what can I do to stimulate it?"
- In Chapter 1, a special section titled "Making Discussion Meaningful" provides guidelines for class discussion.
- Chapter 8 includes sections on describing 11 sources of information ("What to Look for"), on using the Internet, and on avoiding plagiarism.
- A separate chapter (Chapter 6) addresses the problem of motivating students to apply their thinking skills to problems and issues in every college

course, as well as in everyday life. Authorities agree that to be effective, thinking instruction must focus not only on skills but also on dispositions.

- A separate chapter (Chapter 8) explains in detail how to investigate issues quickly, efficiently, and with ingenuity, both inside and outside the library.
- Two chapters—Chapters 14 and 15—assist students in expressing their thoughts persuasively and effectively.
- Warm-up exercises are provided at the end of each chapter, in addition to a generous supply of problems and issues. These exercises are designed to develop students' interest and build their self-confidence, thereby making the formal applications less intimidating.
- Applications are provided following the warm-up exercises in each chapter. In addition, each chapter contains a holistic exercise that includes (1) a succinct description of a significant social or philosophical issue, (2) two brief essays representing opposing viewpoints, and (3) a "class discussion" in which students react to the essays. These holistic exercises offer several advantages over more typical assignments: they more closely reflect the dual way issues are encountered and addressed in college; they demonstrate the quality of thought and expression instructors expect; they encourage students to approach issues analytically rather than viscerally; and they model rigor and civility in discourse (both of which are too often lacking in popular communication).
- An updated Instructor's Manual is available to qualified adopters. The Instructor's Manual offers teaching suggestions on how to stimulate students and create a thinking classroom. Also included are additional exercises and answers to *The Art of Thinking*'s applications.

NEW FEATURES OF THE NINTH EDITION

For the ninth edition, a new section, entitled "Understanding Cause and Effect" has been added to Chapter 2. This section helps students correct the (all too common) belief that causation does not occur in human affairs. It also provides them with a strategy for conducting cause and effect analyses effectively. In addition, Chapter 4 has been expanded to cover critical *listening* and critical *viewing*, as well as critical reading, to reflect the changes in the acquisition of information that have accompanied the advent of the Internet. Finally, the section entitled "Avoiding Plagiarism" in Chapter 8 has been expanded.

VARIATIONS IN TEACHING FORMAT

The Art of Thinking has been used successfully in composition courses and public speaking courses, as well as in creative/critical thinking courses, and in a number of disciplines, including business, the humanities, the social sciences, and the sciences. Instructors who find the book's table of contents not well suited to their courses or their students' needs may wish to consider one of the following alternative sequences.

For Composition Courses

The first half of Chapter 15, "Writing and Speaking Effectively"

Chapter 1, "Developing Your Thinking: An Overview"

Chapter 14, "Persuading Others"

Chapter 2, "Establish a Foundation"

Chapters 3 through 13

For Speech Courses

The second half of Chapter 15, "Writing and Speaking Effectively"

Chapter 1, "Developing Your Thinking: An Overview"

Chapter 14, "Persuading Others"

Chapter 2, "Establish a Foundation"

Chapters 3 through 13

Another Alternative

This alternative is appropriate for students who are already proficient in writing and/or speaking.

Chapters 1 through 4

Chapter 14

Chapters 5 through 13

ACKNOWLEDGMENTS

I wish, first, to express my appreciation to all the men and women—the prophets, the researchers, the risk takers—who labored to advance the cause of knowledge in a subject that for many decades was unfashionable. Without their contributions, this book would never have been written. I also wish to thank the following professors for their constructive criticisms and helpful suggestions for this edition and several previous editions: Larry Beason, University of South Alabama; Michael Berberich, Galveston College; Liz Burke, John F. Kennedy University; Michaela Cosgrove, Keuka College; Kathryn Cowan, Cabrillo College; Adam Brooke Davis, Truman State University; Jeffrey Easlick, Saginaw Valley State University; Maureen Girard, Monterey Peninsula College; Lynne R. Graft, Saginaw Valley State University; Julia Keefer, New York University; Philip M. Keith, St. Cloud State University; Constance Kent, College of the Sequoias; Melinda Kreth, Central Michigan University; Joel Maatman, Lansing Community College; Jane Maulfair, Crest College; Catherine McCartney, Bemidji State University; Donald McDonough, Central Connecticut State University; James Michael Mullins, University of Texas at El Paso; Liz Noblis, Lansing Community College; John Pappas, San Joaquin Delta College; Elizabeth Sawin, Missouri Western State College; Charles Stone, DePaul University; Leila E. Wells, University of Louisville.

Vincent Ryan Ruggiero

Be
Aware

"Every man takes the limits of his own field of vision for the limits of the world," wrote philosopher Arthur Schopenhauer. The wider a person's field of vision, of course, the deeper and more accurate his or her grasp of everyday experiences.

The chapters included in this section of the book will enlarge your understanding of the thinking process; clarify the important and frequently misunderstood concepts of *truth*, *knowledge*, and *opinion*; identify the habits that corrupt thinking; and show you how to become a more critical reader.

1

Developing Your Thinking: An Overview

Is thinking an activity that is done automatically, without conscious effort, or one that we can direct? Is daydreaming a kind of thinking? Are feelings an effective substitute for thinking? Do exceptional thinkers experience mental blocks, lapses in concentration, and confusion the same way average thinkers do? Can thinking skill be acquired, or does one have to be born with it?

In this chapter you will find answers to these questions and other basic facts that will enable you to use this book confidently.

Claude is a high school student. His English teacher has just asked the class to identify the theme of the short story they read for homework. When no one answers, she admonishes them, "Class, you're just not thinking. Get busy and *think.*"

Claude wrinkles up his nose, furrows his brow, scratches his chin, and stares up at the ceiling. "Think, think, I've got to think. What's the theme of that story? The theme, the theme, what could be the theme?" He shifts his gaze to the right and to the left, purses his lips, then reaches down purposefully, opens his book, and begins flipping pages as if looking for something. All the while his mind is repeating, "Think . . . think . . . theme . . . ."

Is Claude thinking? No. He's trying to, hoping to, but not really doing so. His mental motor is racing, but his transmission is in neutral. He's ready to go, but not going.

Let's consider another case. Agatha, a college student, is sitting in the campus cafeteria, drinking her morning coffee. To all outward appearances she is not only thinking but totally lost in thought. Here is what is taking place in her mind:

> So much work to do today . . . must remember to meet Jim at 6 P.M. . . . I'll have to begin my term paper soon . . . That Bertha is such a slob—I wish she'd clean her part of the room sometime this semester . . . my hair looks so awful—if only I could fix it like Martha's, it would look neat, yet demand little attention . . . If winter would only end, I wouldn't be so depressed— why is my mood so dominated by the weather? . . . This coffee is bitter— you'd think the staff here could at least make a decent cup of coffee . . . I can't wait to get home to have a real meal again . . . wonder how much weight I've gained; perhaps jogging is the solution. . . .

Agatha's mental behavior is much closer to thinking than Claude's. Ideas, images, and notions are drifting through her mind, and she is dutifully watching them float by. But her role is passive; she is a spectator to the activity of her mind. Thinking, as we will view in this book (and as most authorities view it), is something more than aimless daydreaming.

WHAT IS THINKING?

What, then, is thinking? To begin with, it is purposeful mental activity over which we exercise some control. *Control* is the key word. Just as sitting in the driver's seat of a car becomes driving only when we take the steering wheel in hand and control the car's movement, so our mind's movements become thinking only when we direct them.

There are, of course, as many different purposes in thinking as there are in traveling. We may be on a business trip or a pleasant drive through the countryside with no particular destination. Similarly, we may drive in varying conditions and with varying degrees of success or efficiency. We may travel in darkness or in light, proceed slowly or quickly, take the correct turn or the wrong one, arrive at our intended destination or a different one, or find that we are hopelessly lost en route. Nevertheless, as long as we are steering our mind, we are thinking.

This does not mean that thinking must always be conscious. The evidence that the unconscious mind can join in purposeful mental activity is overwhelming. The most dramatic example is the fact that insights often come to us when we are no longer working on a problem but have turned away from it to other activities. (We will see a number of examples of this phenomenon in Chapter 9.)

With these important considerations in mind, we can attempt a more formal definition of thinking: *Thinking is any mental activity that helps formulate or solve a problem, make a decision, or fulfill a desire to understand. It is a searching for answers, a reaching for meaning.* Numerous mental activities are included in the thinking process. Careful observation, remembering, wondering, imagining, inquiring, interpreting, evaluating, and judging are among the most important ones. Often, several of these activities work in combination, as when we solve a problem or make a decision. We may, for example, identify an idea or dilemma, then deal with it—say, by questioning, interpreting, and analyzing—and finally reach a conclusion or decision.

There have been many attempts to explain the nature of thinking. One of the most popular notions, now largely discredited, is that thinking is entirely verbal. According to this theory, we arrange words in our minds or silently whisper to ourselves when we think. Yet if this were the case, Albert Einstein would not be considered a thinker. His thinking consisted more of images than of words.[1] Contemporary authorities agree that the form a thought takes in our minds is usually verbal, but not necessarily so. Just as we may *express* an idea in mathematical symbols or pictures, in addition to words, we may also *conceive* of it in that way.

THE IMPORTANCE OF THINKING

Successful problem solving and issue analysis require factual knowledge—that is, familiarity with the historical context of the problem or issue and an understanding of the relevant principles and concepts. But factual knowledge is something already known, whereas in the great majority of cases, solutions are unknown, brand new, and specifically formulated to fit particular problems or issues. For this reason, the possession of factual knowledge does not by itself guarantee success in problem solving. You may, in fact, be the proverbial "walking encyclopedia" and perform quite dismally. To be a successful problem solver, you will need both factual knowledge and proficiency in thinking.

To appreciate the importance of thinking proficiency, consider the various situations in which you are or will be called upon to solve problems, analyze issues, and make decisions. The choice of a major in college and the decision of whom to marry, where to live, what religion (if any) to embrace, and what political party to join are but a few of the most obvious situations. Every day brings new and difficult challenges: how to deal with difficult people, what to do when your parents can no longer care for themselves, how to be a good parent, how to sort through hyperbole and false claims in advertisements, how to manage your investments wisely, how to determine which political candidate will do the most good (or least harm) for the country.

Skill in problem solving, issue analysis, and decision making is increasingly expected of employees. Only a generation or so ago, "scientific management" was still in vogue. In that system, executives did the thinking and other employees merely carried out their assigned tasks. Since the advent of "quality management," employers have learned to value employees who are willing and able to contribute ideas for the improvement of the company. In recent years, this perspective has been reinforced by three developments: the knowledge explosion, the communications technology revolution, and the rise of the global economy.

Improvements in research capability have dramatically increased the information base in virtually every field, making it difficult for anyone to master even a single discipline's knowledge in its entirety. In addition, because new knowledge is not merely being added each year but *multiplied*, before long such mastery will be impossible. More important, the information base acquired in high school and college, which used to be sufficient for an entire career, will in the future become obsolete within a decade or less.

The communications technology revolution has been even more remarkable. Within less than 20 years, the personal computer was developed and hundreds of hardware and software manufacturers sprang into existence, marketing products no one could have imagined a generation earlier. Hundreds of billions of dollars flowed into upstart companies like Microsoft, Intel, Dell, and a host of "dot.coms," ending the seeming omnipotence (and complacency) of such corporate giants as IBM. For individual companies and entire industries, the result has been a loss of stability. Even successful, well-run organizations can experience a rapid change of fortune and be forced to downsize their operations and lay off workers. Individuals who possess problem-solving and decision-making skills are more flexible than others and are therefore (1) less likely to become victims of downsizing and (2) more likely to find satisfactory employment if they are laid off.

The development of a global economy has resulted from the satellite transmission of television programming; the opening of former Soviet bloc countries to trade; the increase in business *competition* from other countries, notably Japan; and the signing of a new generation of trade agreements such as the North American Free Trade Agreement (NAFTA) and the General Agreement on Tariffs and Trade (GATT). Meeting the challenges and seizing the opportunities presented by the global economy require skill in creative and critical thinking. Employees who possess those skills will enjoy a significant advantage over those who do not.

BRAIN AND MIND AT WORK

For well over a century, researchers have deepened our understanding of human thought. We now know that thinking is not a mystical activity, unknowable and unlearnable. Thinking occurs in patterns that we can study and compare to determine their relative objectivity, validity, and effectiveness. This knowledge can be used to reinforce good thinking habits and to overcome bad ones. As James Mursell has observed, "Any notion that better thinking is intrinsically unlearnable and unteachable is nothing but a lazy fallacy, entertained only by those who have never taken the trouble to consider just how a practical job of thinking is really done."[2]

Brain research is providing new insights, notably that the structure of the brain is considerably more complex than previously imagined. The first breakthrough in understanding came when a neurosurgeon began treating patients with severe epilepsy in a new way. He severed the *corpus callosum*, the nerve fibers connecting the two hemispheres of the cerebral cortex, to relieve the symptoms of the disease. The separation made it possible to study the way each hemisphere functioned. The right hemisphere, it was learned, governs nonverbal, symbolic, and intuitive responses. The left hemisphere governs the use of language, logical reasoning, analysis, and the performance of sequential tasks.

Some popularizers of this research have taken it to mean there are "left-brained people" and "right-brained people," and a cottage industry has arisen to help people identify which they are and/or become what they are not. Most researchers regard this development as, at best, an oversimplification of the data. For example, Jerre Levy points out that none of the data "supports the idea that normal people function like split-brain patients, using only one hemisphere at a time," adding that the very structure of the brain implies profound integration of the two hemispheres, the *corpus callosum* connecting them and facilitating their arousal.[3]

William H. Calvin says that researchers who specialize in split-brain research (as he does) tend to regard the popularization "with something of the wariness which the astronomers reserve for astrology." He cites the "behavior and mental processes greater than and different from each region's contribution" as evidence of right/left integration.[4] Others underscore the fact that left-brain/right-brain research has been conducted with severely injured or surgically altered brains and not normal ones. In his Nobel lecture on the subject, for instance, Roger W. Sperry noted that "in the normal state the two hemispheres appear to work closely together as a unit, rather than one being turned on while the other idles."[5]

The extravagance of popularizers notwithstanding, neurophysiological research seems to parallel cognitive psychologists' earlier realization that the mind has two distinct phases—the *production* phase and the *judgment* phase—that complement each other during problem solving and decision making. Proficiency in thinking requires the mastery of all approaches appropriate to each phase and skill in moving back and forth between them. Let's examine each phase a little more closely, noting how good thinkers use each effectively.

The Production Phase

In this phase, which is most closely associated with creative thinking, the mind produces various conceptions of the problem or issue, various ways of dealing with it, and possible solutions or responses to it. Good thinkers produce both more ideas and better ideas than poor thinkers. They become more adept in using a variety of invention techniques, enabling them to discover ideas. More specifically, good thinkers tend to see the problem from many perspectives before choosing any one, to consider many different investigative approaches, and to produce many ideas before turning to judgment. In addition, they are more willing to take intellectual risks, to be adventurous and consider unusual ideas, and to use their imaginations.

In contrast, poor thinkers tend to see the problem from a limited number of perspectives (often just a single narrow one), to take the first approach that occurs to them, to judge each idea immediately, and to settle for only a few ideas. Moreover, they are overly cautious in their thinking, unconsciously making their ideas conform to the common, the familiar, and the expected.

The Judgment Phase

In this phase, which is most closely associated with critical thinking, the mind examines and evaluates what it has produced, makes its judgments, and, where appropriate, adds refinements. Good thinkers handle this phase with care. They test their first impressions, make important distinctions, and base their conclusions on evidence rather than their own feelings. Sensitive to their own limitations and predispositions, they double-check the logic of their thinking and the workability of their solutions, identifying imperfections and complications, anticipating negative responses, and generally refining their ideas.

In contrast, poor thinkers judge too quickly and uncritically, ignoring the need for evidence and letting their feelings shape their conclusions. Blind to their limitations and predispositions, poor thinkers trust their judgment implicitly, ignoring the possibility of flaws in their thinking.

▣ GOOD THINKING IS A HABIT

It is frequently said that good thinkers are born, not made. Although there is an element of truth in this, the idea is essentially false. Some people have more talent for thinking than others, and some learn more quickly. As a result, over the years one person may develop thinking ability to a greater extent than another. Nevertheless, effective thinking is mostly a matter of habit. Research proves that the qualities of mind required to think well, the qualities we noted in our discussion of the production and judgment phases, can be mastered by anyone. It even proves that originality can be learned. Most important, it proves that you don't need a high IQ to be a good thinker.[6] E. Paul Torrance has shown that fully *70 percent* of all creative people score below 135 on IQ tests.[7]

The difficulty of improving your thinking depends on the habits and attitudes you have. Chances are you've had little or no direct training in the art of thinking before now, so you're bound to have acquired some bad habits and attitudes. This book will supply principles and techniques for you to master, and your instructor will supply the guidance. You must supply the most important ingredients: the desire to improve and the willingness to apply what you learn.

If at first the task of changing your habits and attitudes seems impossible, remember that a lot of other tasks seemed so, yet you mastered them: walking, for example, and eating without drooling food out of your mouth onto your high chair, swimming, hitting a baseball, and driving a car. The unfamiliar often seems daunting.

▣ THE STRUCTURE OF THIS BOOK

Becoming familiar with the contents of this book will help you meet its challenge more confidently. The purpose of the book is to *teach you how to think* more creatively and critically. That may seem obvious enough, but it's easily confused with *telling you what to think*. The difference is this: telling you what to think makes you dependent on other people's ideas; teaching you how to think liberates you from dependency on others' ideas and helps you form sound and sensible ideas of your own. You will find this book introducing you to, or deepening your acquaintance with, a host of problems and controversial issues. It will guide the way you consider them—that is, the strategies you apply and the manner in which you apply them. But you will not find this book making up your mind for you. That task is yours alone.

The Art of Thinking is divided into four parts, each with several chapters. "Be Aware" will help you to broaden your outlook and become a critical reader. "Be Creative" and "Be Critical" will demonstrate ways to produce and evaluate ideas more effectively. "Communicate Your Ideas" will help you present your ideas more persuasively to other people.

Don't feel bound by the sequence of the chapters. If you haven't examined the table of contents closely, take a moment and do so now. Whenever you are interested in learning about a topic that appears in a later chapter, read ahead. For example, if you lack confidence in your writing, consult Chapters 14 and 15 now, and apply the advice presented there.

GETTING THE MOST FROM YOUR EFFORTS

At one time it was thought that the same occasions, places, and conditions of work are right for everyone. Today we know better. No two people are exactly alike in their needs. What works for one will not necessarily work for another. Mozart and Beethoven, for example, were both great composers, yet they worked very differently. Mozart thought out entire symphonies and scenes from operas in his head, without benefit of notes. Later he transcribed them onto paper. Beethoven, on the other hand, wrote fragmentary notes in notebooks, often reworking and polishing them for years. His first ideas were so clumsy that scholars marvel at how he could have developed such great music from them.[8]

Imagine what would have happened if Mozart had followed Beethoven's approach, and vice versa. Surely Mozart's output would have been diminished. Given the unsuitability of another approach to his temperament, it might even have been choked off altogether. And Beethoven would have given the world trash.

It is not unreasonable to believe that there are thousands, perhaps millions, of people in the world today who have not begun to glimpse, let alone develop, their potential for achievement *simply because they are using work habits borrowed from someone else or fallen into by chance or force of circumstance.* Your best approach is not to assume that your work habits fit your needs but to experiment a little and find out what really works best for you. What you find may not make a dramatic difference, but even modest improvements in proficiency will continue to pay dividends over the years.

Consider Time.   An hour of prime time will often get better results than two or three hours of the wrong time. When are you in the habit of doing your most important schoolwork? Early in the morning? Late at night? At midday? For the next week or two, try different times and note the effect on your work.

Consider Place.   You can observe students studying in strange places: dormitory lounges, crowded cafeterias filled with people clanging and chattering, and snack bars (often next to a blaring jukebox). You've probably studied in some of these places, too, at one time or another, and for no other reason than that you happened to be there at the time an assignment had to be done. But that is not a good reason. If you need quiet to work efficiently, you should seek a quiet place—if not a dormitory room, then an empty classroom, a park bench, or a parked car. Of course, if you find that a busy place actually stimulates your thinking, by all means work there.

Consider Conditions.   Thinkers throughout history have occasionally needed some strange stimuli. Poet Friedrich von Schiller needed a desk filled with rotten apples. Novelist Marcel Proust needed a cork-lined workroom. Dr. Samuel Johnson demanded a purring cat, an orange peel, and a cup of tea. But you'd do well not to become dependent on gimmicks or bizarre conditions, if for no other reason than that they're hard to maintain. You're better off trying such approaches as taking a walk or a brisk jog across campus before beginning work or playing music while you work.

A word of caution is in order here. Don't confuse what you like with what works best for you. You may, for example, enjoy being in the dormitory lounge in the early evening watching TV or listening to the stereo blare. But these might hinder more than help your efforts to think or write. Similarly, alcohol and drugs may make you feel good (temporarily, at least), but they are definitely counter-productive. Although the notion persists that such substances enhance creativity, researchers are almost unanimous in concluding that they have the reverse effect: They cloud and numb the mind.

USING FEELINGS TO ADVANTAGE

Feelings were greatly emphasized in the 1960s and early 1970s. "Do your own thing," "If it feels good, do it," and "Get in touch with your feelings" were the catchphrases of the time. In light of the neglect of feelings in previous decades, that emphasis was understandable, but it often took the form of a rejection of thought. The proper relationship of thoughts and feelings is harmonious, not mutually exclusive.

The contribution feelings can make to problem solving and decision making is immeasurable. Not only do feelings often yield the hunches, impressions, and intuitions that produce the answers we seek but they also, more importantly, provide the enthusiasm to undertake difficult challenges and persevere in them. Albert Einstein spent 7 years working out his theory of relativity; Thomas Edison spent 13 years perfecting the phonograph; Copernicus devoted more than 30 years to proving that the sun is the center of the solar system. And millions of men and women labor tirelessly to realize the most elusive of goals: victory over disease, poverty, ignorance, and inhumanity. Without deep and abiding feelings about the importance of their work, such people could not sustain their efforts.

The popular notion that only artists feel, that scientists and other practical people approach problems in computerlike fashion, has long been discredited by scholars.[9] Albert Einstein himself affirmed the role of intuition in science. "There is no logical way to the discovery of [complex scientific laws]," he explained.

"There is only the way of intuition, which is helped by a feeling for the order lying behind the appearance."[10] And Arthur Koestler, who studied the lives of innumerable great scientists, observed, "In the popular imagination [they] appear as sober ice-cold logicians, electronic brains mounted on dry sticks. But if one were shown an anthology of typical extracts from their letters and autobiographies with no names mentioned, and then asked to guess their profession, the likeliest answer would be: a bunch of poets or musicians of a rather romantically naive kind."[11]

Of course, not all feelings are good. Some direct us in ways good sense would not have us go. From time to time even the mildest individuals may feel like responding violently to people they don't like, experience a strong urge for sexual contact with those who don't share the sentiment, or be overtaken by the impulse to steal something. For this reason, wisdom demands that we refuse to surrender ourselves to our feelings but instead examine them dispassionately and separate the worthy from the unworthy.

As you proceed through this course, try to become more aware of your feelings. Accept the challenge of finding your best and noblest feelings and allowing them to motivate you.

LEARNING TO CONCENTRATE

Many people have the notion that concentration means a constant, unbroken line of thought. They imagine that scientists, writers, inventors, and philosophers start from point A and move smoothly to point B without distraction. That notion is incorrect. Concentration is not so much something done to *prevent* distraction and interruption as it is something done to *overcome* distraction and interruption when they occur. To concentrate means to return our attention to our purpose or problem whenever it wanders.[12]

Concentrating is much like steering a car. When experienced drivers steer, they don't lock their hands on the wheel in one fixed position; they turn it slightly to the right and to the left to keep the car on course. Even on a straight road, the car stays on course only a small percentage of the time. Drivers must make constant adjustments, many of them almost imperceptible. Experienced drivers are not more talented than inexperienced ones; they have simply learned to make subtle corrections at the right time.

Similarly, the secret of efficient thinkers is not that they experience fewer distractions, but that they have learned to deal with them more quickly and more effectively than inefficient thinkers do. There is no magic in what effective thinkers do. You can learn it as they did, by practicing.

COPING WITH FRUSTRATION

All thinkers have their share of frustration: confusion, mental blocks, false starts, and failures happen to everyone. Good thinkers, however, have learned strategies for dealing with their frustration, whereas poor thinkers merely lament it—thus allowing themselves to be defeated by it. One important study of students' problem-solving processes revealed some interesting differences between good and poor problem solvers. Among them were the following:[13]

Good Problem Solvers	Poor Problem Solvers
Read a problem and decide how to begin attacking it.	Cannot settle on a way to begin.
Bring their knowledge to bear on a problem.	Convince themselves they lack sufficient knowledge (even when that is not the case).
Go about solving a problem systematically—for example, trying to simplify it, puzzling out key terms, or breaking the problem into subproblems.	Plunge in, jumping haphazardly from one part of the problem to another, trying to justify first impressions instead of testing them.
Tend to trust their reasoning and to have confidence in themselves.	Tend to distrust their reasoning and to lack confidence in themselves.
Maintain a critical attitude throughout the problem-solving process.	Lack a critical attitude and take too much for granted.

MAKING DISCUSSION MEANINGFUL[14]

At its best, discussion deepens understanding and promotes problem solving and decision making. At its worst, it frays nerves, creates animosity, and leaves important issues unresolved. Unfortunately, the most prominent models for discussion in contemporary culture—radio and TV talk shows—often produce the latter effects.

Many hosts demand that their guests answer complex questions with simple "yes" or "no" answers. If the guests respond that way, they are attacked for oversimplifying. If, instead, they try to offer a balanced answer, the host shouts, "You're not answering the question," and proceeds to answer it himself. Guests who agree with the host are treated warmly; others are dismissed as ignorant or dishonest. As often as not, when two guests are debating, each takes a turn interrupting while the other shouts, "Let me finish." Neither shows any desire to learn from the other. Typically, as the show draws to a close, the host thanks the participants for a "vigorous debate" and promises the audience more of the same next time.

Here are some simple guidelines for ensuring that the discussions you engage in—in the classroom, on the job, or at home—are more civil, meaningful, and productive than what you see on TV. By following these guidelines, you will set a good example for the people around you.

Whenever Possible, Prepare in Advance

Not every discussion can be prepared for in advance, but many can. An agenda is usually circulated several days before a business or committee meeting. And in college courses, the assignment schedule provides a reliable indication of what will be discussed in class on a given day. Use this advance information to prepare for discussion. Begin by reflecting on what you already know about the topic. Then decide how you can expand your knowledge and devote some time to doing so. (Fifteen or 20 minutes of focused searching on the Internet can produce a significant amount of information on almost any subject.) Finally, try to anticipate the different points of view that might be expressed in the discussion, and consider the relative merits of each. Keep your conclusions very tentative at this point so that you will be open to the facts and interpretations others will present.

Set Reasonable Expectations

Have you ever left a discussion disappointed that others hadn't abandoned their views and embraced yours? Have you ever felt offended when someone disagreed with you or asked you what evidence you had to support your opinion? If the answer to either question is yes, you probably expect too much of others. People seldom change their minds easily or quickly, particularly in the case of long-held convictions. And when they encounter ideas that differ from their own, they naturally want to know what evidence supports those ideas. Expect to have your ideas questioned, and be cheerful and gracious in responding.

Leave Egotism and Personal Agendas at the Door

To be productive, discussion requires an atmosphere of mutual respect and civility. Egotism produces disrespectful attitudes toward others—notably, "I'm more important than other people," "My ideas are better than anyone else's," and "Rules don't apply to me." Personal agendas, such as dislike for another participant or excessive zeal for a point of view, can lead to personal attacks and unwillingness to listen to others' views.

Contribute But Don't Dominate

If you are the kind of person who loves to talk and has a lot to say, you probably contribute more to discussions than other participants. On the other hand, if you are more reserved, you may seldom say anything. There is nothing wrong with being either kind of person. However, discussions tend to be most productive when everyone contributes ideas. For this to happen, loquacious people need to exercise a little restraint, and more reserved people need to accept responsibility for sharing their thoughts.

Avoid Distracting Speech Mannerisms

Such mannerisms include starting one sentence and then abruptly switching to another, mumbling or slurring your words, and punctuating every phrase or clause with audible pauses ("um," "ah,") or meaningless expressions ("like," "you know," "man"). These annoying mannerisms distract people from your message. To overcome them, listen to yourself when you speak. Even better, tape your conversations with friends and family (with their permission), then play the tape back and listen to yourself. And whenever you are engaged in a discussion, aim for clarity, directness, and economy of expression.

Listen Actively

When the participants don't listen to one another, discussion becomes little more than serial monologue—each person taking a turn at speaking while the rest ignore what is being said. This can happen quite unintentionally because the mind can process ideas faster than the fastest speaker can deliver them. Your mind may get tired of waiting and wander about aimlessly like a dog off its leash. In such cases, instead of listening to what is being said, you may think about the speaker's clothing or hairstyle or look outside the window and observe what is happening there. Even when you are making a serious effort to listen, it is easy to lose focus. If the speaker's words trigger an unrelated memory, you may slip away to that earlier time and place. If the speaker says something you disagree with, you may begin framing a reply. The best way to maintain your attention is to be alert for such distractions and to resist them. Strive to enter the speaker's frame of mind and understand each sentence as it is spoken and to connect it with previous sentences. Whenever you realize your mind is wandering, drag it back to the task.

Judge Ideas Responsibly

Ideas range in quality from profound to ridiculous, helpful to harmful, ennobling to degrading. It is therefore appropriate to pass judgment on them. However, fairness demands that you base your judgment on thoughtful consideration of the overall strengths and weaknesses of the ideas, not on your initial impressions or feelings. Be especially careful with ideas that are unfamiliar or different from your own because those are the ones you will be most inclined to deny a fair hearing.

Resist the Urge to Shout or Interrupt

No doubt you understand that shouting and interrupting are rude and disrespectful behaviors, but do you realize that in many cases they are also a sign of *intellectual insecurity*? It's true. If you really believe your ideas are sound, you will have no need to raise your voice or to silence the other person. Even if the other person resorts to such behavior, the best way to demonstrate confidence and character is by refusing to reciprocate. Make it your rule to disagree without being disagreeable.

PRELIMINARY THINKING STRATEGIES

At the end of each chapter in this book, you will find three kinds of challenges. The first kind, warm-up exercises, are intended to provide an enjoyable way for you to experiment with ideas and limber up your thinking. The second kind are applications, which invite you to apply what you learned in the particular chapter and previous chapters to real-life problems and issues. Finally, each chapter has a composition/speech exercise that requires more extended analysis and more formal presentation of your findings.

By the time you reach the end of this book, you will have learned a variety of strategies for applying creative and critical thinking to these challenges. In the meantime, however, you will need some preliminary strategies. The remainder of this chapter will explain seven helpful ones that you can begin using immediately. Because most involve using writing in a way you may not be familiar with, we'll begin by clarifying what that way is.

Although writing is most commonly thought of as a way of expressing thoughts we have already formed, it is also an excellent tool for *discovering* and *clarifying* thoughts. You've probably had the experience of believing you have an idea clearly in mind and then finding out it is hopelessly muddled. It's a common experience. As Ernest Dimnet explains:

> Most men and women die vague about life and death, religion or morals, politics or art. Even about practical issues we are far from being clear. We imagine that other people know definitely their own minds about their children's education, about their own careers, or about the use they should make of their money. The notion helps us to imagine that we ourselves are only separated from decision on these important issues by the lightest curtain of uncertainty. But it is not so. Other people, like ourselves, live in perpetual vagueness. Like us they foolishly imagine they are thinking of some important subject when they are merely *thinking of thinking about it.*[15]

The solution, Dimnet suggests, is to use the technique known as *freewriting.* It consists of focusing on a problem or issue, letting your mind produce whatever associations it will, and writing down the resulting ideas, without pausing to evaluate any ideas (lest you shut off the flow prematurely). This kind of writing is not intended to be read by anyone else, so the rules of composition do not apply. Nor do you have to worry about spelling or penmanship. A variation on freewriting is *listmaking.* Because it involves single words and phrases rather than sentences, it is more efficient than freewriting, which makes it the perfect way to capture those ideas that come suddenly and leave just as quickly.

Once you have recorded your ideas, you can sort them out, refine them, and express them in a way that will be meaningful to others. Generally, that will take the form of stating what you think and why you think it, as well as providing sufficient explanation to overcome any confusion your readers might have.

Following are seven worthwhile strategies to help you meet the challenges at the end of each chapter:

1. If the exercise consists of a single statement to be analyzed, read it again carefully. Be sure you understand what it says. Ask yourself, "Does this make sense?" If you find yourself answering with a firm "yes" or "no," decide precisely what makes you respond that way. Often, that will be what you should explain to your audience.

2. If words fail you at the outset, refuse to sit and stare at the page. If you took a dead-end street by accident, you wouldn't sit in your car staring at the dead-end sign; you'd turn the car around and try moving in another direction. Do the same with difficult challenges. One approach that works well with some problems is to use a diagram. If, for example, you were evaluating the reasoning "All dogs are animals. Fido is a dog. Therefore, Fido is an animal," you might diagram it this way:

   The diagram would suggest the way to explain your analysis:

   It is correct to classify dogs under the general heading *animals.* Moreover, this applies not just to some dogs but also to *all* dogs. There is no other category under which to classify dogs. Fido is correctly classified as a dog, so he must be an animal.

3. When the statement presents as fact something that is not factual, identify the error and explain how it invalidates the statement.

4. When the statement confuses two terms or ideas, identify the confusion and show its effect on the statement as a whole.

5. When the statement presents a conclusion as the only possible conclusion and other conclusions are also possible, present the other conclusions and demonstrate that they, too, are reasonable (perhaps more reasonable).

6. When the statement, or some part of it, is open to interpretation, use the if-then approach to analysis. Consider, for example, the statement "Everyone must die." Here's how the if-then approach works:

   The statement as it stands is ambiguous. *If* it is taken to mean "At present there is no known way for human beings to avoid death," *then* it is a statement of fact. But *if* it is taken to mean "There will never be a way for human beings to avoid death," *then* it is presumptuous. For, however unlikely such a development may seem, we cannot say for certain it will never occur.

   The if-then approach is also useful when you are uncertain of the facts. In other words, you might say, "I am uncertain of the facts in this matter, but *if* they are as stated, *then* the conclusion is sound because. . . . *If,* however, they are not as stated, *then* the conclusion is not sound because. . . ."

7. If the exercise consists of a dialogue, read it several times, each time for a different purpose. First, read it to understand the discussion in its entirety. Then read each person's comments individually, noting the progression of his or her thoughts and the degree of logical consistency. Finally, read for

implications and assumptions; these are ideas that are not stated directly but are nevertheless identifiable by what *is* stated directly. (The dialogue in Sample Exercise 2 contains an unstated idea.)

SAMPLE EXERCISES AND RESPONSES

Each exercise you do will have its own particular details and will therefore demand a special response. For that reason, no one formula can be given for responding to the exercises. The following sample exercises and responses, though fairly typical, are illustrations of what can be done rather than models to be slavishly imitated.

Exercise 1

The Assignment: Analyze the following statement, deciding whether it is reasonable and, if so, to what degree. Explain your thinking thoroughly.

The results of a recent national examination reveal that 75 percent of America's high school students are below average in reading ability.

The Response:

> I don't know if the statement is a factual one. But I can say that it may have different meanings, depending on how the word *average* is interpreted. And the various meanings affect the reasonableness of the statement.
>
> *Below average* may mean "below a score that half the high school seniors have achieved in previous years." Or it may mean "below a score now regarded as an acceptable minimum." In either of these cases, the statement is a reasonable one and could very well be factual.
>
> But there is a more technical definition of *below average*. It may mean "below the arithmetic mean (the score derived from dividing the total scores of all high school students by the total number of high school students)." I am not sure whether it is even mathematically possible that 75 percent could fall below the mean, but I do know that it is highly unlikely. So if this is what the statement is saying, it is not very reasonable.

Exercise 2

The Assignment: Read the following dialogue carefully. Then decide whether what is stated (or implied) makes sense. Explain your reasoning thoroughly.

JOHN: Do you think the masses really have any power in the United States today?

BILL: That depends on what groups you include in "the masses." Would you include professional people—doctors, lawyers, teachers . . .?

JOHN: *Teachers?* They don't make that much money.

The Response:

> John's last comment reveals the assumption that money is the basis for determining professional status. That assumption is unwarranted. If money were the measure, a lawyer with a small practice would not be considered a professional, but a plumber with a good business would be. If an apprentice clerk in a store inherited a large sum of money from his aunt, he would be a nonprofessional one day and a professional the next. No, a professional person is one engaged in one of the *professions:* those fields requiring a liberal arts or science education and some form of subsequent specialization. The amount of money a person earns is beside the point.

Exercise 3

The Assignment: Rowena has three unmarked glasses of different sizes: 3 ounces, 5 ounces, and 8 ounces. The largest glass is full. What can Rowena do to get 4 ounces of liquid into each of the larger two glasses?

The Response: After some initial difficulty trying to work the problem out in your head, you create a visual aid by drawing three glasses on a sheet of paper, as shown here. (You could have instead gotten three actual glasses of appropriate sizes.)

3 ounce   5 ounce   8 ounce

What next? You would pour some liquid into one of the empty glasses, actually or in your imagination. Which glass? It makes no difference. You would just get busy *doing.* If one approach failed, you'd try another.

Try this approach and see if you can solve this challenge by yourself. (You'll find the answer on page 271.)

◼ WARM-UP EXERCISES

1.1   Decide whether the reasoning that underlies the following statement is sound or unsound. Write a paragraph or two stating and explaining your judgment. (If you have difficulty doing this assignment, consult the suggestions on pages 15–17.)

> There's a possibility that the price of postage stamps will be raised again soon. I'll stock up on them now to avoid paying the higher price.

1.2 Follow the directions for Exercise 1.1.

The sun has always risen in the past; therefore, it will rise tomorrow.

1.3 A young child is convinced that the time between two o'clock and three o'clock is longer than the time between one o'clock and two o'clock. Compose a brief explanation, with or without a diagram, that helps the child understand that the time isn't longer.

APPLICATIONS

1.1 For each of the following statements, write a brief response (one or two sentences) stating your position and explaining why you hold it.

   a. Violence is better than reason in dealing with dangerous situations.
   b. Only the good die young.
   c. It's human nature to be greedy.
   d. Capital punishment is a deterrent to crime.
   e. If people are unemployed, they must be lazy. There's a job for everyone who really wants to work.
   f. Everyone has a value system of some kind.
   g. We know ourselves better than others know us.
   h. An unborn fetus is a human being.
   i. If guns are outlawed, only outlaws will have guns.
   j. Truth is an intensely personal matter: What is true for me is not necessarily true for you.
   k. Winning isn't everything—it's the *only* thing.
   l. Challenging another's opinion is a sign of intolerance.
   m. Atheists are generally moral people.
   n. Censorship is evil.
   o. Black people are better athletes than white people.
   p. The oil companies manipulate gasoline prices.
   q. Getting your feet wet can cause a cold.
   r. Homosexuals are as likely to control their sexual urges as are heterosexuals.

1.2 Read the following dialogue carefully, looking for flaws in thinking. If you find a flaw, identify it and explain what is wrong with it in sufficient detail to persuade someone who has read the passage but sees no flaw. If you find two or more flaws, decide which is most serious and limit your discussion to that one. If you find nothing wrong with the thinking in the dialogue, explain why you agree with what is said. (If you have difficulty doing this assignment, consult suggestion 7 on page 16.)

> SALLY: Norma, have you begun your composition yet, the one that's due tomorrow?
>
> NORMA: No, I haven't. But I have done quite a bit of research on the topic. I have a few very interesting facts I plan to refer to. Have you done any reading?

SALLY: Not me. I want to do my own thing in my compositions—you know, be original.

NORMA: Really? Maybe I'd better not use those facts. They could work against me, I guess.

1.3 Follow the directions for Application 1.2.

HOMER: Excuse me, Professor Collins, may I speak to you for a minute?

PROF. C.: Sure, Homer. What can I do for you?

HOMER: It's about the test we had last week. You gave me a 40 on it.

PROF. C.: That's not a very good grade. Had you read all three chapters carefully?

HOMER: *Carefully?* I read each one four times, underlined every important detail, and then studied them for about 10 hours for three nights before the test. I took No-Doz and stayed up until 4:30 A.M. the night before the test.

PROF. C.: I see. That would surely seem to be more than adequate preparation. What do you think went wrong?

HOMER: I think the test was unfair. . . . I mean, it's not. . . . I know you wouldn't make a test unfair on purpose. I think you're a good teacher and all. Sociology is your field and I'm just an amateur, but after all that trying, I wouldn't have got a 40 if the test were fair.

1.4 Follow the directions for Application 1.2.

LILLIAN: Do you think parents should be told when their teenage daughters are given abortion counseling?

ROY: Absolutely. Parents are responsible for their children until they become of age. They have a right to be told.

LILLIAN: I'm not as sure as you. I can see how not telling them is a violation of their rights as parents, and the family has been weakened enough today without its being weakened further. But on the other hand, teenage girls are not just objects. They're people, and therefore, they have rights, such as the right to determine how their bodies will be used. And many times they can't talk to their parents about sex.

ROY: Nonsense. Parents care about their kids. They have their interests at heart more than anyone else, particularly some money-grabbing doctor or abortion-happy feminist. If kids really want to talk to their parents, there's nothing stopping them—except the possibility that they don't want to hear what their parents will say.

LILLIAN: Another thing bothers me, too. Why does the issue always focus on teenage girls rather than teenage boys?

ROY: Check with your local anatomist.

1.5   Follow the directions for Application 1.2.

GUY: Want to know what makes me sick? The tolerance our society has for transsexuals. I can't think of anything more disgusting than a person changing sexes to act out homosexual fantasies or to get more sexual satisfaction.

DARRELL: You obviously don't know much about transsexualism.

GUY: Don't tell me you excuse their perversion, too?

DARRELL: There's nothing to excuse. And you're mistaken in calling it a perversion. It's not.

GUY: What else can it be but a perversion? A man decides to be a woman, or vice versa. It's a mockery of nature. We are what we're born to be, and it's our responsibility to accept that. It ought to be against the law to tamper with nature the way they do.

1.6   The following passage is an excerpt from a student's letter home. Read it carefully. Then decide whether its reasoning is sound or unsound. State and explain your judgment in a paragraph or two, including whatever supporting material you believe will help persuade your reader.

> The one thing that really bugs me about my schedule this term is that required course, "Introduction to Literature." Some students may not know what their future career is. I do. It's to help you, Dad, with the business, and someday to take it over. If we sold books I could see the value of such a course. But literature surely isn't going to make me a better furniture store manager.

■────────────────

ISSUE FOR EXTENDED ANALYSIS

Following is a more comprehensive thinking challenge than the others in the chapter. Read the background note, the two opposing essays, and the class discussion.* Analyze what you have read, conduct additional research where appropriate, and

────────────────

*Note that the essays and the discussions in this exercise, here and in subsequent chapters, are presented in the informal style typically encountered in nonscholarly, journalistic writing. Thus, quotations from authors and mentions of statistical data or other research materials are not accompanied by footnote citations, though in some cases they contain a reference to a book title. This approach creates a different, and in some ways more difficult, burden than that of more scholarly reading, but it is more reflective of everyday reading and discussion.

formulate your assessment of the issue. Then write a composition that explains and supports your assessment. Remember that in addressing one issue, people often raise other issues. Also, keep in mind that the essays and discussion may contain erroneous statements and/or unsound arguments and may neglect important matters. Part of your challenge is to identify new issues as well as errors and omissions.

THE ISSUE: HUMAN NATURE

This issue is an ancient one that has fascinated philosophers, scientists, and most recently, social scientists. Of its many aspects, the one that we will focus on here is the question of whether people are by nature good. Traditional religious believers, notably Jews and Christians, answer "no," claiming that people have a natural predisposition, or at least a vulnerability, to evil. Some conservative Christians go further, arguing that humans are by nature "depraved." Secular humanists and humanistic psychologists tend to take the opposite view, claiming that people are born good and that any bad behavior they may engage in is attributable to social influences and conditions. (This view is borrowed from Romanticism, particularly from the ideas of Jean Jacques Rousseau.) Many current social controversies reflect this controversy over human nature.

THE ESSAYS

People Are Inherently Good
By Asanti Jones

Rousseau was insightful in noting that people are born good and, left to follow their natural inclinations and intuitions, will develop their potential and benefit themselves and those around them. A number of conclusions follow logically from this insight.

First, parents should not impose their beliefs and values on children but instead leave them free to develop their own. This is particularly so in such matters as religion, politics, and morality. No one has a right to say what others should regard as right and proper. Each individual must choose for him/herself. And what each chooses, others should respect.

Secondly, schools should have as few regulations and formalities as possible. Courses should be suggested by teachers, but the final determination of

Nothing More Than Potential
By Inga Nowak

If people are inherently good, it makes sense not to burden them with regimens, rules, and regulations that hinder the natural expressions of their impulses. And the lifting of such burdens should begin at the earliest time of life—in childhood. On the other hand, if people are not inherently good—if goodness like wisdom is not inborn but acquired—then regimens, rules, and regulations are beneficial.

Only a foolish generation would answer such a vital question on the basis of wishful thinking. But that is just what the past couple of generations did. They installed permissivism in both home and school. They let children decide what to think about truth and falsity, right and wrong, beauty and ugliness. They discarded the idea of discipline and let students what to study and how to do so should be the student's. If students find a lecture or other class exercise boring or irrelevant to their needs at the moment, they should be free to choose another activity. Moreover, any assessment of students' achievement should be made by the students themselves—just as they alone know what goals they should set, they alone know how well their have progressed toward reaching those goals.

If all people received such an upbringing, they would be healthy, happy, and successful. Unfortunately, few do, and the result is crime, drug and alcohol addiction, child and spouse abuse, and a host of other social problems. But it is a mistake to meet such problems with more laws and stricter punishment for infractions. The fault lies in society's failure to recognize the inherent goodness of people and to ensure their freedom to be themselves.

decide what they would learn and how they would learn it. They put self-esteem above self-control and eliminated instruction in civics and civility.

Exactly what has been the result of almost half a century of permissivism and self-indulgence? Social chaos. Parents have lost control of their children and have no idea of how to regain it. Teachers are frustrated in their attempts to impart knowledge and often fearful for their personal safety. Young people, intent on following their urges, are making life difficult for themselves and everyone around them, and are filled with resentment without knowing why.

It's about time America saw the notion that people are inherently good for the dangerous nonsense it is. People are not born good or evil but have the potential to be either. And which they become depends partly on the quality of the training they receive and partly on the choices they make.

CLASS DISCUSSION

EDNA: Jones is right. The old saying "As the twig is bent, so grows the tree" supports his view. People, like twigs, start out straight. The bending is supplied by others.

WALLY: Jones's argument is a big cop-out. Efforts to escape personal responsibility are as old as history. They go all the way back to Adam, who blamed Eve, who in turn said the devil made her do it. Today's rapists, child molesters, thieves, and terrorists continue the tradition by blaming their victims. What is different today is that some prominent thinkers tend to side with the perpetrators.

EDNA: Do you deny that bad environments—slums, for example—are more crime-ridden and produce more lawbreakers than the suburbs?

WALLY: Not at all. But I also recognize that two children in the same family, exposed to identical influences, often turn out very differently. One will become a criminal, and the other, a law-abiding citizen; one a narcissist, the other an altruist; one a sinner, the other a saint.

EDNA: There are always exceptions. I'm talking about what happens as a general rule.

WALLY: If Jones were right, then more permissive ages would have fewer social problems than more restrictive ages. Yet over the last few decades, our society has become very permissive, and our social problems have *increased*.

EDNA: Don't kid yourself. The influences of parents, teachers, and other authority figures are every bit as strong today. They're just more subtle.

WALLY: I'm not saying kids aren't influenced by adults. I'm saying that they show the tendency to bad behavior way before such influence takes place. Children who are barely able to crawl display meanness and selfishness. Most parental guidance aims to correct already-existing bad tendencies.

2

Establish a Foundation

Before building a house, you'd want to be sure the ground beneath it was firm. The same sensible approach applies to the challenge of developing your thinking skills. In this chapter, we discuss a number of important issues that will help you decide whether there's any point to being a careful thinker.

For example, are your thoughts and actions under your control, or are they determined by your genes or environment? Can wanting something to be true make it true? Is it possible to know something and still be wrong about it? Can memory be trusted? Does having a right to your opinion make all your opinions right?

If our minds were completely insulated from the outside world—an intellectually germ-free environment—there would be no need for the preliminary work in this chapter. We could just turn to techniques and strategies for thinking and begin practicing them. But that is not the case. We humans are social creatures, and we live in an imperfect world, a world of conflicting ideas and values that affect us, for good or for ill.

Thus, the ideas you have about free will, truth, knowledge, opinion, and the debating of moral issues will make a difference in your development as a thinker. Some ideas will enhance your thinking; others will hinder it. Still others may paralyze it altogether. It is therefore important to examine these matters closely before proceeding, by sorting out helpful from harmful notions and establishing a firm conceptual foundation. First, we'll consider the question of *free will*.

FREE WILL VERSUS DETERMINISM

Are you reading this chapter out of choice or compulsion? By *compulsion* I don't mean your instructor's direction, "Read Chapter 2 for tomorrow." That is a kind of gentle (and benevolent) pressure, but it is not compulsion. Compulsion is a force you are virtually powerless to resist. Some psychologists would argue that you have no free will and so you are not reading through choice but through compulsion.

"Wait a minute," you say. "I know I have free will because right at this minute there's a party in my friend's room, and I had to struggle with my conscience to read this chapter instead of going there." The psychologists smile patiently and say, "Sorry, that struggle was an illusion. There's no choice—just a stimulus–response bond. You've been conditioned to behave in a certain way, and so you behave that way."

"Oh, yeah?" you respond. "Then watch this." You slam shut the book and head for the door. They yawn and say, "Quite unconvincing. All that your dramatic action shows is that you've been conditioned to be stubborn in the face of a disagreeable idea."

At this point, your fists are clenched and you're beginning to grind your teeth. That's a normal reaction. And a lot of scholars and intellectuals—yes, and a lot of other psychologists—react similarly. Many of them have wisely given up arguing with the strict determinists. They realize that it's as impossible to win with someone whose rule is "Anything you say will prove my point" as it is to play cards with someone who stacks the deck.

This is not to say that reasonable people reject the idea of conditioning. On the contrary, they reject only the extreme notion that *all* human action is governed by conditioning. They take the moderate view that though we are all influenced by our surroundings and background—sometimes very strongly—we usually retain a significant measure of free will. Reasonable people would say that it is possible you are reading this chapter because of some compulsion but more likely that you are doing so because you *chose* to read rather than to attend the party. What role has conditioning in your choice? They would say it increases or decreases the probability of one choice over another. A student who has acquired the habit of putting responsible action before self-indulgence would be more likely to do so in any particular situation.

It is important for you to accept this more moderate view for a number of reasons. First, you can discuss moral issues meaningfully only if you affirm that people have some control over their behavior and to that extent are responsible for it. (There is little point in discussing which of two actions is preferable if no one has the ability to choose between them.) In addition, you can profitably discuss social issues like nuclear disarmament, prison reform, or the treatment of the elderly only if you affirm that individuals or whole societies can change their policies and priorities. Most important, you can become motivated to approach problems creatively and critically only if you affirm that you have control over what you say and do, only if you believe that careful thinking can make a difference.

WHAT IS TRUTH?

We live in an age that has made the true–false test not only the basis of educational achievement but also the staple of one of our most durable (if lamentable) forms of entertainment: the game show. For this reason, it is ironic that so much confusion exists about truth. Even otherwise intelligent people can be heard saying things such as "Everyone makes his or her own truth," "One person's truth is another person's error," "Truth is relative," and "Truth is constantly changing." All of these ideas undermine thinking.

If everyone makes his or her own truth, then no person's idea can be better than another's. All must be equal. And if all ideas are equal, what is the point in researching any subject? Why dig into the ground for answers to archaeological questions? Why probe the causes of tension in the Middle East? Why search for a cancer cure? Why explore the galaxy? These activities make sense only if some answers are better than others, if truth is something separate from, and unaffected by, individual perspectives.

Consider, for instance, this interesting, though hardly momentous question: What are the most popular street names in the United States? If the truth here is relative, any answer is as good as any other. One person says, "Maple," another, "Roosevelt," still another, "Grove," and so on. Many people would say, "Broadway" or "Main." (After deciding on your answer, check page 273.)[1] If every answer were equally correct, few people would be interested in the question. Yet progress depends on the curiosity and interest of people, the drive to find the *right* answer, the desire to know the truth.

Truth is *what is so* about something, the reality of the matter, as distinguished from what people wish were so, believe to be so, or assert to be so. From another perspective, in the words of Harvard philosopher Israel Scheffler, truth is the view "which is fated to be ultimately agreed to by all who investigate."[2] The word *ultimately* is important. Investigation may produce a wrong answer for years, even for centuries. *The Man with the Golden Helmet*, a well-known and often-reproduced seventeenth-century painting, was long considered the work of Rembrandt. Only in recent years was it established to be the work of an unknown contemporary of Rembrandt.[3] Though generations of art experts proclaimed the work to be Rembrandt's, the truth remained unaltered.

At various times and places, some very strange ideas were widely accepted as true—for example, the idea that a horsehair turns into a snake when placed in water. (Even Shakespeare believed this one.)[4] The reason people were deceived is obvious to anyone who has observed how refraction of light in water makes any object appear to be moving.

Similarly, many people believed erroneously that small flies, moths, and bees are babies of larger ones.[5] And the history of medicine includes an interesting and often bizarre collection of folk cures—for example, curing a headache by putting a bowl on the head, cutting the hair around the bowl, and then burning the hair; curing an earache by having someone spit tobacco juice in the affected ear; curing pneumonia by cutting a live chicken in two and placing it over the person's lungs; and curing weak vision by piercing the ears.[6]

We laugh at these ideas today, and rightly so. But it is important to realize that our laughter underlines the fact that people do not *create* truth. If they did, how would scientists ever test theories? The very creation of a theory would be documentation of its validity, and every theory would thus be equally acceptable. This, of course, is nonsense. We know from everyday experience that some theories prove accurate and others inaccurate. The test of a theory's validity must lie outside the theory itself.

But if people do not create their own truth, what do they do? They reach out to apprehend it and construct expressions that they hope represent it faithfully. Sometimes they succeed, and sometimes they fail. Novelist H. G. Wells summed up the challenge and the difficulty of the task in a simple metaphor: "The forceps of our minds are clumsy forceps and crush the truth a little in taking hold of it."[7]

Does the truth ever change? No. It may sometimes seem to, but on closer inspection it will be found not to. Some years ago, for example, a previously unknown species of fish was accidentally found deep in the Pacific Ocean.[8] We might think that the truth was that no such fish existed at first and that the truth changed when the fish was discovered. But think of just how foolish that idea is. It asks us to believe that there was no such fish swimming in the water and that someone in a deep-diving machine "looked" it into existence. How much more reasonable it is to believe that the fish existed but we didn't know that it did—in other words, that the truth of the matter was the same before and after the discovery, and only our knowledge of it changed.

Consider another very different example: the case of the authorship of the first book of the Bible, the book of Genesis. For centuries, Christians and Jews alike believed that the book had a single author. In time, this view was challenged and eventually replaced by the belief that as many as five authors contributed to Genesis. Then the results of a five-year linguistic analysis of Genesis were published, stating that there is an 82 percent probability of single authorship, as originally thought.[9] Has the truth about the authorship of Genesis changed? No. Only our belief has changed. Perhaps one day we will have final and conclusive proof, or perhaps, like an unsolved crime, the matter will never be resolved. In any case, the truth will not be changed by our knowledge or by our ignorance.

One easy way to spare yourself any further confusion about truth is to reserve the word *truth* for the final answer to an issue. Get in the habit of using the words *belief*, *theory*, and *present understanding* more often. This will have the added benefit of making you more willing to revise your views when new evidence appears and casts doubt on them.

■
WHAT IS KNOWING?

Here's a brief quiz. Don't read ahead until you have completed it.

1. Who said, "I only regret that I have but one life to give for my country"?

2. What was the agreed-upon signal that Paul Revere was to be given from the church tower if the British were coming?

3. What was Cinderella's slipper made of in the original story?

4. What is a camel's hair brush made of?

Most people could answer these questions quite readily. But the answers that come quite readily to those who are sure they "know" are often wrong. (See page 274 for the correct answers.)[10] The point is that *thinking we know* is not the same as *knowing*. We can think we know, be certain we know, proclaim loudly that we know, and yet not know at all. Our ideas do not constitute knowledge unless they correspond to reality.

Reality, unfortunately, can be deceptive. In 1972, 17-year-old college student Lawrence Berson was held for more than a week on multiple rape charges—until another man, Richard Carbone, 20, confessed to the crime. A glance at photographs of the two (Figure 2.1) will explain why the victims who identified Berson "knew" he was the rapist.[11]

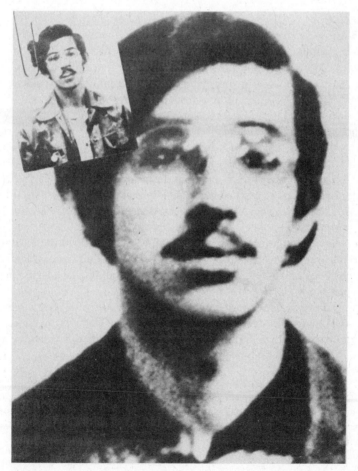

FIGURE 2.1 Lawrence Berson (inset) and his look-alike, Richard Carbone.
Copyright © 1974 by the New York Times Company. Reprinted by permission.

It is obvious that situations in which we believe we know but really *don't* know pose an obstacle to effective thinking. Why should anyone go to the trouble to investigate a matter or listen to opposing testimony if one believes one knows already? It is important, therefore, to understand the dynamics of knowing: how we come to know and what kinds of knowledge are most trustworthy.

WAYS OF KNOWING*

We can obtain authentic knowledge in any one of three ways: personal experience, observation, and report from others. The first is the most reliable, but as we will see, even that one is far from perfect.

Experience

We do not just receive experiences and store them, hermetically sealed, in our minds. We compare them with previous experiences; classify, interpret, and evaluate them; and make assumptions about them. All these processes may occur quite unconsciously, without our being aware of them. And any flaw in them makes our experiences seem different from the reality we encountered.

Consider this situation. Agnes has grown up in a religious family. She went to a parochial school and celebrated all the feasts of her church, including Christmas. She knows that Christmas is a Christian feast, and throughout her lifetime, it has always been a sacred time. From her knowledge, she unconsciously creates the idea that it has always been so, throughout the history of Christianity. In time, this vague idea becomes a certainty in her mind. She can even imagine herself hearing it expressed in a classroom. Yes, she *knows* that Christmas has always been a major Christian feast.

Alas, she is wrong. In fact, in seventeenth-century England the Puritans forbade the celebration of Christmas. They felt it was a pagan custom. Similarly, it was banned in colonial New England. Christmas was not made a legal holiday in Massachusetts until 1856.

Here is another, even more common, example. All of us have experienced childhood as a stage in our development. Most of us have never conceived of anyone *not* experiencing childhood, so it is easy for us to believe with certainty

---

*Our concern here is with the most commonly discussed kind of knowing: *knowing that.* Its focus is information. Another, equally important kind of knowing is *knowing how.* Its focus is procedures and strategies. The measure of knowing how, or know-how, is not the possession of a body of content but the performance of a skill. The strategies you will learn in later chapters for approaching problems and issues will constitute "know-how."

that childhood always existed. Yet research shows this idea to be false. Historian J. H. Plumb writes:

> The world that we think proper to children—fairy stories, games, toys, special books for learning, even the idea of childhood itself—is a European invention of the past four hundred years. The very words we use for young males—boy, *garçon, Knabe*—were until the seventeenth century used indiscriminately to mean a male in a dependent position and could refer to men of thirty, forty, or fifty. There was no special word for a young male between the age of seven and sixteen; the word "child" expressed kinship, not an age state.[12]

Because our perceptions are not passively received but are influenced by our emotional states and mental processes, they seldom mirror reality precisely. At times, in fact, they seriously distort reality.

Observation

It is certainly possible to observe accurately, but we often fall short of doing so. We usually see the world through glasses colored by our experiences and beliefs. If we believe that blacks are more athletic than whites, we are likely to "see" a particular black athlete outperforming a white athlete in a basketball game— even if that is not occurring. If we believe that Italians are violent by nature, we are likely to "see" an Italian man making threatening gestures and preparing to strike another person when we observe him in a spirited discussion—even when those gestures are not unfriendly. Exactly how such distortions of observation occur may be explained as follows:

> We are told about the world before we see it. We imagine most things before we experience them. And those preconceptions, unless education has made us acutely aware, govern deeply the whole process of perception. They mark out certain objects as familiar or strange, emphasizing the difference, so that the slightly familiar is seen as very familiar, and the somewhat strange as sharply alien. They are aroused by small signs, which may vary from a true index to a vague analogy. Aroused, they flood fresh vision with older images, and project into the world what has been resurrected in memory.[13]

Report

This source of knowledge covers most of what we are taught by our parents and teachers, what we hear reported in the news, and what we read in books and magazines. Most people who present ideas to us are undoubtedly trying to teach accurately and do not deliberately misinform us; they themselves believe what they tell us. Yet, because they are human and therefore capable of error, it is likely that a fair percentage of what we have been taught is at least partly incorrect.

An interesting example of the extent to which error can creep into news reports was revealed by George Seldes. Here is an original news story, together with the actual facts, as later determined by Seldes:[14]

The Story

Belgrade, Oct. 27—A few moments before she should have appeared on the stage at the Lioubliana Theater last night, Mme. Alla Behr, a Slovene actress, was found hanging dead in her dressing room. The reason for the suicide is unknown.

The Facts

After the first act. Not at the Lioubliana, but the Klägenfurt. Her name, Ella Beer. Not Slovene, but Viennese. Not in her dressing room, but in her hotel. The reason was known.

How could the reporter make such a total botch of the story? It's really not too difficult to imagine. He probably arrived at the scene late, found the area cordoned off, and got his details from bystanders or police keeping the crowd back—in other words, from people whose only knowledge was the fragments of fact and hearsay that had circulated among them.

Errors are sometimes made from simple carelessness. For example, it was reported in an upstate New York daily newspaper that Thomas Simmons was arrested for striking Carl Peterson on the head. A day or two later, a corrected version was published. It seems Peterson had struck Simmons.[15] All those who read the first version but missed the second "knew" what had happened, but they were wrong.

But what of magazine articles and books? These are researched more carefully than newspaper articles and therefore ought to be more accurate. Edwin L. Clarke explains how they, too, can be flawed:

> It is well known that secondary sources are likely to be written to harmonize with generally accepted beliefs and prejudices. Most popular histories, for instance . . . make heroes more heroic, villains more wicked, battles bloodier, and peaces more glorious than the best primary sources warrant. In short, they tend to present historical events, not as they were, but as the author likes to think of them, or as he believes his public likes or ought to think of them.[16]

THE PROBLEM OF REMEMBERING

Finally, all three ways of knowing (experience, observation, and report) are subject to another problem, one that occurs days, months, or years later: inaccurate remembering. This assertion may seem far-fetched because, in the popular view, memory is an unimpeachable mental recording of events—a videotape, as it were, that does not fade with the passing of time and can be played back on demand. However, this notion is erroneous. As Elizabeth Loftus, a University of Washington experimental psychologist and expert on memory, explains:

> Most theoretical analyses of memory divide the process into three separate stages. First the acquisition stage, in which the perception of the original event is put into the memory system; second, the retention stage, the period of time that passes between the event and the recollection of a particular piece of information; and third, the retrieval stage, in which a person recalls stored information. Contrary to popular belief, facts don't come into our memory and passively reside there untouched and unscathed by future events. Instead, we pick up fragments and features from our environment and these go into memory where they interact with our prior knowledge and expectations—information that is already stored in our memory. Thus experimental psychologists think of memory as being an integrative process—a constructive and creative process—rather than a passive recording process such as a videotape.[17]

In her widely replicated experiments, Loftus has demonstrated that memory is amazingly malleable. For example, after showing videos of events and asking people to remember what they saw, she can by subtle suggestion "plant" details of people, places, and things that were not present in the original experience. But psychologists' subtle suggestions aren't the only influences on memory. Our own present attitudes can cause us to delete some parts of a memory, condense others, and invent things that were not part of the original experience.[18]

Even eyewitness testimony is subject to this distortion. "It has been found," one report states, "that [eye]witnesses have a tendency both to perceive and to remember things, first, according to their expectations, second, according to their emotional bias, and third, according to their private notions as to what would be the natural or reasonable way for things to happen."[19]

A simple example, of a kind that everyone has experienced at one time or another, will illustrate how easily we can manipulate our memories. Professor Sage is sitting captive at a faculty meeting as a long-winded administrator drones on and on. Seeking escape, he opens a book and begins to read. Suddenly he hears his name spoken: "Dr. Sage, may I have your attention, please?" Caught off guard, he looks up awkwardly, accidentally drops his book, and stammers, "Uh ... I was listening ... sort of ... sorry."

As he is driving home after the meeting, his mind ranges over the responses he could have made to the speaker. In the one he likes best, he rises to his feet dramatically and replies in his most withering tone, "Sir, my attendance at this meeting may be required, but my attention must be *earned*." Several months later, Professor Sage is talking with a friend and recounts the experience as it exists in his memory. Which version does he tell? The one he has come to believe really happened: the imagined one.

This may seem a rather pessimistic view of knowing and remembering, but you shouldn't be discouraged by it. It is not the whole story, only the neglected side. Although knowing accurately and remembering with little or no distortion do not happen automatically, they are still possible if we strive for them.

WHAT ARE OPINIONS?

Opinions are intensely personal, so it is understandable that people have strong feelings about theirs. But many people carry those feelings beyond the boundaries of good sense. They take the valid idea "Everyone has a right to his or her opinion" to the ridiculous extreme of "Everyone's opinion is right." No one can hope to be a good thinker without acquiring a mature understanding of the nature of opinion.

The basic problem with the word *opinion* is that it is too general. It is made to carry a heavier load than it can bear, covering both expressions of taste and expressions of judgment.

Expressions of Taste

Expressions of taste describe internal states and preferences. They say essentially, "I like this" and "I dislike that." For example, one may say, "I find bald men attractive" or "I wouldn't buy any car but a Buick" or "When I look at a painting of a cow, I want to see something resembling a cow, not a swirl of color" or "Yellow and purple go well together." All these statements are expressions of taste. We may share the preferences or find them deplorably vulgar, but we have no business asking someone to defend these statements. No defense is necessary.

Expressions of Judgment

Expressions of judgment are assertions about the truth of things or about the wisdom of a course of action. Thus, if people say, "Bald men get more colds than hirsute men" or "Buicks are more economical cars than Fords" or "Paintings of cows that are unrecognizable as cows are inferior paintings" or "Yellow and purple combinations are a sign of aesthetic disability," they are not expressing taste (though their taste may be lurking in the background). They are expressing judgment every bit as much as if they had commented on the question of whether the death penalty deters crime or whether the voting age should be raised.

It is not impolite or undemocratic to challenge an expression of judgment. Judgments are only as good as the evidence that supports them. History is filled with examples of judgments based either on insufficient evidence or a narrow interpretation of evidence. In many cases, they did untold harm because people were timid about challenging them.

For centuries, people accepted the idea that the heart rather than the brain is the center of human consciousness. As late as the seventeenth century, people believed that the planets were guided in their orbits by angels. (Even the renowned astronomer Johannes Kepler did not question this belief.)[20] Fossils, which were known to exist long before Charles Darwin's day, were interpreted as relics of plants and animals destroyed by Noah's flood, as creations of Satan to deceive religious people, or as tests of religious faith put in the ground by God.[21]

Similarly, at various times our ancestors believed that disordered behavior was caused by demons and that the most effective cure was either magic, an enema, imprisonment in an asylum, beating, spinning in a rotating machine, or stoning to death.[22] And as late as 1902, books were being written proclaiming that black people were created along with animals to serve Adam, that they possessed minds but not souls, that Adam's temptress was a black servant, and that Cain married a black woman and so mixed the blood of men and beasts.[23]

The fact that human judgment can be not only wrong but also ludicrous is the best reason to base your judgments on sufficient evidence, carefully interpreted, rather than on prejudice, whim, or blind faith. You also need to be quick to reconsider your judgments when new evidence challenges them.

UNDERSTANDING CAUSE AND EFFECT[24]

A clear understanding of cause and effect relationships is crucial to the responsible formation of opinions. Unfortunately, there is a great deal of confusion about such relationships, and this can cause a number of errors. One error is to see cause and effect relationships where there are none. Another is to see only the simple and obvious cause and effect relationships and miss the complex and/or subtle ones. A third is to believe that causation is relevant only to material forces and is unrelated to human affairs. To avoid such confusion, you must understand four facts.

1. One event can precede another without causing it. Some people believe that when one event precedes another, it must be the cause of the other. Most superstition is rooted in this notion. For example, breaking a mirror, having a black cat cross your path, or walking under a ladder is believed to cause misfortune. You don't have to be superstitious to make this mistake. You may believe that your professor gave an unannounced quiz today because students were inattentive the day before yesterday, whereas he may have planned it at the beginning of the semester. Or you may believe the stock market fell because a new president took office when other factors might have prompted the decline.

The problem with believing that preceding events necessarily cause subsequent events is that such thinking overlooks the possibility of *coincidence*. This possibility is the basis of the principle that "correlation does not prove causation." In order to establish a cause and effect relationship, it is necessary to rule out coincidence or at least to make a persuasive case against it.

2. Not all causation involves force or necessity. The term "causation" is commonly associated with a physical action affecting a material reality. For example, a lightning bolt striking a house and the house catching fire and burning. Or a flower pot out the window being accidentally dropped out a window and then falling to the ground and breaking. Or a car speeding failing to negotiate a curve, careening off the highway, and crashing into a tree. In such cases, a scientific principle or law applies (combustion, gravity, inertia) and the effect is inevitable or at least highly predictable.

That type of causation is valid, but it would be a mistake to think of it as the *only* type. Causation also occurs in the non-material realities we call human affairs—more specifically, in the processes of emotion and thought. This type of causation has little if anything to do with scientific principles or laws, is almost never inevitable, and is often difficult to predict.

If we are to avoid oversimplification, we need to define causation in such a way as to cover both material and non-material realms. We will therefore define causation as *the phenomenon of one thing influencing the occurrence of another.* The influence may be major or minor, direct or indirect, proximate or remote in time or space. It may also be irresistible, as in the examples of combustion, gravity, and inertia mentioned above; or resistible, as in following parental teaching or the example of one's peers. In the latter case, and in other matters involving ideas, the influence (cause) does not *force* the effect to occur but instead *invites, encourages,* or *inspires* it. Consider these examples:

> The idea that criminals are not responsible for their behavior has inspired criminal defense attorneys to transfer blame from their clients to parents, teachers, and society in general. Such appeals have encouraged some judges and juries to treat criminals more leniently than they previously did.

> The idea that taking up arms against others is morally wrong has led some people to believe not only military aggression is never acceptable, even in the defense of one's country against unprovoked attack. That belief, in turn, makes some people reluctant to consider "just war" arguments.

> The idea that intelligence is genetically determined led early twentieth century educators to conclude that thinking cannot be taught, and thus to emphasize rote learning and expand vocational curriculums.

> The idea that feelings are a reliable guide to behavior has led many people to set aside restraint and follow their impulses. This change has arguably led to an increase in incivility, road rage, and spouse abuse, among other social problems.

> The idea that self-esteem is prerequisite to success changed the traditional idea of self-improvement, inspired hundreds of books focused on self-acceptance, and led educators to more indulgent views of homework, grading, and discipline.

In each of these examples, one idea influenced the occurrence of an action or belief and, in that sense, *caused* it. Columnist George Will no doubt had this view of causation in mind when he encountered the claim that "no one has ever dropped dead from viewing 'Natural Born Killers,' or listening to gangster rap records." Will responded, "No one ever dropped dead reading 'Der Sturmer,' the Nazi anti-Semitic newspaper, but the culture it served caused six million Jews to drop dead."[25]

3. There is a wild card in human affairs—free will. To say that human behavior is less predictable than material phenomena does not mean that human behavior is not predictable at all. When two ideas, or an idea and a behavior, are strongly linked, one is a good indicator of the other. Samuel Johnson was acknowledging this fact when he wrote: "He that overvalues himself will undervalue others, and he that undervalues others will oppress them." Also, when he remarked about an acquaintance: "But if he does really think that there is no distinction between virtue and vice, why, Sir, when he leaves our houses let us count our spoons."

Other indicators of behavior are habit and fashion. Habit inclines smokers to continue smoking, liars to continue lying, and selfish people to go on being selfish. As for fashion, when leading designers say "hemlines should be raised," hordes of women comply. When oversized beltless denim jeans are in vogue, hordes of young men waddle down the street, tops of pants below hips and crotches touching knees. When iconic athletes shave their heads, legions of fans shave theirs.

Some fashions develop incrementally, sometimes occurring over two or three generations. In that case, people's responses change so gradually that they are unaware they have changed at all. Consider the case of sexual content on TV and in films.

In the 1950s, little violence and sex were shown on-screen and what was shown was tame. Then viewers were given glimpses of blood and gore and brief peeks at naked flesh. Year by year, the number of such scenes increased and the camera drew a little closer and lingered a little longer over them. Over time, one thematic taboo after another was broken. Eventually, violence and sexuality were joined, and themes of rape, child molestation, and even cannibalism were introduced. More recently, the industry crafted a new vehicle for assaulting the senses—the forensics program, which depicts rape-murders as they happen, then presents every gory detail of the autopsies in extreme close-up, accompanied by frequent, graphic flashbacks to refresh the shocking details of the crimes.

Each of these changes provoked serious protests. In time, however, as sensational images became familiar, the protests diminished to the point where those who object to graphic sex and violence are considered odd. Simply said, over time sensationalism became familiar and that fact caused it to be accepted.

So far we have noted that causation occurs through force or necessity in material events, but through influence in non-material events—that is, in human affairs. Also, that in human affairs, effects are to some extent predictable but much less so than in material events. Now we need to consider why they are less predictable. The answer is because *people possess free will*—that is, the capacity to respond in ways that oppose even the strongest influences. Free will is itself a causative factor, and one that can trump all others. This explains why some people who grow up in the worst of circumstances—for example, in dysfunctional, abusive families or in crime-ridden neighborhoods in which the main sources of income are drug-dealing and prostitution—resist all the negative influences and become decent, hard-working, and law-abiding. (Also, why people who are more fortunate economically and socially fall short of those ideals.)

It has been rightly said that people can seldom choose the circumstances life places them in, but they can always choose their responses to those circumstances. In any investigation of causes and effects in human affairs, the factor of free will must be considered.

4. Causation is often complex. When a small pebble is dropped into a serene pool of water, it causes ripples in every direction and those ripples can affect even distant waters. NASA researchers have found a similar process at work in the atmosphere: tiny particles in the air called aerosols can have a rippling effect on the climate thousands of miles away from their source region.

Effects in human affairs can also be complex. In an effort to cut costs, the owner of a chemical plant may dispose of chemicals in a nearby stream which flows into a river. This action may result in effects he did not intend, including the pollution of the river, the killing of fish, and even the contracting of cancer by people living far from his plant. Those effects will be no less real because he did not intend them.

A woman in the early stages of influenza, unaware that she is ill, may sneeze while on a crowded airplane and infect dozens of her fellow passengers. As a result, they may lose time at work; some may have to be hospitalized; those with compromised immune systems could conceivably die. Given her lack of knowledge of her condition, no reasonable person would consider her culpable (morally responsible) for the effects of her sneeze, but there would still be no doubt that she caused them.

A car is driving on the Interstate at night. In rapid succession, a deer jumps out, the driver slams on his brakes but still hits and kills the deer. The car traveling closely behind slams into his car, and five other cars do likewise, each crashing into the car in front. As a result of this chain reaction, the drivers and passengers suffer a variety of injuries—minor in the case of those wearing seat belts, major in others. The task of identifying the causative factors requires careful attention to the details. The initial cause was the deer's crossing the road at an unfortunate time, but that is not the only cause. The first driver caused the deer's demise. Each of the other drivers caused the damage to the front end of his/her car and back end of the car in front.[26] And the passengers who did not fasten their seat belts caused their injuries to be more severe than those of other drivers and passengers.

These examples contain a valuable lesson about the need for care in investigating causes and effects. But this lesson will be even clearer if we examine a case in the way investigation usually proceeds—*backwards* in time from the latest effect to the earliest causative factor; that is, to the "root" cause.

For example, it has been clear for some time that the number of people of Middle Eastern origin living in Europe has increased so dramatically that before long, according to some observers, Europe might well be called "Eurabia." What *caused* this change? Analysts found that for decades European companies, with their governments' blessing, have been inviting foreigners to work in their countries and these workers brought their families, formed their own enclaves, built their own mosques and churches, and "planted" their own ethnic cultures. The next question was what *caused* the governments to approve this influx of workers? The answer is that the native population of European countries had declined to a point near or below "replacement level" and there were too few native-born workers to fill the available jobs and thus fund older people's pensions and health care services.

What *caused* the population decline? The availability of effective birth control techniques in the 1960s and 1970s and the choice of more and more families to employ those techniques. What *caused* so many families to limit the number of their children? One factor was the century-long population movement from rural areas to cities, where children are an economic burden rather than an asset. Others were the growing emphasis on self-fulfillment and the corresponding tendency to regard child-rearing as self-stifling.

As even this brief analysis of causes and effects suggests, facile responses to complex issues—in this case, "Middle Easterners are trying to take over Europe" or "The Crusades are here again, in reverse"—are not only unhelpful but unfair. The following tips will help you avoid oversimplification in your analyses:

Remember that events seldom, if ever, "just happen." They occur as the result of specific influences, and these influences may be major or minor, direct or indirect, proximate or remote in time or space; also irresistible (forced or necessary) or resistible (invited, encouraged, or inspired).

Remember, too, that free will is a powerful causative factor in human affairs, and it is often intertwined with other causes. In the case of the changes in European society, the movement of people from farm to city and the use of birth control were individual choices, but the greater availability of jobs in the cities (an economic reality) and birth control technology (a scientific development) were not.

Be aware that in a chain of events, an effect often becomes a cause. For example, the decline in population in Europe caused the importation of foreign workers, which in turn caused a change in the ratio of native-born to foreign citizens, which may in time alter the continent's dominant values and attitudes.

When dealing with human affairs, outcomes can be unpredictable. Therefore, in determining causes, you may have to settle for probability rather than certainty (as you would in matters that lend themselves to scientific measurement). In other words, you might conclude that something is *more likely than not* or, when the probability is very high, *substantially more likely*, to be the cause. Either of these conclusions has significantly more force than mere possibility, but it falls short of certainty. The difference is roughly analogous to the difference in legal standards of judgment: in civil cases, the standard is "a preponderance of the evidence" or "clear and convincing evidence," whereas in criminal cases, it is the more demanding standard of "beyond a reasonable doubt".

DEBATING MORAL QUESTIONS

Nowhere is modern thinking more muddled than over the question of whether moral issues are debatable. Many argue they are not, saying it is wrong to make "value judgments." This view is shallow. If value judgments were wrong, ethics, philosophy, and theology would be unacceptable in a college curriculum—an idea that is obviously silly. As the following cases illustrate, it is impossible to avoid making value judgments.

Raoul Wallenberg was a young Swedish aristocrat. In 1944, he left the safety of his country and entered Budapest. Over the next year, he outwitted the Nazis and saved as many as 100,000 Jews from the death camps (he was not himself Jewish). In 1945, he was arrested by the Russians, charged with spying, and imprisoned in a Russian labor camp. He undoubtedly perished there.[27] Now, if we regard him as a hero (as there is excellent reason to do), we are making a value judgment. Yet, if we regard him neutrally, as no different from anyone else, we are also making a value judgment. We are judging him to be neither hero nor villain, only unexceptional.

Consider another case. A 20-year-old mother left her three infant sons unattended in a garbage-strewn tenement in New York City.[28] Police found them there, starving, the youngest child lodged between a mattress and a wall, covered with flies and cockroaches, and the eldest playing on the second-floor window ledge. The police judged the mother negligent, and the court agreed. Was it wrong for them to judge? No. Judging was unavoidable. Either she was negligent or she was not.

No matter how difficult it may be to judge such moral issues, we *must* judge them. Value judgment is the basis of our social code as well as our legal system. The quality of our laws is directly affected by the quality of our moral judgments. A society that judges blacks inferior is not likely to accord blacks equal treatment. A society that believes a woman's place is in the home is not likely to guarantee women equal employment opportunity.

Other people accept value judgments as long as they are made *within* a culture and not about other cultures. Right and wrong, they believe, vary from one culture to another. It is true that an act frowned on in one culture may be tolerated in another, but the degree of difference has often been grossly exaggerated. When we first encounter an unfamiliar moral view, we are inclined to focus on the difference so much that we miss the similarity.

For example, in medieval Europe animals were tried for crimes and often formally executed. In fact, cockroaches and other bugs were sometimes excommunicated from the church.[29] Sounds absurd, doesn't it? But when we penetrate beneath the absurdity, we realize that the basic view—that some actions are reprehensible and ought to be punished—is not so strange. The core idea that a person bitten by, say, a dog has been wronged and requires justice is very much the same. The only difference is our rejection of the idea that animals are responsible for their behavior.

Is it legitimate, then, for us to pass judgment on the moral standards of other times or places? Yes, if we do so thoughtfully, not simply concluding that whatever differs from our view is necessarily wrong. We can say, for example, that a culture that treats women as property or places less value on their lives than on the lives of men is acting immorally by denying women their human rights. Consider the following cases.

In nineteenth-century Rio de Janeiro, Brazil, a theatrical producer shot and killed his wife because she insisted on taking a walk in the botanical gardens against his wishes. He was formally charged with her murder, but the judge dismissed the charge. The producer was carried through the streets in triumph. The moral perspective of his culture condoned the taking of a woman's life if she disobeyed her husband, even in a relatively small matter. A century later, that perspective had changed little. In the same city, in 1976, a wealthy playboy, angry at his lover for flirting with others, fired four shots into her face at point-blank range, killing her. He was given a two-year suspended sentence in light of the fact that he had been "defending his honor."[30]

Surely it is irresponsible for us to withhold judgment on the morality of these cases merely because they occurred in a different culture. It is obvious that in both cases the men's response—murder—was out of all proportion to the women's "offenses" and therefore demonstrated a wanton disregard for the women's human rights. The men's response is thus properly judged immoral. And this judgment implies another: the culture condoning such behavior is guilty of moral insensitivity.

THE BASIS OF MORAL JUDGMENT

On what basis should moral judgment be made? Certainly not the majority view—that is too unreliable. In the 1976 murder in Rio, for example, a radio poll revealed that 90 percent of the people surveyed agreed with the verdict. Hitler enjoyed the support of a majority of the German people. The American people at one time supported slavery. And more recently, the majority first opposed abortion, then approved it. Nor should the basis of moral judgments be feelings, desires, or preferences. If it were, then we would be forced to conclude that every rapist, every murderer, every robber is acting morally. Conscience provides a better basis for judgment, but it, too, can be uninformed or insensitive. (After all, the most vicious criminals sometimes feel no remorse.)

The most reliable basis for moral judgment, the basis that underlies most ethical systems, is the principle that people have rights existing independently of any government or culture. The most fundamental is the right to be treated with respect and left undisturbed as long as one does not infringe on others' rights. Other rights—such as "life, liberty, and the pursuit of happiness"—are extensions of that right.

The basic principle, of course, is not itself adequate for a judgment of complex moral questions. Additional working principles are needed. The following four are found in most ethical systems and provide common ground for the discussion of issues, even among people of very different ethical perspectives:

1. Relationships with other people create *obligations* of various kinds, and these should be honored unless there is compelling reason not to do so. There are, for example, formal agreements or contracts, obligations of family membership (parent to child, child to parent, and spouse to spouse), obligations of friendship, employer–employee obligations, and business and professional obligations.

2. Certain *ideals* enhance human life and assist people in fulfilling their obligations to one another. These should be honored whenever possible. Among the most important ideals are tolerance, compassion, loyalty, forgiveness, peace, brotherhood, justice (giving people their due), and fairness (being impartial, as opposed to favoring selected people).

3. The *consequences* of some actions benefit people, whereas those of other actions harm people. The former actions should be preferred over the latter. Consequences, of course, can be emotional as well as physical, momentary as well as lasting, and subtle as well as obvious.

4. *Circumstances* alter cases. Generalizations have their place, but too often they are used as a substitute for careful judgment. "Taking a human life is wrong" is useful as a general moral outlook, but it provides little help in deciding real cases. It blurs important distinctions. A "hit man" for the mob takes a life when completing a contract. So does a police officer who kills a robber in self-defense. And so does a small child who mistakes a real pistol for a toy and accidentally shoots a sibling. But all three acts are very different from one another. Good thinking about issues means getting beyond generalizations and examining the particulars of the case.

To achieve depth in your examination of moral issues and wisdom in your judgment, you must deal effectively with complexities. The presence of two or more conflicting obligations or ideals creates complexity. So does the likelihood of multiple consequences, some beneficial and some harmful. Here is an easy-to-follow guide for dealing with such complexities.

1. Where two or more obligations are in conflict, decide which is the most serious obligation or which existed first.

2. Where two or more ideals are in conflict, ask which is the highest or most important ideal.

3. Where multiple consequences exist, some good and some bad, ask which are most significant and whether the good effects outweigh the bad, or the reverse.

Let's look at an actual moral issue and see how these considerations apply. Ralph is a middle-aged man. In his youth, he was a good athlete, and his son Mark grew up sharing his father's enthusiasm for sports. In seventh grade, Mark went out for three sports but was rather poor in two of them. Basketball was his best sport; in that, he was fair but not outstanding. Ralph decided that Mark could be a first-string player only if he received some assistance. So Ralph struck up a friendship with the junior varsity and varsity basketball coaches. He invited them to his house for dinner, opened his personal sports library to them, and got them tickets to professional games through his business contacts.

Through his friendship with the coaches, Ralph was able to help his son. He spoke to them often about Mark's intense desire to excel in basketball and asked whether they would mind giving Mark some tips to improve his game. The coaches were happy to help Mark; their help was an expression of their friendship with Ralph. They opened the gym to him on weekends and took personal responsibility for developing his skills.

Soon Mark was playing junior varsity basketball. Ralph took every opportunity not only to remind the coaches of Mark's dedication but also to point out other players' weaknesses and apparent lack of dedication. Mark received more playing time in each game than his skills alone justified, and in time he became the team's scoring leader. When he moved up to the varsity, Mark received further special treatment. He was almost never benched, even when his team was far ahead; instead, he was kept in to raise his point total. During his senior year, most of the team's plays were designed for him. And Ralph persuaded the coaches to write letters praising Mark's playing to a number of college coaches.

Did Ralph behave morally? Let's apply the principles we discussed earlier and see. There are three important obligations involved in this case: Ralph's obligation to guide his son responsibly to manhood, through teaching and example; obligations of friendship between Ralph and the coaches; and the coaches' obligation to help all their players develop their potential and learn the values associated with sports.

The ideals that should be considered are sensitivity to others' needs, justice, and fairness. The first applies to Ralph: He should have appreciated the other players' (his son's teammates') needs for encouragement, support, and equal opportunity. The other two ideals, justice and fairness, apply to the coaches: They should have considered giving each player on the team the attention and help he deserved, rather than concentrating their attention on one player. (This, of course, does not mean that it would be an injustice to give special attention to an outstanding player; Mark, remember, was only a fair player at the outset.) And the coaches should have considered treating players impartially (fairly). One way they could have done this was by opening the gym on weekends to all players who wished to practice, instead of only to one.

The clearest and most certain consequence was that Mark's skills were developed and the other players were shortchanged because they did not have the same opportunities. Other probable consequences were that Mark's teammates developed a feeling of bitterness and cynicism over the coaches' favoritism and that Mark acquired the attitude that it was permissible, even desirable, for him to disregard other people's rights and needs to achieve his own goals.

It is clear that though Ralph's actions achieved some good (the development of his son's skills), they also caused a great deal of harm to a number of people.

The obvious harm was to the other players. But Ralph's actions also caused the coaches to put friendship over responsibility to their players and to violate the ideals of justice and fairness. (The main responsibility for the coaches' actions was, of course, their own. They could have resisted Ralph's influence.) Moreover, Ralph's actions probably harmed even his son. The self-serving attitude created in him far outweighed the development of his modest athletic skill.

In light of these considerations, we would find Ralph's actions morally wrong. Further, the fact that he knew what he was doing and actually *planned* it makes him even more blameworthy.

DEALING WITH DILEMMAS

Moral issues frequently pose dilemmas, situations in which a number of choices are available, but no choice is completely satisfactory. Such situations are frustrating. No matter what choice we consider, it seems the wrong one. "It's impossible to decide," we tell ourselves. Such situations are best approached with a clear strategy in mind. The following strategy will help you get beyond confusion and indecision:

1. Remember that you needn't classify your choices into simple good-versus-bad terms. You can view them in a more sophisticated way. To do so, ask where each choice fits on the following scale:

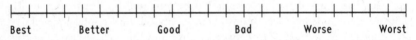

| Best | Better | Good | Bad | Worse | Worst |

Note: This approach will help you to distinguish between choices that at first glance seem equally moral.

2. In situations where the choices are all good, decide which is the *greater good*. In situations where none of the choices is really good, decide which is the *lesser evil*.

☐ WARM-UP EXERCISES

Remember that the warm-up exercises have no special relation to the chapter and generally concern matters of less consequence than the applications. They are intended mainly to "limber up" your thinking, so be as daring and imaginative as you wish in responding to them.

2.1 Your niece, a preschooler, asks you the following question: "Is it possible to remember the future?" Compose an answer simple and clear enough for her to understand.

2.2 If I say, "I'll see you tomorrow," three days in a row, am I saying the same thing each time? Explain your answer thoroughly.

2.3 A man is walking up on the down escalator, and it is moving down faster than he is moving up. Is he going upstairs or downstairs? Explain thoroughly.

APPLICATIONS

2.1 Read the following dialogue carefully, looking for flaws in thinking. If you find a flaw, identify it and explain what is wrong with it in sufficient detail to persuade someone who has read the passage but sees no flaw. If you find two or more flaws, identify and explain your thinking about each.

> CLEM: Can you believe that stuff Chapter 2 says about truth and opinion? I mean, it's a lot of garbage.
>
> CLYDE: I don't know. . . . It sort of made sense to me.
>
> CLEM: Come on, man, you've got to be kidding. How can some egghead textbook writer tell *me* what truth is for me? He's himself, not me. How can he see through my eyes or make up my mind? Only I can do that.
>
> CLYDE: But wait a minute . . .
>
> CLEM: Wait, nothing. You're taken in by all the words, man. Like that stuff about opinion. This is a democracy, isn't it? In a dictatorship, the government can say which opinion is right, but not here. My opinion is as good as anyone else's. It says so right in the Constitution.

2.2 When jazz musician Billy Tipton died at age 74, it was learned that "he" was a woman. Tipton had apparently begun the deception early in life to enhance "his" chances of success as a musician. Virtually everyone who knew, or knew of, Tipton (including "his" three adopted sons) was certain "he" was a man. Did the fact that millions of people believed Tipton was a man change the truth of the matter? Does your answer support or challenge the popular notion that people create their own truth?

2.3 Turn back to Application 1.1. Select one of the statements there (a–r) and recall your response to it. Examine that response in light of what you learned in this chapter about knowledge and opinion. That is, determine the source(s) of your view and its soundness.

2.4 The quotation that follows is by a famous American politician. Does it challenge any idea you read in this chapter? If so, identify the idea it challenges, and decide which view is more reasonable. If it does not challenge anything, identify the part of the chapter it is most in agreement with.

> It is a great and dangerous error to suppose that all people are entitled to liberty. It is a reward to be earned, not a blessing to be

gratuitously lavished on all alike;—a reward reserved for the intelligent, the patriotic, the virtuous and deserving;—and not a boon to be bestowed on a people too ignorant, degraded and vicious, to be capable either of appreciating or of enjoying it. (John C. Calhoun)[31]

2.5 Each of the following situations involves possible cause and effect relationships. Consider each in light of what you learned in this chapter:

a. The U.S. Congress has given "favored nation" status to certain foreign countries. The governments in several of those countries provide the funding for terrorist training camps. Religious leaders in the same countries promise a heavenly reward to those engaging in acts of terrorism. Instructors in the training camps teach young people to build explosive devices, hide them on their persons, and detonate them in crowded places. The young people do as they were taught, killing many unsuspecting and innocent people. Which of the individuals/groups specified can reasonably be said to have caused the deaths? Explain.

b. A skilled computer technician creates a virus that will erase the hard drives of all those who download it. He devises a clever e-mail guise for this virus and proceeds to send it to 50 people. Before they realize their computers will be affected, each of the fifty people forwards the deadly e-mail to others. Those recipients do the same and in a matter of weeks, thousands of individuals have their hard drives wiped out. Describe the causative role, if any, played by the various individuals.

c. Many commentators have expressed concern over the decline of civility in America. Be prepared to discuss whether any of the following could have played a causative role in this decline: Slogans such as "No rules, just right" (Outback Steakhouse); "Have it your way" (Burger King); and "On planet Reebok there are no rules." Glamorization of rule-breakers and even, in some instances, lawbreakers in movies. Displays of crudeness, vulgarity, and lack of self-control on shows like *The Jerry Springer Show*. Verbal assaults and rule-breaking behavior in professional wrestling. The frequent interruptions and shouting over others permitted, if not encouraged, on TV talk shows. The encouragement to express our urges, be assertive, and/or reject traditional standards of behavior offered by the authors of self-help books.

2.6 Each of the following cases involves a moral question. (Some also involve legal questions that do not concern us here.) Identify the important moral considerations in each, and then judge the morality of the action that was taken (or is proposed). Be sure to explain your reasoning carefully.

a. A doctor in Waltham, Massachusetts, was convicted of raping a nurse at the hospital where he was employed. While free, pending appeal of his conviction, he applied for a position at a Buffalo, New York, hospital. The Waltham hospital administration reportedly wrote him a strong letter of recommendation and did not mention the rape case. (Buffalo hospital officials learned of his conviction only when a new rape charge, involving patients, was filed against him in Waltham.)[32] Did the Waltham officials behave morally in withholding information concerning his rape conviction?

b. In Montpelier, Vermont, 11-year-old Ana Sola was struck by a car and rushed to the hospital. When her father, a Jehovah's Witness, denied permission for the blood transfusion that the doctors felt was imperative, a judge revoked the parents' custody of the girl and gave it to the state so the transfusion could be administered.[33] The judge's behavior was within legal limits, but was it moral?

c. The law tends to oppose sterilization of mentally impaired people unless they understand the nature of the operation and freely consent to it. But some years ago, the parents of three girls with severe mental impairment brought court action to gain the legal right to make the decision for their daughters.[34] Is their position morally acceptable?

ISSUE FOR EXTENDED ANALYSIS

Following is a more comprehensive thinking challenge than the others in the chapter. Analyze and respond to it as you did the challenge at the end of Chapter 1. Also, review "The Basis of Moral Judgment" and "Dealing with Dilemmas" in this chapter.

THE ISSUE: TREATMENT OF BRAIN-DAMAGED PATIENTS

A Florida woman, Terri Schiavo, had been brain damaged for 15 years as result of an accident. In 2005, her husband who had been living with another woman for several years and had fathered her children, said Terri wouldn't want to continue living in a "persistent vegetative state (PVS)" and petitioned the court to have her feeding tube removed. Her parents argued that she was not in a PVS and offered to take responsibility for her care. After several appeals, the court ordered her feeding tube to be removed. Two weeks later, she died. The fact that many more Americans are reaching old age and experiencing physical and mental debilitation has made this issue (and related end-of-life issues) especially relevant.

THE ESSAYS

The Right to Die
By Curt Weber

Few decisions are more personal than the decision about how one dies. In 2005 America watched the pathetic spectacle of a team of lawyers working every angle to prevent Terri Schiavo from having her personal wishes carried out.

Long before the accident that left her in a permanent vegetative state, Terri had told her husband that she would not ever want to live that way. But when he sought to honor her request, her parents proceeded to put one obstacle after another in his path. Only when all their legal appeals were exhausted was he able to allow her to die with dignity.

Terri's parents understandably found it difficult to see her life ended. They loved her and continued to hope for her eventual recovery. But that hope was without foundation. The eye movements she made in response to a floating balloon were nothing more than reflex responses. No one has ever recovered from such injuries to the brain.

The courts made the right decision in refusing legal maneuvers to reinsert her feeding tube. Had those maneuvers succeeded, she might have existed in that subhuman condition for years, without meaning or purpose to her life. Her husband would have been prevented from getting on with his life. Her parents and siblings would have maintained their tragic delusion. And countless hours and dollars of medical attention would have been wasted on a individual who had, by any reasonable measure, died many years earlier.

"Keep Them from Harm"
By Jessica Torres

"I will apply dietetic measures for the benefit of the sick according to my ability and judgment; I will keep them from harm. ..." So said the original Hippocratic Oath for doctors, the oath the courts determined should be violated in Terri Schiavo's case.

Terri Schiavo wasn't terminally ill. Everyone agreed she had a good chance of living many years—some say that is precisely why her husband sought to have her feeding tube removed. Nor was she receiving extraordinary care, such as being hooked up to a respirator. She was simply receiving ordinary nourishment.

Technically, Terri's husband was her legal guardian, but from all indications he lacked the basic requirement of guardianship in that his personal interests were in conflict with hers. Her death probably benefited him financially and certainly benefited him socially and morally by freeing him to remarry. The courts should have asked whether these factors disqualified him to be guardian. They also should have questioned whether his recollection of her spoken intentions seven years after her accident was too convenient to be relied upon.

A week or two after Terri Schiavo was starved to death, a school of dolphins became beached in Florida. Volunteers splashed water on them to keep their skin from drying out. Others bottle-fed them. How ironic—and how tragic—that the state of Florida treated those animals more humanely than it treated Terri Schiavo.

CLASS DISCUSSION

MILA: The Schiavo case had nothing to do with the sanctity of life, as conservatives claim. It was a right-to-die issue, pure and simple. The court wisely decided that the terminally ill should be able to choose to die with dignity.

JOE: You've got your facts wrong. Terri Schiavo wasn't terminally ill, and it's not at all clear that she wanted to die. Furthermore, the court didn't act on Terri's behalf. They simply decided that the husband's desire to be free of the burden of a bedridden wife trumped the parents' desire to care for her.

MILA: Look, her husband was her legal guardian, so he was the one to make the decision. And he chose to allow her to die peacefully. Medical authorities used the word "euphoric" to describe her final days.

JOE: I wish people would stop describing Terri's last days as "dignified" and "euphoric." There's nothing dignified about having one's body dry up and become emaciated, with one organ after another shutting down for lack of nourishment. There's also nothing euphoric about starving to death. If serial killers or even animals were treated that way, every human rights group would be up in arms.

MILA: You're ignoring some important considerations. She was in a "permanent vegetative state," as later confirmed by the autopsy. Also, she was taking up space in a hospice facility that could have been better used for a conscious person. And she was medicated to ensure that she felt no pain.

JOE: She shouldn't have been in a hospice facility in the first place because she wasn't terminally ill. Besides, the parents were eager to take her into their home. You're ignoring the most important, and dangerous, fact of all. The trend of treating human beings as disposable and allowing the courts to decide who should be denied food and water threatens all of us, and particularly the most vulnerable.

CHAPTER

3

Broaden Your Perspective

Have you noticed that many of the people who claim to be individuals dress, talk, and act exactly like other people? Is it possible that all the people who shave their heads, sport tattoos, or wear earrings in unusual places were not influenced by others?

In this chapter, we consider what it means to be an individual. We also discuss the habits that will help you reinforce *genuine* individuality and develop your capacities.

Do you know the story of the six blind men and the elephant? Able to rely only on their sense of touch, they reached out and touched an elephant to learn about it. One touched its side and decided that an elephant was like a wall. The second touched its trunk and decided—a snake. The third touched its tail— a rope; the fourth, its ear—a fan; the fifth, its leg—a tree; the last, its tusk—a spear. Now each had a clear picture of the elephant in mind. But because all the pictures were based on a limited perspective, all were wrong.[1]

All too often we are like the six blind men in our perspective on the world. We see narrowly, and our thinking suffers as a result. The first and perhaps saddest way we are victimized by narrow perspectives is in our view of our own potential. Most of us never come to know ourselves fully. We see only what we are and never realize the larger part of us: *what we have the capacity to be.* We never appreciate just how much of what we are is the result of accident.

Our development, for example, and our degree of success are strongly influenced by the way others regard us. In one experiment, researchers administered an intelligence test to an entire elementary school. The researchers told the faculty that the test would identify students who were ready to undergo a "learning spurt." Actually, the test did no such thing: the testers merely selected some students at random and identified them as the ones whose learning would enjoy a spurt. Teachers were subsequently observed using the same materials and methods for these students as for others. Nevertheless, at the end of the year, when the researchers again tested the student body, they found that the students who had been singled out had gained twice as many IQ points as the other students.

What was responsible for this gain? Obviously, the teachers had formed favorable attitudes toward these students and unconsciously transmitted their attitudes to the students. The students' self-images, in turn, were ultimately changed.[2]

If that experiment seems surprising, the following one, similar in its design, will seem astounding. Laboratory assistants were assigned the task of teaching rats to run a maze. They were told the rats were in two groups: fast learners and slow learners. Actually, all the rats were identical. After the test period, the rats that had been designated fast learners were found to have learned the maze better than the other rats. Like the schoolteachers, the lab assistants had formed preconceived notions about the rats, and those notions had not only affected the degree of patience and the amount of attention and encouragement the assistants displayed with the rats but also *influenced the rats' performance.*[3]

Studies show that confused, defeatist, helpless reactions are not inborn in us. They are *learned.* In one study, people were given problems they were told could be solved but that in fact could not be. As their efforts to solve the problems failed, the subjects experienced increasing frustration, until they finally accepted their helplessness and gave up. The real point of the study, though, came later. When the same people were given solvable problems, they continued to act helpless and to give up without really trying.[4]

What do these studies suggest about everyday life? That parents who are inconsistent in their demands and unpredictable in their reactions, teachers who focus on the negative rather than the positive, and coaches and activity leaders who ignore actual performance or contribution can rob us of our confidence, lead us into the habit of failure, and blind us to our real potential.

One of the distinguishing marks of many successful people is their refusal to define themselves by other people's assessments. Winston Churchill was branded a slow learner. Martha Graham was told that she did not have the right kind of body to become a dancer. Thomas Edison was urged to quit school because he was considered hopelessly stupid. Later, on his first job, working for the railroad, he set a train on fire with one of his experiments and was dismissed. And Albert Einstein's early record was even worse. Here are some of the details:

- He was not only an unimpressive student; he was told flatly by one teacher, "You will never amount to anything."
- At age 15 he was asked to leave school.
- When he took his first entrance exam to Zurich Polytechnic School, he failed and was required to spend a year in a Swiss High School before he could be admitted.
- At Zurich, he did mediocre work and was so unimpressive to his professors that he was rejected as a postgraduate assistant and denied a recommendation for employment.

- He eventually obtained a job as a tutor at a boarding school but was soon fired.
- He submitted a thesis on thermodynamics for a doctoral degree at Zurich. The thesis was rejected.
- Four years later, he submitted his special theory of relativity for a doctoral dissertation at the University at Bern. It was rejected.

"Wait," you may be saying, "Churchill, Graham, Edison, and Einstein were very special people. The question is whether *the average person* can overcome negative assessments." The answer is yes. To cite just one example, a teacher noticed that when students saw themselves as stupid in a particular subject, they unconsciously conformed to that image. They believed they were stupid, so they behaved stupidly. He set about changing their self-image. And when that change occurred, they no longer behaved stupidly.[5]

The lesson here is not that legitimate criticism or advice should be ignored nor that one can achieve competency in any field merely by belief. It is that you should not sell yourself short; your potential is undoubtedly much greater than you have ever realized. So when you catch yourself saying, "I'll never be able to do this" or "I don't have the talent to do that," remember that the past does not dictate the future. What people call talent is often nothing more than knowing the knack. And *that* can be learned.

BECOMING AN INDIVIDUAL

All the philosophers and sages tell us that individuals are rare. Yet the curious thing is that virtually all people consider themselves individuals. (Think about it: have you ever met anyone who admitted, "I am *not* an individual"?) If the philosophers are right, then most people are wrong in their self-assessment. The source of the error lies in the assumption that having unique genes and a unique collection of experiences guarantees individuality. If that were the case, no one could be a conformist. But there *are* conformists. Therefore, the assumption is unwarranted. Individuality is not inborn but acquired.

The key to becoming individuals is to look at ourselves honestly and objectively. This takes courage because it often involves abandoning wishful thinking and destroying cherished illusions about ourselves. How serious is *your* lack of individuality? Let's see. Ever since you lay helpless and gurgling in your crib, you have been learning. The moment you were able to use your senses, impressions rushed in on you. You received literally millions of impressions before you could interpret them with any sophistication. By the time you were able to interpret effectively, you had long since acquired a large repertoire of actions and reactions—by imitation. You endlessly practiced speaking and walking and, yes, *thinking* as your parents and siblings did.

Later, you attended school, and accepted your teachers' information and beliefs, often imitating their habits and attitudes. You learned, too, from your friends and classmates, and in time (when peer acceptance became more important), you said and did many things not because they seemed appropriate or mature or because you especially wanted to, but because you believed those things would gain you the crowd's acceptance. If you are like most people, you are still selecting your words and actions at least in part by what others want or expect from you.

But the greatest shaper of your attitudes, habits, and values has probably not been your parents, siblings, teachers, or friends. It has very likely been popular culture. According to a 2002 study of children's TV viewing, the average boy watches just under three hours a day, and the average girl, just over two and a half hours a day.[6] This means that from preschool through high school the average young person spends about 14,000 hours in front of the TV set, compared to about 11,000 hours in the classroom. And this doesn't take into account the time spent reading popular magazines, playing video games, and listening to music.

How does popular culture affect people? By placing viewers in the role of spectators, television tends to promote passivity. By bombarding people with print advertisements and commercials—an estimated 750,000 by age 18—advertising encourages people to be gullible and to accept biased testimony as fact. By building frequent scene shifts and commercial breaks into programs, television prevents viewers' attention spans from developing. By urging self-indulgence, impulsiveness, and instant gratification, advertising undermines self-discipline. By devoting forests of newspaper and magazine space to entertainers and providing them with talk-show platforms to parade their opinions, the media make it difficult for people to distinguish between excellence and mediocrity.

The process of being exposed to society—home, neighborhood, church, school, and so on—sociologists call *acculturation*. Essentially, it involves settling into our culture. The way we settle in, the way the culture shapes us, can be powerfully affected by our families' socioeconomic condition, their religious and political views, and the quality of the care they give us.

Acculturation can occur subtly, creating the illusion that our values, attitudes, and ideas were formed independently of other people and circumstances. Erich Fromm was referring to this kind of illusion when he noted that much of the time when we say we think something, we really ought to say, "It thinks in me."[7]

It's not hard to understand how we are deceived about our independence. We are much more acutely aware of the fact of having ideas than of the circumstances in which we received them. What we feel and believe are current experiences for us, so we tend to forget their origins. What we think, moreover, seems as much a part of us as the beating of our heart. The idea that our thoughts are borrowed from others is foreign and offensive, so we resist it.

To be an individual means more than claiming independence. It means achieving it. Here are three steps that will help you begin to achieve your individuality:

1. Acknowledge the influences that have shaped your thinking. Say to yourself, "My mind is full of other people's ideas and attitudes, which I received uncritically and accepted because I was young and trusting. Many of those ideas and attitudes are now hardened into principles and convictions. Yet some of them are surely erroneous or unworthy." Identify the people you have especially admired or been close to: your mother and father, an aunt

or uncle, a coach or teacher, a celebrity. Consider each person's convictions and actions. Decide exactly how those convictions and actions have contributed to your ideas and attitudes.

2. Sort out and evaluate your ideas and attitudes, even your most cherished ones. Ask, for example, what your political philosophy is. (That question, of course, means more than "Are you a Democrat or a Republican?" It includes your views on the proper role of government and on citizens' responsibility in a democracy.) Ask, too, about your views on religion, race, nationality, marriage, morality, and law. Compare your ideas and attitudes with other people's. Make your beliefs prove themselves, not on the basis of their familiarity or their compatibility with other ideas, but on their reasonableness in light of the evidence.

3. Choose the best ones. Decide as objectively as you can which ideas deserve your endorsement and which attitudes are worth striving to acquire. Remember that you are never being more an individual than when you resist the pressure of habit and change the way you think about a subject or issue because the evidence prompts you to do so.

Real individuality, of course, cannot be attained in a single sitting, or even in a hundred. It is an ongoing task, the occupation of a lifetime, but one that everyone who wants to be a good thinker must undertake.

■

HABITS THAT HINDER THINKING

In your effort to become more of an individual, try to identify any habits of mind interfering with clear thinking. Some of these habits will be peculiar to your own situation and depend on your unique background and experience. But there are a number of habits that victimize everyone to some extent. The most significant deserve close attention. They are the *mine-is-better* habit, *face saving, resistance to change, conformity, stereotyping,* and *self-deception.*

The Mine-Is-Better Habit

This habit is natural enough. It begins in early childhood. As children, we all said, "My bike is better than your bike"; "My dad is stronger than your dad"; "My mom is prettier than your mom." We believed what we said, too. Whatever we associated with was an extension of ourselves. Asserting its superiority was an expression of ego.

The habit does not go away easily as we grow up. "In later life," writes Rowland Jepson, "we are apt to think that the world in which we grew up was the best of all possible worlds, and to regard the customs and notions which helped to mold our own selves as the acme of wisdom and sound sense, never reached before or since."[8] And we tend to regard our present ideas, values, groups, and political and religious affiliations as superior, too.

Mine-is-better is undoubtedly as old as humankind. Primitive societies tend to regard those who are different—foreigners, criminals, the mentally deranged, the physically or emotionally handicapped, other races, other religions, and other social classes—as lesser beings. "The creature who does not 'belong' to the tribe, clan, caste or parish," they reason, "is not really human; he only aspires or pretends to be 'like us.' "⁹ From that, it is only a short step to the decision that such "different people," being subhuman, have no human rights, as some cultures have decided.¹⁰

We are appalled at such a view, yet our mine-is-better habit leads us to similar—if considerably less extreme—thinking and acting. If a friend proposes a change, we call her a reformer; if an enemy proposes a change, we call him a troublemaker or a fanatic. Likewise, the differences between a traitor and a defector, a religious denomination and a cult, a politician and a statesman or stateswoman depend on how close the person or subject is to us and our view.

The mine-is-better habit hinders our thinking. It destroys objectivity and prompts us to prefer self-flattering errors to unpleasant realities. If you wish to be a good thinker, you must learn to control this habit and keep your ego from interfering with your search for truth.

Face Saving

Like the mine-is-better habit, face saving is a natural tendency arising from our ego. Unlike mine-is-better, it occurs *after* we have said or done something that threatens to disturb our self-image or the image others have of us. Psychologists call face saving a *defense mechanism*, meaning it is a strategy we use to protect our image.

One common form of face saving is the excuse most children and many adults employ at one time or another: "It wasn't my fault—he [or she] made me do it" or "It wasn't my fault—I had no alternative." This excuse, though an obstacle to good thinking, at least has the virtue of acknowledging that something wrong or undesirable has occurred. The dishonesty lies in pointing the finger away from oneself.

A more dangerous form of face saving is called *rationalizing*. Rationalizing is a dishonest substitute for reasoning whereby we set out "to defend our ideas rather than to find out the truth about the matters concerned."¹¹ Let's say, for example, that you are a heavy smoker. As the evidence linking smoking to serious diseases mounts, you begin to realize that your habit harms you. You feel like a fool. But instead of admitting that smoking is harmful or at least examining the evidence and deciding whether it is valid, you say, "The case against smoking isn't conclusive" and "The relaxation of tension smoking achieves for me more than balances any minor harm it may cause me." That's rationalizing.

Although rationalizing sometimes resembles honest reasoning, there is a simple way to tell the difference between them. You are reasoning if your belief follows the evidence—that is, if you examine the evidence first and then make up your mind. You are rationalizing if the evidence follows your belief—that is, if you first decide what you'll believe and then select and interpret evidence to justify it.¹²

The process of face saving and its effect on thinking are effectively summed up by Rowland Jepson:

> When we have once adopted an opinion, our pride makes us [reluctant] to admit that we are wrong. When objections are made to our views, we are more concerned with discovering how to combat them than how much truth or sound sense there may be in them; we are at pains rather to find fresh support for our own views, than to face frankly any new facts that appear to contradict them. We all know how easy it is to become annoyed at the suggestion that we have made a mistake; that our first feeling is that we would rather do anything than admit it, and our first thought is "How can I explain it away?"[13]

To control your face-saving tendency, be alert for occasions when your ego is threatened; and remember this adage: A person who makes a mistake and refuses to admit it is thereby compounding the mistake.

Resistance to Change

Resistance to change is the tendency to reject new ideas and new ways of seeing or doing without examining them fairly. It has been the recurrent reaction to creativity throughout the ages. Galileo came close to losing his life when he suggested the sun, not the earth, was the center of the solar system. The inventors of the plow, the umbrella, the automobile, and the airplane were scoffed at, as were the individuals who first advocated using anesthetics during surgery, performing autopsies to determine the cause of death, and extending voting rights to women. Even the ending of child labor, which we now regard as eminently reasonable, was initially scorned: critics called it a Bolshevik attempt to nationalize children.

One cause of our tendency to resist change is simple laziness. Having got used to things one way, we resent being asked to regard them another way; doing so makes us break our routine. Another reason is excessive regard for tradition. The old ways must be best, we believe, because our parents and grandparents used them. New ideas and approaches seem an affront to our ancestors.

But what is tradition, really? Is it the best way of seeing or doing? In some cases, it certainly is. But in others, it is more like the path in the following verse by Sam Walter Foss:

> One day through the primeval wood
> A calf walked home as good calves should;
> But made a trail all bent askew,
> A crooked trail as all calves do.
> Since then three hundred years have fled,
> And I infer the calf is dead.
> But still he left behind his trail,
> And thereby hangs my moral tale.
> The trail was taken up next day
> By a lone dog that passed that way;

And then a wise bellwether sheep
Pursued the trail o'er hill and glade
Through those old woods a path was made.
And many men wound in and out
And dodged and turned and bent about
And uttered words of righteous wrath
Because 'twas such a crooked path;
But still they followed—do not laugh—
The first migrations of that calf,
And through this winding wood-way stalked
Because he wobbled when he walked.
This forest path became a lane
That bent and turned and turned again;
This crooked lane became a road,
Where many a poor horse with his load
Toiled on beneath the burning sun,
And traveled some three miles in one.
And thus a century and a half
They trod the footsteps of that calf.
The years passed on in swiftness fleet,
The road became a village street;
And thus, before men were aware,
A city's crowded thoroughfare.
And soon the central street was this
Of a renowned metropolis;
And men two centuries and a half
Trod in the footsteps of that calf.
Each day a hundred thousand rout
Followed this zigzag calf about
And o'er his crooked journey went
The traffic of a continent.
A hundred thousand men were led
By one calf near three centuries dead.
They followed still his crooked way,
And lost one hundred years a day;
For thus such reverence is lent
To well-established precedent.[14]

In situations where tradition is nothing more than "well-established precedent," or following in the footsteps of those who have gone before, it is more of an insult to our ancestors to follow them than to explore new paths.

Another more significant reason for resisting change is fear. Each of us has developed habits of thinking and acting. These habits, like old shoes, are comfortable. The very idea of trading them for something new is frightening: "How could I ever cope with daily situations?" Our imagination conjures up a hundred apprehensions, all of them intensified by being nameless. So we choose to resist the new rather than welcome it. Sometimes, we avoid feeling ashamed by pretending we are really being honorable and acting on principle.

Unfortunately, if we are resistant to change, we are resistant to discovery, invention, creativity, progress. Each of these, after all, first comes to the world as a new idea. *To resist change is to set our minds against our own best and most worthwhile ideas.*

Being open to change does not mean embracing every new idea uncritically; many new ideas prove, on examination, to be worthless or unworkable. Rather, it means being willing to suspend judgment long enough to give every new idea, no matter how strange it seems, a fair chance to prove itself.

Conformity

Not all conformity is bad. We put our out-of-town letters in the out-of-town post office slot, say hello instead of good-bye when we answer the phone, try to spell correctly and not violate the rules of grammar, and stop for red lights when driving. Such actions, and thousands of others like them, are a sensible kind of conformity. If we were to try nonconformity in such matters, we would waste valuable time, confuse or annoy those around us, or threaten the safety of ourselves and others.

Harmful conformity is what we do instead of thinking in order to belong to a group or to avoid the risk of being different. Such conformity is an act of cowardice, a sacrifice of independence for a lesser good. In time, it makes us more concerned about what others think than about what is right and true and sensible. Once we begin to conform, we quickly find ourselves saying and doing not what we believe is best, but what we believe others want or expect us to say and do. That focus dulls our ability to think creatively and critically.

It's not always easy to avoid conforming. Our friends, families, and associates may exert considerable pressure on us. It takes courage to say, "I disagree" or "That's wrong," when the group is firm in its view. If you've ever tried it, you know how painful that you're-being-a-traitor look can be. That's why so many people give in again and again until they have completely surrendered their individuality. One widely repeated laboratory experiment documented this surrender dramatically. The experiment involved two subjects, who were told they were participating in a memory test. One assumed the role of teacher; the other, the role of student. When the student gave a wrong answer, the teacher was supposed to deliver an electric shock. With each wrong answer, the shock increased.

The situation, of course, was rigged. There was really no electric shock, and the "student" was really an actor instructed to say he had a heart condition, to plead with the "teacher" to stop, and even to claim chest pains. At the highest level of shock, he remained silent, and since he was in another room, the "teacher" must have considered the possibility that the shock had killed him.

The result of the experiment? Fully 65 percent of the "teachers" administered the shocks up to the highest level. Most protested to the experimenter that they didn't want to inflict pain on the student, but when the experimenter insisted, they obeyed.[15]

Perhaps we would behave differently in that experiment. Perhaps not. In any case, the effects of conformity are all around us. Abraham Maslow observed:

> Too many people do not make up their own minds, but have their minds made up for them by salesmen, advertisers, parents, propagandists, TV, newspapers and so on. They are pawns to be moved by others rather than self-determining individuals. Therefore they are apt to feel helpless, weak, and totally determined; they are prey for predators, flabby whiners rather than self-determining persons.[16]

It would be a mistake to fight conformity by refusing to believe and act as others do, to be different for the sake of being different. That is no more thoughtful than mindless conformity. The right way to fight conformity is to think for yourself and not worry about how many people share your view.

Stereotyping

Stereotyping is an extreme form of generalizing. Generalizations classify people, places, and ideas according to their common elements. Thus, we may say that most basketball players are tall, that medical doctors study for years before being licensed to practice, that Honda Civics get better gas mileage than Corvettes. These are fair and reasonable generalizations. Some generalizations go beyond the boundaries of reasonableness; these are called *overgeneralizations*. The beliefs that, for example, city residents are less friendly than rural folk and that athletes don't do well in their studies are overgeneralizations.

Stereotyping, however, is a deeper and more serious problem than overgeneralization. A stereotype is a fixed, unbending generalization, irrationally maintained. As Walter Lippmann explains:

> Stereotypes are loaded with preference, suffused with affection or dislike, attached to fears, lusts, strong wishes, pride, hope. Whatever invokes the stereotype is judged with the appropriate sentiment. Except where we deliberately keep prejudice in suspense, we do not study a man and judge him to be bad. We see a bad man. We see a . . . sainted priest, a humorless Englishman, a dangerous [communist], a carefree Bohemian, a lazy Hindu, a wily Oriental, a dreaming Slav, a volatile Irishman, a greedy Jew, a 100% American. . . . Neither justice, nor mercy, nor truth, enters into such a judgment, for the judgment has preceded the evidence.[17]

The most common stereotypes are racial, religious, and ethnic. There is the stereotype of the black, the fundamentalist Christian, the Italian. But there are many other types as well, no less firm for being less common. There are stereotypes of homosexuals, the clergy, college dropouts, feminists, male chauvinists, New York City, singles' bars, motherhood—even God.

Stereotyping sets up a nice, neat mental warehouse for ideas. Everything has its own compartment. There is no comparing, no sorting, weighing, or selecting, just storage. Everything is presorted, predetermined, and prejudged. Thus, stereotyping impedes the mind's dynamic activity, forcing life's infinite variety, the myriad people and circumstances around us, into ready-made categories.

Many people find it difficult to overcome stereotypes because they tend to see them as accurate descriptions of the world, even as insights. Yet it is important to make the effort to expose them, for they distort our view of reality.

Self-Deception

A boy once went fishing with several friends. Someone suggested they all share whatever fish were caught. It seemed a reasonable idea, so the boy agreed. Then, as the day wore on and he caught more fish than his friends, his attitude began to change. By the end of the day, he was violently opposed to sharing and objected loudly, arguing that good anglers shouldn't be penalized for others' incompetence.[18]

That boy engaged in one of the many kinds of self-deception that tempt us all. "One of the most disturbing habits of the human mind," Katherine Anne Porter observed, "is its willful and destructive forgetting of whatever in its past does not flatter or confirm its present point of view."[19]

One of my colleagues often begins his classes in informal logic by asking students to do this exercise: "Think of the guy or girl you most resented in high school. In a couple of sentences, explain why you resented him or her." He has read hundreds of students' answers and has found that the great majority say, "That guy had the terrible habit of . . ." or "That girl lacked. . . ." Only one or two out of ten will say, "*I* was jealous (or immature or insecure)." In other words, any resentment is clearly the other's fault and not one's own. A similar kind of self-deception occurs when students who get low grades because of missing class, failing to hand in homework, or refusing to prepare for examinations accuse their teachers of favoritism and prejudice.

People with symptoms of serious diseases—cancer, for example—sometimes lie to themselves that the matter is not serious enough for them to see a doctor. Many divorced people deceive themselves about the reasons for the breakup of their marriages. Most alcoholics lie to themselves about their alcohol dependence; "I can stop anytime I want to" is the common lie. And most marijuana or crack smokers deceive themselves that they smoke because they want to, rather than as a means of escape from unpleasant experiences and frustrations. If they smoke heavily, they may also persuade themselves that they are not getting burned out, even when their symptoms—loss of memory, listlessness, and confusion, among others—are obvious to everyone around them.

In addition, many people deceive themselves about their competency, first pretending to others that they are knowledgeable and then coming to believe the pretense themselves. Edwin L. Clarke describes their behavior this way:

> Persons who, for instance, would consider it the height of presumption to advise an engineer how to plan a simple culvert, have no hesitation in speaking with an air of authority on far more complex questions such as Portuguese immigration or the nature of a desirable currency, subjects on which their knowledge is very superficial and only too often derived from inaccurate and biased sources.[20]

To be a good thinker, you must be able to decide honestly what information you need to solve a problem and then, after acquiring that information, to evaluate it fairly. You will be able to do these things only if you have learned to be honest with yourself.

All six of the habits that hinder thinking—the mine-is-better habit, face saving, resistance to change, conformity, stereotyping, and self-deception—can become deeply ingrained and therefore difficult to overcome. Nevertheless, they can all be overcome with desire and effort. The following section explains how to attack them.

OVERCOMING BAD HABITS

The key to overcoming the bad habits we have been discussing is to examine your first impressions of problems and issues, particularly strong ones prompting you to take a stand immediately without examining the evidence or weighing competing arguments. By closely examining such impressions, you will often be able to determine that a particular bad habit—resistance to change, for example, or stereotyping—is interfering with your thinking.

Marvin and Martha both read the same magazine article, which discusses a scientific book on the subject of life after death.[21] The article explains that the book is a study of 116 people's near-death experiences and their subsequent memories of floating out of their bodies and, in some cases, traveling down a dark tunnel toward a bright light. It also points out that the author is a medical professor who began his study as a skeptic and conducted his investigations in a thoroughly scientific manner. Finally, it notes that although the author personally believes in life after death, he neither claims that his studies prove that it exists nor offers his findings in support of any particular religious perspective.

As Marvin begins reading the article, a strong feeling rises in him: "Here it is—proof that there's life after death—just what we need to show the skeptics, the doubters, those of little faith." Because he merely yields to the feeling without examining it, Marvin fails to realize that it masks mine-is-better thinking, stereotyping, and conformity. Later that day, he may be heard in the snack bar proclaiming that the book's author is a champion of Marvin's own religion and that the "entire scientific community" has now "conceded" that Marvin's view of an afterlife is "unquestionably true."

A very different, but equally strong, feeling rises in Martha as she reads the article: "More nonsense from mindless religious quacks who can't face the reality of oblivion." She, too, yields to the feeling unquestioningly and so fails to realize that it is a mixture of the same errors: mine-is-better thinking, stereotyping, and conformity. At lunch the next day, she tells her friends that the book says nothing of value, calling it a "pathetic attempt" to brainwash people.

Marvin's and Martha's self-deception may seem laughable, but it is really sad. Without realizing it, each has read without profit, remaining in a state of self-flattering ignorance instead of learning and growing. Each has substituted what Henshaw Ward termed *thobbing* for considering and evaluating ideas.

The term combines the *th* from *thinking,* the *o* from *opinion,* and the *b* from *believing.* Whenever people think the opinion that pleases them and then believe it, they are thobbing.[22]

Your best protection against thobbing is to develop the habit of *thinking about your thinking.* (The technical name for this activity is *metacognition.*) More specifically, be aware of your initial impressions of problems and issues, particularly those impressions that prompt you to take a stand immediately without examining the evidence or weighing competing views. When such feelings arise, control them instead of yielding to them, and force yourself to be objective.

 ## WARM-UP EXERCISES

Remember that unlike the applications, the warm-up exercises have no special relation to the chapter contents. They may demand creative thinking, critical thinking, or both.

3.1   As soon as you enter the room, your roommate challenges you. "You're taking a course in thinking, so answer this: If perfection in anything is beyond human attainment, what's the point in striving to be better in anything?" What do you reply?

3.2   Your little niece looks puzzled. You ask her what's wrong, and she says, "It doesn't make sense: We blow on our hands to warm them when they're cold, but we blow on our food to cool it when it's hot. How can blowing make things both hot and cold?" Construct a clear and meaningful reply.

3.3   In a dorm gripe session, Bertram advances the following argument. Decide whether it is a reasonable one and explain your view thoroughly.

> I could understand the teacher's failing me in the course if I hadn't handed in my homework. But I did hand it in, faithfully.
> Therefore, I didn't deserve to fail.

APPLICATIONS

3.1   Read the following dialogue carefully, looking for flaws in thinking. If you find one, identify it and explain what is wrong with it in sufficient detail to persuade someone who has read the passage but sees no flaw. If you find two or more flaws, identify and explain your thinking about each.

> EDNA: Professor, I don't like to complain, but I don't feel I'm getting as much out of this composition course as I should be getting.

PROF.: Really? Where do you think the problem lies?

EDNA: Well, you've got us writing just about every other day if we include the brief responses to the readings as well as the longer compositions. Yet so much of the writing seems wasted: You only correct about half the assignments.

3.2 Look back at the exercises for Chapters 1 and 2. Recall your responses. Decide whether those responses were influenced by any of the bad habits discussed in this chapter. Discuss your findings. (*Note:* In doing this assignment you should expect yourself to resist admitting such influences. Overcoming that resistance is a mark of thinking effectively.)

3.3 Reread the paragraph beginning "How does popular culture affect people?" (page 53). Then examine television programs, commercials and print advertisements, and magazines to determine the extent of the influences specified in that paragraph. Be prepared to share your findings with the class.

Note: In doing the following applications, your first objective should be to examine the ideas that occur to you and to decide whether they are the most reasonable responses to the problem or issue. Modify flawed ideas; where appropriate, change your mind completely. The more carefully you conduct this examination process, the more impressive your written and spoken contributions will be.

3.4 When Rae Landau and Isaac Perlstein were divorced, Ms. Landau won custody of their 8-year-old son. The boy's observance of Jewish dietary laws was one provision of the divorce agreement. Ms. Landau admittedly failed to honor that provision for a period of five years. As a result, a New York Supreme Court justice ruled that Ms. Landau had to surrender custody of the boy to his father.[23] Do you agree with the judge's ruling? Explain your position.

3.5 An 18-year-old San Francisco resident sued the high school from which he graduated, contending that the faculty were responsible for his inability to read and write adequately.[24] Do you think such a suit is reasonable? What factors would you consider if you were responsible for judging its merits?

3.6 It is common for high school coaches to forbid their players to drink alcohol. If a coach has such a rule and catches a player drinking, is it reasonable for the coach to dismiss the player from the team for the rest of the season? Should the coach treat the team's star player differently from a benchwarmer?

3.7 Apparently, a sizable number of Americans believe in astrology and think the stars govern their lives. How reasonable is this view? Explain your thinking.

3.8 A minister in Pontiac, Michigan, was arrested and charged with practicing medicine without a license—a felony—after he sprinkled blood from a freshly killed rooster on an ailing person. The minister said the authorities were stifling his constitutional rights. Do you agree with him? Explain your position.[25]

ISSUE FOR EXTENDED ANALYSIS

Following is a more comprehensive thinking challenge than the others in the chapter. Analyze and respond to it, following the instructions for extended analysis at the end of Chapter 1. Also, review "The Basis of Moral Judgment" and "Dealing with Dilemmas" in Chapter 2.

THE ISSUE: PEDOPHILIA

The *Oxford English Dictionary* defines pedophilia as "sexual desire directed toward children." Technically, a person can be a pedophile without acting on his or her desires. But the designation usually denotes action—for example, taking sexual photographs of children, exposing one's genitals to them, or having sexual contact with them. All such actions are classified as crimes. In recent years, there has been considerable public outcry for more protections against pedophiles, even after their release from prison.

THE ESSAYS

Protect the Children
By Daleesha Ford

To take advantage of anyone is wrong. To take advantage of a child is more offensive. To do so in a way that causes lasting emotional pain is reprehensible. In fact, the only thing more reprehensible is society's refusal to prevent such offenses from occurring.

The harm done by pedophiles is well documented. They violate innocence, destroy their victims' trust in adults, and leave them in a state of fear. In many cases, they also create in their victims a sense of shame and guilt and make it difficult, if not impossible, for them to achieve intimacy later in life. All this for a momentary selfish, perverted pleasure.

Pedophiles Deserve Fairness
By William Murphy

Today's psychology community takes a more tolerant view of pedophilia than it once did. Many therapists argue that its effects on victims are less severe and lasting as was once thought. Such therapists reject the image of pedophiles as monsters bent on corrupting young people, seeing them instead as lonely people searching for closeness and intimacy. A few therapists go so far as to approve pedophilia. Dr. Ralph Underwager, for example, sees pedophilia as an "acceptable expression of God's will for love and unity among human beings."

Admittedly, Underwager's view is extreme. But it is not extreme to view

Also well documented is the fact that pedophilia cannot be cured—once a pedopohile, always a pedophile. Thus, the idea that once a criminal pays his debt to society, he should have his liberties restored is not applicable to pedophiles. In fact, when released from prison, pedophiles are likely to be even more dangerous—they will have learned to be more stealthy and, in many cases, have added violence to their repertoire.

For these reasons, upon release from prison, pedophiles should not only be required to register wherever they reside, but they should also be forbidden to live near any places where children congregate, such as a school or a public playground. Most important, they should be required to wear a tracking device so that their movements can be monitored by the police. To those who say this constitutes an unfair burden, I say not as great as the lifelong emotional burden they inflict on their victims.

pedophilia as an illness and pedopohiles as victims of urges beyond their control. And where there is no control, there can be no legal or moral responsibility for the action.

The fairest and most sensible approach to dealing with convicted pedophiles is rehabilitation in a therapeutic facility rather than imprisonment with criminals. And when treatment is completed and pedophiles learn to control their urges, their rights as citizens should be fully restored.

We don't place restrictions on rapists, thieves, or even murderers after they pay their debt to society. Nor do we subject them to the humiliation of segregation, registration, or wearing tracking devices. And the crimes of such people are arguably much more serious than the crime of pedophilia.

Fairness demands that we treat rehabilitated pedophiles with an equal measure of mercy and compassion.

CLASS DISCUSSION

WARD: I agree with most of what Daleesha Ford has written. My only objection is that her stand isn't tough enough. I don't think a person who is convicted of pedophilia should be let out of prison at all.

DOROTHY: I can't believe you think Daleesha Ford isn't tough enough. She's much too tough. For example, she says pedophiles should not be allowed to live near schools, playgrounds, or anywhere else children congregate. By my estimate, that leaves only three places: deserts, jungles, and deserted mountaintops. Such a requirement is patently ridiculous.

WARD: It's the government's job to protect the rights of citizens, especially those least able to protect themselves. That means children. If it is established that someone is certain to or even highly likely to prey on children, as it is in the case of pedophilia, the government has an obligation to keep that person off the streets.

DOROTHY: Most of the talk about how to treat convicted pedophiles is filled with statistics about repeat offenders and psychiatric opinions about the impossibility of curing pedophilia. Such information obscures the fact that people can beat the odds and overcome all sorts of compulsions and addictions. To say that pedophiles *cannot* change is to deny them both hope and opportunity. And that is wrong.

HANK: There's another factor to consider. From what I've read on the subject, the effects of pedophilia may not always be as dire or as lasting as most people think. If the harm of pedophilia has been exaggerated, we may not need either indeterminate prison sentences or special requirements after release from prison.

DOROTHY: I'm personally revolted by the very idea of someone using a child for sexual gratification against his or her will, so I am not against punishment for pedophiles. I'm only against unreasonable extremes.

WARD: I don't know what you might have read, Hank, other than more of the bilge that Murphy quotes Dr. Underwager as promoting. I've never seen the slightest evidence that the effects of pedophilia are anything but horrific and lifelong.

4

Be a Critical Reader, Listener, and Viewer

You may be thinking, "This chapter doesn't apply to me. I have no trouble comprehending the messages I read, hear, and see." But this chapter isn't about basic comprehension. It is about analyzing and evaluating the messages you receive and deciding whether they are worthy of acceptance. Chances are you haven't had much training in this kind of reading, listening, and viewing.

In this chapter, you'll learn specific strategies for analyzing and evaluating messages.

Not long ago, while searching the Internet, I encountered a reference to an article describing "Pepper Power Bear Spray," which was created by a survivor of a grizzly bear attack for defense against bears, lions, and moose. The manufacturer promises "quick access and potent stopping power." If I were going camping in the deep woods, I thought to myself, I'd certainly feel safer if I had a good supply of that product.

Then my glance fell on the *very next* response to my search request. It read, "Bears attracted to repellent, researcher says." My curiosity aroused, I read the news article. It seems that though pepper spray can indeed stop a charging bear if sprayed in its face, it has the *opposite* effect if sprayed on clothing, camping equipment, or the ground around a campsite. A camper who sprayed it around his tent was soon surrounded by a bunch of brown bears. A pilot who sprayed it on his plane's pontoons returned to find them chewed up.

The lesson in that experience was don't believe everything you read, hear, or view. Unfortunately, many people have never learned this lesson. They erroneously assume that if something is published or broadcast, it must be true. In reality, even honest, well-intentioned communicators make mistakes; imperfection is an unavoidable part of being human.

The consequences of being misinformed by what is written or broadcast are not always as dramatic as being visited by a family of wild and presumably hungry beasts, but are no less real. Every day people undermine their health, make disastrous investments or career moves, or harm their marriages by uncritically accepting something they've read, heard, or viewed. The best safeguard against such misfortunes is to develop the habit of critical evaluation.

CRITICAL EVALUATION DEFINED

Critical evaluation* is active, thoughtful examination, as opposed to passive acceptance, of what you read, hear, and see. The standard of judgment in such evaluation is not how closely the author's view matches your own, but whether it is accurate and reasonable. Consequently, those who evaluate messages critically are less vulnerable to deception and manipulation than other people.

Our age is not the first to realize the importance of critical evaluation. Almost 400 years ago, Francis Bacon warned about the danger of reading improperly. He advised people not to dispute an author's view nor to accept it uncritically, but to "weigh and consider" it. In the nineteenth century, British statesman Edmund Burke expressed the same view in more dramatic terms: "To read without reflection is like eating without digesting." The following explanation by a twentieth-century scholar expands on this idea:

> There is one key idea which contains, in itself, the very essence of effective reading, and on which the improvement of reading depends: *Reading is reasoning.* When you read properly, you are not merely assimilating. You are not automatically transferring into your head what your eyes pick up on the page. What you see on the page sets your mind at work, collating, criticizing, interpreting, questioning, comprehending, comparing. When this process goes on well, you read well. When it goes on ill, you read badly.[1]

By extension, Bacon's and Burke's observations apply to listening and viewing as well as to reading. (When they made their observations, of course, cinema, television, and the Internet did not yet exist.) In addition, the intense mental activity they describe is not required for every message. A bus schedule or a menu can be read with virtually no reflection; an encyclopedia article, light fiction, or a TV weather report requires relatively little evaluation. Critical evaluation is most relevant, and necessary, when the message is intended to *persuade* people; that is, when one perspective or opinion is presented as superior to others. Persuasive

---

*Don't be confused by the fact that the word *critical* is also used to mean "finding fault with." That is not the meaning intended here.

communication can be found in every subject—from politics, psychology, finance, religion, popular culture, and business management to sports, chess, and even gardening. Although persuasive communication is typically associated with editorials, opinion essays, and letters to editors, it can also be found in TV talk shows, commercials, and even in news reports and textbooks. Wherever it is found, you are challenged to evaluate the message critically.

MAKING IMPORTANT DISTINCTIONS

A fundamental requirement for critical evaluation is making distinctions. The most important and most often overlooked ones are the following.

The Distinction Between the Person and the Idea

Your reaction to a sentence beginning "Adolf Hitler said . . ." would probably be very different from your reaction to one beginning "Winston Churchill said. . . ." In the first instance, you might not even continue reading. At the very least, you would read with great suspicion and be ready to reject what was said. There's nothing strange about that. You've learned things about Hitler and Churchill, and it's difficult to set this information aside. In one sense, you *shouldn't* set it aside. Yet, in another sense, you *must* set it aside to be a good thinker. After all, even a lunatic can have a good idea, and a genius will, on occasion, be wrong.

If you do not control your tendency to accept or reject ideas on the basis of who expresses them, your analysis of everything you read, hear, and view is certain to be distorted. You will judge arguments on whether the speaker is of your race, religion, political affiliation, or generation. Consequently you might embrace nonsense and reject wisdom. Aristotle's contemporaries tell us he had very thin legs and small eyes, favored conspicuous dress and jewelry, and was fastidious in the way he combed his hair.[2] It's not hard to imagine some Athenian ignoramus muttering to friends the ancient Greek equivalent of "Don't pay any attention to what Aristotle says—he's a wimp."

To guard against confusing the person and the idea, be aware of your reactions to people and try compensating for them. That is, listen more carefully to people you are inclined to dislike and more critically to people you are inclined to like. Judge the arguments as harshly as you wish, but only on their merits as arguments.

The Distinction Between Matters of Taste and Matters of Judgment

In Chapter 2, we saw that there are two broad types of opinion: *taste* and *judgment*. They differ significantly. In matters of taste we may express our personal preferences without defending them. In matters of judgment, however, we have an obligation to provide evidence—that is, supporting material that provides a basis for our view. Only when evidence is sufficient in both quality and quantity to remove all reasonable doubt and establish certainty does it qualify as *proof.* Evidence may take a variety of forms, notably factual details, statistics, examples, anecdotes, quotations, comparisons, or descriptions.

Many people confuse taste and judgment. They believe their right to hold an opinion is a guarantee of the opinion's rightness. This confusion often causes them to offer inadequate support (or no support at all) for views that demand support. For example, they express judgments on such controversial issues as abortion, capital punishment, the teaching of evolution in the schools, mercy killing, discrimination in hiring, and laws concerning rape as if they were matters of taste rather than matters of judgment.

Keep in mind that whenever someone presents an opinion about the truth of an issue or the wisdom of an action—that is, whenever someone presents a judgment—you, as a critical thinker, have not only the right but also a duty to judge that opinion by the evidence. To be a careful thinker, you *must* do so.

The Distinction Between Fact and Interpretation

A *fact* is something known with certainty, something either objectively verifiable or demonstrable. An *interpretation* is an explanation of meaning or significance. Frequently, facts and interpretations are so intertwined that we have difficulty deciding where one leaves off and the other begins. Here is an example of such intertwining:

This paragraph presents facts from research conducted by others. (The author cites his source in a footnote.)

Poverty causes crime? According to James Q. Wilson and Richard Herrnstein, "During the 1960s, one neighborhood in San Francisco had the lowest income, the highest unemployment rate, the highest proportion of families with incomes under four thousand dollars a year, the least educational attainment, the highest tuberculosis rate, and the highest proportion of substandard housing. . . . That neighborhood was called Chinatown. Yet, in 1965, there were only five persons of Chinese ancestry committed to prison in the *entire* [emphasis added] state of California."

The first four sentences are factual statements. The final sentence is the author's interpretation.

Roxbury, Massachusetts, a predominantly black and impoverished area, sits next to South Boston, a predominantly white and impoverished area. Both contain the same percentage of single-parent households, and public housing accounts for the same percentage of the population. Yet, the violent crime rate in Roxbury, the black area, is four times the rate of that in South Boston. If poverty caused crime, one would expect the numbers to be closer to equal.

This entire paragraph is the author's interpretation of the facts he presented in the previous paragraphs.

No, the formula is more likely the other way around: crime causes poverty. The more crime, the less incentive for businesspeople to locate businesses in that area. Store owners must charge consumers more to offset losses caused by theft and higher insurance premiums. Homeowners, apartment dwellers, and business people pay increased security costs to combat the ever-present threat of theft or violent crime. *This* impoverishes neighborhoods.[3]

The danger in failing to distinguish between fact and interpretation is that you will regard uncritically statements that ought to be questioned and contrasted with other views. If the habit of confusing the two is strong enough, it can paralyze your critical sense.

The Distinction Between Literal and Ironic Statements

Not everything that is said is intended to be taken literally. Sometimes, a writer makes a point by saying the exact opposite of what is meant—that is, by using irony or satire. Suppose, for example, you encountered this passage in your reading:

> Congress is right in reducing the taxes of the wealthy more than those of the working classes. After all, wealthy people not only pay more into the treasury but they also have a higher standard of living to maintain. If the cost of soybeans has risen, so also has the cost of caviar; if the subway fare has increased, so has the maintenance cost of a Rolls-Royce and a Lear jet. If the government listens to the minor grumbling and whining of the unemployed, it surely should be responsive to the plight of the affluent.

On the surface, this certainly looks like a plea on behalf of the rich. But on closer inspection, it will be seen as a mockery of that plea. The clues are subtle, to be sure, but undeniable: the reference to the higher standard of living, the comparison of travel by Rolls-Royce or jet with travel by subway, the reference to the "plight" of the rich. Such tongue-in-cheek writing can be more biting and therefore more effective than a direct attack. Yet you must be alert to the subtlety and not misread it, or the message you receive will be very different from the message that has been expressed.

The Distinction Between an Idea's Validity and the Quality of Its Expression

The way an idea is expressed can influence people's reactions. This is why a mad leader like Hitler won a large popularity even among intelligent and responsible people and why Jim Jones's followers killed their children and committed suicide in Guyana. Impassioned, eloquent expression tends to excite a favorable response, just as lifeless, inarticulate, error-filled expression prompts a negative response. Compare these two passages:

1. Ain't right to treat some folks good and others bad. If a man don't treat all equal, he ain't much of a man.

2. To achieve success in a competitive world, you must honor the first principle of success: Treat well those people who can benefit you, and ignore the others.

The first passage may seem less appealing than the second. And yet it contains an idea most philosophers would enthusiastically endorse, whereas the second contains an idea most would find reprehensible. Careful thinkers are able to appraise the passages correctly because they are aware that expression can deceive. Such thinkers make a special effort to separate form from content before judging. Thus they are able to say, "This idea is poorly expressed but profound" and "This idea is well expressed but shallow."

The Distinction Between Language and Reality

Language is our principal means of understanding reality and communicating that understanding to others. Words come so naturally and become so closely associated with what they represent that we may unconsciously regard them as synonymous with reality. That can be a costly mistake. A people's language develops according to its insights and observations, and because no single group has equal insight into all dimensions of reality, no language is perfectly suited to express all realities. For example, Eskimos have many words for snow, each word denoting a certain kind of snow (heavy and wet versus light and fluffy, small and fine versus large and dense, and so on), so they can speak with much greater precision about snow than can English-speaking peoples. Similarly, the ancient Greeks had a number of words for love, each representing a distinct type of love (love of God, love of family, romantic or sexual love, and so forth), whereas we require our word *love* to bear an excessive burden and thereby create confusion in our discourse.

The word *self* is another good example of a term that is made to carry more meaning than it can bear. We say, "I made myself resist that triple chocolate truffle cake," "You really ought to give yourself a chance to get over one lousy relationship before entering another," and "Bill is not himself these days." In each of these constructions there seem to be two distinct selves: in the first, the one controlling and the one controlled; in the second, the giver and the receiver; and in the third, Bill and not-Bill. As Peggy Rosenthal has shown, the problem is not limited to informal, everyday expression but is found in psychological discourse as well:

> One thing [writers about psychology] often seem to have in mind is that *self* is a goal of some kind. But the kind varies. It can be the goal of what sounds like a treasure hunt (the familiar "finding of one's self"), a trip ("the long journey to achieve selfhood"), a vegetable ("the maturation of the self"), or a vaguely Aristotelian process ("self-actualization is actualiza-tion of a self"). Sometimes, though, *self* seems not to be a goal but to have goals of its own: "the [mature] self now expresses ... its intentions and goals." ... [It can even be] a sort of balloon that expands and contracts with our moods: there's "that enlargement of self that goes into feeling good," whereas "in despair we have a reduced sense of self."[4]

Rosenthal notes that some writers use *self* and *sense of self* interchangeably. "But how can this be?" she asks. "Can the sense, or awareness, of something be equal to the thing itself?" The ultimate confusion, she suggests, is found in a pas-sage written by Carl Rogers in which he uses *self* to mean "both the considering agent and the object of consideration in the same sentence."[5]

The reality of the *self* would be no less complex if we had half a dozen words, each designating a single aspect, instead of merely one word, but our dis-course would undoubtedly be less confusing and we might well achieve a deeper, more accurate understanding of that reality. In any case, keeping in mind the dis-tinction between language and reality will help you approach both your thinking and your communication with appropriate care and humility.

A STRATEGY FOR CRITICAL READING

So much for the distinctions essential to critical evaluation. Now we'll consider a five-step strategy for critical reading: *Skim, Reflect, Read, Evaluate,* and *Express Your Judgment.* We'll examine each in turn. (Strategies for critical *listening* and *viewing* will be discussed later in this chapter.)

Step 1: Skim the Work

To skim is to glance at selected parts of a book or article in order to gain an overview of it. On average, skimming should take about 15 or 20 minutes for a book and 5 or 10 minutes for an article. When done effectively, skimming will not only make your reading easier and more effective, but it will also save you time by sparing you the chore of *rereading* all or part of the work.

Skimming should answer these questions: *What issue is the author writing about? What is the author's position on this issue? What are the main divisions (subtopics) of the book or article? How much evidence does the author offer in support of his or her view? What type(s) of evidence?*

In the case of a book, skim the preface or introduction for a statement of the author's purpose in writing and essential message, the table of contents for the breakdown and sequence of the contents, the beginnings and ends of one or two chapters to learn whether the author provides previews or summaries (if they are provided, skim them for each chapter), and the endnotes and/or bibliography to see how well documented the book is and the kinds of sources the author has used. If time permits, skim the entire concluding chapter to learn what judgments and/or recommendations the author makes. Sometimes the final chapter will summarize the main argument presented in the book.

For articles, skim the introduction, the section headings, the first paragraph following each heading, and the conclusion.

Step 2: Reflect on Your Views

Ask yourself: *What ideas do I have about this subject that could create a bias for or against the author's view and prevent me from giving it a fair hearing?*

Bias can occur in one of two ways. The more obvious way is to have thought carefully about the issue, considered the opposing views, and decided that the evidence supports one better than the others. Far from being shameful, this process is praiseworthy—the purpose of thinking, after all, is to form conclusions. But is it fair to *prejudge* one author's presentation on the basis of our prior conclusion about some *other* author's presentation? No. The author we are reading now may have compelling new evidence or may expose an error in our thinking. The only way we can be sure is to set aside our prior conclusion long enough to read fairly.

The other way in which bias can occur is more subtle, so subtle in fact that we may be unaware of it. Each of us has many ideas that we did not form for ourselves, ideas that slipped into our minds when we were not paying close attention. Such ideas include the ones our parents and teachers expressed while we were growing up, statements made by people on talk shows or characters in films, advertising jingles, and all our casual perceptions, impressions, hunches, and assumptions. Many of these ideas have no doubt faded, but others—notably the popular ones that we have heard repeated time and again—are still present and can impact our thinking. These repeated ideas may become so familiar and comfortable that we are inclined to defend them, even though we have never evaluated them and, for that reason, they are not really our own. Because this kind of bias is both unconscious and irrational, it can pose a greater problem than the more obvious kind.

The purpose of reflection is to become aware of both kinds of bias and to control them during the remaining steps.

Step 3: Read the Work

If you have skimmed well, this step will be relatively easy. You will already know what the author is saying; you will also understand the sequence of the author's points and the kind and amount of evidence presented. Now your task is to deepen and refine your understanding. Read the entire work carefully, at a single sitting if possible. Keep a pen or pencil in hand while reading and underline the most important sentences. Try to limit your underlining to one sentence per several paragraphs. Where appropriate, add your questions and thoughts in the margin.

In the case of a book or a long article, it is a good idea to *summarize* what you have read. To do this, review the sentences you have marked as important. Consider how many sentences you can combine without changing the author's meaning. Next write your summary in complete sentences, keeping to the original phrasing and the original order of presentation as much as possible to avoid distortion. Then briefly note in your own words the evidence offered by the writer. Do not attempt to elaborate on the evidence as the author did, or your summary will be too long to be useful.

If you have summarized effectively, you should now have a brief version of the original work that is faithful in content yet much easier to analyze. A whole book can be reduced to several paragraphs in this way; a full-length magazine article, to seven or eight sentences or less. Whenever you summarize, however, keep in mind the danger of distortion and oversimplification. It is not only unfair but also pointless to criticize an author for something he or she did *not* say.

Step 4: Evaluate What You Read

Begin by reading your summary carefully so that you grasp the author's main points *and* the evidence offered for each. Then answer the following questions. (Note: Some questions will require you to reexamine the work itself and not just your summary of it. In such cases, your summary will help you determine in which chapter or section to look.)

Are any of the author's terms vague or ambiguous (open to more than one meaning)? In such cases, you will have to decide what meaning is implied.

Does the author use emotionally charged language as a substitute for evidence? Words like *harassment, terrorism, rape, censorship, diversity, multicultural, human rights, family values, justice, empowerment, freedom, liberty, rights,* and *choice* tend to evoke an emotional response. Persuasive writing may make us feel as well as think, but when it makes us feel *instead* of think, it is dishonest.

Is the author's evidence relevant to the issue? No matter how comprehensive and authoritative evidence may be, if it has no bearing on the issue under discussion, it does not deserve our consideration.

Did the author omit any significant evidence? Often, the weakness in an argument lies in what the author does *not* say. For example, let's say an author stated that several years ago, an American engineer and his wife visited the Congo, trying to find evidence of a dinosaur-like creature reportedly living there; and also that they returned with a picture that they said documented their sighting of the creature. Everything in the statement is correct.[6] However, one important detail is missing: the picture was severely underexposed and therefore worthless as documentation.

Are the author's examples and cases typical and comprehensive? The author's citation of some examples and cases does not necessarily establish the argument's validity. If the cases are extraordinary—exceptions rather than typical instances—they are worth very little. Similarly, if they represent one narrow aspect of the issue, they may not adequately support the author's argument.

If the author cites a scientific study, has it been replicated? The practice of the scientific community is to withhold endorsement of any researcher's findings until they have been independently confirmed. This is a wise approach, for some studies are proven to be "flukes."

If the author cites a survey, what organization designed and administered it? How large was the sample? Was it random? A survey that does not conform to established statistical principles is worthless as evidence.

Are the sources of information cited by the author still current? There is nothing necessarily wrong with old sources. Something written in 1800 may still be valid today. But later findings may have discredited older views.

Are the experts cited by the author authoritative and reliable? The fact of being well known does not make one an authority. A Nobel Prize winner in physics may be totally incompetent in psychology or government. And even if the person cited is an authority in the field in question, the view is open to question if the person has been guilty of unreliability (professional dishonesty, for example) in the past.

Do other experts agree with the experts cited by the author? In controversial matters, there is seldom any more agreement among experts than among nonexperts. A little investigation may reveal that the experts cited by the author hold the minority view!

What criticisms and counterarguments would someone who holds a different position make about this book or article? Nothing reveals the flaws on one side of an issue better than hearing the other side.

Does the author commit any errors in logic? For example, does the author overgeneralize, oversimplify, or assume facts not in evidence?

Is the author's conclusion about the evidence the most reasonable one, or is another conclusion more reasonable? Like the rest of us, authors sometimes yield to their biases and interpret evidence in a way that flatters their prior opinions. In such cases, an objective assessment of the evidence may produce a different conclusion.

As you no doubt realize, the answers to many of these questions are not likely to be found either in the book or article you are evaluating or in your own head. To answer them will require further investigation on your part. Be sure to conduct whatever investigation is necessary before making your final judgment.

Step 5: Express Your Judgment

One mistake readers commonly make in evaluating a book or article is to assume that they must agree completely or disagree completely with the author. More often than not, the most reasonable response is to accept some parts of an author's argument, reject others, and perhaps be uncertain about still others. The following guidelines will assist you in expressing your judgment.

1. If you agree in part and disagree in part, explain exactly what your position is and support it carefully. Remember that good thinkers will judge your arguments as closely as you judge other people's arguments.

2. If some vagueness or ambiguity in the author's argument prevents you from giving a flat answer, don't attempt one. Rather, say, "it depends," and go on to explain. The if-then approach is very helpful in such cases. Here's how it works. Suppose someone had written, "A human being is an animal." You might respond as follows.

   > It depends on what you mean by *animal*. If you mean *human being* is included in the broad classification *animal,* as opposed to *vegetable* or *mineral,* then I agree. But if you mean a human being has nothing more than animal nature, no intellect and will that distinguish him or her from other members of the animal kingdom, then I disagree. I believe that . . .

3. If you must deal with conflicting testimony and cannot decide your position with certainty, identify the conflict and explain why you cannot be certain. If you believe that circumstances seem somewhat in favor of one side, explain those circumstances and why you are inclined to judge them as you do.

An example of conflicting testimony occurred some years ago in the highly publicized trial of Jack Henry Abbott. Abbott, who had spent 24 of his 37 years behind prison bars, was paroled after Norman Mailer arranged for Abbott's book, *In the Belly of the Beast,* to be published. Six weeks after his parole, Abbott stabbed a waiter in a dispute over the use of a restroom. Abbott testified that he thought the waiter had pulled a knife first and that he lunged forward with his knife in self-protection. A passerby, however, witnessed the incident and testified that the waiter had made what appeared to be a "conciliatory gesture" and turned to walk away when Abbott raced after him, reached over his shoulder, and stabbed him with "terrible ferocity," then taunted him as he lay dying.[7]

In this case, you might reasonably say that although you cannot be certain which testimony is correct, circumstances seem to favor the witness's testimony. You would go on to explain that Abbott's testimony was more likely than the witness's to be colored by emotion and self-interest.

These guidelines may seem to encourage evasion or straddling the fence. They are not intended to do so and should not be used for that purpose. Apply them when reasonableness demands a qualified answer, not in situations in which timidity prompts you to avoid answering.

A SAMPLE EVALUATION AND JUDGMENT

To see how a typical evaluation might proceed, imagine you are evaluating a magazine article arguing that "inferior" people should be sterilized at puberty. You have completed the first three steps in the critical reading process and have summarized the author's argument as follows. (For reference purposes, the sentences and items of evidence are numbered.)

1. A serious world population problem exists today.

2. The ideal solution is for everyone to be responsible in deciding whether he or she should reproduce.

3. However, few people make that decision rationally—emotion overwhelms logic.

4. Moreover, the least talented and least intelligent are likely to have the most children.

5. In time, this tendency may set the process of evolution in reverse.

6. The best and most practical solution is to identify inferior people and force them to be sterilized at puberty.

As evidence in support of the argument, the article presented:

7. UN statistics on world population.

8. Selected UN statistics on world poverty, illiteracy, and disease.

9. A research study showing that more affluent, better-educated, higher-IQ couples tend to have fewer children.

10. Quotations from geneticists showing the favorable genetic effects that would occur if only higher-IQ individuals were to reproduce.

11. Quotations from medical authorities showing the benefits that would accrue to world health if people with hereditary diseases did not reproduce.

Your evaluation of the argument and evidence might look like this (parenthetical numbers refer to the preceding statements and evidence).

Concerning the Clarity of the Argument:

Several terms are ambiguous. Do *talented* and *intelligent* (4) refer to the broad range of abilities or to some specific ones? People with mild mental impairment often possess considerable talent and intelligence if measured by a broad definition of the terms. Does the *process of evolution* (5) mean survival of the physically fit or the perpetuation of culture as we know it? And does *inferior people* (6) mean those with hereditary diseases, the mentally impaired, neurotics, nonconformists, or all of these?

Concerning the Questions Informed Critics Might Raise:

These are the most probable ones: Isn't it possible that forced sterilization might pose even worse dangers to civilization than a reversing of evolution (5)? Might it not lead to totalitarianism? Wouldn't a better and more practical solution (6) be to improve the distribution of wealth among nations, to find cures for disease, to share technology, and to expand educational opportunity (including education in birth control methods)?

Concerning the Kind and Quality of the Evidence:

One significant question about some of the evidence (10, 11) concerns how typical and comprehensive it is. Is the view expressed in the quotations one that is shared by most geneticists and medical authorities, or is it a minority position? An even more important question concerns the evidence that is omitted. Surely psychologists, sociologists, and historians could contribute to this issue. Some of the questions they could answer are these: What psychological effects would forced sterilization have on those subjected to it? A feeling of worthlessness, perhaps, or rage? What social behavior would be likely to result from such effects? Violence? Revolution? What historical precedents are there to help us measure the probable effects?

In light of these considerations, you might conclude that although the world population problem and the related concerns of poverty, illiteracy, and disease are serious and should be addressed, the idea of forced sterilization should be opposed—at least until its advocates clarify their terms and answer the important critical questions. If you were to make a formal response to the argument in an analytical paper or article, you would develop your ideas thoroughly, meeting the same standards you expect of others. (For a discussion of the principles and approaches used in analytical writing, see Chapter 14.)

■
A STRATEGY FOR CRITICAL LISTENING

In one respect, critical listening is little different from critical reading. Both involve the evaluation of messages expressed in words, so both require all the careful distinctions described earlier in the chapter. Yet in other respects, critical listening is very different from critical reading. In listening, there is no opportunity to get an overview of the message before it is delivered—in other words, there is no activity comparable to *skimming* a piece of writing. Once uttered, the spoken word is gone, and there is no way to go back and hear what we missed because of some distraction (unless, of course, the message was recorded). Another difference is that listening is a more emotional activity than reading. In listening, we do not just receive the message—we also hear a human voice, with its inflections, its emphases, and its passion. If the speaker is physically present, we see his or her body and notice the gestures and facial expressions that accompany the words. These sounds (and sights) can make the message seem more or less insightful than it actually is. They can also make us more absorbed in the message or, conversely, distracted from it.

The importance of critical listening is nowhere more evident than in politics. For example, no presidential candidate since John F. Kennedy has been more enthusiastically received than Barack Obama, who combines attractive physical appearance with extraordinary eloquence. His speeches contain allusions to inspiring leaders such as Abraham Lincoln, Winston Churchill, and Martin Luther King, Jr. They are also filled with phrases such as "change we can believe in," "the unfinished business of perfecting our Union," and "a new birth of freedom upon this Earth," as well as frequent references to hope, justice, and opportunity. Such language evokes powerful feelings that tend to *suppress* critical questioning.[8] Here is a four-step strategy for listening critically, even in cases in which the force of the message and the quality of the delivery discourage critical evaluation.

Step 1: Set Aside Preconceptions

Preconceptions are the previously formed beliefs and attitudes that you bring to an issue. Unless you set them aside, your listening is almost certain to be biased in favor of what you already believe. To set aside your preconceptions, you must first admit that you have them, and then be alert for their influence, which will usually take the form or strong feelings—more specifically, positive feelings toward speakers you agree with and negative feelings toward speakers you disagree with. Such feelings will often arise even before the speaker has finished speaking. This is especially so in the case of negative feelings, which can prompt you to block out what the speaker is saying. (The most blatant example of such behavior is the habit of many talk-show guests of interrupting and shouting down those with whom they disagree.) Whenever you start to experience strong feelings, positive or negative, about a speaker, remind yourself that they can block the understanding you will need for critical evaluation.

Step 2: Focus on the Message

Even when your preconceptions are in check, your mind may tend to wander from what the speaker is saying. For example, if the speaker expresses an opinion that differs from yours, you may feel the urge to begin framing your response. That is a natural reaction and there is nothing wrong with it *when the time is right*. The problem is that if you give in to that urge while the person is speaking, you will stop listening and thus miss his or her elaboration of the opinion—that is, the further descriptions, qualifications, and supporting data. In that case, however carefully you may construct your response, it will not fit what the speaker actually said but only your speculations about what he or she might say. On the other hand, if you resist the urge to frame your response and continue to focus on what the person is saying, you will gain the understanding necessary to construct a truly effective response. A special caution is in order here: when you are listening to a point of view that disagrees with your own, you will probably not encounter a single temptation to stop listening, but *multiple* temptations. Resist them all.

Step 3: Identify Key Assertions and Supporting Information

All coherent *spoken* presentations of ideas have the same basic components as *written* presentations—a main assertion or claim and the evidence and/or reasoning that supports that claim. Longer or more complex presentations may also have *secondary* assertions or claims, together with supporting evidence/reasoning. The third step in critical listening consists of identifying these assertions and the information offered in support of them. Put more simply, the third step consists of answering these questions: What viewpoint does the speaker hold, and why does he/she hold that viewpoint? The best way to answer these questions is to record the presentation and replay it as often as necessary for understanding. If recording is not possible or practical, take notes during the presentation. If the presentation is followed by a question-and-answer period, ask for clarification of any vague or ambiguous statements.

Steps 4 and 5: Evaluate the Message and Express Your Judgment

These steps are essentially the same as those explained in steps 4 and 5 of the "A Strategy for Critical Reading" discussed earlier in the chapter. The only difference is that in critical *listening* you will not be aided by a written summary of the speaker's message but will have to rely on your record of his or her key points.

■———————————————

A STRATEGY FOR CRITICAL VIEWING

Technological advances in communication and entertainment have inspired new and more varied uses of visual material and have led to a new subdiscipline known alternatively as "visual communication" and "visual rhetoric." These developments have made critical *viewing* as important as critical reading and critical listening.

One form of visual communication is statistical graphics. Some people tend to be less critical of graphs and charts than they are of words alone, as if graphs and charts were less open to error. But that is a mistake. Edward Tufte, a leading scholar of graphics, describes them as "instruments for reasoning about quantitative information" and as "pictures of . . . numbers." Noting that graphics are as open to error as prose, Tufte explains that graphic distortion—that is, error—occurs when the picture of the numbers is at odds with the numbers themselves or the facts that are represented by the numbers. He adds that the danger is increased by the fact that "mass market graphics are usually done by people with artistic but not statistical backgrounds. They aim for beauty rather than 'statistical integrity.' The consequence is 'over-decorated and simplistic designs, tiny data sets, and big lies.' "[9]

To view graphics critically, decide on the meaning of the data from the data itself rather than from the form in which it is presented. Remember that the design of the graphic has the power to distort as well as to reveal meaning.

Another form of visual communication is the advertisement in either the static form of print or the dynamic form of the television commercial. The primary aim of advertising, unlike that of statistical graphics, is more to stir the emotions than to appeal to the mind. Walter Dill Scott, an advertising executive and early theorist, argued that "suggestion is of universal application to all persons, while reason is a process which is exceptional, even among the wisest." Scott advised advertisers to appeal to emotions, particularly to sympathy.[10] John Watson, the founder of Behaviorism and a consultant to advertisers, went much further than Scott, arguing that people are not moved by reason at all but only by emotion. He therefore saw the job of advertising as manipulating the public's emotions in much the same manner that Pavlov had manipulated the physiological responses of dogs.[11] Although some modern advertisers disavow the philosophy of Scott, Watson, and their followers, it continues to dominate the field.

To view advertising critically, you must remember that it is usually aimed at your feelings rather than at your mind. Then you should ask: What feelings is this ad designed to evoke in me? What words does it employ to evoke that feeling? What pictures and sounds? What people? Admired celebrities? People I envy or pity? Answering these questions takes the advertisement out of the realm of feelings and into the realm of thinking, where you can evaluate it.

A third form of visual communication is the dramatic presentation. This form can be traced back to the ancient Greek comedies and tragedies, but the presentations we are most familiar with are television programs and movies. Critical viewing of dramatic presentations is also as old as the form itself, and the basic questions remain the same today: How do the characters relate to one another and how do their personal qualities contribute to those relationships? What is the plot or story line and how does it unfold? What specific conflict or conflicts are central to the plot? What is the setting and how does it contribute to the action? What is the theme or meaning (previous generations preferred the term *lesson* or *moral*) of the presentation—that is, what idea does it convey about people or life?

The last question has been difficult to answer because dramatists have traditionally eschewed *preaching* but instead allowed the action and the interrelationships among the characters to *suggest* the theme. Today the question is even more difficult to answer, not because dramatic presentations have become more sophisticated (the opposite is often the case), but because cinematic technology has made it possible to create dramas filled with excitement yet lacking in meaning—for example, a series of chase scenes, explosions, and sexual encounters with little or no plot or character development.

To view dramatic presentations critically, ask the basic questions about characters, plot, setting, and theme. In addition, decide how realistic and believable the presentation is. Look in particular for signs that story has been contrived to serve the author's personal agenda. Typical signs include stereotyped characters, oversimplified relationships, and slanted dialogue.

WARM-UP EXERCISES

4.1   Make up as many new words—*non*words like *garrumptive*—as you can to reflect people's moods. In each case, indicate the specific mood each word reflects. Be sure to list many possible words before choosing the *best one.*

4.2   Make up a new name for yourself (both first name and last), one that fits the special qualities you have or are striving for. Be sure to consider unusual names (Honor Trueblood, Rick Decent), and list many possibilities before choosing the best one.

4.3   Your young nephew is confused. He has learned "He who hesitates is lost" and "Haste makes waste." The sayings seem to oppose each other, and he wants to know which is right. Answer in a way he will understand.

APPLICATIONS

4.1   Read the following dialogue carefully. Decide which statements are reasonable and which are not. Provide a brief explanation of why you consider any statement unreasonable.

[Scene: A college dormitory room. A bull session is in progress. George and Ed, freshmen at Proudly Tech, are discussing academic affairs with their sophomore roommate, Jake.]

GEORGE: When I arrived on campus last month, I went to see my adviser to get my freshman English course waived. I didn't get to first base with him. "Everyone takes freshman English," he said. "Everyone!" I'll bet he's got that line taped and just plays it whenever a student raises the question. It really burns me having to take that course. I can see it as a requirement for most students. But I earned straight Bs in high school English. Why should I spend more time on that stuff in college?

ED: You're right, George. This place is like home—everybody's on your back making you do things you don't want to do. I should have gone to Bloomville State instead of to this dump.

JAKE: What's so great about Bloomville State?

ED: They let you take whatever courses you want. No required courses at all.

JAKE: Look, my uncle went there after the Vietnam War. He told me a lot about his college days. But he never mentioned that.

ED: It's true. Listen, there was this guy I was talking to at the bar in the train station when I was coming up here. He goes to Bloomville, and he told me they had no required courses.

GEORGE: That really bugs me. Straight Bs. And still I've got to take this crappy course. . . .

JAKE: Listen, pal. You're lucky you were born talented in writing. I wish I had that gift. For me, nothing but Ds and Fs. Hopeless.

ED: Who'd you have for English, Jake?

JAKE: Crawford. An OK guy, I guess, but sort of scholarly. Talks over everybody's head, always quoting some writer or other.

ED: I've got Mr. Schwartz. What's the word on him?

JAKE: Three of my friends had him last year and two got Bs and one a B+. A guy who grades like that has got to be a winner.

GEORGE: I'm glad somebody's luck held. Mine certainly didn't. For the two comps I've written so far, I've got a D+ and a C–.

JAKE: Who have you got?

GEORGE: Mr. Stiletto.

JAKE: He wasn't here last year.

GEORGE: I'll bet he's just out of graduate school. Or maybe he never went. At any rate, he sure has it in for me. Maybe he's prejudiced against Germans.

ED: Maybe you picked the wrong side of the issue to write on—you know, the one he disagrees with.

GEORGE: Hey, you may be right. The first topic was birth control, and I'm sure he's Catholic because I saw a little statue of Jesus on his car dashboard when his wife dropped him off outside the building last week. I wrote in favor of abortion. Wow. What a jerk I am. Hey, and come to think of it, that second comp. . . .

JAKE: I should have taken him for comp. I'm Catholic.

GEORGE: That second comp was on civil rights. And I know he's against blacks. The guy who sits next to me is black, and Stiletto really cut him down just because he was late a few times. And there's a black girl he always calls on for the tough questions. No wonder I got a C–.

JAKE: Wait till you guys take psych next year. I don't know if I'll be able to last till the end of the term. It's the boringest subject ever thought up. Professor Clifford walks in, opens his book, and begins reading from his notes in a low mumble: "Mmmm ... Freud says ... mmmmmm ... Oedipus complex ... repression ... mmmmm." Deadliest stuff you ever heard. I'm glad I don't need another social science course. Those guys are really out of it.

ED: Doesn't he ever let you discuss what you read?

JAKE: Yeah, once in a while. Yesterday, for example, we were talking about some guy named Frankl, and Clifford said that according to this Frankl, boredom causes people more problems than distress does. Some kids in the class gave examples of how that's so—you know, there are always some guys looking to agree with the prof to make some points. ...

ED & GEORGE: Yeah.

JAKE: ... And so I raised my hand and said that that guy Frankl was all wet, that everybody knows that distress causes more problems than boredom. I told him that my own experience proved it because five years ago, when my father lost his job, my family really had to struggle for more than a year. We had problems, believe me, and they weren't caused by *boredom*!

GEORGE: What did he say to that?

JAKE: Well, he mumbled something about Frankl not meaning that. And then he started tossing around a lot of statistics and examples to try to get me confused. He couldn't corner me, though. I finally said, "Frankl's entitled to his opinion; I've got my own."

GEORGE: Hey, that's great. I bet he cursed you out under his breath. You really nailed him.

JAKE: Yeah, I guess I did. When I get mad, I can argue pretty good. Now I've just got to be careful he doesn't take it out on me in my grade.

ED: Say, fellas, I've got to cut out. I'm going to the library and prepare for tomorrow's English class.

GEORGE: What's your assignment?

ED: Oh, a piece by Orwell. We just have to read it and be ready to discuss it. I've read it five times already, but I can't find anything wrong with it, nothing to disagree with. I'll just have to read it again. Be seeing you.

4.2 Follow the directions for Application 4.1. In addition, decide what action you would recommend if you were a school board member. Explain why you think that action is best.

[Scene: The Alertia, Indiana, town hall. The members of the Alertia school board are meeting with a group of parents concerned about the school's new sex education program for seventh- and eighth-graders.]

CHAIR: I'd like to welcome the guests of the board to our regular meeting. As you all know, the board agreed to Ms. Jackson's request for an opportunity for those who wished to present their views on the school's new program in sex education. As we know, sex was around for quite a while before this program began, heh, heh. *[Silence]*

MS. SCHULTZ: It's exactly that sort of levity about this dangerous program that worries me.

CHAIR: I'm sorry, Ms. Schultz. I only meant that as a little joke.

MS. SCHULTZ: Well, there's nothing funny about a program that introduces raw sex into the minds of innocent young children.

MS. JACKSON: The reason we asked for this meeting is that we feel that what is taking place in sex education class goes beyond the bounds of decency.

CHAIR: Could you be more specific, please? Just what is taking place?

MS. JACKSON: Someone told me that Ms. Babette encouraged the students to touch each other freely to overcome any inhibitions they might have about sex. Can you deny that such encouragement goes beyond the bounds of decency?

CHAIR: No, I certainly wouldn't deny that. But . . .

MS. BROWN: I heard that last week she asked two students to come to the front of the room and demonstrate what petting means.

MS. GREEN: That doesn't surprise me a bit. She *does* have a sluttish manner, you know. Those miniskirts, that long hair. The way she talks to men is most provocative, positively lewd. If my daughter dressed and acted like that, I'd feel I had failed as a parent.

CHAIR: Ladies, please. We've got to have a little more order. Mr. Lessrow has had his hand up for some time.

MR. LESSROW: Thank you. Of course, I agree with the good ladies who have spoken thus far. But with all respect to them, I think they may be missing the real nature of this threat to the morals of our young people. We must not forget that those young people are the United States citizens of tomorrow. And let me ask you, just who will stand to profit if they are corrupted, if their preoccupation with the flesh stays them from their duties and obligations as citizens? Let me ask ...

MEMBER 1: Who *will* stand to profit, Mr. Lessrow?

MR. LESSROW: I was getting to that point, sir. Who else but the Muslim extremists?

MEMBER 1: Are you suggesting that the Muslim extremists are in some way responsible for sex education in American schools, for the course in our school?

MR. LESSROW: I am saying precisely that. Sex education is a plot to lure our children into lives of lustful hedonism. It is a plot designed and supported by those who would overthrow our country. All a person needs to do is a little reading, have a little concern for the truth, and not be like these hothouse liberals who believe that the only real enemy is conservatives. The liberals are either misguided dupes of the extremists or willing accomplices.

MEMBER 2: Now that's surely a very extreme interpretation of ...

MR. LESSROW: It's an extreme plot! Extreme situations demand extreme responses.

MEMBER 2: As I started to say, it's an extreme interpretation of a very complex issue. Surely we should be a little less quick to jump at every wild accusation, be a little more open-minded.

MS. SCHULTZ: A person should be open-minded while searching for the truth but not after finding it.

MS. JACKSON: I just can't understand how people can resist common sense. It should be clear enough to everybody—even to the teachers of this school—that when you bring sex into the classroom, you dignify it. When you encourage the young to talk about it openly in school, they'll talk about it openly out of school. And talking is a very short step away from acting. I for one don't want my teenagers to become promiscuous just because some so-called educators in this town persist in denying the obvious.

MS. OVERLOOK: I don't see the need for a sex education course in the first place. Surely, if parents know enough to raise their children in other respects, they are qualified to teach them about sex. Sex is a moral matter—and the school has no business butting into the moral upbringing of the young. The school should stick to the three Rs and leave moral and spiritual matters to the home and church.

MS. SCHULTZ: If the school were as anxious to guard the innocence of the young as it is to fill their heads with sex ideas, perhaps our society wouldn't be slipping so badly today.

MEMBER 2:   I'd like to go back to something Ms. Jackson said a few minutes ago about promiscuity. Ms. Jackson, no one wants to make teenagers promiscuous. The whole effect of the program in sex education, as I understand it, may be to prevent just that development. There is a great deal of emphasis on sex in advertising today and an increasing tendency toward frankness in the arts. The board had only a brief explanation of the objectives and approaches of this course, but we were told by the principal that the faculty committee that developed the course consulted numerous statistical studies, and every one showed that most young people receive very little direct, honest, and accurate information about sex. Despite appearances, he said, they're woefully ignorant, in many cases, about the facts of life. That is what the course and its teacher, Ms. Babette, are trying to overcome: misinformation and ignorance.

MS. GREEN: *[Turning to Ms. Brown and whispering]* It's obvious why he speaks that way. I've seen the way he looks at Ms. Babette. Those bachelors and their filthy minds.

MS. SCHULTZ: A course in sex education is a strange way of decreasing promiscuity. Why is it that since courses like this have been added to curricula around the country, the incidence of rape, out-of-wedlock pregnancy, and venereal disease has risen so dramatically?

MEMBER 2:   I'm not sure I understand the point you are making. Are you suggesting that . . .

MS. SCHULTZ: I'm suggesting that I'm in favor of ridding our society of its preoccupation with sex. I confess I don't know quite how to do that. But I do know where to start. Right here in Alertia—by ridding our school of that course.

MR. LESSROW: *[Applauding vigorously]* My sentiments exactly. If we're not going to defeat our country's enemies, including those in Washington, at least we can stop their insidious campaign against our youth at home. I voted for you for the school board—probably most of us in this room did. We had confidence in your ability to act wisely, to do the right thing. You now know the facts in this matter. It's time to act on them. You can justify our confidence in you by demanding that that course be discontinued immediately.

CHAIR: *[After a minute or two of silence]* Well, I believe the board has a good idea of the nature of your concern about this course. If there are no more comments at this time, I'd like to thank you ladies and gentlemen for coming out tonight and to assure you that we will give your position our careful consideration. If the board members will remain, we'll continue with our meeting in a few minutes.

4.3 Evaluate the argument in the following letter to the editor, using the approach explained in this chapter. State your judgment and support it thoroughly.

Dear Editor:

I enjoyed your recent series of articles on religious views. I believe religious values occupy the central place in one's being. Today an increasing number of young people are giving up their religion because of the vocal skepticism of those who find religious values too restrictive. If more of us who do believe were as vocal, the young would surely see the relevance of religion and not be so easily deceived by those who wish to mislead them.

It is fashionable today among so-called humanists to place people's reason above religious faith. They say a person must follow his or her own lights, affirm what he or she believes is true. But are they really so open-minded and humble as that view makes them seem? I think not. For underneath that view lies the fact that they exalt their own judgment. When they accept the word of an authority, it is only because they agree with that authority. And they do not accept one authority without, by that very acceptance, rejecting other authorities. In short, they are superegotists who refuse to accept what transcends their understanding and who try to fit God into their understanding. Their efforts are in vain, for God will not fit into the finite mind. A god who can be understood by human beings is no god at all, but a poor imitation.

I do not believe that any intelligent, honest person can place his or her confidence in human intelligence and reason. Human learning is too sparse and fragmentary to warrant such trust. Human knowledge and understanding change all too quickly. Yesterday's theories gather dust in the attics of libraries, and history judges all things mercilessly. But the Bible, God's own word, remains. It stands as an immutable beacon to all who love the truth. One need only put aside his or her probing and questioning and doubting, become like the little children, and accept it.

Sincerely yours,

Mrs. Joan Truly

4.4 The following letter appeared in the *New York Times Magazine.*[12] Evaluate the argument it presents by using the approach explained in the chapter. State your judgment and support it thoroughly.

To the Editor:

As a man whose past is considerably peppered with the buckshot of imprisonment including four years at Attica prison, I am in a position to state that William R. Coons's article, "An Attica Graduate Tells His Story" (Oct. 10), is equipped with built-in blinders. The reader can look in only one direction: at the brutal guards, the butcher doctors, the unfeeling, unconscionable warden, etc. A cartoon, therefore, forms in the mind of the reader. He sees a huge, hairy monster, frothing fangs bared, labeled "Penal System" and crushing the life out of a ragged, pity-evoking figure labeled "Defenseless Convict."

I wonder why Mr. Coons omitted the worst handicap facing the inmate who is sincerely interested in rehabilitation—his own "brothers" in gray?

Contrary to what Mr. Coons would have the reader believe, prison populations are not made up solely of misunderstood, slightly tarnished angels unjustly sentenced to hundreds of years for merely stealing wormy apples.

Many—let me lean on that word—many convicts are incorrigible scum whose sole purpose in life closely parallels that of a demented crocodile. They wouldn't lead an honest life if guaranteed a thousand dollars per week and half of God's throne in the hereafter.

They are the ones who steal from their fellow inmates, who collect "protection money" from the weak and frightened, who force others with "shanks" pressed to their throats to commit homosexual acts, whose roaring animal voices fill the cell blocks until your brains vibrate from the obscene cacophony and you couldn't write your own name without misspelling it. They are the ones who will grip prison reform by the throat and choke it, exploit it, mangle and tramp on it until, in disgust, the administration rescinds it.

The first step toward lasting prison reform is to collect all the incorrigible scum, the human cockroaches who infest prison populations, and place them in separate institutions. Let them prey on each other. Let them, if it comes to it, kill each other off . . . incurable cancers devouring each other.

Unless this step is taken, prison reform, however great and shining, will fade into the limbo of things that might have worked.

Name Withheld

4.5 Visit the following Web site and sample the links on visual communication. http://www.uiowa.edu/~commstud/resources/visual.html. For each of the links you sample, write a brief explanation of what you learned.

4.6 The following Web site presents a variety of examples of photo tampering. http://www.cs.dartmouth.edu/farid/research/digitaltampering/ After examining those examples, write a brief description of how they have complemented and/or added to your understanding of critical viewing.

ISSUE FOR EXTENDED ANALYSIS

Following is a more comprehensive thinking challenge than the others in the chapter. Analyze and respond to it, following the instructions for extended analysis at the end of Chapter 1. Also, review "The Basis of Moral Judgment" and "Dealing with Dilemmas" in Chapter 2.

THE ISSUE: THE IRAQ WAR

The central question about the Iraq war is "Was it *just*—that is, justified?" As George Weigel points out, classical just-war theory has six requirements. In question form, they might be expressed thus: *Is the cause for going to war just? Are the stated intentions for going to war defensible? Do the leaders of the nation going to war have the authority to do so? Is there a reasonable chance for the war effort to be successful? Will the good that the war accomplishes outweigh the harm that it does? Have less drastic means of achieving the desired outcome been exhausted? (In other words, does the particular war in question represent the last resort?)*

THE ESSAYS

The Iraq War Was Just
By Pedro Blanco

The infamous attack on "nine-eleven" took 3,000 innocent lives, and that alone was sufficient reason for the U.S. to go to war. True, the perpetrators wore no uniforms and carried no country's flag; they were, instead, a group of international thugs who sought sanctuary in various countries. But these facts in no way diminished the horror and injustice of their actions.

The Iraq War Was Unjust
By Wendy Walker

All war is a failure or an abandonment of reason and is therefore an inappropriate response to difficulties between nations. Since violence can never be the solution to violence, all war must be considered evil. Some philosophers claim that, in rare circumstances, this form of evil may be unavoidable. The Iraq War, however, does not fall into this category because, to put it simply, there was nothing "just" about it.

The Bush administration repeatedly tried to get international support, both through the U.N. and through direct diplomacy with other nations, for the Iraq War. Some large and influential nations refused to support the war because, as was later revealed, they were profiteering from the Oil for Food program. And the U.N. had warned Iraq several times that noncompliance with its directives could have dire consequences. All the U.S. did was to carry out the threat that the U.N. was unwilling to carry out. And more than 20 other nations joined the U.S.

The main reason for singling out Iraq was the threat of Weapons of Mass Destruction (WMD). For a decade virtually all U.S. officials, including those in the Clinton administration, were convinced Saddam had WMD, and with good reasons—he had used them against his own citizens and most intelligence showed that he still had a huge stockpile. The fact that WMD could not be found after the war does not prove they didn't exist; Saddam could easily have sent them to Syria. In any case, the U.S. decision to go to war was made in good faith and on the best available intelligence. And it freed millions of people from tyranny.

Most important, the war was conducted so as to minimize harm to civilians. For the first time in military history, pinpoint bombing was used, and wherever possible, Iraq's infrastructure was spared. Finally, when Saddam was ousted, the U.S. did not attempt to colonize Iraq but helped the Iraqi people establish a democratic government. For all these reasons, and by any fair measure, the Iraq war was just.

To begin with, there was no provocation for the U.S. to invade Iraq. True, the attack on "9/11" claimed 3,000 innocent lives, but that outrage was perpetrated by a group of terrorists that, though they had bases in several nations, were formally aligned with none. There was never any proof that the terrorists acted on behalf of the nation of Iraq or, for that matter, that they had any more support for the attack from Iraq than from any other nation. Given that all of the terrorists on 9/11 were Saudis, a better case could have been made for a U.S. attack on Saudi Arabia.

Second, the Iraq War was not a "last resort," decided upon after all diplomatic avenues had been exhausted. It was a *first* resort. Moreover, the Bush administration did not bother to get either the support of the United Nations or the (required) consent of Congress. Instead, the administration acted hastily, recklessly, and unilaterally.

A third reason for considering the Iraq War unjust is that it was conducted inhumanely. Not only were hundreds of noncombatants killed, but prisoners were detained without the filing of formal charges and without benefit of legal counsel. Worse, there were credible charges of torture at the Guantanamo Bay prison camp and humiliation and sexual mistreatment at Abu Ghraib. (Disgusting photos documenting the latter abuse were circulated in the world press.)

Far from being a just war, the Iraq War was a stain on our national character.

CLASS DISCUSSION

NICK: There's no such thing as a just war because all war violates the ethical requirement of loving our neighbors and treating them with kindness. The "just war" theory is simply a clever way of defending the indefensible.

MARGARET: War exists because human nature is flawed—that is, because people *and nations* don't always behave as they should. Whenever the leaders of one nation commit atrocities against their own people or acts of aggression against weaker nations, it is not only right and proper but also neighborly for other nations to wage war against the offenders.

AGNES: I believe the just war criteria need to be revised to cover the new forms of aggression that have arisen in recent decades. The aggressors no longer wear uniforms or represent specific countries. They don't march in columns or attack others openly but, rather, work to conduct their operations secretly. They rely on terror and make no distinction between enemy soldiers and innocent people. The kind of war they are waging calls for different kinds of responses.

NATHAN: I agree that the strong have an obligation to protect the weak and defenseless. But they can't just rush off to war willy-nilly the way the U.S. did in Iraq. They have to gain the cooperation of other nations.

MARGARET: The idea that the president made no effort to get the cooperation of other nations is false. He not only made efforts; he also got the support of more than 20 other nations. The only reason he failed to get the U.N. support for the war is that the representatives of some key nations were taking bribes from Saddam.

NATHAN: What about all the ballyhoo about WMD? The administration knew there were no such weapons—they manufactured the idea as an excuse to attack.

MARGARET: The term "Monday morning quarterback" fits Iraq war critics perfectly. They can tell you exactly how any "game" should have been played *after the game has been played*. It's easy to say the Bush administration should have known there were no WMD, but given the circumstances of the time, there was no way anyone could have known. Furthermore, to say the Bush administration manufactured the idea of WMD is irresponsible. Well before Bush came to office, President Clinton and virtually all other leaders of both political parties believed WMD existed.

PART II

Be Creative

What is the greatest difficulty people have in thinking about problems and issues? The standard answer is "the difficulty of evaluating the various solutions and choosing the best one." In some cases, this may be true. But two other difficulties are equally troublesome: *identifying problems and issues before they become crises,* and *getting beyond common, unoriginal solutions to creative ones.*

The first chapter in this part introduces the creative process. The other chapters expand this introduction, showing you how to search for challenges, express and investigate problems and issues, and produce many and varied solutions. By the end of Part II, you will have developed a proactive approach to problems and issues and learned how to stimulate your imagination.

The Creative Process

Have you heard any of these sayings: "Creativity can't be learned," "The way to be creative is to ignore traditional ways of doing things," "It takes a high IQ to be creative," "Taking drugs enhances a person's creativity," or "Creativity is related to mental illness"? They've all been around for a long time. But guess what? *They're all wrong.*

This chapter sets the record straight about creativity. It also details the characteristics of creative people, provides an overview of the creative process, and offers a strategy you can use to develop and apply *your* untapped creative potential.

The human mind, as we have seen, has two phases. It both produces ideas and judges them. These phases are intertwined; that is, we move back and forth between them many times in the course of dealing with a problem, sometimes several times in the span of a few seconds. To study the art of thinking in its most dynamic form would be difficult at best. It is much easier to study each part separately. For this reason, we will focus first on the production of ideas (Chapters 5 through 9) and then turn to the judgment of ideas.*

Although everyone produces and judges ideas, the quality of the effort varies greatly from person to person. One individual produces a single common or shallow idea for each problem or issue and approves it uncritically, whereas another produces an assortment of ideas, some of them original and profound, and examines them critically, refining the best ones to make them even better.

---

*Because it is impossible to separate the two completely, minor elements on judging will be included in our treatment of creativity, and vice versa.

The terms *creative thinking* and *critical thinking*, as we will use them throughout the remaining chapters, refer to the latter kind of effort.

KEY FACTS ABOUT CREATIVITY

Before the mid-1950s, creativity received little scholarly attention. Then one researcher examined more than 121,000 listings of articles recorded in *Psychological Abstracts* during the previous 23 years. He found that only 186 articles—less than two-tenths of 1 percent of the total—had any direct concern with creativity.[1] Since that finding, interest in creativity has increased considerably, and many books have been published on the subject.[2] Researchers have examined the lives of creative achievers, probed the creative process, and tested creative performance in every conceivable circumstance and at every age level.

Researchers' efforts have helped deepen our understanding of creativity and overcome the many misconceptions that for so long went unchallenged. You have undoubtedly been exposed to some of these misconceptions and therefore have developed some false impressions about what creativity is and how it works. Replacing those false impressions with facts is an important first step in developing your creative potential. The facts that follow are the most important ones. Some we mentioned briefly in Chapter 1. All are worth returning to and reflecting on from time to time.

"Doing Your Own Thing" Is Not Necessarily a Mark of Creativity. "For many people," George F. Kneller observes, "being creative seems to imply nothing more than releasing impulses or relaxing tensions. . . . Yet an uninhibited swiveling at the hips is hardly creative dancing, nor is hurling colors at a canvas creative painting."[3] Creativity does involve a willingness to break away from established patterns and try new directions, but it does not mean being different for the sake of being different or as an exercise in self-indulgence. It is as much a mistake to ignore the accumulated knowledge of the past as it is to be limited by it. As Alfred North Whitehead warned, "Fools act on imagination without knowledge; pedants act on knowledge without imagination."[4] Being creative means *combining* knowledge and imagination.

Creativity Does Not Require Special Intellectual Talent or a High IQ. The idea that highly creative people have some special intellectual ability lacking in the general population has been widely accepted for centuries. When the IQ test was devised, that idea was given new currency, and anyone who achieved less than a genius-level score (135 and above) was considered to have little or no chance for creative intellectual achievement.

However, when researchers began studying the lives of creative people and comparing IQ test performance with creativity test performance, they made two discoveries. They found that creativity depends not on the possession of special talents, but on the *use* of talents that virtually everyone has but most have never learned to use. In addition, they found that the IQ test was not designed to measure creativity, so a high score is no indication of creative ability, and a low score, no indication of its absence. In fact, they found that the great majority of creative achievers fell significantly below the genius level.[5]

The Use of Drugs Hinders Creativity.   Although many people seem determined to resist this fact, it has long been acknowledged by those who have studied creativity. If liquor and other drugs have been such a boon to original thought, one researcher asks, why hasn't the corner saloon produced more creative achievers? No one, as yet, has answered this question satisfactorily. Nor is anyone likely to. The reason drugs harm creativity, Brewster Ghiselin explains, is that "their action reduces judgment, and the activities they provoke are hallucinatory rather than illuminating." What is needed, he argues, is not artificial stimulation of the mind, but increased control and direction.[6]

The use of drugs and liquor as stimulants is sometimes part of a larger misconception that might be termed the *bohemian mystique*. This misconception is the notion that a dissipated lifestyle somehow casts off intellectual restraints and opens the mind to new ideas. Eliot Dole Hutchinson offers an assessment that most researchers would endorse: "Narrow streets, shabby studios, undisciplined living, and artistic ballyhoo about local color may all have their place in pseudo artistry, but they have little to do with genuine creation. Nor is the necessary creative freedom clearly associated with them at all. Bohemianism squanders its freedom, returns from its hours of dissipation less effective. Creative discipline capitalizes its leisure, returns refreshed, reinvigorated, eager."[7]

Creativity Is an Expression of Mental Health.   One common image of the creative person is reinforced by a number of low-budget horror films. That image depicts a wild-eyed mad scientist, shuffling nervously around a laboratory (pronounced *lab-or'-a-try* in an ominous tone of voice), rubbing hands together evilly and drooling. Many people really believe the image: They view *creative person* and *lunatic* as near synonyms. They are wrong.

In the following passage, Harold H. Anderson summarizes a leading psychological view concerning the relative sanity of creative people. (Endorsers include such respected thinkers as Erich Fromm, Rollo May, Carl Rogers, Abraham Maslow, J. P. Guilford, and Ernest Hilgard.)

> The consensus of these authors is that creativity is an expression of a mentally or psychologically healthy person, that creativity is associated with wholeness, unity, honesty, integrity, personal involvement, enthusiasm, high motivation, and action.
>
> There is also agreement that neurosis either accompanies or causes a degraded quality of one's creativity. For neurotic persons and persons with other forms of mental disease [who are, at the same time, creative] such assumptions as the following are offered: that these persons are creative in spite of their disease; that they are producing below the achievements they would show without the disease; that they are on the downgrade, or that they are pseudo creative, that is, they may have brilliant original ideas which, because of the neurosis, they do not communicate.[8]

CHARACTERISTICS OF CREATIVE PEOPLE

Studies of creative achievers have identified a number of characteristics they share.[9] The following characteristics are among the most prominent.

Creative People Are Dynamic.   Unlike most people, creative people do not allow their minds to become passive, accepting, unquestioning. They manage to keep their curiosity burning, or at least to rekindle it. One aspect of this intellectual dynamism is *playfulness.* Like little children with building blocks, creative people love to toy with ideas, arranging them in new combinations, looking at them from different perspectives. It was such activity that Isaac Newton was referring to when he wrote, "I do not know what I may appear to the world; but to myself I seem to have been only like a boy playing on the seashore, and diverting myself in now and then finding . . . a smoother pebble or a prettier shell than ordinary whilst the great ocean of truth lay all undiscovered before me."[10]

Einstein was willing to speculate further. He saw such playfulness as "the essential feature in productive thought."[11] But whatever the place of playfulness among the characteristics of creative people, one thing is certain: it provides those people a richer and more varied assortment of ideas than the average person enjoys.

Creative People Are Daring.   For the creative, thinking is an adventure. Because they are relatively free of preconceived notions and prejudiced views, creative people are less inclined to accept prevailing views, less narrow in their perspectives, and less likely to conform with the thinking of those around them. They are bold in their conceptions, willing to entertain unpopular ideas and seemingly unlikely possibilities. Therefore, like Galileo and Columbus, Edison and the Wright brothers, they are more open than others to creative ideas.

Their daring has an additional benefit: It makes them less susceptible to face-saving than others. They are willing to face unpleasant experiences, apply their curiosity, and learn from those experiences. As a result, they are less likely than others to repeat the same failure over and over.

Creative People Are Resourceful.   Resourcefulness is the ability to act effectively and to conceptualize the approach that solves the problem—even when the problem stymies others and the resources at hand are meager. This ability is not measured by IQ tests, yet it is one of the most important aspects of practical intelligence. One dramatic example of this quality was reported in *Scientific American* more than half a century ago. A prisoner in a western state penitentiary escaped but was recaptured after a few weeks. The prison officials grilled him for days. "Where did you get the saw to cut through the bars?" they demanded. In time, he broke down and confessed how he had managed to cut the bars. He claimed he had picked up bits of twine in the machine shop, dipped them in glue and then in emery, and smuggled them back to his cell. Night after night for three months, he had "sawed" the one-inch-thick steel bars. The prison officials accepted his explanation, locked him up, and made sure he never visited the machine shop again.

That, however, is not the end of the story. One dark night about three and a half years later, the man escaped again, and the prison officials found the bars cut in exactly the same manner. Though he was never recaptured, the way he escaped is legendary in the underworld. He'd lied about using material from the machine shop the first time. He had been much more resourceful than that. He had used woolen strings from his socks, moistened them with spit, and rubbed them in dirt on his cell floor.[12]

Creative People Are Hardworking. "All problems," states William Gordon, "present themselves to the mind as threats of failure."[13] Only people who are unwilling to be intimidated by the prospect of failure, and who are determined to succeed no matter what effort is required, have a chance to succeed. (Even for them, of course, there is no guarantee of success.) Creative people are willing to make the necessary commitment. It was that commitment Thomas Edison had in mind when he said, "Genius is 99 percent perspiration and 1 percent inspiration"; so did George Bernard Shaw when he explained, "When I was a young man I observed that nine out of ten things I did were failures. I didn't want to be a failure, so I did ten times more work."

Part of creative people's industriousness is attributable to their ability to be absorbed in a problem thoroughly and to give it their undivided attention. But it is derived, as well, from their competitiveness, which is unlike most people's in that it is not directed toward other people but toward ideas. They take the challenge of ideas *personally*. Lester Pfister was such a person. He got the idea of inbreeding stalks of corn to eliminate weaker strains. He began with 50,000 stalks and worked by hand, season after season. After five years, he had only four stalks left, and he was destitute. But he had perfected the strain.[14] Where others would have succumbed to frustration and disappointment, he persevered because he was unwilling to accept defeat.

Creative People Are Independent. Every new idea we think of separates us from other people, and expressing the idea increases the separation tenfold. Such separation is frightening, especially to those who draw their strength from association with others and who depend on others for their identity. Such people are not likely to feel comfortable entertaining, let alone expressing, new ideas. They fear rejection too much. Creative people are different. This is not to say that they don't enjoy having the acceptance and support of others or that the possibility of losing friends doesn't bother them. It means that however much they may want acceptance and support and friendship, they don't need them the way others do. Instead of looking to others for approval of their ideas, they look within themselves.[15] For this reason, they are less afraid of appearing eccentric or odd, are more self-confident, and are more free to speak and act independently.

Knowing these five characteristics can help you develop your creative potential if you are willing to make the effort to acquire them—or if you already possess them, to reinforce them. It is never an easy task; old habits resist replacement. But even modest progress will make a difference in the quality of your thinking.

APPLYING CREATIVITY TO PROBLEMS AND ISSUES

The two broad applications of creativity that are of special concern to us are solving problems and resolving controversial issues. The terms *problem* and *issue* overlap considerably. Both refer to disagreeable situations that challenge our ingenuity, situations that have no readily apparent, satisfactory remedy. But an *issue* has an additional characteristic. It tends to divide people into opposing camps, each sure that it is right and the opposition wrong.

The most important ways to apply creativity to problems and issues include taking a novel approach, devising or modifying a process or system, inventing a new product or service, finding new uses for existing things, improving things, and inventing or redefining a concept. Let's look at some examples of each.

Taking a Novel Approach

D. B. Kaplan's, a Chicago delicatessen, approaches menu writing with its tongue well in cheek (and in some cases, in the sandwich). Items include Tongue Fu, the Italian Scallion, Chive Turkey, Ike and Tina Tuna, Dr. Pepperoni, the Breadless Horseman, Annette Spinachello, and Quiche and Tell. The ingredients are as creative as the names.

Humane Society inspectors who found two dogs in a closed car in brutal 92-degree heat used a novel approach in dealing with the dogs' owners. They offered them an alternative to being charged with cruelty to animals: spend an hour inside the closed car themselves in the same heat the dogs endured, while the dogs spent the hour in the air-conditioned Humane Society building.[16]

A judge in a Michigan divorce court took a novel approach to the issues of custody and the right to live in the family home. He awarded the house to the *children* until the youngest reached 18. The parents would take turns living in the house and paying the bills. (Both parents lived in the area, so this housing arrangement was workable.)[17]

To instill in students a sense of obligation to help those in need, Tulane University Law School set the unusual graduation requirement of performing at least 20 hours of volunteer legal work for the poor.[18]

The city of Venice, Italy, sits on a number of small islands in an Adriatic lagoon and has long been subject to periodic flooding. Now there is reason to fear that the rising sea level will eventually flood the city. The most publicized and widely accepted proposal to prevent this disaster is to build 79 moveable, hollow gates at the entrance to the lagoon. These gates could be filled with air and caused to rise up, preventing rising waters from flooding Venice. Not everyone accepts this novel plan, however. Some scientists say the gates' design is based on outdated tide tables, and thus the gates would eventually have to be replaced. And environmentalists have raised concerns about the increased pollution the gates could cause.

Devising or Modifying a Process or System

The Dewey decimal system and the Library of Congress system are two techniques that were invented for classifying books. (Even more basic to learning, of course, is the invention known as the alphabet.)

In recent decades, a new surgical procedure has been devised for combating periodontal disease and making it possible for people to keep their teeth throughout their lives. The procedure involves cutting back diseased gum tissue and scraping accumulated plaque from the teeth. (Left untreated, periodontal disease can cause teeth to loosen and fall out.)

Over the years, several procedures have been developed for determining the health of a fetus. Both amniocentesis and chorionic villus sampling involve the extraction of amniotic fluid; ultrasound involves the bouncing of sound waves off the fetus to form an image.

Between the 1880s and the 1980s the principal tool of criminal investigation was the fingerprint. Since then it has been DNA testing. Every individual who ever lived has his or her own distinctive genetic makeup. A strand of hair or a spot of urine, saliva, or semen left at a crime scene can be compared with a DNA sample of a suspect and be a significant factor in determining guilt or innocence.[19]

Reacting to widespread criticism of the 1988 presidential campaign as superficial, a member of Congress from Indiana, Lee Hamilton, proposed a change in the traditional debating format. His idea was to have each candidate speak alone for an hour, presenting his or her ideas on a single issue and responding to in-depth questioning by a panel of experts. The presentations would be videotaped simultaneously for sequential televising at a later time.[20] (Unfortunately, the idea has not been implemented in subsequent presidential campaigns.)

Inventing a New Product or Service

In 1845, a man needed money quickly to pay a debt. "What can I invent to raise some money?" he thought. Three hours later, he had invented the safety pin. He later sold the idea for $400. Virtually all the products we use every day have similar, though perhaps less dramatic, stories. The hammer, the fork, the alarm clock, the electric blanket, the toothpaste tube, the matchbook—these and thousands of other products first occurred as ideas in a creative mind. And new ideas are occurring every day. Two you may not have heard of are Graffiti Gobbler, a chemical compound that can remove ink or paint from wood, brick, or steel,[21] and the Moto-Stand, a three-wheeled, upholstered, motorized truck invented by a man paralyzed from the chest down. The vehicle permits him to maneuver around the house in a standing position.[22]

The laundromat, the car wash, and the rent-a-car agency are examples of successful services that have been invented. When the rent-a-car service became quite expensive, some enterprising people invented rental services providing older, high-mileage cars in good working condition. (One such agency is called Rent-a-Wreck; another, Rent-a-Heap.) A public-spirited psychiatrist invented a service for insomniacs called Sleepline that offers an eight-minute recorded message ("Sleep is coming . . . slower . . . deeper . . .") to help people sleep.[23]

Finding New Uses for Existing Things

No matter how old something is, new uses can always be devised for it. Consider how many kinds of nails, nuts, bolts, and brushes have been developed from the original ideas. Even the water bed, a relatively new variation on the bed, has been given a new use: to simulate the warmth and protection of the womb for premature babies.[24] In some cases, apparently useless objects can be put to good use. For example, a St. Louis barber combines hair clippings with peat and other substances to form an unusually rich potting soil that he believes may help restore drought-ravaged soil in parts of Asia and Africa. And at least one college student devised a use for empty beer and soda cans: He punched holes in the top and bottom, ran heavy cord through them, and hung the cans in close rows as window curtains.

Agricultural crops have long been used for unusual purposes. Cotton lint, for example, is used to manufacture explosives, and ground-up tobacco is used for insecticide. Now scientists have found new uses for the largest surplus crop in the United States: corn. These uses include de-icing materials, adhesives, disposable bottles, and biodegradable garbage bags. Such creative ideas promise to reduce dependency on oil imports and to reduce pollution.[25]

New uses for the computer and the laser continue to multiply, such as this one that combines the two: A Cleveland firm markets a computer device that measures a person for a suit of clothing and then telephones the information to a factory where lasers cut the fabric.[26]

Improving Things

Far more patents are issued each year for improvements in existing things than for new inventions. There is a very good reason. Nothing of human invention is perfect; everything can be made better. Consider the development of the light, from the pre-historic torch to the latest flashlight, or that of the camera and the automobile.

Recent developments in the telephone, for example, include call block, call trace, priority call, return call, repeat call, and caller ID. Each of these features was developed in response to a particular need that was not being met by the existing equipment.

The use of creativity to improve things is nowhere more evident than in the computer industry. Every few months a significant breakthrough is announced in hardware or software, and minor improvements are constantly being made.

Inventing or Redefining a Concept

We tend to regard the many concepts that help us think and deal with reality as fixed and eternal. Yet that is not so. Concepts are invented, just as products and services are. The concepts of taxation and punishing criminals, for example, may be very old, but they were once new. Numerous other concepts are relatively recent. It is hard to imagine how mathematics could even be used without the concept of zero. Yet that concept was invented by a Hindu around A.D. 500. Similarly, the concept of the corporation originated in the sixteenth century, and our ideas of progress and worldly success in the seventeenth. The concept of the zip code is very recent.

The concept of childhood we are familiar with—as a stage of innocence with its own special characteristics—dates back only a few centuries. Before then, chil-dren were treated as little adults. The historian J. H. Plumb writes: "Certainly there was no separate world of childhood [in earlier times]. Children shared the same games with adults, the same toys, the same fairy stories. They lived their lives together, never apart. The coarse village festivals depicted by Bruegel, show-ing men and women besotted with drink, groping for each other with unbridled lust, have children eating and drinking with the adults."[27]

STAGES IN THE CREATIVE PROCESS

Being creative means more than *having* certain traits. It means *behaving creatively*, addressing the challenges we encounter with imagination and originality. In short, it means demonstrating skill in applying the creative process. Although authorities disagree over the number of stages in this process—some say three, others say four, five, or seven—the disagreement is not over substantive matters. It is merely over whether to combine activities under one heading or several. There is no real disagreement about the basic activities involved.[28]

For ease in remembering and convenience of application, we will view the creative process as having four stages: searching for challenges, expressing the particular problem or issue, investigating it, and producing a range of ideas. Each of these stages will be the subject of a separate chapter, but a brief overview of the process will enable you to begin using it right away.

The First Stage: Searching for Challenges

The essence of creativity is meeting challenges in an imaginative, original, and effective way. Often, challenges need not be sought out; they come to you in the form of obvious problems and issues. For example, if your roommate comes home night after night at 2 or 3 A.M., crashes into the room, and begins talking to you when you are trying to sleep, you needn't be very perceptive to know you have a problem. Or if you find yourself in the middle of a raging argument over whether abortion is murder, no one will have to tell you that you are addressing an issue.

However, not all challenges are so obvious. Sometimes, the problems and issues are so small or subtle that few people notice them; at other times, there are no problems and issues at all, only *opportunities to improve existing conditions*. Such challenges arouse no strong emotion in you, so you will not find them by sitting and waiting—you must look for them.

The first stage of the creative process represents the habit of searching for challenges, not at one specific time, but constantly. Its importance is reflected in the fact that you can be creative only in response to challenges that you perceive.

The Second Stage: Expressing the Problem or Issue

The objective in this stage is to find the best expression of the problem or issue, the one that will yield the most helpful ideas.** "A problem properly stated," noted Henry Hazlitt,[29] "is partly solved." Because different expressions open different avenues of thought, it is best to consider as many expressions as possible. One of

---

**In the case where there is no real problem or issue but only an opportunity to improve an existing condition, you would treat the situation *as if it were* problematic, saying, for example, "How can I make this process work even more efficiently?"

the most common mistakes made in addressing problems and issues is to see them from one perspective only and thus to close off many fruitful avenues of thought.

Consider the prisoner deciding how to escape from prison. His first formulation of the problem was probably something such as "How can I get a gun and shoot my way out of here?" or "How can I trick the guards into opening my cell so I can overpower them?" If he had settled for that formulation, he would still be there (where he belonged). His ingenious escape plan could have been devised only as a response to the question "How can I cut through those bars without a hacksaw?"

Often, after expressing the problem or issue in a number of ways, you will be unable to decide which expression is best. When that happens, postpone deciding until your work in later stages of the process enables you to decide.

The Third Stage: Investigating the Problem or Issue

The objective of this stage is to obtain the information necessary to deal effectively with the problem or issue. In some cases, this will mean merely searching your past experience and observation for appropriate material and bringing it to bear on the current problem. In others, it will mean obtaining new information through fresh experience and observation, interviews with knowledgeable people, or your own research. (In the case of the prisoner, it meant closely observing all the accessible places and items in the prison.)

The Fourth Stage: Producing Ideas

The objective in this stage is to generate enough ideas to decide what action to take or what belief to embrace. Two obstacles are common in this stage. The first is the often unconscious tendency to limit your ideas to common, familiar, habitual responses and to block out uncommon, unfamiliar ones. Fight that tendency by keeping in mind that however alien and inappropriate the latter kinds of responses may seem, it is precisely in those responses that creativity is to be found.

The second obstacle is the temptation to stop producing ideas too soon. As we will see in Chapter 9, research has documented that the longer you continue producing ideas, the greater are your chances of producing worthwhile ideas. Or as one writer puts it, "The more you fish, the more likely you are to get a strike."

There is one final matter to be clarified before you will be ready to begin practicing the creative process: How will you know when you get a creative idea? By what characteristics will you be able to distinguish it from other ideas? A creative idea is an idea that is both imaginative and effective. That second quality is as important as the first. It's not enough for an idea to be unusual. If it were, then the weirdest, most bizarre ideas would be the most creative. No, to be creative an idea must work, must solve the problem, or must illuminate the issue it responds to. A creative idea must not be just uncommon—it must be *uncommonly good*. This is the standard you should apply when looking over the ideas you produced.

When you have produced a generous number of ideas, decide which seems to be the best. Sometimes that will be a single idea; other times it will be a combination of two or more ideas. At this point your decision should be tentative. Otherwise, you will be tempted to forgo the valuable critical thinking process by which ideas are *evaluated*.

WARM-UP EXERCISES

5.1 Four friends have a large garden in the following shape. They want to divide it into four little gardens the same size and shape, but they don't know quite how to do this. Show them.

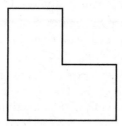

5.2 How many uses can you think of for old socks, stockings, or panty hose? Be sure to guard against setting unconscious restrictions on your thinking and to resist the temptation to settle for too few ideas.

5.3 Every change of season brings a new clothing fashion for men, women, and children. Invent as many new fashions as you can. (If you wish, you may include out-of-date fashions in your list, as long as they have not been popular in recent years.) Observe the cautions mentioned in Exercise 5.2.

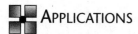 APPLICATIONS

5.1 For each of the following problems, apply stages 2 through 4 of the creative process. Record all your thoughts as they occur, and be prepared to submit them to your instructor. When you have finished with the last stage, state which of your solutions is best and briefly explain why.

  a. Barney has early classes five days a week. Yet he has attended few of them because he just can't seem to wake up in the morning. If he doesn't find a solution to his problem soon, he'll surely flunk out of college.

  b. The campus library has been losing articles from magazines and even pages from expensive books. Irresponsible students just tear them out, hide them in their book bags, and walk out of the library. But yesterday a student was caught leaving with ripped-out pages. Some of the library staff favor making an example of her by expelling her from school and pressing criminal charges against her. Others favor merely charging her for the mutilated books.

    c. Virtually every building with a public bathroom has a graffiti problem. Even when the messages are not offensive, they create maintenance problems.

    d. Shoplifting cuts deeply into store owners' profits. Owners and managers would welcome a solution to this problem.

    e. Many elderly and handicapped people live lonely lives. No longer active in careers, they are often forgotten by former associates and neglected by family and friends. Many lack transportation to community affairs.

5.2   Think of the most unpleasant task you ever had to do. Use your creativity to make it more pleasant. Follow the directions given at the beginning of Application 5.1.

5.3   Think of your biggest pet peeve about other people, the thing they do that aggravates you most. Use your creativity to reduce or eliminate that aggravation. Follow the directions given at the beginning of Application 5.1.

ISSUE FOR EXTENDED ANALYSIS

Following is a more comprehensive thinking challenge than the others in the chapter. Analyze and respond to it, following the instructions for extended analysis at the end of Chapter 1. Also, review "The Basis of Moral Judgment" and "Dealing with Dilemmas" in Chapter 2.

THE ISSUE: OUTSOURCING U.S. JOBS

"Outsourcing" means exporting jobs overseas. The best-known instances of outsourcing are in the manufacturing sector—for example, most athletic shoes and many articles of clothing are made in Third-World or developing countries. Less well-known instances are in the technical and professional sectors—for example, computer technical support is done largely in India. Many Americans consider this a betrayal of American workers; others believe it is a boon to the economy; all agree it is the wave of the future.

THE ESSAYS

Outsourcing Is Unfair
By Kalif Ali

    They called it "free trade" when it started a few decades ago. The idea was that outsourcing low-paying jobs like assembling garments would bring prosperity to Third-World countries and help us sell more of our goods

Outsourcing Is Fair
By Louie Lefebvre

    For more than half a century, labor unions have had enormous power in America. In the beginning, they used that power to establish fair working conditions, pay schedules, and health and retirement benefits.

overseas. The promise was that our higher-paying jobs would not be affected. But that promise was quickly forgotten. The flow of high-paying jobs out of America is increasing. A Forrester Research study estimates that by 2020 almost 3.5 billion more jobs, most of them white-collar and representing over $130 billion, will be outsourced.

At this very moment millions of jobs in machine tooling, steel processing, computer services, banking, medical services, aircraft design and manufacturing, insurance, graphic design, and engineering are performed offshore. Call for computer assistance, and you'll likely speak to someone in India. Go for an X-ray or an MRI, and it will be read by a radiologist in Japan or the Philippines. The list of countries participating includes Canada, China, Sri Lanka, Pakistan, Burma, Hong Kong, Mexico, and Panama.

Some of the companies are American; others are multinational corporations, many based in America. All are obsessed with maximizing profits. Their greed has driven millions of Americans who had well-paying jobs into minimum-wage jobs or unemployment. Lost, too, are their health insurance and retirement benefits. Taken together, these developments have created a massive burden on American taxpayers.

The impact on the countries receiving the American jobs is not much better. Because there are no labor unions and often no governmental regulations, workers often work in unsanitary sweatshops for 14 or 15 hours a day. The pay is meager and health care and retirement plans are nonexistent. In many cases, even

But after achieving equity for their workers, they kept demanding more and more considerations from management. The unreasonableness of their demands is a main cause of the outsourcing phenomenon.

The unions depict corporate executives as greedy monsters totally without conscience or compassion. In reality, they are no different from the rest of us, except that the challenges they face are greater. They must control the costs and maintain work standards so that they can meet the often formidable challenge of international competition. Far from being their own bosses, they are answerable to their customers, who want the highest value at the lowest price, as well as to their stockholders, who want a profit on their investments.

Consider the case of Sudhakar Shenoy, CEO of Information Management Consultants, Inc., who had a choice of paying over $3 million for a job that could be done in India for less than $400,000. He chose India, as would any reasonable person. To do otherwise would have been a violation of his company's trust.

Critics complain that outsourcing puts Americans out of work, but that is a one-sided perspective. From the view of the other country, people are being employed. True, they may make only $2 a day compared with the $50 a day their American counterparts might make. But that $2 may be two or three times the average wage of other workers in their country. Moreover, that two dollars multiplied by millions of workers creates capitalism in entire countries and makes freedom and democracy possible. We Americans value those things for ourselves. Why should we deny them to others?

children are forced to work in these slavelike conditions.

Far from being a boon, free trade and outsourcing of labor have proved to be a blight on rich and poor nations alike.

Outsourcing is a central feature of the new "global economy," and that economy is here to stay. American workers had better come to terms with that fact and find a way to live with it.

CLASS DISCUSSION

ANNE: My main concern with outsourcing is that companies tend to choose the lowest-bidding countries; and those countries pay the lowest wages and have the worst working conditions. Many engage in child labor and even slave labor. Those practices are wrong, and American consumers should not be forced to support them. We should refuse to profit from other people's misery.

GIOVANNA: I'm sure the abuses you mention exist in other countries. They may even exist in our own. I agree we should make our concerns known. But we shouldn't ignore the greater benefits offered by outsourcing.

MARTIN: Some complain that computer manufacturers outsource their technical support operations to India. But I'm glad they do. I've had occasion to speak to many Indian technicians and have always found them polite, informed, and eager to help. That's more than I can say for many American technical support people.

GIOVANNA: People talk about buying American, but when it comes to their actual purchases, they aren't willing to pay the higher prices for American-made products. And I can't really blame them for bargain shopping.

MARTIN: I don't know whether the unions are at fault, as Louis Lefebvre says. But I do know that the current salaries and generous benefits being paid to American workers are making it increasingly difficult for American companies to compete in world markets.

ANNE: I can't see any merit in the wholesale abandonment of American workers. It seems to me that they have a *right* to keep their jobs, particularly if they've given 10, 20, or more years of faithful service to their employers. It's immoral to force them into unemployment or minimum-wage positions. The government should take control of the situation and prevent this travesty.

MARTIN: Competition has made America great. In countries that have replaced it with a government-controlled economy, the result has been chaos. That is why the old Soviet Union no longer exists. No, the only way for American companies to meet the challenge of world competition is to continue outsourcing. If they try to maintain their American workforces, they'll eventually go out of business, have to lay off all their workers, and cease to contribute to the U.S. tax base. I can't see that as a solution for Americans.

BENJAMIN: Outsourcing seems to be a mixed blessing. On the positive side, it enables people in poor countries to raise their standard of living and thus reduces social unrest throughout the world. On the negative side, it causes America's standard of living to decline. Americans may be unenthusiastic about that fact, but from a global perspective, it is a worthwhile trade-off.

6

Search for Challenges

Chapter 5 presented an overview of the four stages of creative think-

ing. In this chapter, we take a closer look at the first stage: searching

for challenges. You'll learn that curiosity plays a central role in creativ-

ity and that most people begin life with considerable curiosity but lose

it in childhood. Most important, you will learn six helpful techniques

for *regaining* your curiosity and applying it in your everyday life.

Dennis was sitting at the breakfast table, reading the morning paper, when he first noticed that the pictures and descriptions of two missing children were printed on the side of the milk carton. A public service organization employee, Dennis was impressed with the idea. "Such an obvious idea," he thought, "using the milk carton for a public service advertisement. Now why didn't I think of that?" He asked the question rhetorically, assuming it was unanswerable, and returned to reading his newspaper.

The question, however, is answerable. People fail to think of new ideas because they are mentally *re*active rather than active. That is, they go through each day unimaginatively, oblivious of problems and issues until someone else solves them, unaware of opportunities until other people transform them into achievements. At that point, they spend a few moments envying the other person for her or his "luck" and then slip back into their daily routine, never realizing that, as Robert P. Crawford observed, "Luck is often simply a sensing of an opportunity—an opportunity that is there for all of us to see."

It is one thing to possess thinking skills and quite another to use them in everyday situations. By the end of this course, you will undoubtedly have mastered the various skills of creative and critical thinking. Yet that mastery will be meaningless if you have not also developed the desire to use those skills and a heightened sensitivity to the challenges and opportunities that surround you. This chapter assists you in this development.

THE IMPORTANCE OF CURIOSITY

Curiosity, useful in every stage of thinking, is indispensable in the first stage—searching for challenges. Curiosity is not a quality reserved for the gifted few; virtually every child is boundlessly curious. A researcher once recorded all the *why* questions asked by a child slightly under five years of age over a four-day period. Read the following transcript of that recording carefully; it will help you recall your own childhood and the state of mind you felt so comfortable with then. (One asterisk indicates no answer was given; two asterisks, no answer and the question was not repeated. Italics are used for the mother's responses.)

1. Why do you have this box for your feet?

2. Why did they bring the bed down from the attic?

3. *Take your dollies in now, Joyce!* Why?

4. *Fix the rug! You caught your feet under the edge of it!* Why? Why did I?

5. Why did you take two cookies?

6. Why does the watering pot have two handles?

7. Why did he put the solder in so many places?

8. *The song sparrow isn't pretty to look at.* Why isn't he pretty?

9. *The bobolink has a brown coat in winter.* Why?* Why?

10. *It was careless of you to lose your shovel.* Why?* Why?

11. *This is your orange juice.* Why?**

12. *You are to sit here, in Daddy's place.* Why?*—Please, Mother, tell me why.

13. Do we have bangs at the back of our heads? *No!* Why?* Why, Mother?

14. *And then he made a mast for his little boat.* Why? Please tell me why he made a mast.

15. Why do you wash the hair off (the razor)?

16. (Putting on bathrobe without putting her arms in the sleeves) Is this good? *No. Why?*—(impatiently) Why? Speak out! (but then without waiting for an answer) Because it wouldn't stay on. *There, you thought it out for yourself, didn't you?*

17. Why did you stub your toe? *Because I wasn't watching out.* Why?

18. *I will tell you a story about this willow plate.* Why?**

19. *Please hurry, Joyce!* Why?* Because you want me to wash?* Why didn't you wash first? Because you knew I wanted to go with Daddy?

20. See the little tea things! Why did we buy them? *Why do you think?* Because we might use the others all up.

21. Why did you use both a fork and a spoon in making that cake?

22. Why did you sit in that chair, Mother?

23. *Please don't climb in that chair!* Why?**

24. Why are you putting up that screen?**

25. Why are you opening that window?**

26. Why does the little chicken grow in the shell?

27. *You can't win by jumping up and down!* Why?

28. Jeremiah, Jeremiah. He got into a pit, didn't he? Why did they put him into a pit?

29. *Please be careful not to break the bean plants.* Why?

30. I saw your blue apron through a crack in the door. I thought it was a spider. *A spider isn't blue, dear!* Why?* Please, Mother, tell me why a spider isn't blue.

31. *You shouldn't talk about a visitor's beard, Joyce, until he has gone!* Why?* Please tell me why.

32. Why don't you have a beard, Mother?

33. I want to cut my eyebrows in half! *Oh! You wouldn't want to do that!* Why? Because I would look funny?

34. Why do we have eyebrows?

35. Why must I hurry?

36. Why should I wait for candy until after supper?

37. Why did you speak to that man?

38. *Please don't bang the car door!* Why?*

39. Why did the chickens walk in front of the car?

40. *It is time to go home for dinner now!* Why?*[1]

Some of the questions, of course, were merely designed to get her mother's attention. But judging from both the content of the question and the child's expression when asking it, the researcher concluded that 13 of the 40 questions were genuine expressions of curiosity. Considering that the list contains only *why* questions, and omits *how, where, who,* and *when* questions (which also express curiosity), it is clear how marvelous a child's curiosity is.

HOW CURIOSITY IS LOST

Unfortunately, many children who at age 4 bombarded their parents with questions have lost their curiosity by age 18. How this happens is clear enough, at least in broad overview. Their parents grow weary of answering and begin to discourage questions. "Don't ask so many questions," they scold. And they warn, "Curiosity killed the cat." Then the children enter school and find the teacher has little time to answer. There are too many other boys and girls in the room, the schedule must be followed and the material covered, and time is short.

Nor are parents and teachers the only agents suppressing curiosity. The various media contribute to the problem. Most television programming aims to entertain the audience rather than inform them or explore complex issues with them, thereby fostering a passive spectator mentality. (Curiosity is, by definition, an *active* response to life.)

The publishing industry seldom serves curiosity much better. Popular magazines stimulate morbid curiosity about intimate details of celebrities' lives rather than healthy curiosity about the challenges of life. And book publishers tend to be more interested in fiction than in nonfiction and in physical rather than intellectual development. Diet and bodybuilding books are marketed with an enthusiasm that used to be reserved for literary classics. Even so-called self-improvement books, which might be expected to emphasize developing important qualities of mind, frequently offer little more than advice on dressing well or playing office politics or inflicting oneself on others.

Thus, the suppression of curiosity begins in childhood and continues indefinitely. The result is that most people lose the habit of raising meaningful questions about the world around them.

REGAINING YOUR CURIOSITY

At first thought, it may seem impossible to regain your childhood curiosity. Yet it is possible. Many people have done so. The first step is to realize that lack of interest and the tendency to take everything for granted are not natural, but acquired, characteristics; in other words, that lack of curiosity is a bad habit that can be broken.

A number of years ago, as a young industrial engineer, I had the privilege of working for a man who realized this and shared his realization with his subordinates. The first day I arrived on the job, this man, the chief industrial engineer, gave me these instructions: "For the next week I want you to do nothing but walk around the plant (a large mail-order company), question everything you see, and keep a record of your questions. Screen nothing out; record even the silliest and most obvious questions. At the end of each day I'd like to meet with you for half an hour and have you share those questions with me." At first I thought the direction strange. "What good can come from this?" I wondered. But I obeyed. I walked through the various departments—shipping and receiving, accounting, merchandising, order filling—and I wrote down my questions.

As the week passed, my list grew, and each day's conversation with the chief engineer increased my understanding of my assignment. He wanted me (and every other new engineer) to develop a special work style: to see things with heightened curiosity as if through a child's eyes, so that I might think more effectively about what I saw. "What is being done in this operation? Is it all necessary? If so, in what other ways might it be done? Are any of those ways simpler, quicker, safer, more economical? Who is doing it? Could a less highly paid employee do it? How might the work of several people be reduced to the work of one? Is it done at the right time, in the best place, with the most appropriate materials and equipment?" The four years I spent as an engineer were filled with such questions—and the answers saved the company tens of thousands of dollars. Yet they all proceeded from that first strange lesson in regaining my curiosity.

Anyone can regain his or her curiosity in much the same way that atrophied muscles can be rebuilt—by appropriate exercise. In the case of curiosity, the pay-off is not merely in personal satisfaction but also in increased career effectiveness. A curious person is able to understand and solve many of life's problems before others have moved beyond grumbling about them.

SIX HELPFUL TECHNIQUES

Fortunately, it isn't necessary to pretend you are a child again and go about asking a child's kind of questions. (If you were to try it, your friends would probably report you to the campus psychologist.) Nor is it necessary to adopt an industrial engineer's approach; though this approach works well in the right context, it might not fit your situation. There is a better approach, which fits a wide variety of situations. It includes six specific techniques.

1. Be observant.

2. Look for the imperfections in things.

3. Note your own and others' dissatisfactions.

4. Search for causes.

5. Be sensitive to implications.

6. Recognize the opportunity in controversy.

Be Observant

Some people are oblivious of what is going on around them. They are so involved in their own internal reverie that they miss much of what is happening. Subtle hints are wasted on them; they never really learn much from experience. How can they? They aren't really in touch with the external world.

Even if you are not such a person, chances are your powers of observation can stand improvement. Here's a little test to help you decide how observant you are.

1. Does your instructor wear a wedding band?

2. What color are your mother's eyes?

3. How many gas stations are there in your hometown (or neighborhood)?

4. How many steps are there on your front porch at home (or on the stairway to your apartment)?

5. How many churches are there in your hometown (or neighborhood)? What denominations are they?

6. Are there any trees in your best friend's yard? If so, how many? Are there any flowers? If so, what kind?

7. What color are the walls in your old high school hangout?

8. Can you describe your high school's band uniforms in detail? Can you describe the athletic uniforms (any sport)?

Most people are surprised at how little they know about supposedly familiar people, places, and things. You've probably heard the stories about people who have lived in a city or town all their lives, yet can't give directions to a stranger. The reason is that they travel the same route over and over in a daze, automatically, like robots.

Begin looking at and listening to people, places, and things more closely. Try to pick up details you'd ordinarily miss. See how people behave. For example, next time you are in the cafeteria or dining hall, watch people's actions. Note how many enter alone. Compare the way those alone and those with others behave. How at ease do those alone seem? Do they seem more or less relaxed? Do they seem nervous as they look for a table? What clues do they give about their feelings?

When you are sitting in a group of people discussing something, note the mannerisms of the group. What speech patterns are repeated? How do they look at one another? Do certain people tend to dominate? If so, in what ways? How does their behavior affect the others?

What clues do you get from people you pass in the hall (students, professors, administrators) about their states of mind? How courteous are people to one another? Do people look and speak differently to those they especially like? What manner betrays their attitude?

What excuses do people give for their behavior? How many of your friends accept responsibility as easily as they give it to others? When your friends go to parties, do their personalities seem to change in any way? Do they behave very differently from when they are in the company of professors? What are your friends' prejudices? How do they reveal them (other than by telling you directly)?

The types of observations you can make about people could be extended indefinitely. But remember, too, not just to be observant about other people. Observe yourself as well: the way you act and the broad or subtle clues you give about your attitudes and values.

Look for the Imperfections in Things

This advice will seem at first to contradict what most parents teach their children. "Don't expect things to be perfect," they say. "Learn to accept things as they are and be happy they aren't worse." But there is no real contradiction. Seeking imperfections does not mean being chronically dissatisfied, a complainer about life. It means realizing where improvements can be made.

Research suggests that productive thinkers and creative people have a keen sense of imperfection and that this sense is one of the sources of their achievement. They recognize that all ideas, systems, processes, concepts, and tools are inventions and therefore open to improvement.[2]

In some cases, creative people go out of their way to find imperfections. Walter Chrysler, for example, the mechanical genius who founded Chrysler Corporation, was just a young railroad mechanic on a meager salary when he saved enough money to buy a Pierce Arrow automobile. It cost $5,000, at that time a huge sum of money. His purpose was not to drive around and play the big shot but to take the car apart bolt by bolt—to see what parts and assembly design he could improve.[3]

Look around you at any manufactured object: the classroom blackboard and desks, your bed, your clothes, your car, the library's cataloging system, the rules governing your favorite sport, our democratic system of government. All of these in their present form evolved from earlier inventions. And every step in their evolution was an attempt to overcome imperfection. Consider the broad development of two inventions.

Artificial Lighting	Writing Implements
The torch	The hammer and chisel
The candle	The stylus
The oil lamp	The quill pen
The electric lamp	The fountain pen
The battery-powered lamp	The ballpoint pen
The fluorescent lamp	The felt-tip pen
The flashlight	The hard-point flowing pen

More important than the evolution to the present is evolution beyond the present. Everything is still imperfect. There is literally no need to curse the darkness: you can invent a new kind of light.

Note Your Own and Others' Dissatisfactions

Each day brings its share of disappointments and frustrations. There's no way to avoid them. But there is a way to capitalize on them. The common responses to such experiences, of course, are anger, resentment, and anxiety. Though these responses are understandable, many people wallow in them, letting dissatisfaction ruin their days.

Starting today, take note of the dissatisfactions you feel, like your resentment when your professors' sneak quizzes catch you unaware or when your younger sister orders you around to make herself look important. Notice, too, your irritation when your car refuses to start at the most inopportune moment and your impatience at having to stand in line at the supermarket. Also, when you converse with other people, listen carefully for their expressions of dissatisfaction, even the minor ones that are mentioned only briefly in passing.

Instead of surrendering yourself to your own feelings of dissatisfaction or plunging into other people's laments, pause and remind yourself that viewed positively, every dissatisfaction is a signal that some need is not being met. In other words, regard the situation not merely as a nuisance but also as a challenge to your ingenuity, and consider how the situation can best be improved.

A good example of how dissatisfaction can be used to produce creative ideas is consumer activist Ralph Nader's proposal for a new measure of the state of the economy. Disturbed over the fact that the gross national product focuses on things (notably production) instead of on people, Nader has proposed recording how many people are being fed rather than how much food is being produced and how many people have shelter rather than how many houses are being constructed.[4]

Search for Causes

The people who make breakthroughs and achieve insights are those who wonder. And their wondering extends to the *causes* of things: how they got to be the way they are and how they work.

For example, it was known for years that the disease known as *anthrax* remained in the soil indefinitely. However, that process was a puzzle to scientists. Then one day, while visiting a farm, Louis Pasteur's curiosity was aroused. He observed that one patch of soil was a different color than the soil around it. When he asked the farmer about it, the farmer explained that he had buried some sick sheep there the previous year. Pasteur wondered why that should make a difference. So he examined the soil more closely, noticed worm castings, and theorized that worms bored deep into the earth and carried the anthrax spores up with them. His later laboratory experiments proved him right.[5]

Similarly, diabetes might still be a mystery if it weren't for the curiosity of a research assistant engaged in unrelated research. When he noticed flies gathering around the urine of one dog used in an experiment, he wondered what in that dog's urine would attract flies. His search for the cause ultimately led to the understanding and control of diabetes.[6]

The key to searching for causes is to be alert to any significant situation or event you cannot explain satisfactorily. One especially good time to practice this alertness is while reading the news or watching it on television. For example, if you read the report of the man who killed his wife in a dispute over a penny on Valentine's Day, your curiosity would be aroused. (Legally separated, they were meeting to discuss their property division. She refused to give him a valuable Indian-head penny, and he shot her to death.)[7] "What makes a person lose his or her sense of priorities?" you might wonder and thus identify a challenging problem about human behavior. (For more information on causation, turn back to Chapter 2.)

Be Sensitive to Implications

As a child you probably enjoyed throwing pebbles in a still pond and watching the ripples reach out farther and farther until they touched the shore. Through those ripples, the tiniest pebble exerts an influence out of all proportion to its size. So it is with ideas. Every discovery, every invention, every new perspective or interpretation makes an impact whose extent is seldom fully realized at first. Good thinkers usually recognize that impact before others because they are sensitive to implications. Several examples will illustrate this sensitivity.

In August 1981, the Kinsey Institute released a study of homosexuality that challenged the traditional theories about its cause. The researchers concluded that homosexuality seemed to derive from a deep-seated predisposition that may be biological.[8] The report immediately stirred controversy, so no careful thinker would leap to the conclusion that it was the final word in the matter. Yet a person sensitive to implications would quickly realize that if the report proves correct—if homosexuality is determined by biology—homosexuality cannot fairly be considered immoral behavior because homosexuals have little or no choice in the matter.

Some years ago, research suggested that in about one-third of all cases, shyness is caused by a genetic predisposition rather than by environmental factors, and that in those cases it is especially difficult to overcome.[9] The person sensitive to implications would consider how shyness affects performance and immediately think of school and career. That would raise, among other questions, the question of whether it is fair to judge students on class participation and whether career guidance should be offered at much earlier ages than at present.

At about the same time, another study demonstrated that some people have a genetic predisposition to commit crimes and that measurements of brain waves, heart rates, and the skin's electrical properties can predict the onset of criminal behavior as early as 10 years in advance. The study also made clear that it is possible to overcome such a predisposition and avoid criminal behavior.[10] One serious implication was immediately recognized by the legal profession: whether testing for evidence of criminal tendencies (in the schools, for example) would constitute a violation of the test subjects' rights.

One final example: In 1982, the Georgia Supreme Court decided that a convicted murderer engaging in a hunger strike while in prison had a legal right to starve himself to death.[11] One interesting, if subtle, implication of this decision concerns the question of suicide. Traditionally, suicide has been considered a crime. (Technically, a person attempting suicide and failing can be legally charged for the attempt.) The Georgia decision implied that one has a right to take one's own life, thereby challenging the tradition. Since that time Dr. Jack Kevorkian has become famous (and was successfully prosecuted) for assisting people to commit suicide.

Recognize the Opportunity in Controversy

Many people do little more than rant and rave when a controversial issue is mentioned, rambling on about the wisdom of their side and damning those who disagree. They miss the real opportunity in controversy: the opportunity to be adventurous, explore new perspectives, and enrich their understanding.

What, after all, is a controversial issue? It is a matter about which informed people disagree—not just any people, but *informed* people. If such people disagree, there must be some basis for disagreement. Either the facts are open to more than a single interpretation, or there are two or more competing values, each making a persuasive demand for endorsement.

Therefore, *it is probable that neither side in a controversy possesses the total truth, that each side has a part of it.* Is each side 50 percent right, or is the ratio 51:49, 60:40, or perhaps 99:1? What does the latest evidence suggest? Have I perhaps been mistaken in my views? In these questions lie the challenge and the opportunity.

Mistakes, after all, are common, even about issues regarded as settled once and for all. For example, until recently, most scientists agreed that the age of the universe is 20 million years. The available data supported that view, and the matter was considered closed. Then a team of astronomers produced new data that suggested that the universe is really closer to 10 billion years old.[12] The controversy was alive again—and with it the adventure.

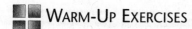

▪ WARM-UP EXERCISES

6.1 Most high school athletic teams have rather predictable, uncreative, and sometimes offensive names: Bulldogs, Indians, Warriors, and so on. Think of as many creative names as you can for high school teams, names you have never heard used before. Be sure to guard against setting unconscious restrictions on your thinking and to resist the temptation to settle for too few ideas.

6.2 List as many ideas as you can for new products or services—that is, products or services that do not now exist but for which there is a need.

6.3 Divide the circle below into as many parts as you can, using four straight lines.

APPLICATIONS

6.1   Spend some time in the dining hall, snack bar, or some other place where people congregate, and listen carefully to their conversations. (Do the same with conversations you are participating in and with conversations you hear on the radio or see on television.) Note all the things people complain about, including procedures, policies, other people's actions, tools, and machines (cars, washing machines, and so on); note, too, the nature of their complaints. Keep a record of your findings.

6.2   Visit a general department store (Wal-Mart, for example) and browse in every department, looking for items whose design could be improved. Make a list of those items. Add to that list any items, from a shoehorn to a toaster, whose imperfections you have had personal experience with.

6.3   Think of as many experiences as you can that caused you to be dissatisfied or frustrated, experiences that posed a challenge to your ingenuity but that you were too irritated to see. Describe the experiences and state the challenges you now see.

Note: To make seeking out challenges a habit you use every day, continue to do Applications 6.1, 6.2, and 6.3 each day for the rest of the term, in addition to your other assignments. Set aside a special notebook for this use, and make your daily entries in journal fashion. (Consult your instructor for special format directions.)

6.4   In each of the following situations, the causes of the behavior are not self-evident. Speculate about those causes, first listing as many possible explanations as you can think of and then deciding which explanation seems most reasonable in each case. Explain your choices.

    a. Many athletes who use anabolic steroids reportedly do so with full realization that such use may result in serious physical injury and even death.

    b. Many people who have decided their parents' Jewish, Protestant, or Catholic faith is irrelevant to this age of science and technology have become devotees of belief systems that science long ago rejected as sheer superstition, systems such as astrology, tarot cards, and channeling (giving over one's body to beings from other spheres to receive enlightenment).

    c. Three high school students doing research on shoplifting entered a large drugstore in an upper-middle-class neighborhood and, with the knowledge of the owner, walked up and down aisles, stuffing their pockets with large and small items: candy, magazines, watchbands, perfume, a hair dryer, and more. More than

100 shoppers were in the store, and at least 50 of them saw what was happening. Yet every one of the shoppers either walked away or turned his or her head.[13] How do you explain their reaction?

6.5 Each of the following cases is (or could be viewed as) a controversy as defined in the chapter. Examine each carefully, decide whether you agree or disagree with the decision reached or action taken, and explain your view. In addition, identify any implications suggested by each case and any connections with other issues.

a. Robert L. Race of Toddsville, New York, believed the state has no authority to require that everyone have a driver's license, so he turned in his license and publicly announced his intention to drive without it. In his view, driving is not a privilege but a right.[14] Many would disagree with his view.

b. Anthony Broussard raped and murdered his girlfriend, then threw her body into a ravine. Later, before the crime was discovered by authorities, he bragged about it to friends and took some of them to the ravine to see the body. One friend, 16-year-old Kirk Rasmussen, kicked leaves over the body. After the crime was discovered and Broussard was arrested, Rasmussen was charged with being an accessory after the fact. He was found guilty and sentenced to three years in a reformatory.[15] Many would argue that Rasmussen's sentence was excessive. Some would say he shouldn't even have been charged.

ISSUE FOR EXTENDED ANALYSIS

Following is a more comprehensive thinking challenge than the others in the chapter. Analyze and respond to it, following the instructions for extended analysis at the end of Chapter 1. Also, review "The Basis of Moral Judgment" and "Dealing with Dilemmas" in Chapter 2.

THE ISSUE: VIOLENCE IN SCHOOLS

In a highly publicized case at Columbine High School in Littleton, Colorado, two high school students killed twelve classmates and a teacher and then killed themselves. Similar scenarios occurred in schools in Conyers, Georgia; Springfield, Oregon; Fayetteville, Tennessee; Jonesboro, Arizona; West Paducah, Kentucky; and Pearl, Mississippi. Innumerable other, less dramatic incidents of assaults and threats of assault on students, teachers, and other school personnel are occurring in small and large schools around the country. Concerned individuals and groups are trying to understand these tragic events and find ways to prevent future ones.

THE ESSAYS

Eliminating School Violence
By Christopher Giordano

The current concern over school violence is not only appropriate but overdue. Over the last 20 or so years, acts of violence among young people have increased both in number and in viciousness. Something must be done to make the nation's schools safe again, and the responsibility to take action rests with parents and teachers.

Dr. Helen Smith, author of *The Scarred Heart* and other studies of violence in children, claims it is a mistake to blame youthful violence on violent movies, rap music, and Satanism. She notes that the "most common thread among school killers" is inexpressible rage over feelings of rejection or stress. The best hope to solve the problem of school violence, in her view, is for schools to hire more counselors, get tough with "bullying and ostracism," and take kids' concerns more seriously.

Another excellent source of ideas for combating school violence is "Best Practices of Youth Violence Prevention." The practices recommended include providing students with films and workshops on problem solving, role-playing, anger management, stress-coping strategies, and other nonviolent alternatives to violence. A parallel practice, outside the school, is to have community organizations develop programs to help parents improve their child-raising skills.

Among the most important objectives of such programs should be building students' self-esteem; promoting

The Real Villain Is Pop Culture
By Hamzah Muhammed

Most social critics blame school violence on the home and the school. Accordingly, the solutions they propose center around parents guiding their children to settle differences with words instead of fists and teachers adding classroom lessons on self-esteem and diversity.

Though well-intentioned, such approaches fail to address the real problem: popular culture's glorification of aggressive, violent behavior.

The central role of popular culture in youth violence can be confirmed by simply turning on the TV set, listening to popular CDs, or checking out video games. We'll limit our focus to TV because children and teens spend considerably more time watching TV than in any other activity, in or out of school. Not only are TV programs filled with violence, but the presentations are so vivid and dramatic that they make a deep and lasting impression. Worse, after viewers see a thousand of them, they are likely to be attracted rather than repulsed.

Why are the critics and pundits blind to these facts? Because they believe TV industry moguls' claims that what we see in movies and on TV has no effect on us. A mountain of research contradicts that claim.

One good source is Liebert and Sprafkin's *The Early Window*, which summarizes hundreds of studies, including the U. S. Surgeon General's report, almost all of which conclude that TV violence increases aggressive/violent behavior, particularly among impressionable people. Also, deeper understanding of racial, cultural, and ethnic diversity; and developing in students the habit of negotiating differences.

If all these strategies were pursued at the local and state levels across the country, the problem of school violence would be greatly diminished in a few years and virtually eliminated within a decade.

that people who are emotionally disturbed tend to seek out violent programs and thus tend to be even *more* affected by them.

Better parenting and improved teaching are worthy goals. But until we do something about violence in popular culture, there is virtually no chance of solving the problem of violence in the schools.

CLASS DISCUSSION

FLORENCE: Home and school have an important role, but it's not to make students feel better about themselves. Instead, it's to enforce both the general rules of courtesy and etiquette and the specific standards of conduct set by institutions to promote civility and social harmony. Violations of those rules and standards should be punished.

SUSAN: I side with the entertainment industry leaders. No one was ever assaulted or molested by a book or a movie.

FLORENCE: That argument is disingenuous. Books and films are inanimate objects, so they obviously cannot *perform* any action, good or bad. But they can urge, motivate, inspire, provoke, or otherwise *influence* people to take action, good or bad. They can also provide a blueprint and/or model for doing so.

SUSAN: Are you saying that people are not personally responsible for their actions?

FLORENCE: Not at all. People have the primary responsibility for what they say and do. But whoever or whatever influences them to speak and act has secondary responsibility. I'm speaking of moral responsibility, of course, but there is also a legal parallel—it's called "complicity before the fact."

SUSAN: I think you're letting parents off the hook. If they taught their kids the virtues of nonviolence and turned off the violent TV shows, school violence would disappear.

FLORENCE: You're underestimating the power of peer pressure. Though conscientious parents may be able to block exposure to violent material in the home, they can't prevent their kids from contact with children who have been exposed to it in their homes, act out what they have seen, and thus model aggressive behavior to those around them.

SUSAN: It sounds to me as if you are in favor of censorship of the entertainment media. I think that's a violation of the right to freedom of expression.

FLORENCE: If censorship were the only course of action, I would probably support it. But I think there is a more acceptable alternative. It's for informed people to speak out about the dangers of violent entertainment and to persuade others to pressure the entertainment industry to behave more responsibly.

7

Express the Problem or Issue

Imagine that a certain kind of question would help you produce many and varied kinds of solutions to problems. Imagine, too, that other questions would enable you to cut through confusion and get to the heart of controversial issues and that knowing those questions would make you a more confident and successful thinker.

The good news is that such questions do exist. This chapter identifies them and shows you how to use them.

This stage in the creative process is the one most often neglected. The reason is not that people decide to be stubborn and to proceed without having identified the best expression of the problem or issue. Rather, it is that they are convinced that the problem is self-evident and that it would be a waste of their valuable time to consider alternative ways of formulating it.

Such thinking is wrong. Like our first impressions of people, our initial perspectives on problems and issues are likely to be limited or superficial. We see no more than what we have been conditioned to see, and stereotyped notions block clear vision and crowd out imagination. Most important, all this happens without any alarms sounding, so we never realize it is occurring.

You can avoid this narrowness of perspective by developing the habit of expressing every problem or issue in as many different ways as you can. Before discussing the most effective forms of expression, we will note how to distinguish between problems and issues.

DISTINGUISHING PROBLEMS FROM ISSUES

As noted earlier, problems and issues differ in some respects. A problem is a situation that we regard as unacceptable; an issue is a matter about which intelligent, informed people disagree to some extent. Solving problems therefore means *deciding what action will change the situation for the best,* whereas resolving issues means *deciding what belief or viewpoint is the most reasonable.*

Whenever you are uncertain whether to treat a particular challenge as a problem or an issue, apply this test: Ask whether the matter involved tends to arouse partisan feelings and to divide informed, intelligent people. If it does not, treat it as a problem. If it does, treat it as an issue. Here are some sample problems: a student trying to study in a noisy dormitory, a child frightened by the prospect of being admitted to the hospital, a businesswoman dealing with subtle sexual harassment from her boss. And here are some sample issues: a public school teacher leading students in prayer in a public school classroom, a member of Congress proposing a cut in Social Security benefits for the elderly, an anthropologist stating that human beings are by nature violent.

Each of the situations in the first group is properly considered a problem because there is nothing about the situation itself that is likely to divide informed, intelligent people. Of course, someone, somewhere, might conceivably take an unusual view of a situation—for example, challenging the right of a student to a quiet dorm atmosphere—but that is likely to be a remote possibility. However, each of the situations in the second group is likely to provoke considerable disagreement because each involves *a matter that is itself controversial.*

EXPRESSING PROBLEMS

Both problems and issues are best expressed as questions, but the form of the question is different for each. The form most effective in expressing problems is the "How can . . . ?" form. Let's consider an actual case and see how this form applies. Some years ago, almost 7000 public schools around the country closed their doors because of declining enrollments, budget cuts, and inflation.[1] Here are the various ways school officials might have expressed this problem.

- How can school enrollments be increased?
- How can school budgets be reduced?
- How can the impact of inflation on education be lessened?
- How can school buildings best be used after the schools are closed?
- How can the unused space in school buildings be used to generate income so the school will not have to be closed?
- How can school buildings be used in evenings and on weekends to generate income?
- How can the empty buildings be used after the schools are closed?
- How can the unemployed teachers be used after the schools are closed?

Let's consider another problem, the drug problem, arguably the greatest social challenge of our time. Here are just a few of the many ways this problem can be expressed.

- How can people be taught to shun drugs?
- How can people be discouraged from dealing in drugs?
- How can celebrities be persuaded to use their influence to combat drug use?
- How can the media assist in the antidrug effort?
- How can individual citizens support the federal government's antidrug program?
- How can law enforcement agencies be made immune to corruption by drug lords?
- How can the support of drug-producing countries be enlisted?
- How can crops of drug-producing plants be spotted and destroyed before harvest?

There is room for disagreement about which expression of a problem is best. But there can be no disagreement that we are in a better position to make that decision, and to produce a creative solution, if we take the time to identify and consider all of the questions, because *each question opens a different avenue of thought*. The kinds of solutions for teaching people to shun drugs are very different from those for destroying drug crops.

EXPRESSING ISSUES

The question forms most effective in expressing issues are the "Is . . . ?" "Does . . . ?" or "Should . . . ?" forms. Using such questions, in the sense we are considering here, does not mean asking for simple facts. Rather, it means probing the central elements of dispute. To determine these elements, just note the main points each side uses in its arguments, and turn them into questions.

For example, in the abortion issue, the pro-life side argues that the fetus is a human being and therefore should be entitled to the protection of the law. The pro-choice side argues that a woman's body is hers alone and therefore she alone should have the right to decide the fate of her fetus. Thus, your expression of the issue would be

Is the fetus a human being?

Does the fetus deserve the protection of the law?

Is a woman's body hers alone?

Should a woman have the right to decide the fate of her fetus?

In the issue of capital punishment, the pro side argues that when a person has been convicted of a capital crime, the government has the right to decide whether he or she should live or die. The anti side argues that capital punishment constitutes cruel and unusual treatment and is therefore a violation of a person's constitutional rights. Thus, your expression of this issue would be

> Does the government have the right to decide whether someone convicted of a capital crime will live or die?
>
> Is capital punishment cruel and unusual treatment?
>
> Does capital punishment violate a person's constitutional rights?

The main points in an argument will be either directly expressed or at least clearly implied. They may, of course, be more numerous than those in the preceding examples.

The fact that "How can . . . ?" questions are the best kind for expressing problems and "Is . . . ?" "Does . . . ?" or "Should . . . ?" questions are best for expressing issues does not mean that other kinds of questions are without value. It means only that they have a different purpose than to focus a challenge. Questions that demand information—such as "Who?" "What?" "When?" and "Where?"—are useful in the investigating stage.* And questions that analyze—such as "Why?" and "How?"—are useful in the evaluation and refinement of ideas.

■───────────────────

WHEN PROBLEMS BECOME ISSUES

It is possible to create a controversial issue where none existed. The way we express the problem (or, at a later stage, the specific solution we choose) may provoke serious objection. Consider, for example, the last expression of the drug problem: "How can crops of drug-producing plants be spotted and destroyed before harvest?" Even people strongly committed to the war on drugs might respond as follows: "Most of the plants used for drugs could be used for other purposes. It is morally wrong to destroy such plants, especially if they are found in foreign countries on the lands of poor farmers."

Concerned about the high number of dropouts in West Virginia high schools (a problem in other states as well), officials devised an ingenious way to keep students in school: taking away the driver's licenses of students aged 16 to 18 who miss classes. The school notified the Department of Motor Vehicles, which sent a letter telling the offender to return to school or surrender his or her license.[2] This solution, however, was controversial. Some people argued that it violated the rights of students or that it transferred jurisdiction over minors from the parents to an agency of the government.

Good thinkers are sensitive to the implications of both their questions and their assertions. Whenever your questions or assertions create an issue, address it immediately. In the case of destroying drug plants, that would mean asking, "Are there any situations in which it would be morally wrong to destroy such plants?" and resolving the matter. (If you decided the most reasonable answer was affirmative, of course, you would either revise or delete the question "How can

───────────────────

*When the subject is noncontroversial, "Is . . . ?" and "Does . . . ?" are also in this category.

crops . . . be spotted and destroyed?") And in the case of the West Virginia school action, it would mean asking, "Does this action violate the rights of students? Does it transfer jurisdiction from parents? Is doing so defensible?"

GUIDELINES FOR EXPRESSING PROBLEMS AND ISSUES

1. *Identify the challenge.* The moment you are aware that something you have experienced or read about is bothering you or that you are dissatisfied with some person, object, or situation (stage 1), examine the situation and raise your negative feeling to the conscious level. Ask yourself, "What exactly am I feeling? Sadness? Anger? Frustration? What is the source of this feeling?" Then decide whether what bothers you is best treated as a problem or as an issue.

2. *Express the problem or issue.* Using the appropriate form of questions—"How can . . . ?" for a problem, "Is . . . ?" "Does . . . ?" or "Should . . . ?" for an issue—express the problem or issue on paper rather than merely in your mind. There are two important reasons for writing your expressions. First, joining mental and physical effort and externalizing ideas often help clarify them. Second, as any composition teacher will verify, *the very act of writing an idea has a way of triggering other ideas.* Press yourself to produce as many expressions of the problem or issue as you can.

3. *Refine your expression.* After you have expressed the problem or issue in as many ways as you can, refine the expressions. That is, replace vagueness with exactness and general words with specific ones. An expression is too vague or general whenever you can't be sure what kind of solution it points to. For example, "How can the school enrollment problem be solved?" and "How can the drug problem be eliminated?" point nowhere in particular and therefore should be revised.

BENEFITS OF CAREFUL EXPRESSION

It Helps You Move Beyond the Familiar and Habitual

The first perspective that occurs to you will usually be slanted heavily toward familiar, habitual ways of seeing and interpreting experiences. Thus, it is more likely than later perspectives to reflect bad thinking habits: mine-is-better, face saving, resistance to change, conformity, stereotyping, and self-deception. Creativity is not likely to arise out of these habits.

It Keeps Your Thinking Flexible

Once you adopt a perspective, even tentatively, it becomes difficult to entertain a different one. This is especially true with issues. Once you have reached a postion on an issue, even casually, without any real analysis, you will be tempted to become inflexible about it. Thus, you will have difficulty considering it further, even in light of dramatic new evidence.

To appreciate the speed with which you can "lock into" a perspective and the difficulty of entertaining another perspective once you do so, look closely at each of these pictures for at least a minute. Then continue reading.

In the left-hand figure, you should be able to see both an old woman and a young girl; in the right-hand figure, both a vase and two faces. In each case, many people see one image quite readily but have difficulty seeing the other until it is pointed out to them. (If you still haven't seen both, turn to pages 271–272 for assistance.) Once you have seen both, however, you are able to move back and forth between them freely and quickly. It is much the same with perspectives on issues. If you force yourself to entertain a variety of perspectives, you are better able to maintain flexibility.

It Opens Many Lines of Thought

Once you have settled on a perspective, you close off all but one line of thought. Certain kinds of ideas will occur to you, but only those kinds and no others. Thus, if the handicapped man who invented the motorized cart had defined his problem as "How to occupy my time while lying in bed" rather than "How to get out of bed and move around the house," he would never have conceived his invention.

Have you ever looked closely at the wheels on a railroad train? They are flanged. That is, they have a lip on the inside to prevent them from sliding off the track. Originally, train wheels were not flanged; instead, the railroad *tracks* were. Because the problem of railroad safety had been expressed as "How can the tracks be made safer for trains to ride on?" hundreds of thousands of miles of railroad track were manufactured with an unnecessary steel lip. Only when someone thought to redefine the problem as "How can the wheels be made to grip the track more securely?" was the flanged wheel invented.[3]

The tendency to limit the lines of thought that are considered is one of the reasons that breakthrough ideas take years, even centuries, to develop. The development of modern periodontal surgery is a case in point. Before the idea of recording human history was invented, some toothless, elderly person may have wondered, "How can I prepare food to make it edible without teeth?" Having asked the question, he or she may have hit upon the idea of pounding food with a rock to grind it into powder or paste. Later, history tells us, the ancient Etruscans asked, "How will we chew our food after our teeth have fallen out?" and proceeded to invent false teeth. But thousands of years passed before some dentist thought to ask, "How can we restore the gums to good health and make loose teeth more secure in the underlying bone?" and thereafter invented periodontal surgery. Undoubtedly, some creative person is at this very moment asking, "How can people's gums be permanently protected from disease?"

Keeping more than one line of thought open is especially urgent when dealing with issues. The human drive to make sense of things (a healthy drive, we should acknowledge) will often lead you to take sides too quickly in disputes. And once you have taken a side, ever afterward you are burdened with a powerful temptation to ignore all arguments and all evidence for the other side—indeed, to ignore the very questions that intellectual honesty requires you to ask.

For example, a strict creationist, who believes that the earth is only a few thousand years old, will tend to avoid pondering the question "Is it likely that scientific techniques for dating rocks and other materials are as inaccurate as my belief would suggest?" Similarly, a strict evolutionist, who attributes all that exists to strictly material causes, will tend to avoid pondering the question "Is it possible that a Supreme Being created the evolutionary process by which all things come into existence?" Surely both would be better thinkers for asking the questions they tend to ignore.

Keeping many lines of thought open when you address problems and issues can enable you to produce ideas that are ahead of your time and to avoid narrow-mindedness.

A SAMPLE PROBLEM

A situation that occurred some time ago in a college town illustrates the approach discussed here. Jean, a middle-aged woman, returned to college after many years to complete her degree. She was living off campus, in an apartment house. Directly below her apartment lived a young woman who played her stereo loud enough to reach Vladivostok with a favorable wind. At least it seemed that way to Jean. The sound and the woman's rudeness infuriated her. She pondered the problem and came up with these expressions of it.

How can I persuade her to turn it down?

How can I compel her to turn it down?

How can I frighten her into moving?

How can I escape the noise?

How can I bother her as much as she bothers me?

Deciding that the first expression of the problem was the best, Jean investigated how she might approach the woman. She tried to recall similarly difficult situations in the past that she had experienced or heard others tell about. Then she brainstormed the possible approaches she might take. After producing a generous number of ideas, she chose the best one, went to the woman, and tried it. It failed; the music continued to blare.

Disappointed, Jean looked at her list of expressions again and decided, probably because of her anger, that *compelling* might succeed where persuasion hadn't. She investigated again, produced ideas again, then selected and carried out not one, but two of them: reporting the matter to the apartment house's owner and registering a complaint with the police. The result was disheartening. The owner made a feeble appeal to the woman and the police gave her a halfhearted warning. After a day or two of quiet, the music blared again.

Now Jean decided her last expression of the problem was the best of the remaining ones. She gleefully listed dozens of hateful ideas for *bothering* the woman (including boring a hole in the floor and pouring water on the stereo). Then the insight came to her. An athletic woman, Jean loved to play tennis and jog. Why not use exercise as a weapon? So she did. She bought herself a jump rope and every morning, promptly at 4:00 A.M., she jumped rope in her bedroom—right over the sleeping woman's head. Wham, whump, thump. How sweet was revenge.

What happened next proved Jean's idea to be even more creative than she had realized. In a few days, the woman knocked on Jean's door and explained sheepishly that Jean's jumping was keeping her awake. Jean seized the opportunity and said, "I'll tell you what: I'll stop jumping rope if you'll turn the stereo down." The woman agreed, and the problem was solved.

A SAMPLE ISSUE

The following situation illustrates how the expression of an issue would differ from that of a problem.** You read a newspaper story explaining that a national chain of convenience stores has decided no longer to sell magazines with a sexual emphasis. The chain's decision, the story says, reflects increasing public objection to all forms of pornography. You decide to address the challenge implicit in this subject.

Your first step is to decide whether the subject should be considered a problem or an issue. Because pornography divides informed, intelligent people—some regarding it as harmless and others as harmful—you decide it is an issue. Next, you consider the essential elements of dispute found in the pro and con arguments concerning pornography. Those who believe pornography is harmless

---

**Because an adequate treatment of the issue illustrated here would demand greater space than is available, the discussion, unlike that of the sample problem, is limited to the expression of the issue.

often argue that (1) countries that take a liberal approach to the dissemination of pornography have no higher incidence of sex crimes than the United States, (2) looking at pornography provides a healthy release for sexual tension, and (3) the right of free speech applies to pornographers. On the other hand, those who believe pornography is harmful often argue that (4) it promotes a distorted view of sexuality and a negative view of women, and (5) it encourages irresponsible, immoral sexual behavior, including sadomasochism and sex between children and adults.

This consideration of the elements of dispute would lead you to the following expressions of the issue (the numbers correspond):

1. Is the incidence of sex crimes lower in countries that take a liberal approach to pornography?

2. Does looking at pornography provide a healthy release for sexual tension? In everyone? In certain people? Does the answer depend on the kind of pornography viewed?

3. Is the right of free speech applicable to pornographers?

4. Does pornography promote a distorted view of sexuality? A negative view of women? Does it do so for some people but not others? Is age a factor here?

5. Does all pornography encourage irresponsible, immoral sexual behavior, including sadomasochism and sex between children and adults? Does some pornography encourage these?

Careful exploration of these questions would prepare you to address the more general expression of the issue: Should the sale and distribution of pornography be in any way restricted?

■■ WARM-UP EXERCISES

7.1 A hunter sees a squirrel on the trunk of a tall tree. The hunter approaches quietly, but the squirrel hears him and scampers to the other side of the tree. The hunter follows the squirrel around the tree, but the squirrel is very clever: it keeps moving at just the right pace to be on the side of the tree opposite the hunter. Around and around they move that way, on into the night. The question is: Does the hunter ever go around the squirrel? Explain your answer.

7.2 Is it possible for you to think of a city or a country that you have never been to? Explain your answer thoroughly.

7.3 Read the following dialogue carefully. Then state what you think Kenneth should say next to ensure that Karl will have no reasonable comeback.

KENNETH: Every circle has an inside and an outside.

KARL: I'll bet you can't prove that statement.

KENNETH: Sure, I can . . .

KARL: Remember, you said *every* circle. That's what you have got to prove.

APPLICATIONS

7.1   Select three entries from the lists you developed in response to Applications 6.1 and 6.3. Decide whether each of those entries represents a problem or an issue, and express it, following the guidelines in this chapter.

Note: Do each of the following applications in this manner: First, express the problem or issue, using the guidelines explained in this chapter. Then investigate, as necessary, and produce as many ideas as you can to solve or resolve it. (Record all your thoughts as they occur to you, and be prepared to submit them to your instructor.) Finally, state which of your ideas you believe is best, and briefly explain why.

7.2   A Los Angeles woman and her husband were convicted of prostitution charges in an unusual case. The couple admitted accepting money from men for sexual favors, but they claimed that the sex acts were part of a religious ritual rather than prostitution. The husband testified he had a revelation from God to revive a 5000-year-old Egyptian religion. In his church, he explained, men's sins are absolved by having sex with the priestess, his wife.[4]

7.3   James Cook, president of the Thomas Alva Edison Foundation, noted that the number of patent applications in the United States had declined steadily and that a large number of the applications filed came from foreigners. He believed that the main reason for the apparent lack of interest in invention here was the poor image technology enjoyed, particularly among young people. He cited a UN study of the understanding level and appreciation of technology among the people of 19 industrialized countries. Japan scored first, the United States last.[5]

7.4   Rocco is the manager of a movie theater. In recent years a number of competitors have cut into his business, and cable television and video rental stores have reduced the number of moviegoers still further. Rocco desperately needs to get more people to patronize his theater, particularly since he has begun to hear the owners talk of closing it and dismissing him if box office receipts don't improve.

7.5   Many authorities agree that one of the important reasons for the high divorce rate in this country is the naively romantic view of love many people have when they enter marriage.

7.6   Gail has always slept well, but lately, she has been waking up at about 3 A.M. and having trouble getting back to sleep.

ISSUE FOR EXTENDED ANALYSIS

Following is a more comprehensive thinking challenge than the others in the chapter. Analyze and respond to it, following the instructions for extended analysis at the end of Chapter 1. Also, review "The Basis of Moral Judgment" and "Dealing with Dilemmas" in Chapter 2.

THE ISSUE: JUDICIAL ACTIVISM

"Judicial activism" refers to the philosophy under which judges do not just interpret the law—in particular, the Constitution—but also, in effect, *revise* it. Supporters of such activism claim that the law—in particular, the Constitution—is a living entity that must be revised to fit new circumstances and insights. Opponents argue that the legislature alone should legislate and the courts should only decide whether a law is constitutional. The debate over this issue became especially heated during the George W. Bush administration, when some senators used the filibuster to prevent some of his federal court nominees from being voted on.

THE ESSAYS

Judicial Activism is an Abomination
By Hannah Andersen

America has been blessed with bountiful natural resources, but the greatest resource of all is the U.S. Constitution. For over 200 years that document has provided us a finely balanced political system and a legal foundation that is the envy of the world. Today, however, the Constitution—and our liberty—are threatened by judicial activism. Thurgood Marshall, the late Supreme Court justice, expressed that philosophy simply: "You do what you think is right and let the law catch up."

A Blend of Old and New
By Benjamin Ward

The passing of time changes human understanding, and over the last 200 years, the changes have been astounding. When the U.S. Constitution was written, the biological and physical sciences were primitive, and the academic disciplines of psychology, sociology, and anthropology did not even exist. The insights since gained in those areas, as well as in philosophy and history, give us a much greater and deeper understanding of ourselves and our institutions.

As Mark Levin has documented in *Men in Black*, judicial activism has led jurists to base their decisions on their personal opinion or international law rather than on the Constitution. In so doing, they have usurped the legislative function. For example, they have created "rights" that are nowhere to be found in the Constitution: notably, the "right" to abortion, to privacy in the bedroom, to affirmative action, to welfare assistance for illegal aliens, to flag burning, and to legal status (in U.S. courts) for enemy combatants.

But unlike members of Congress, federal jurists cannot be voted out of office—they serve for life. And that is exactly the problem. It is outrageous to have a small number of individuals decide for several million Americans what is fair and unfair, just and unjust, legal and illegal on the basis of *their personal desires and preferences*. The courts should be using a clear, objective standard that, Supreme Court Justice Antonin Scalia suggests, reflects the *original meaning* of the Constitution as it was written and as it was understood at that time. Any other approach is a violation of the founders' and our trust.

Judicial activism is not a Democrat-versus-Republican issue. It's between individuals in both parties who believe our country should be guided by the Constitution and individuals who prefer to be guided by the intellectual fashion of the day. President Franklin D. Roosevelt (a Democrat) was one of the former; as he argued, the job of the judiciary is to "do justice under the Constitution and not over it."

Any suggestion that a 200-year-old treatise in physiology, astronomy, or physics should remain the standard for contemporary judgments would be greeted with derision. I submit that the view that America's legal system should remain chained to the past is equally laughable and even more dangerous.

Today's jurists know everything that the authors of the Constitution knew about democracy and law. In addition they have 200 years' worth of knowledge that has accumulated since the founders' time. This reality is neither a credit to modern jurists nor a discredit to the founders, and it certainly does not imply any criticism of the Constitution. It is merely an acknowledgment that past ideas, however noble in their time, are inadequate to present situations.

Because society and the law evolve, today's jurists serve us best when they are guided but not constricted by the Constitution—in other words, when they blend the ideas in the Constitution with contemporary insights. Harvard law professor Lawrence Tribe argues that such *constructing* of legal interpretations is more honest than the more passive approach of *discovering* them, as long as the interpreter presents "a forthright account, incomplete and inconclusive though it might be, of why one deems his or her proposed construction of the text to be worthy of acceptance. . . ."

CLASS DISCUSSION

HARRY: Mr. Ward's essay is right on the mark. His argument reveals the weakness of Hannah Andersen's old-fashioned view of the law.

EDWARD: Your own words betray the error of Ward's view. Law is not a matter of fashion, whether old or new. When it is made so, it becomes vulnerable to whatever nutty ideas happen to be popular.

HARRY: There's nothing "nutty" about keeping the Constitution up to date and having it reflect the latest insights of psychology, biology, and the other academic disciplines.

EDWARD: The problem with that perspective is that it's seldom possible to tell whether the latest idea is an insight or a fallacy until it has been tested. Besides, many of the supposed insights ignore the findings of the disciplines. The issue of abortion is a perfect example of this tendency. Geneticists have documented that human life begins at conception, yet in *Roe* v. *Wade* the Supreme Court embraced the pretense that it begins whenever a pregnant woman wishes it to begin.

EDWARD: You have to admit that it's anti-intellectual to cling to the views embodied in the Constitution, views that are now over 200 years old.

HARRY: The test of any idea is not how *old* but how *wise* it is. The U.S. Constitution is the most profound and practical set of ideas ever proposed for governing a nation. To swap it for the latest intellectual fad is not only absurd but dangerous.

CHAPTER

8

Investigate the Problem or Issue

It would be convenient if every problem or issue came in a kit containing all the information necessary to solve it. Unfortunately, that is seldom the case—we've got to search out the facts for ourselves.

In this chapter, you'll learn numerous sources of information and how to use them efficiently and imaginatively. You'll also learn how to conduct your own research whenever possible.

It may seem strange to learn that investigation is a creative stage. You may think of it as a dull, plodding effort involving very little thinking of any kind, let alone creative thinking. In part, that is right. The way many people actually carry out their investigation involves little or no thinking—which is why their investigation is so often unproductive.

Investigation, as we define it, means more than routinely getting the same information as everyone else. It means getting information others overlook by searching in ways and places that never occur to the uncreative. It means using our resourcefulness and originality, being imaginative in our search.

Not every problem you encounter requires significant investigation. If, for instance, you decide to go beyond grumbling and kicking your gym locker when the string in your sweatpants slips out, you can apply the creative process without using the investigative stage at all. You can identify the problem in a number of ways—"How can I insert the string again easily?" "How can I avoid having it slip out again in the future?" "How can I eliminate the need for a string?"—and then go directly to the third stage of the creative process: producing as many solutions to the problem as you can.

In many other cases, however, the investigative stage is a crucial step in the process. The scientists who developed the creative surgical procedure in response to periodontal disease first had to investigate the nature of the disease—that is, its cause, its progress from initial infection to tooth loss, and the various technological methods, medical tools, and approaches available to be used. In the case of unwanted graffiti, the invention of Graffiti Gobbler depended on (1) a knowledge of what techniques had been unsuccessfully tried and (2) a basic understanding of chemistry. "Inspiration," wrote Louis Pasteur, "is the impact of a fact on a well-prepared mind." The investigation stage provides the mental preparation.

Investigation is especially important in complex or controversial issues. In such matters, unless you know all the relevant facts, including the various viewpoints involved and the different lines of reasoning people follow, you are not likely to make sound judgments and develop workable solutions. A. E. Mander makes the point vividly:

> The fewer the facts [one] possesses, the simpler the problem seems to him. If we know only a dozen facts, it is not difficult to find a theory to fit them. But suppose there are five hundred thousand other facts known—but not known to us! Of what value then is our poor little theory which has been designed to fit, and which perhaps fits, only about a dozen of the five hundred thousand known facts![1]

Sometimes a single fact can make a significant difference, as in a study of multiple personality disorders that revealed that 97 percent of the victims had been abused as children.[2]

The point is not that you should feel daunted by difficult problems and issues and give up—that would certainly not help you to become a better thinker. It is that you should appreciate the importance of being thorough in your investigations and refusing to rush in, like the proverbial fool, where angels fear to tread.

WHAT TO LOOK FOR

Broadly speaking, the information necessary to solve problems or resolve issues consists of facts and informed opinions. Following are the most common sources of information.

Eyewitness Testimony

Such testimony is usually associated with the courtroom but in the more general sense it consists of any observation recounted by the person who made it. A report of what transpired at a committee meeting by someone who was present constitutes eyewitness testimony, as does the statement of someone who witnessed an automobile accident.

Eyewitness testimony is commonly thought to be highly reliable, but that is a misconception. Research has shown that perception can be clouded by a number of factors, including time of day, atmospheric conditions, emotional state, and degree of alertness. In addition, memories change over time, as Elizabeth Loftus explains:

> The "drawers" holding our memories are obviously extremely crowded and densely packed. They are also constantly being emptied out, scattered about, and then stuffed back into place. . . . As new bits of information are added into long-term memory, the old memories are removed, replaced, crumpled up, or shoved into corners. Little details are added, confusing or extraneous facts are deleted, and a coherent construction of the facts is gradually created that may bear little resemblance to the original event.[3]

Because eyewitness testimony may or may not be accurate, you should not accept it at face value. Instead, wherever possible, try to verify it.

Unpublished Report

This kind of information sometimes reflects real knowledge and sometimes merely hearsay. If you are familiar with the game "Rumor,"* you know that the more a story is told, the greater the likelihood of its being changed, often dramatically. Unpublished reports abound in e-mail. Even if you have only a few correspondents, you may receive a number of these reports every day. Sometimes they take the form of a warning to do or avoid doing something lest harm befall you or your computer. Often as not, they are false. Therefore, it is prudent to verify the accuracy of unpublished reports before accepting them or repeating them.

Published Report

This kind of information is found in books, magazines, professional journals, radio and television broadcasts, such reference works as encyclopedias, almanacs, and dictionaries, and (sometimes) on the Internet. When the information is documented in a footnote or endnote, as it sometimes is, you can check the original source for verification. If documentation is not provided, you should consider whether the author's and/or publisher's reputation for reliability is solid enough for you to trust the information. (Remember, too, that even trustworthy people can make mistakes.)

Expert Opinion

Expert opinion is generally much more trustworthy than most other sources of information because experts are better acquainted with the complexities of their subjects than laypeople and better able to distinguish typical incidents and events from nontypical ones. However, the knowledge explosion has made it more difficult to stay abreast of the developments even in a single area of a discipline, let alone an entire discipline. Thus, a person can be world renowned in one special area of his or her discipline yet uninformed about other areas. Before accepting

---

*This game is played with a group of people. It begins with one person whispering a statement to the person next to him or her. That person then whispers the statement to the next person, and so on around the room. When the last person whispers it to the person who originated it, that final version is compared with the original statement.

expert opinion, it is best to (1) be sure the person is qualified in the *specific* area in question and (2) check to see whether or not the expert's view is shared by other experts. And never confuse celebrity with expertise.

Experiment

An experiment is a controlled procedure undertaken to test the validity of a hypothesis, a statement that predicts or explains phenomena or behavior. The researcher begins the experiment by formulating one or more hypotheses. Next, the researcher decides what behavior characteristics can be measured, rated, or scored; these characteristics are known as *variables*. Finally, the researcher constructs and conducts the experiment and analyzes the resulting data.

There are two broad categories of experiment: the laboratory experiment and the field experiment. The laboratory experiment has the advantage of controlled conditions, which permit more accurate determinations of cause and effect. However, it has the disadvantage of the experimenter unintentionally influencing the outcome. The results of a laboratory experiment can be trusted if it has been replicated by other researchers; the conclusions of a field experiment can be trusted if they have been independently confirmed.

In one well-known psychological experiment, Haney, Banks, and Zimbardo tested the hypothesis that the roles people choose or are assigned strongly influence the way they behave. The researchers had college students volunteer (for pay) to take part in a six-day "prison" experiment in the basement of a university building. Some students were randomly assigned to be "prisoners" and others were assigned to be "guards." In a relatively short time, the "prisoners" developed one or more emotional symptoms, including depression, helplessness, apathy, anger, and panic. The "guards" quickly adopted the characteristics common to prison workers. Some were kind and fair, but others were cruel and abusive, even when the "prisoners" gave them no reason to be so. When the experiment ended, all the "prisoners" were relieved, but most of the "guards" were disappointed: they had found their position of power enjoyable and were reluctant to relinquish it.[4]

In another well-known experiment, Solomon Asch tested the hypothesis that people will contradict their own perceptions and judgments if they are under group pressure to conform. Asch's experiment was quite simple. One by one, eight students were shown a sheet of paper containing a 10-inch line and three other lines marked A, B, and C. They were then asked which of the three other lines matched the 10-inch line. The correct answer was A, the other lines being obviously shorter or longer. Unknown to the eighth student, all the students who answered before had been secretly directed to choose line B. By the time the eighth student answered, the pressure to conform was strong. Predictably, a majority of students yielded to the pressure and gave the wrong answer.[5] In this experiment, as in the previous one, the researcher's hypothesis was validated.

Statistics

The term *statistics* refers, in the broadest sense, to quantified information. Used more narrowly, it means information obtained by accounting for every individual in a group. Examples of statistical information are the voting records of members of Congress, the patterns of immigration over the last 50 years, and the comparative incomes of various racial and ethnic groups. When carefully collected and honestly presented, statistical information is very reliable. In considering any statistical information, determine the completeness and currency of the data as well as the reputation of the statistician.

Survey

Like statistics, a survey produces quantified information. However, a survey is done with a *representative sample* of a group rather than with the entire group. A survey identifies the opinions, beliefs, or behaviors of a particular group of people, the technical name for which is a *population*. If the population is small enough, all members may be surveyed. However, if the population is too large, a more limited number, or *sample,* is surveyed. The sample must be representative of the total population, and to ensure that this is the case, researchers are required to take a systematic approach, selecting, for example, every tenth or twentieth or one-hundredth name on a list of members of the population. The actual survey may be mailed (or otherwise delivered) and self-administered, or it may be conducted in person or by telephone. Survey questions are typically fill-in or multiple-choice and designed to identify the subject's feelings, thoughts, or behaviors concerning the issue being investigated. For the survey to be valid, all questions must be clear, unambiguous, and free of bias.

Observational Study

As the name implies, this approach consists of closely examining an event or activity as it is taking place, for the purpose of understanding it and, in some cases, finding ways to improve it. The researcher may be either a participant or a bystander. In the latter role, his or her physical presence is not necessarily required; a videotape of the activity might suffice. For example, an executive charged with improving a company's customer service department might spend a week or so performing that job or, instead, arrange to videotape customer service staff interacting with customers. (The staff would, of course, be informed that they were being taped.) From this study, the executive would learn the kinds of situations customer service representatives are required to deal with, the variation in the time necessary to complete transactions, the difficulties and frustrations that accompany the job, and the relative effectiveness of the strategies employed to achieve customer satisfaction.

The conclusions reached by formal observation are generally reliable if (a) they were of sufficient duration to ensure that the group's behavior was not unusual, (b) the observer did not influence the group's behavior by his or her presence, and (c) the conclusions are not overgeneralized beyond the group observed to other groups that might be different.

Research Review

As the term implies, a research review draws together and compares the results of a number, often dozens or hundreds, of individual studies. Because it can reveal broad areas of agreement and disagreement among researchers, it is among the most valuable and reliable kinds of information, provided that it does not omit any relevant research.

Your Personal Experience

This is often the most vivid information because you know it intimately and have greater confidence in it. Unfortunately, that confidence could lead you to assume that an experience is typical when it might not be and to end your investigation prematurely. The best approach is to combine your personal experience with the other information rather than use it as a substitute.

Your personal experience may be more substantial and more relevant than you realize. This is especially so if, like many people, you regard every subject, and every aspect within a subject, as neatly and permanently separated from every other one. In that case, you might never dream of finding a scientific insight in a poem or a clue to an ethical problem in a math book. Yet many of the most creative insights come from just such unexpected places.

The forklift, for example, which makes it possible to move the heaviest objects effortlessly, was first conceived of when the inventor was standing in a bakery. He noticed how the doughnuts were lifted out of the oven on steel "fingers" and thought, "Why shouldn't that same idea work in the warehouse?"[6] Similarly, the idea of the printing press first occurred to Johannes Gutenberg while he was watching a winepress operating. He had long pondered how to achieve quicker book production; the current method was to carve words laboriously on blocks and then to rub paper against them. The winepress suggested the idea of transferring an image to paper by pressing an inked lead seal against it.[7]

What connection is there between a secretary's desk and an operating room? Or between the dolphins at Florida's Ocean World and the education of children with Down syndrome? "No connection at all," most people would say. And yet creative people have seen a very valuable connection. Surgeons are now using staples in place of sutures to save time and blood loss. And David Nathanson, a professor of psychology at Florida International University, has demonstrated that young people with Down syndrome learn to speak more quickly and remember words longer when they are placed in pools with trained dolphins. He got the idea for the experiment when he noticed that these children, who couldn't sit still and pay attention to a teacher, would play with a puppy for a quarter of an hour. Speculating on how this interest in animals could best be used in teaching, he decided to use dolphins.[8]

In addition to searching for connections among ideas you encounter now, you can also search for connections you overlooked in past experiences and observations. You surely have thousands of experiences classified under only one heading that could be classified under several. For example, you may have gone swimming as a child, got a little too far from shore, struggled, panicked, and almost drowned, until a friend saved you. That experience and the circumstances surrounding it are probably etched in your mind as *narrow escape from drowning*. But think of the other possible classifications: *effects of fear on performance, importance of children's obedience to parents, role of personal sacrifice in friendship*. By seeing more connections between past experiences and observations, you multiply your store of useful information.

The Experiences of People You Know

Other people's experiences can be as valuable to you as your own. To tap your friends' experiences, approach them skillfully, with questions that stimulate their thinking and assist them in remembering. Let's say your problem is how to overcome your fear of heights. You could ask a friend, "Have you ever been afraid of high places?" but that wouldn't be the best way to phrase the question. Any of your friend's fears might give you helpful information, so your first question should be broader. And you should be ready with subsequent questions to direct your friend's recall in ways that seem helpful to you. Here's how you might proceed:

YOU: Have you ever had a nagging fear you wanted to overcome?

FRIEND: I don't know . . . I guess so. Hmmm . . . *[Trying to remember something specific]*

YOU: *[Stimulating recall]* I mean, like a fear of being closed in; or dogs; or high places.

FRIEND: Yeah, when I was about 12. I can remember being terrified of the dogs on my paper route.

YOU: Tell me about it. How did you feel?

Later in the conversation, you would ask how the fear began and, more important, how your friend coped with and overcame it. You'd also ask whether he or she ever received any advice from others that proved helpful or knows any books and articles that speak to the question of overcoming fear. You might even share your fear with your friend and ask for a reaction.

Any time you try to draw on other people's experience in this way, keep two points in mind. First, some people are more helpful than others. You'll always do better asking a good thinker rather than a poor thinker or an open, talkative person rather than a shy, secretive one. Second, successful questioning depends not only on your ability to ask the right question at the right time but also on your willingness to listen at other times, to open yourself to the person's experience and not let other thoughts (even analytical ones) intrude.

It is also a good idea not to rely solely on your memory. Instead, get in the habit of taking notes. In most cases, this is better done soon after the conversation rather than during it because many people will be distracted if you write while they speak.

USING THE LIBRARY

Perhaps you think of the library as a gathering place for dull people, a place of little use to anyone who is lively and creative. That is a mistaken view. In fact, the library is best seen as *a formal meeting room for interviews with authorities not otherwise available.* That's precisely the way the very best thinkers regard it.

If your aversion to the library is based instead on the fear of lingering too long, you'll be pleased to learn that the people who use the library most often—professional writers, speakers, and scholars—have even more reason than you to save time. They often have difficult deadlines to meet. Efficiency is not just a matter of preference with them; it's a dollars-and-cents concern. Yet they don't avoid the library; they simply use it more effectively.

The first step in using the library as professionals do is to determine all the headings and subheadings that might apply to your subject. Because the information sought may appear under different headings in the library's various sources, this is an important step. Start by giving free rein to your imagination and listing as many headings as you can. For example, for *crime,* you may think of the subtopics *homicide, rape, shoplifting, kidnapping, vandalism,* and *burglary.* Next, expand your list of headings by consulting two sources available in most college libraries: the index volume of *Encyclopedia Americana* and the *Thesaurus of Psychological Index Terms,* a companion volume to *Psychological Abstracts.* You'll find such additional headings as *felonies, misdemeanors, antisocial behavior, behavior disorders, psychosexual behavior,* and *infanticide.*

Once you have determined the headings under which the information you are looking for is classified, get the information by using these simple and efficient approaches.

1. Consult a good encyclopedia for a broad overview of your subject. *Encyclopaedia Britannica* and *Encyclopedia Americana* are generally considered the best. Note important facts. In addition, note special terms that might be useful in further research.

2. Consult an almanac, a collection of miscellaneous facts and statistical information about a wide variety of subjects. On the subject of crime, for example, you can find information under as many as two dozen specific listings. Most almanacs are published once a year. Thus, you can obtain comparative data— say, for 1970, 1980, and 1990—quickly and easily.

3. Consult the appropriate indexes. Indexes do not present the information you are looking for, but they tell you where to find it and so save you much time and energy. The following are among the most generally useful indexes. (Your librarian will be able to suggest others.)

   • For information in nontechnical periodicals—*The Readers' Guide to Periodical Literature.*
   • For information in specialized and technical publications—

   Applied Science and Technology Index
   Art Index
   Biography Index
   Biological and Agricultural Index
   Book Review Index
   Business Periodicals Index
   Education Index

    Engineering Index

    Essay and General Literature Index

    General Science Index

    Humanities Index

    Index to Legal Periodicals

    Magazine Index

    Music Index

    Philosopher's Index

    Psychological Abstracts

    Religion Index One: Periodicals

    Social Science Index

- For information in newspaper reports—the *New York Times Index*.
- For information in government publications—the *Monthly Catalog of United States Government Publications* and the *Monthly Checklist of State Publications*.

4. Consult computer databases and abstracting services. Data searches are easier than ever with modern information-retrieval technology. Your librarian can explain the databases available to you. Ask, too, about abstracting services such as *Sociological Abstracts, America: History and Life,* and *Dissertation Abstracts International*.

5. Use the *subject heading* feature of your library's online catalog for books on your subject. Use broad subject headings as well as narrow ones; often a book that treats a larger subject will have a chapter or two on your subject.

6. Obtain and read the books and articles that are most relevant to your subject. Though the number of books and articles you read will depend on the scope of your project, the first five steps of the process should be followed for all but the very briefest of treatments.

These reference works are only the basic ones. For that reason, it is important to remember that your most important resource in the library is the people who work there: the librarians and their assistants. They can suggest other research materials and help you expand your expertise.

USING THE INTERNET

In a relatively short time the Internet has become one of the most popular and useful research tools. One important reason is that you don't have to leave home to access it. All you need is a computer and an Internet Service Provider (ISP). Then you just dial up the ISP, get online, and you're free to surf the Web. You can visit commercial sites, designated by .com; organizational sites (.org); government sites (.gov); and education sites (.edu).

The main challenge of using the Internet is finding the information you are looking for quickly and efficiently. If you happen to know the address of the Web site you are looking for, all you have to do is type it in the address box and hit "enter." (*Note:* It is essential that you get the address exactly right. Change a character or add a space and you'll end up nowhere, or somewhere unintended.) If you don't have a specific address, you will have to use a "search engine." One of the best is Google—the address is http://www.google.com. If you were to type that address into your ISP address box, you would get the Google home page shown in Figure 8.1. If you were to click on any of the blue words on that home page, a window would open, providing you with information on that topic.

Next, if you were to type in the term "media bias" in the search box and click on "Google Search," you would get a page like the one shown in Figure 8.2. Notice near the top right of the page how many results the search produced. The page shown here contains only some of the results shown on the actual Web page. At the bottom of that page you can choose to access the next ten results, and so on. You can access any one of the items by clicking on its title. By clicking on "Cached" at the end of an item, you can get a snapshot of what Google found when it accessed the item. If you find an item is especially appropriate, you can click "Similar pages" at the end of the entry and get more focused results.

Use Google when you don't know which Web site is likely to provide the information you are seeking, or when you wish to expand your search. On the other hand, if you do know the most likely Web site, start your search there. Here are some special-purpose Web sites.

For Finding Hoaxes and Fake Viruses

If you've ever passed on an e-mail warning to your friends only to learn later that it was a hoax, you know how embarrassing the experience can be. By checking the following sites *before* you pass on the message, you can spare yourself that embarrassment:

> http://www.snopes2.com (the best general-purpose site)
>
> http://www.cdc.gov/search.htm (this is run by the Centers for Disease Control (CDC); when there, type "hoaxes" in the search box)
>
> http://hq.mycio.com/dispHoax.asp?virus_k=99436 (this McAfee site helpful in detecting virus hoaxes)
>
> http://www.fraud.org (The National Fraud Information Center site)

For Evaluating the Quality of a Web Site

> http://www2.widener.edu/Wolfgram-Memorial-Library/webeval/ eval1198/index.htm (an outstanding slide show by Jan Alexander and Marsha Ann Tate)

For Informed Opinion

Conservative

> http://www.townhall.com (click on "columnists," and then click on any of the featured columns or on any name in the list of contributors)

FIGURE 8.1 www.google.com, November 13, 2002, 11:00 A.M.

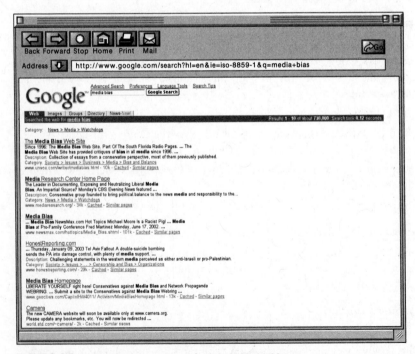

FIGURE 8.2 www.google.com, November 13, 2002, 11:02 A.M.

http://www.jewishworldreview.com/ (click on any of the names in the "Insight" column on the home page)

Liberal

http://www.prospect.org (click first on "columnists" and then on "find other authors")

http://www.demsonline.net/home.htm (click on "links")

Varied

http://www.blueagle.com/index.html (this site lists 700 columnists, many cartoonists, and links to political Web sites)

For News

http://www.foxnews.com (the Fox News Channel site)

http://www.ap.org (the Associated Press site)

http://www.cnn.com (the CNN site)

For Reference Materials (including encyclopedias; thesauruses; dictionaries; collections of quotations; guides to English usage, religion, and literary history)

http://www.bartleby.com/reference/

http://www.infoplease.com (the Information Please site)

For Quotations on a Variety of Subjects

http://www.toinspire.com

For Legal Information

http://www.legalengine.com

For Health

http://www.nih.gov

http://www.medlineplus.gov

For General Up-to-Date Information on Search Engines

http://www.searchenginewatch.com

MAINTAINING A QUESTIONING PERSPECTIVE

When dealing with published ideas, particularly those of well-known authorities, you may be tempted to surrender your judgment. To let that happen is a mistake. Being human, authorities are subject to making the same errors as anyone else. They can, for example, be blinded by personal preferences, cling stubbornly to outmoded views, and suffer lapses in reasoning.

Even when they manage to avoid such elementary errors, they may miss important new developments in their field or related fields, or they may misinterpret the significance of such developments. Research is constantly being done in every field, and the findings of such efforts often overturn previous conclusions. For example, for years, expert medical opinion was in agreement that eating fats increased the risk of heart disease, that heavy salt consumption caused a rise in blood pressure, that the frequent consumption of eggs caused an increase in serum cholesterol, and that obesity in adulthood depended on childhood eating habits. Then new studies were published that challenged each of these conclusions and caused expert opinion to be modified.[9]

Complicating the matter further is the fact that new insights often take years to become general knowledge among the members of a profession. Psychologist Carol Tavris's excellent study *Anger: The Misunderstood Emotion,* which demolished the traditional assumption that venting hostility is beneficial, was published in 1982. Yet articles are still being written endorsing the earlier idea, the authors apparently oblivious of Tavris's work or irrationally committed to an erroneous view.

Accordingly, as important as it is to seek out authoritative opinion, it is equally important to maintain a questioning perspective. The best ways to do so are to consult several authorities of differing perspectives, to ask probing questions of each, and to compare their responses.

MANAGING AN INTERVIEW

Chances are, most of your investigation will be done in the library or on the Internet. But you may, on occasion, have the opportunity to interview an authority (for example, a professor on your campus who has done special research in the area you are investigating). In such cases, follow this basic rule: be considerate of the interviewee, who is donating valuable time and shouldn't be taken for granted. Here are some specific ways to show consideration.

1. Call or write ahead for an appointment. Explain exactly what you wish to discuss and how long you'll take. (Keep the time as brief as you can, preferably under half an hour.) Make yourself available at a time that fits the interviewee's schedule best.

2. Before the interview, make an effort to learn the fundamentals of the subject you will be discussing. If the subject is controversial, know the issues in dispute and have at least a general notion of the competing arguments.

3. Prepare your questions carefully in advance. Make them clear and brief. Try to avoid those that can be answered yes or no; they won't be very helpful. For instance, instead of asking, "Do you agree with the governor's position?" ask, "What is your reaction to the governor's statement?" If you are sufficiently informed about a view that opposes the interviewee's views, ask, "Dr. _____ says such-and-such. How would you respond?" If you are insufficiently informed about opposing views, ask, "On what matters do those who oppose your view differ with you, and how would you respond to their disagreement?"

4. Anticipate the responses to your initial questions, and prepare follow-up questions to probe those responses you feel don't go far enough or don't address the points you wish addressed.

5. Arrive on time. When you begin the interview, get right to the point. Keep your questions crisp and clear. Avoid thinking ahead to your next question. Instead, listen carefully to the reply. If any of your interviewee's comments open up an aspect of the issue you did not consider but is worth pursuing, be sure to pursue it. However, try not to overstay your welcome.

6. If at all possible, don't make the person wait while you take notes. If you can't take shorthand or write rapidly in longhand, consider the possibility of taping the interview. (Always obtain permission to tape an interview. Never merely assume taping is acceptable to the other person.)

If an in-person interview is not possible, consider a telephone interview. Such an interview is conducted the same as the preceding, with two additional requirements. First, be sure to call or write in advance to determine when the interview will be most convenient. It is boorish to assume that because you are ready, your interviewee is, too. Second, remember that when conducting a telephone interview, it is especially important to speak clearly and to ask clear, concise questions.

AVOIDING PLAGIARISM[10]

Once ideas are put into words and published, they become "intellectual property," and the author has the same rights over them as he or she has over a material possession such as a house or a car. The only real difference is that intellectual property is purchased with mental effort rather than money. Anyone who has ever wracked his or her brain trying to solve a problem or trying to put an idea into clear and meaningful words can appreciate how difficult mental effort can be.

Plagiarism is passing off other people's ideas or words as one's own. It is doubly offensive in that it both steals and deceives. In the academic world, plagiarism is considered an ethical violation and is punished by a failing grade for a paper or a course, or even by dismissal from the institution. Outside the academy, it is a crime that can be prosecuted if the person to whom the material belongs wishes to bring charges. In the eyes of the law, stealing ideas and/or the words used to express them is as criminal as stealing the computer on which they were recorded.

Some cases of plagiarism are attributable to intentional dishonesty, others to carelessness. But many, perhaps most, are due to misunderstanding. The instructions "Base your paper on research rather than on your own unfounded opinions" and "Don't present other people's ideas as your own" seem contradictory and may confuse you, especially if no clarification is offered. Fortunately, there is a way to honor both instructions and, in the process, to avoid plagiarism.

Step 1: When you are researching a topic, keep your sources' ideas separate from your own. Begin by keeping a record of each source of information you consult.

For an Internet source, record the Web site address, the author and title of the item, and the date you visited the site. For a book, record the author, title, place of publication, publisher, and date of publication. For a magazine or journal article, record the author, title, the name of the publication, and its date of issue. For a TV or radio broadcast, record the program title, station, and date of transmission.

Step 2:   As you read each source, note the ideas you want to refer to in your writing. If the author's words are unusually clear and concise, copy them *exactly* and put quotation marks around them. Otherwise, paraphrase—that is, restate the author's ideas in your words. Write down the number(s) of the page on which the author's passage appears.

If the author's idea triggers a response in your mind—such as a question, a connection between this idea and something else you've read, or an experience of your own that supports or challenges what the author says—write it down and put brackets (not parentheses) around it so that you will be able to identify it as your own when you review your notes. Here is a sample research record illustrating these two steps:

> **Adler, Mortimer J. *The Great Ideas: A Lexicon of Western Thought* (New York: Macmillan Publishing Co., 1992, pp. 867, 869)**   Says that throughout the ages, from ancient Greece, philosophers have argued about whether various ideas are true. Says it's remarkable that most renowned thinkers have agreed about what truth is—"a correspondence between thought and reality." 867 Also says that Freud saw this as the scientific view of truth. Quotes Freud: "This correspondence with the real external world we call truth. It is the aim of scientific work, even when the practical value of that work does not interest us." 869 [I say true statements fit the facts; false statements do not.]

Whenever you look back on this record, even a year from now, you will be able to tell at a glance which ideas and words are the author's and which are yours. The first three sentences are, with the exception of the directly quoted part, *paraphrases* of the author's ideas. The fourth is a direct quotation. The final sentence, in brackets, is your own idea.

Step 3:   When you compose your paper, work borrowed ideas and words into your writing by judicious use of quoting and paraphrasing. In addition, give credit to the various authors. Your goal here is to eliminate all doubt about which ideas and words belong to whom. In formal presentations, this crediting is done in footnotes; in informal ones, it is done simply by mentioning the author's name.

Here is an example of how the material from Mortimer Adler might be worked into a composition. (Note where the footnote is placed and the form that is used for it.) The second paragraph illustrates how your own idea might be expanded:

> Mortimer J. Adler explains that throughout the ages, from the time of the ancient Greeks, philosophers have argued about whether various ideas are true. But to Adler the remarkable thing is that, even as they

argued, most renowned thinkers have agreed about what truth is. They saw it as "a correspondence between thought and reality." Adler points out that Sigmund Freud believed this was also the scientific view of truth. He quotes Freud as follows: "This correspondence with the real external world we call truth. It is the aim of scientific work, even when the practical value of that work does not interest us."[1]

This correspondence view of truth is consistent with the common sense rule that a statement is true if it fits the facts and false if it does not. For example, the statement "the twin towers of New York's World Trade Center were destroyed on September 11, 2002" is false because they were destroyed the previous year. I may sincerely believe that it is true, but my believing in no way affects the truth of the matter. In much the same way, if an innocent man is convicted of a crime, neither the court's decision nor the world's acceptance of it will make him any less innocent. We may be free to think what we wish, but our thinking can't alter reality.

[1]Mortimer J. Adler, *The Great Ideas: A Lexicon of Western Thought* (New York: Macmillan Publishing Co., 1992), pp. 867, 869.

Three problems commonly arise in quoting and/or paraphrasing. Here is an explanation of each, together with a practical way to solve it:

Problem 1: Deciding whether to quote or paraphrase. The general rule is to quote only when a statement is so well and concisely expressed that a paraphrase would add unnecessary length and/or lose the force of the original. Such instances are rare. Most passages can be stated as well—some can actually be improved—by being paraphrased.

Statements that should be quoted rather than paraphrased:

"No act of kindness, no matter how small, is ever wasted." Aesop

"What we think, we become." Buddha

"It is impossible for a man to learn what he thinks he already knows." Epictetus

Statements that should be paraphrased (with suggested paraphrasing). (Notice that the source of the material is stated in the paraphrase, so that appropriate credit is given for the idea.)

"As a man thinketh in his heart, so is he." Proverbs 23-7 (Paraphrase: As the Book of Proverbs reminds us, we are what we think.)

"He does not believe who does not live according to his belief." Thomas Fuller (Paraphrase: To be genuine, belief must be practiced.)

Problem 2: Converting the author's words to your words. Constructing a paraphrase is mentally taxing because it involves thinking of alternative ways to express ideas. It is tempting to say, "The way the author said is it is the only way," and to settle for a quotation. But if you do that you will quickly find that most of your paper requires quotation marks. Not wanting to appear so obviously imitative, you may decide to leave the quotation marks off. But then you will have committed *plagiarism*!

The solution to this problem is to acknowledge that there are always alternative ways to express an idea and that to find them you just have to put forth a little effort and invest a little imagination. Here is an example of an effective paraphrase of a passage from Shelby Steele's book, *White Guilt*. (For the purpose of this exercise, five passages that appear on different pages are joined together, with the junctures indicated by ellipses.)

Original Passage

". . . This new black consciousness [of the 1960s] led blacks into a great mistake: to talk ourselves out of the individual freedom we had just won for no purpose whatsoever except to trigger white obligation . . . The goal of the civil rights movement had escalated from a simple demand for equal rights to a demand for the redistribution of responsibility for black advancement from black to white America, from the 'victims' to the 'guilty.' This marked a profound—and I believe tragic—turning point in the long struggle of black Americans for a better life . . . Black militancy, then, was not inevitable in the late sixties. It came into existence *solely* to exploit white guilt as a pressure on white America to take more responsibility for black advancement . . . Thus, since the sixties, black leaders have made one overriding argument: that blacks cannot achieve equality without white America taking primary responsibility for it. Black militancy became, in fact, a militant belief in white power and a correspondingly militant denial of black power . . . But this sad symbiosis overlooks an important feature of human nature: human beings, individually or collectively, cannot transform themselves without taking *full* responsibility for doing so. This is a law of nature. Once full responsibility is accepted, others can assist as long as it is understood that they cannot be responsible. But no group in human history has been lifted into excellence or competitiveness by another group." Shelby Steele, *White Guilt: How Blacks and Whites Together Destroyed the Promise of the Civil Rights Era* (New York: HarperCollins, 2006), 45, 58, 59, 60, 62.

Paraphrase

Shelby Steele contends that blacks in America have allowed whites to overcome their guilt for the evils of slavery and discrimination by treating blacks as victims and taking over all responsibility for black people's advancement. This he regards as a serious error because "no group in human history has been lifted into excellence or competitiveness by another group."

*Note: 1) The first four words make clear that the author is paraphrasing Steele. 2) Some **individual** key words that appear in the original, such as "advancement" and "responsibility," also appear in the paraphrase. Such repetition is* *often unavoidable and does not constitute plagiarism. 3) The only* **group** *of words that is repeated appears in quotation marks. To omit the quotation marks would have constituted plagiarism. 4) Although the paraphrase embraces the entire idea expressed in the original, it is more compressed. This is a typical feature of paraphrasing.*

Problem 3: Constructing ideas of your own to blend with paraphrased and/or quoted material. If the subject is unfamiliar or complex, you may wonder what you can possibly add to what the authors you consulted have said. Using the Shelby Steele passage as an example, here is how you might solve this problem. After presenting your paraphrase of his ideas, you could do one or more of the following: 1) Elaborate on Steele's views by mentioning some of the evidence he offers in the book to support them. 2) Present the views of other authors who *share* Steele's perspective and the evidence they offer in support of their views. 3) Present the views of authors who *disagree* with Steele on this issue and the evidence they offer. (In all three of these steps, you would, of course, exercise the same care in paraphrasing, quoting, and citing your sources.) 4) Present your evaluation of the issue, explaining which author(s) you agree with and which you disagree with, in each case presenting *your reasons* for thinking as you do.

This fourth step makes the composition or research paper uniquely your own. It represents your thinking and your expression. The more carefully you approach it—explaining thoroughly, providing evidence, anticipating and answering objections—the better its quality will be.

CONDUCTING YOUR OWN RESEARCH

The approaches considered so far in this chapter constitute the first and most fundamental line of investigation—determining *what is already known.* In many cases, such an investigation will produce all the evidence you need to solve the problem or resolve the issue. Sometimes, however, you will need to go beyond what is already known and develop *new knowledge* by conducting your own research. Here are two suggestions.

Consider Doing a Survey

Among the survey topics that might be interesting to investigate on a college campus are students' attitudes toward cheating, the campus community's position on the issue of whether women's athletic teams should receive the same level of funding as men's teams, and the professors' attitudes toward open parking on campus.

Consider Doing an Observational Study

Examples of observational studies that would be appropriate on a college campus are a study of the dynamics of a committee meeting to determine areas of inefficiency and ineffectiveness, and a study of the flow of people through the campus cafeteria during peak volume periods to identify how and where bottlenecks occur.

Before you attempt either of these approaches, reread the explanation provided earlier in the chapter.

KEEPING CREATIVITY ALIVE

As crucial as the investigation stage is in the solution of many problems, it can threaten creativity. The more information you accumulate, the greater the potential for confusion. To keep creativity alive, you will have to overcome that confusion. Here is how to do so.

Whenever you are confused by the amount or complexity of the information you have obtained and have difficulty sorting it out, pause for a moment, look back at your statement of the problem (stage 2), and use that statement to decide what is relevant and what is not. If you are dealing with an especially difficult problem, you may have to use this approach many times. Even the best and most creative thinkers lose their bearings from time to time, but they don't allow themselves to become discouraged. They just find their bearings again and continue.

A large amount of information can also have a daunting effect on your confidence. The more you probe a problem, the more you are likely to realize its complexity. In time, you may find yourself thinking, "I didn't realize it would be this difficult. Maybe there is no solution. If other, more qualified people have been unable to find a solution, what business do I have trying?" When such thoughts occur, remind yourself that others may not have solved the problem precisely because they gave in to their feelings of apprehension—the ones that at this very moment threaten your creativity—or because, despite their expertise, they lacked the techniques for unlocking and applying their creativity. (After all, creativity is not a formal subject taught in most schools and colleges, so it is not surprising that otherwise educated people should be uninformed about it.) Remember, too, that whatever difficulties arise in thinking, there are effective methods for dealing with them, and your resources for producing creative responses to problems and issues are, as the next chapter will demonstrate, considerable.

WARM-UP EXERCISES

8.1 Read the following dialogue carefully. Then decide what you would say next if you were Veronica. Make your response so clear and effective that the matter would be settled.

PERRY: The only book a person ever needs to read is the Bible.

VERONICA: I don't agree. Other books surely have something to offer.

PERRY: Let me show you how wrong that is. If other books agree with the Bible, they are unnecessary. And if they disagree, they are irreligious and should be avoided.

8.2 Create as many new food recipes as you can. Include ingredients and preparation instructions.

8.3 Old toothbrushes are usually thrown in the trash. But are they really useless? Think of as many uses as you can for them.

APPLICATIONS

8.1 Each of the following cases was reported in the news. Most readers undoubtedly viewed them narrowly, believing each was entirely irrelevant to any but the most obvious subject. Yet, to someone searching for more than surface connections, each case offers some interesting possibilities. For each of the following cases, list as many implied subjects or issues as you can. Be sure to specify what those implications are.

    a. Some research findings suggest that personality differences among individuals are more a result of heredity than of environment. For example, University of Minnesota psychologists who studied 400 sets of adult twins found a strong genetic link for such qualities as anger, cautious behavior, and social-political religious conservatism. And a Pennsylvania State University study of 700 sets of twins estimated that environment counts for only 10 percent of personality differences.[11]

    b. A 9-year-old boy known as Robert M. pointed a toy gun at a New York City bank teller and robbed her of $118. He was placed on two years' probation after his attorney argued he was only playacting during the robbery. Then, a year later, the same boy, with two accomplices, was arrested for stealing a sled from two boys at knifepoint.[12]

    c. Three-year-old Chad Chancey was expected to be the youngest trial witness in Oklahoma's history. He was the only person with any knowledge of the events that took place the night his mother and sister were murdered. Chad reportedly heard a loud argument in the next room, women's screams, a sound he described as a loud handclap, then silence. He later identified the man who had been in the apartment that night from a police file photo. The defense attorney expressed concern that the child might be too young to separate fact from fantasy.[13]

    d. In 1945, Charles Jamison was found badly wounded on a Boston dock. He carried papers identifying him as a first mate on the USS *Cutty Sark*. Yet no records could be found of the existence of such a ship, and all further investigations about the man revealed nothing. Interviews with him disclosed only that he had no family, had gone to sea at age 13, and believed his ship had been torpedoed. He remained in a Boston hospital until his death 30 years after his discovery on the dock.[14]

e. Dr. Martin Orne, a psychiatrist and an expert on memory and
    hypnosis, and Dr. Elizabeth Loftus, a psychologist and memory
    expert, presented information to the American Association for
    the Advancement of Science that suggested that using hypnotism
    to get witnesses to recall details of past events may be ill
    advised. Their research showed that memory may be uninten-
    tionally altered by the form of the hypnotist's questions. "If the
    hypnotist has certain beliefs," said Dr. Orne, "he will create
    memories in the subject's mind." [15]

f. A human fetus survived to full term after it was extracted from
    its mother's womb for surgery and then returned to the womb
    following surgery. The surgery, which took place in the twenty-
    fourth week of pregnancy, corrected a life-threatening urinary
    tract obstruction. [16]

8.2   Woebegone College is having a problem with grade inflation. The
average grade submitted by many professors is a B+, even though
the average entrance examination score of Woebegone's students has
declined steadily over the past decade. It appears that work that
would have received a C 10 or 15 years ago is now being given a B
or B+. One effect has been that 60 percent of the student body is on
the dean's list. Find the best expression of this problem. Then investigate it, as necessary, using the approaches explained in the chapter,
and produce as many solutions as you can. (Record all your
thoughts as they occur to you, and be prepared to submit them to
your instructor.) Finally, state which of your solutions you believe is
best, and briefly explain why.

8.3   Every so often, someone writes an article about the poor state of
composition teaching, usually with a title such as "Why Dick and
Jane Can't Write" or "The Scandal in the English Classroom." The
public then gets excited and calls for a study of the problem, and the
media explore methods of developing students' language skills. But
no lasting creative solution to the problem ever seems to be found.
Identify and solve this problem, following the directions in
Application 8.2.

8.4   Alcohol and drug abuse are associated with crime in the streets,
health problems, the breakdown of the family, and poor job performance. Identify and solve this problem, following the directions in
Application 8.2.

8.5   In many states, the schools are financed primarily by property taxes.
This system, of course, tends to favor wealthy areas over poor areas
and often results in inequality of educational opportunity. Identify
and solve this problem, following the directions in Application 8.2.

8.6   On the one hand, the federal government forbids cigarette advertising on radio and television and requires health warnings to be
printed on every pack of cigarettes sold. On the other hand, the

same government heavily subsidizes tobacco farming. Address this challenge, following the directions in Application 8.2.

8.7 The U.S. Patent and Trademark Office announced in 1987 that it considered "non-naturally occurring non-human multicellular living organisms, including animals, to be patentable subject matter. . . ." A year later a patent was issued to Harvard University for a new breed of genetically altered mice. Some people consider this scientific advancement. Others consider it a dangerous precedent.[17] Address this challenge, following the directions in Application 8.2.

ISSUE FOR EXTENDED ANALYSIS

Following is a more comprehensive thinking challenge than the others in the chapter. Analyze and respond to it, following the instructions for extended analysis at the end of Chapter 1. Also, review "The Basis of Moral Judgment" and "Dealing with Dilemmas" in Chapter 2.

THE ISSUE: U.S. FOREIGN AID

Every year the United States donates billions of dollars in cash, goods, and services to other countries. Many Americans believe our foreign aid programs are a shining example of our compassion and generosity. Others believe the programs not only fail to achieve their objectives but, in some cases, are *counter*productive.

THE ESSAYS

Expand U.S. Foreign Aid
By Mirra al-Nur

It is commonly believed that the United States is the most generous country in the world. This is simply not the case. Statistical comparisons of the foreign aid contributions of major industrialized countries consistently show the United States near last place. For example, in 2004, only one industrialized country (Italy) scored lower. Those scoring higher included Canada, Ireland, Finland, and even tiny Luxembourg!

If this fact is surprising, it is only because the ratings are based not on total dollars given but instead on what percentage of each country's gross

End the Foreign Aid Fiasco
By Mary Robinson

America is the most generous country in history. We contribute money and services to countries stricken by earthquakes, hurricanes, tsumanis, and disease epidemics. We help countries ravaged by war. We even help restore countries with whom *we ourselves* have been at war—notably Nazi Germany and Imperial Japan after World War II.

Despite our generosity, however, we are the most hated country in the world. In the UN and elsewhere world leaders accuse us of lacking compassion and even of being bullies and imperialists. It is not uncommon to national product (GNP) the contribution represents. That is a much more reasonable measure, and by it our contribution is embarrassingly low. After all, we are the richest and most powerful nation in the world. Our generosity is essential to overcoming the devastation of poverty and disease in the Third World.

To say that U.S. foreign aid should be increased is not to suggest that the existing model for that aid is perfect. The largest amounts of our aid now go to Egypt, Russia, and Israel. If they were to receive less, nations with more basic and serious problems could receive more. In addition, our aid programs tend to pay little attention to the use to which the aid is put and the effectiveness of distribution efforts. It would be wise for us not merely to trust the leaders of foreign countries to be honorable but to require verification.

We also should consider giving more of our aid in the form of technical assistance. There is much insight in the old saying, "Give a man a fish and you feed him for a day. Teach him to fish and you feed him for a lifetime."

But however much we may revise our aid model, we should increase its funding. A great nation should lead the world in generosity.

see the American flag and effigies of our leaders burned in public squares.

The fact that our efforts are so unappreciated would be reason enough to rethink our foreign aid policy. But there is an even better reason—our foreign aid is not working. This is not exactly a news flash. In 1986, in a research study titled "The Continuing Failure of Foreign Aid" James Bovard pointed out that "foreign aid has rarely done anything that countries could not have done for themselves. And it has often encouraged the recipient governments' worst tendencies." Bovard argues that in dumping free food in other countries, our Food for Peace program bankrupts local farmers. He also feels that the Agency for International Development (AID) helps corrupt governments take charge of entire industries and thus stifle private enterprise, strengthen their hold over the people, and block democratic movements.

The situation has actually gotten worse since he wrote those words. Dictators and their lackeys have become more sophisticated at diverting aid from their people to their own bank accounts or, worse, to the coffers of terrorists. The time has come to admit that foreign aid doesn't work and to end it. There are more than enough good uses to which our money can be put in this country.

CLASS DISCUSSION

ALEXIS: I think al-Nur's view is more balanced than Robinson's. She admits that the aid could be divided more evenly among the recipient countries. And she acknowledges the problem of ensuring that the aid reaches the people it is intended to help. Yet she also points out the fact than the United States is providing far less aid than it could and should.

BRUCE: I applaud her balance, but when all is said and done, she is championing a failed program. I see no virtue in that. It's simply throwing good money after bad.

ALEXIS: The virtue lies in helping people in need. Acts of kindness are the cornerstone of religion and morality. In Judaism, they are known as *mitzvahs* (good deeds); in Buddhism, as metta (acts of loving kindness). And Jesus admonished his disciples that "whatever you do to . . . the least of my brethren, you do unto me."

BRUCE: It's true that religion urges, even demands, that *individual people* help neighbors in need. But to my knowledge no religion teaches that *governments* have any such responsibility.

ALEXIS: There are so many poor people and nations, and their needs are so great, that governmental aid is absolutely essential. Individuals couldn't meet the need even if they wanted to, and I'm not sure that a sufficient number of people want to.

BRUCE: You're mistaken. There are thousands of private aid programs, including many religious ones. Millions of people support those programs. And the programs do a more efficient and effective job in distributing aid than any government does.

CHAPTER

9

Produce Ideas

So far our examination of the creative process has demonstrated how to recognize problems and issues, express them clearly, and gain essential insights into them. There is one additional stage in the creative process: producing possible solutions.

In this chapter you will learn the advantage of producing a wide range of solutions rather than settling for a few. You will also learn how to stimulate your imagination, how to be more original, and how to overcome the obstacles most common at this stage of creativity.

Imagine a pearl diver on an island in the South Seas. He pushes off his canoe from the shore, paddles out into the lagoon, dives deep into the water, picks an oyster off the bottom, surfaces, climbs into his boat, paddles to shore, and opens the shell. Finding nothing but an oyster inside, he sets off in his canoe again and begins paddling into the lagoon. "Wait a minute," you're probably thinking. "He's wasting an awful lot of time. The right way to do it is not to paddle back to shore with one oyster but to dive again and again, fill the canoe with oysters, and then return to shore."

You're right. Pearls are rare; a diver must open many oysters before finding one. Only a very foolish diver would waste time and energy making a separate trip for each oyster.[1] *And it's exactly the same with producing ideas.* Foolish people think of a single solution to a problem and then proceed as if that solution *had* to be creative. But creative ideas, like pearls, occur infrequently. So sensible people produce many ideas before expecting to find a creative one.

Researchers have found a clear relationship between the number of ideas produced and the quality of the ideas. The more ideas produced, the better the chances of having one or more good ones.[2] There are two reasons for this. The first is a matter of simple probability. Creative ideas are statistically uncommon. As Alfred North Whitehead explains, "The probability is that nine hundred and

164

ninety-nine of [our ideas] will come to nothing, either because they are worthless in themselves or because we shall not know how to elicit their value; but we had better entertain them all, however skeptically, for the *thousandth* idea may be the one that will change the world."[3]

The second reason is that initial ideas are usually poorer in quality than later ideas. Just as water must run from a faucet for a while to be clear and free of particles, so thought must flow before it becomes creative. "Early ideas," Herbert Spencer warned, "are not usually true ideas."[4] Exactly why this is so is not known, but one very plausible hypothesis is that familiar and safe responses lie closest to the surface of our consciousness and therefore are naturally thought of first.[5] In any case, success in creative thinking depends on continuing the flow of ideas long enough to purge the common, habitual ones and produce the unusual and imaginative.

In dealing with problems, the ideas you should seek to produce are answers to the "How can . . . ?" questions you asked in expressing the problem. In dealing with issues, your ideas should be broader, including not only direct answers to your "Is (Are) . . . ?" "Does . . . ?" and "Should . . . ?" questions, but also all other ideas that can help you answer those questions. Not infrequently, the idea that provides a key to resolving an issue will seem, at first consideration, irrelevant.

STIMULATING YOUR IMAGINATION

Producing a large quantity of ideas is the first way to produce creative solutions, but it is not the only way. Another important way is to stimulate your imagination. Most people behave unimaginatively not because they lack imagination, but because they fear the reaction their ideas will receive. In time, they grow used to suppressing ideas that differ from the norm, ideas that might raise eyebrows. They do themselves a great disservice because creativity depends on imagination. "No great discovery is ever made without a bold guess," observed Sir Isaac Newton.[6] And Albert Einstein added, "I believe in imagination . . . Imagination is more important than knowledge."[7]

It takes more than determination to stimulate your thoughts, of course, particularly if you have gotten into the habit of suppressing them. You'll need some strategies for activating your creative imagination. Following are seven effective strategies. Some will fit problems better than issues; others, the reverse.

1. Force uncommon responses.

2. Use free association.

3. Use analogy.

4. Look for unusual combinations.

5. Visualize the solution.

6. Construct pro and con arguments.

7. Construct relevant scenarios.

Force Uncommon Responses

We noted that common, familiar ideas tend to come first. Nothing can be done to avoid this pattern. Therefore, your best approach is to expect them, even encourage them, to free your mind for more original ideas. Begin by asking yourself what responses most people would think of. Write them all down. When you have produced a number of these, and you can't think of any others, ask yourself what responses others would probably *not* think of. Press yourself for as many as you can produce.

One predictable outcome of this effort is the listing of some outrageous or silly ideas. Chances are you will feel a little uncomfortable with such ideas. "How can they be helpful?" you'll think. "Problems and issues are serious matters—no room for foolishness here." *Resist that feeling.* Playfulness, as we saw, is one important characteristic of creative people; it contributes to their dynamism. There's nothing wrong with writing even the most ridiculous ideas on paper. Listing them is not the same as endorsing them; you can always cross them out later. But don't screen them out now; you might inadvertently discard an original insight in the process.

Don't misunderstand this advice. It doesn't mean you should try to be outrageous or ridiculous. It means you should tolerate being so when it occurs as a natural consequence of striving for uncommon ideas.

Use Free Association

Free association means letting one idea suggest another. It differs from forced response in that you are not directing your mind at all but giving it free rein, relaxing your control over it momentarily and observing what ideas and associations result. Some of them may be quite unexpected and may point out interesting and profitable directions. As with forced responses, you should not screen any associations as they occur to you. Rather, write them all for later examination. Often, what seems totally irrelevant when it occurs to you may later prove valuable.

A word of warning is in order. The purpose of this strategy is to help you retrieve relevant information you originally classified too restrictively. Because this strategy involves relaxing mental control and allowing your thoughts to drift, it can slip into aimless daydreaming. You should therefore use it as a variation on other strategies and not as a substitute for them.

Use Analogy

An analogy is a reference to one or more similarities between two otherwise very different things. An analogy might be made, for example, between a football halfback's broken-field running and the movements of a jaguar or cheetah.

The history of creative achievements documents the value of analogical thinking. Creative breakthroughs often occur when a person makes a connection between something outside his or her field. (This fact suggests the value of a broad education. Narrowness of training all too often breeds a narrowness of perspective that hinders creativity.) When Gutenberg observed a winepress in operation and conceived of the printing press and when the inventor of the forklift got his insight from the doughnut machine, they were using analogical thinking.

To use analogy in your thinking, simply ask what the problem or issue is like, what it reminds you of. Where appropriate, you may also ask more specific questions, such as "What does this *look* like (or sound, taste, smell, or feel like)?" or "What does this *function* like?"

Look for Unusual Combinations

Sometimes, the best solution to a problem will be to combine things not usually combined. The miner's cap (combining a flashlight and a protective hat), the wheelchair, and the clock radio are examples of how combinations result in invention. Perhaps the most common example of this kind of invention is the recipe. Every time a cook blends different ingredients to make a dish differently, he or she is inventing by combination. The first person to put a slice of mozzarella cheese on a veal cutlet invented veal parmigiana, and the ingenious person who couldn't afford veal and substituted a slice of meatloaf invented meatloaf parmigiana.

This same strategy works well in other kinds of creativity as well—finding solutions to social problems, for example. One problem of growing concern today is the increasing cost of our prison system. Someone wrestling with that problem might well consider combining prisons with factories—that is, having convicts work for private industry behind bars and be paid for their efforts, and reimbursing the taxpayers for the cost of the imprisonment. (The idea might even come through analogy, by noting that prisons sometimes resemble large factory complexes.)

Visualize the Solution

This strategy consists of imagining the problem solved and visualizing what it would look like then. For example, before the problem of automobile travel on snow- and ice-covered roads was solved, a man forced to drive in such conditions would have pictured in his mind not the reality of tires mired in snow or spinning on ice but the condition he *wished for:* wheels turning smoothly and tires biting into the snow and grasping the ice firmly. His imagination thus stimulated, he'd have asked himself, "What would those tires look like if they were able to perform the way I wish?" And he might just have visualized pieces of metal wrapped around the tire (chains) or spikes protruding from the tire to grip the road (studs).

Construct Pro and Con Arguments

This strategy, an essential one in dealing with issues, consists of listing all conceivable arguments that might be advanced on either side of the issue. To use it, simply address your expression(s) of the issue—"Is . . .?" "Does . . .?" or "Should . . .?"—and list as many "yes" responses as you can, together with the reasoning that supports them, and as many "no" responses as you can, together with the reasoning for them. If, for example, the issue you examined was whether technology has had a positive or negative effect on human society, you would include these points, among others. (For the sake of brevity, supporting arguments are omitted.)

Positive-Effect Arguments	Negative-Effect Arguments
Has shortened the workweek, creating more leisure time for workers.	Has made many jobs very routine, increasing workers' boredom.
Has increased the variety of goods and services available.	Has decreased the quality of goods and services in many cases.
Has created many new skilled occupations.	Has eliminated many unskilled jobs.
Has increased the monetary reward to both employers and employees.	Has caused many workers to hate what they do for a living.
Has created the need for new kinds of education—vocational and technical.	Has undermined the role of the liberal arts in education.

An important warning: expect yourself to be biased, and expect your bias to affect your efforts to construct arguments. Unless you are perfectly neutral about the issue, an unlikely circumstance, at the very outset of this strategy you will believe one side of the issue to be right, and that belief will incline you to construct your list accordingly. In other words, consciously or unconsciously you will present more and better arguments for the side of the issue you prefer. The only safeguard against such bias is to *go out of your way to think of arguments that might be advanced on the other side of the issue*. If your investigation of the issue gave a fair hearing to both sides, this safeguard should not be too difficult to accomplish.

Construct Relevant Scenarios

We often tend to think of ideas exclusively as *assertions,* claims about what is or should be, such as "Respect for the rights of others is decreasing in our society" and "Ethics instruction belongs in the nation's schools." Those are ideas, to be sure, but so are *scenarios,* which are imaginatively conceived examples of situations and events that are relevant to the issue under consideration. Well-constructed scenarios have a special value that assertions lack: they represent reality itself and not just conclusions about reality.

Let's say that the issue you are analyzing concerns whether a woman must have offered "earnest resistance" to a man's sexual advances for a rape charge to be filed in the courts. (This was still a legal requirement in some states as recently as 1982.) Here are three scenarios you might construct.

- A woman has just returned from a date with a young man whom she has known for some time, has dated previously, and has had sexual intercourse with on several occasions. She invites him into her apartment and proceeds to engage in sexual foreplay. When he proposes that they have intercourse, she says "no" several times but does not stop him from performing the act.
- A woman is lying in a hospital bed, heavily sedated after experiencing a nervous breakdown. A male nurse realizes she is unable to resist his advances and so assaults her sexually.

- Walking from the campus library to her dormitory one evening, a college student passes through a dimly lighted wooded area. Suddenly, two men jump out at her, one brandishing a knife and warning that if she resists sexual intercourse with them, he will kill her. Fearing for her life, she submits.

A close reading of these scenarios will reveal the importance of constructing more than a single scenario and of taking care that those constructed cover the broad range of possibilities. All of these are believable—an indispensable qualification that every scenario must meet. However, they do not shed equal light on the issue of whether "earnest resistance" is a reasonable legal requirement. Taken alone, the first scenario might be considered to support an affirmative answer. Yet, as the other two make clear, such an answer would be shallow. Under the very plausible circumstances they present, the requirement of "earnest resistance" is quite unreasonable.

These seven strategies will give you significant help in activating your imagination. But don't expect to be able to use them smoothly right away. Give them time to become familiar. If you are inclined to give up after a few tries, remind yourself how awkward you felt the first time you dribbled a basketball or drove a car. That, too, seemed impossible to learn, but you mastered it. Whenever turning from one strategy to another confuses you, simply look back at your statement of the problem, regain your bearings, and continue producing ideas.

AIMING FOR ORIGINALITY

In the popular view, originality is a kind of genetic endowment. Either you have it or you don't, and if you don't have it, you have no hope of learning it. Research has demolished this idea. Like every other creative skill, *originality can be learned*. If you don't produce original thoughts, it is only because you have acquired the habit of being unoriginal. One study revealed that originality can be stimulated simply when the person knows it is expected.[8]

To achieve originality in your thinking, demand it of yourself. Remind yourself that there is nothing mysterious about originality; it lies just a step or two beyond the commonplace. Don't restrict your ideas to those you have heard or thought of before. Every time you address a problem and try to find solutions, stretch your mind a little, reach for thoughts a little more daring than you have entertained before.

There is one additional method that can help you be more original: *watch your fringe thoughts*. The term *fringe thoughts* was coined by Graham Wallas.[9] It means thoughts occurring on the edge or fringe of consciousness, much the same way objects appear on the periphery of our vision. When walking down the street or driving a car, we focus our gaze in one direction but continue to see objects outside that focus. When something unusual or unexpected appears there, we are able to turn our attention to it. Since original ideas often appear first on the fringe of consciousness, the more alert you are to what is happening there, the more original ideas you will discover.

WITHHOLDING JUDGMENT

Judgment is an essential part of thinking. Without it, we wouldn't be able to distinguish between good and bad solutions or select the best and most workable one. But the timing of our judgment can make all the difference. Most people don't time their judgment well: they are impulsive, evaluating ideas as soon as they are produced, sometimes even screening out certain ideas before they are fully conceptualized. At the first inkling of an idea, they say, "No, that's no good" or "This is silly" or "That can't be a solution."

Yet often, the most creative ideas are the ones that seem silliest at first. Rushing to judgment, therefore, causes some of the best ideas to be discarded—and the least creative ones to be approved mindlessly. Ironically, it ensures that people will be uncreative just when they want most to be creative.

Research has documented that thinkers who resist judging ideas during the idea-producing stage and who extend their effort to produce ideas beyond the point where they are tempted to stop are rewarded with a greater proportion of good ideas.[10] As you do the applications for this and subsequent chapters, and whenever you look for solutions to problems outside this course, don't allow yourself to judge any idea until after you have produced as many ideas as you can. Don't set artificial limits on the number of your ideas. When you find yourself thinking, "I've got 10 (or 20 or 30) ideas now—that's enough," remember that the best solution to the problem very likely lies 10 or 20 ideas beyond that point. It can be reached only by pressing on. Moreover, just to be sure you are not unconsciously setting limits on your thinking, look back occasionally at previous efforts—the applications you did in the last few chapters, for example—and decide whether you stopped producing ideas too soon.

OVERCOMING OBSTACLES

The three most common obstacles to the effective production of a large and varied number of ideas are thinker's block, vagueness and confusion, and inflexibility. Learning how to recognize each, and mastering a few simple responses, can prevent your problem-solving efforts from being frustrated.

Thinker's Block

Like writer's block, which prevents an author from putting words on the page, thinker's block prevents us from producing ideas. It makes us sit idle and grow increasingly nervous, waiting for ideas that do not come. Poor thinkers are not the only ones afflicted with thinker's block. Everyone experiences it from time to time. But good thinkers have learned that they needn't be victimized by it, that there are effective methods for dealing with it.

The best way is to minimize the chance of its occurring by doing something we have already discussed: *developing the habit of withholding judgment while you are producing ideas.* Every time you stop the flow of ideas to make a judgment, even if you stop for only a second or two, you run the risk of not being able to start again. On the other hand, the more you resist the temptation to stop and instead sustain your idea production, the less trouble thinker's block will cause you.

When it occurs despite your best efforts to avoid it, try one or more of the following approaches, in the order they are presented.

1. Look back at the ideas you have written. Read them carefully, concentrating on each as you read it. Usually, one of those ideas will suggest another that you have not written. As soon as it does, write it. Now that the ideas are flowing again, don't stop until you have to. It doesn't matter if the first few ideas are off target. You can gently direct the flow back to the problem or issue.

2. Run through the strategies for stimulating your imagination again. That is, force uncommon responses (however outrageous), use free association and analogy, look for unusual combinations, and so on through the list of strategies. You'll seldom get beyond the first or second strategy before the ideas are flowing again.

3. Copy your list of ideas over again and again, concentrating on each idea as you are writing it. Be alert to the appearance of a new idea on the fringe of your consciousness. This approach will keep you active and will prevent frustration and apprehension.

4. Walk away from the problem for a time (an hour, a day, a week). Return to it only when you can take a fresh look at it, unburdened of anxiety.

5. If all else fails, go back to the second stage of the process and consider other expressions of the problem or issue.

Vagueness and Confusion

Even the greatest thinkers experience this obstacle to problem solving. Einstein, for example, began considering the problem that led to his relativity theory when he was 16 years old. He struggled with it for seven years before reaching a solution. During that time he experienced vagueness, confusion, and puzzlement to the point of depression and despair.[11]

Whether this obstacle appears during the investigating stage or the idea-producing stage, it is most often caused by losing sight of the problem. The best way to overcome it is the way noted in Chapter 8: *look back at your statement of the problem or issue and get your bearings.* In the beginning, you may have to stop the flow of ideas to take this backward look, but with a little practice, you will be able to do it without stopping the flow. You will merely slow it down a little. It's much like steering a car. A beginning driver often has to come to a complete stop to straighten the car's direction, but very soon, he or she learns to make slight corrections with the steering wheel while maintaining speed.

You will find this kind of mental steering easier to master if you write your expression of the problem on a card or sheet of paper and keep it handy while working on the problem.

Inflexibility

This obstacle is characterized by too many ideas of one type, with little or no variation. It is caused by unconsciously directing your thinking along one narrow line of thought. Whenever you find this obstacle in your work (a simple glance back over your ideas will reveal whether it is present), make a special effort to stimulate your imagination. Any of the seven strategies we discussed may be used, but the first two and the last—forcing uncommon responses, using free association, and constructing relevant scenarios—are especially helpful.

HOW INSIGHT OCCURS

The most dramatic experience of the idea-producing stage—indeed, of the entire creative process—is the arrival of an insight. The moment of insight has been described in many ways. One is the *Aha!* reaction, such as Archimedes experienced when he sat down in a tub of water, noticed the displacement of the water by the mass of his body, and instantly conceptualized the principle of specific gravity. "Eureka!" ("I have found it!") he is said to have shouted as he ran naked through the streets. (Apparently the law against indecent exposure was not well enforced then, or else he ran very fast. In any case, he seems to have escaped arrest.) Another way of describing the moment of insight is an intense feeling of satisfaction, such as we get when we find a missing puzzle piece. But perhaps the most common experience is sudden illumination, like the lightbulb glowing above the head of a cartoon character.

For some reason, many insights come during moments of rest. One of the building blocks of modern science, an idea called "the most brilliant piece of prediction to be found in the whole range of organic chemistry," occurred at such a time. Friedrich August von Kekulé lay dozing by the fire one day in 1865 and suddenly realized that the molecules of certain organic compounds were not open structures, but ring-shaped. Here's how he described the experience:

> I turned my chair to the fire and dozed . . . . Again the atoms were gambolling before my eyes. This time the smaller groups kept modestly in the background. My mental eye, rendered more acute by repeated visions of this kind, could now distinguish larger structures, of manifold conformation; long rows, sometimes more closely fitted together; all twining and twisting in snakelike motion. But look! What was that? One of the snakes had seized hold of its own tail, and the form whirled mockingly before my eyes. As if by a flash of lightning I awoke.[12]

The fact that many imaginative leaps have come during periods of leisure or rest has led to the misconception that insight comes without effort. Authorities on the creative process are in agreement that insight is not associated with idleness. (If it were, the village loafer would hold the record for creative achievement.) Nor does it arrive during any type of leisure. Rather, it arrives during the leisure that follows periods of intense activity, in which the thinker grapples with the problem or issue, is momentarily defeated by it, and turns away in frustration. Authorities theorize that the conscious mind then turns the problem over to the unconscious, which continues working. Insight comes from that effort.[13]

Sudden insights, like all dramatic experiences, tend to be more widely publicized and more memorable than everyday occurrences. However, the fact is that many, sometimes the vast majority, of creative solutions come about more quietly. They are the result of alertness to details and careful analysis of ideas. Such solutions, though they arrive without fanfare, are no less valuable for that. And they have one great advantage over sudden insights. We can, to a significant extent, *make* them happen.

◼ A SAMPLE PROBLEM

You are a bill collector for a magazine. You have wasted countless hours in waiting rooms, hoping to see the magazine's debtors. But most secretaries have been instructed to let you wait until you get tired and leave. You examine the problem from all sides and consider a number of expressions of the problem. Finally, you decide that the best expression is "How can I get to see debtors despite their secretaries' refusal to let me do so?" Here is how your production of ideas might proceed.

You begin listing all your ideas. The first ones are outrageous, but that doesn't bother you. You know you shouldn't stop to evaluate them.

- Carry a shotgun and threaten the secretary.
- Threaten to kidnap the debtor's wife and kids.
- Bring an attack dog to the office.
- Scale the building and climb in the debtor's window.
- Tell the secretary you are the boss's brother or sister.
- Tie up the secretary and barge into the office.

You encounter thinker's block, so you apply one or more of the strategies recommended in the chapter for overcoming this obstacle. The ideas begin to flow again.

- Sweet-talk the secretary.
- Call and make an appointment first.
- Send a letter requesting payment.
- Fax the debtor repeatedly.
- Change jobs.
- Take a course in quick thinking.
- Cancel the debtor's subscription.
- Take legal action.
- Sit and wait until the office closes.
- Take an attorney with you.
- Send someone else to wait in your place.

At this point, you become confused; you believe you've lost sight of the problem. A glance back at the ideas you've just produced confirms this. They do not address the problem as you expressed it. You reread your expression and begin producing again.

- Bother the secretary.
- Give him or her a box of candy.
- Take him or her to lunch.
- Try bribery.
- Beg to see the debtor.
- Wait for the secretary to go to lunch and then barge in.

You run dry again, so you start once more with the first strategy, looking back over the ideas you have produced. Starting with the most recent, you read, "Wait for the secretary to go to lunch . . . beg to see the debtor, bribery . . . ." Suddenly you realize your inflexibility: you have slipped into producing ideas of the same type, with little or no variation. You try to stimulate your imagination, first by forcing uncommon responses. The ideas begin again.

- Pretend to be someone else.
- Catch the debtor outside the office.
- Bother the other people in the waiting room.
- Cause a disturbance.
- Be obnoxious.

The ideas stop once more, so you stimulate your imagination. When you fail to force uncommon responses, you turn to free association. Several of your ideas suggest a number of associations. Specifically, "Pretend to be someone else" suggests

- A telephone repairer
- A janitor
- A job applicant
- A police officer
- An office-supplies salesperson
- A priest or nun
- An electrician
- A newspaper reporter
- A magazine contest representative (to award a prize)
- A window washer

"Bother the secretary" suggests

- Ask to be announced every few minutes.
- Sit on the secretary's desk.
- Talk to him or her incessantly.

"Bother the other people in the waiting room" suggests

- Talk loudly about your recently contracted contagious disease.
- Tell everyone loudly that the debtor has been named in a paternity suit.
- Tell them the truth about the debtor's bill.

"Cause a disturbance" suggests

- Fall down and feign a seizure.
- Practice the tuba.
- Yell, "Fire!"
- Jump up and down on a whoopee cushion.
- Sing off-key.
- Pitch a tent (literally).
- Make howling noises.
- Put up signs saying, "This guy doesn't pay his bills."

"Be obnoxious" suggests

- Put on a horrible mask and fake blood.
- Rub your clothing with garlic and onions.
- Soak your clothes in skunk spray.

At this point, you'd have produced enough good ideas, including a number of creative ones, to stop producing and select your best one. (This selection, remember, will be tentative, pending your application of critical thinking.) Which idea would that be? A real bill collector, Andy Smulion of London, uses the very last one with great success. He soaks his clothes in skunk spray, walks quietly into the debtor's office, and hands the secretary a note saying, "I'll leave when you pay." Needless to say, he doesn't have to wait long.

■——————————————————

A SAMPLE ISSUE

You read in the newspaper that the Television Information Office, an organization financed by the television industry, has issued a six-page research paper arguing that television is not the cause of declining reading scores in the nation's schools. The research paper claims that children's reading scores have more to do with "socioeconomic factors" than with the amount of television they watch and that heavy viewing doesn't cause reading problems but is the result of those problems. It states, "Children having difficulty with classroom study and with homework will turn to television . . . precisely because of their reading difficulties."[14]

You realize that this is a matter that informed people disagree about, so you approach it as an issue and decide that the best expression of it is "Is television viewing in any way a causative factor in declining reading scores?" After reading several scholarly articles in the library and interviewing an education professor and a reading-skills instructor (both of them on your campus), you develop ideas as follows.*

————————————————

*The form and content of this sample do not reflect what you would typically do. You would undoubtedly list your ideas in fragmentary fashion so as not to interrupt the flow of thought; yet, for the sake of clarity, ideas are presented here in complete sentences. Moreover, your analysis would involve actually conducting investigations and then reflecting on each to generate more ideas, whereas here, because of space limitations, the investigations are only suggested. The emphasis here is not on research completeness but on the process by which one strategy leads to another and produces ideas.

The television industry financed the study, so it could be biased.

The conclusion says television doesn't cause reading deficiencies. That makes me more suspicious, though it proves nothing.

[A move to interpretation] The claim that reading scores have more to do with "socioeconomic factors" suggests that the disadvantaged are the only ones with reading problems. Yet that's not the case.

Middle- and upper-class students' reading deficiencies must be caused by something else.

What about reading problems causing heavy television viewing? Sounds odd, but the authorities I consulted agreed that it can happen.

How exactly would this happen? Let's see . . .

[Now constructing a scenario] Kids have trouble reading in school, grow frustrated, and so are motivated not to pick up a book but to escape. They come home, switch on the television set, and watch the evening away.

It makes sense. In cases like this, reading deficiencies probably do cause excessive television viewing.

[Now playing devil's advocate] But how are those kids any different from the average kid? Don't many good readers watch television just as much? If reading problems don't cause them to be enslaved by the boob tube, maybe they don't always cause poor readers to do so. Is it possible that the study is in error, that television viewing does cause reading problems, after all?

What would have to happen in order for television viewing to be the cause? It would have to *precede* reading deficiencies. Kids would first have to be hooked on television. Let me get a clearer picture of the sequence.

[Now another scenario] First, the TV viewing. When, exactly? In early childhood. How? The kid plays while a parent is busy. The parent leaves the television set on as a kind of baby-sitter. The kid watches it, hour after hour, day after day, from age 1 to age 5. By the time the child begins learning to read, at age 6 or so, he or she has already watched thousands of hours of TV . . . .

That's not only plausible, it's what actually happens in many cases. TV does exert influence in a child's life much earlier than formal education.

[Now an attempt to interpret] What exactly is the influence of television? What happens on television that could affect reading?

[Now yet another scenario, this one of a typical television hour, during a soap opera] The hour begins with a cluster of commercials, then for 10 minutes or so moves back and forth among two or three story lines. Then there's another cluster of three or four commercials and perhaps a newsbreak before returning to the several story lines . . . .

What does all of that translate into? Frequent shifts from scene to scene, frequent commercial breaks, frequent shifts of the viewer's attention, no demands on the mind, no difficulties or challenges—no wonder reading seems impossibly difficult by comparison.

At this point you will no doubt be inclined to conclude that television viewing is indeed a causative factor in declining reading scores. But before you can be fully confident that this is the correct conclusion, you will have to apply critical thinking and evaluate your thinking. Chapter 10 introduces the critical thinking process.

WARM-UP EXERCISES

9.1 Many performers drop their given names and take stage names that are easy to remember and that project a particular image. Thus, the cinema had Theda Bara (her last name was derived by reversing *Arab*) and Victor Mature. Wrestling has Hulk Hogan, and music had Prince (until he grew tired of the name). Think of as many creative stage names as you can. The image you aim to project may be macho male, female sex symbol, charming child, or any other you wish.

9.2 Think of as many creative names as you can for a restaurant. Consider all types of establishments, from the fancy high-priced variety to the lowly coffee shop, as well as all types of cuisines.

9.3 Most of us complain that we don't have enough closets. Yet we seldom use very efficiently the closet space we already have. Redesign your closet at home (or if you prefer, the one at college) to achieve maximum use of its space. Do "before" and "after" sketches of the closet.

APPLICATIONS

For each of the following applications, find the best expression of the problem or issue, investigate it as necessary, and then produce as many ideas as you can, applying what you learned in this chapter. (Record all your thoughts as they occur to you, and be prepared to submit them to your instructor.) Finally, state which of your ideas you believe is best, and briefly explain why.

9.1 You've entered a snow sculpture contest. The most important judging criterion, according to the organizers of the contest, will be creativity. There is no special theme, nor are there any restrictions on size or form.

9.2 In Chapter 8, we noted that the problem of having the string slip out of your sweatpants can be expressed in a number of ways, but we did not discuss that problem's solution.

9.3 In some cultures, the elderly are greatly respected and made to feel important. Their views are considered especially valuable because they are formed out of a lifetime of experience. In our culture it is quite different. Most of those over 70 are regarded as having nothing to offer society.

9.4 Many people, notably students, believe that extracurricular activities in high school complement the curriculum and provide valuable opportunities for personal growth and achievement. Yet many communities are finding the cost of financing today's schools an intolerable burden and are looking for ways to reduce that cost. Some are deciding, reluctantly, that they must cut extracurricular activities (including varsity sports) from the school budget.

9.5 The American Lung Association is looking for ways to warn teenagers about the dangers of cigarette smoking. Assist the association.

9.6 Going to the hospital for the first time can be a frightening experience, particularly for small children. Think of as many ways as you can to make the children's ward of a hospital a nonthreatening, cheery place.

9.7 Some states still consider adultery a crime and can legally impose monetary fines or prison sentences on anyone convicted of it.

ISSUE FOR EXTENDED ANALYSIS

Following is a more comprehensive thinking challenge than the others in the chapter. Analyze and respond to it, following the instructions for extended analysis at the end of Chapter 1. Also, review "The Basis of Moral Judgment" and "Dealing with Dilemmas" in Chapter 2.

THE ISSUE: AFFIRMATIVE ACTION

There is little controversy about the theoretical concept of "affirmative action," which refers to any program that aims to achieve racial/ethnic balance in education and in the workplace by actively seeking out minority candidates. The controversy concerns some of the strategies certain programs have employed, notably "set asides," quotas, and various forms of preferential treatment. Some people believe such strategies are both necessary and fair; others strongly disagree.

THE ESSAYS

Affirmative Action: A Good Thing
By Lawrence Bertrand

However free of prejudice white people can be, they cannot understand the burden of slavery's legacy. Nor can they perceive how many slights, insults, and deprivations are *still* inflicted (whether intended or not) on black people. Thus, white people cannot fully appreciate the critical importance of affirmative action to the black community. To their credit, of course, many white people accept the testimony of spokespeople of the black community—notably Jesse Jackson and Al Sharpton—and vigorously support affirmative action.

The case for affirmative action rests on two amply supported conclusions: it is necessary and fair. Why necessary? Because there is no other way for significant numbers of black citizens to make up for centuries of discrimination and the denial of educational and employment opportunities. Imagine a marathon race with many participants. Imagine, too, that 90 percent of the runners start at 9:00 A.M. but the remaining 10 percent are held back until 10:00 A.M. No matter how naturally gifted and determined the 10 percent may be, they will have no chance of winning the race.

The situation of those handicapped runners is analogous to that of black Americans in school and at work. They have entered the "competition" for education and employment that the only way for them to have a chance at "winning" is to have their handicap removed. Present opportunity

End Affirmative Action
By Kimberly Jones

The government's affirmative action program was designed to achieve justice but instead has created a new injustice, not just to the white majority but also, and most significantly, to the black community it was intended to help.

Unlike civil rights and voting rights legislation, which is necessary to prevent racial discrimination, affirmative action is unnecessary and unfair. To begin with, it emphasizes people's race over more important considerations, including the role of effort in achievement, the ideal of merit, and the necessity of being qualified for a level of academic pursuit or a particular job. (Interestingly, the very idea of affirmative action ignores Martin Luther King, Jr.'s plea to value the content of a person's character more than the color of his or her skin.) By substituting entitlement for merit, affirmative action also robs black youth of the motivation to achieve and erodes their confidence and sense of self-worth.

Many people in the black community accept the notion that white liberal supporters of affirmative action are their friends and conservative critics of the program disrespect them. The truth is exactly the reverse. The real reason white liberals are so committed to affirmative action is one they won't express publicly: they don't think blacks are *capable* of making it in school or on the job without government assistance.

is fine, but it does not restore the education and jobs black people could and should have had. Preferences alone ensure parity.

The second conclusion concerns the fairness of affirmative action. Some say it is manifestly *unfair* to allow black students to enter college with lower test scores than white students or to set aside a certain number of jobs for black applicants. They are mistaken. Extreme situations demand unusual responses, and no situation is as extreme as a history of slavery and discrimination. Affirmative action is therefore the fairest possible response to the situation of black Americans.

A number of distinguished black authors have recognized these facts and have spoken out strongly against affirmative action. Among those individuals are Ward Connerly, Walter Williams, William Raspberry, Thomas Sowell, and Shelby Steele. For example, in *Losing the Race* Berkeley professor John McWhorter argues academic underachievement among black students is not caused by lack of opportunity but by liberal conditioning that they are victims who don't have to conform to traditional academic standards.

Simply said, affirmative action does more harm than good and should be abolished.

CLASS DISCUSSION

KAREN: I've heard all the arguments for affirmative action, but the one fact that stands out to me is that it gives one group of people preferential treatment. I think that is unfair, and I'm heartened to know that Martin Luther King, Jr. had the same view.

EMMA: How fair is it to have denied millions of black Americans the opportunities historically enjoyed by other Americans?

KAREN: It wasn't fair at all but the solution is not to treat other people unfairly. Doing that merely compounds the problem. The only real solution is to guarantee everyone equal opportunity. That was the original idea behind the Civil Rights movement. Affirmative action is a corruption of that idea.

EMMA: I agree that fairness to everyone is a worthy ideal. But that doesn't make up for past injustices.

KAREN: It doesn't make up for past injustices because it can't do so—the vast majority of the people who were treated unjustly are long dead. Giving preferences to their great-grandchildren in no way removes the injustice to them. It just transfers the injustice to another group and perpetuates it.

EMMA: Not really. Affirmative action is both a powerful symbol of the nation's regret and a spur to black success.

KAREN: Wrong on both counts. The symbol is an empty exercise in assuaging white guilt. And affirmative action doesn't spur black success—it creates a false sense of entitlement that hinders success. Jones cited a number of black authors who take that view.

EMMA: Those authors are traitors to their race.

KAREN: It's offensive for you, a white woman, to make such a judgment.

PART III

Be
Critical

Both solving problems and resolving issues involve two complementary thinking activities: creative thinking to produce ideas and critical thinking to evaluate them. In Part II we discussed creative thinking. Now, in Part III, we will turn our attention to critical thinking. The focus in critical thinking is on reasoned judgment. Chapter 10 provides an overview of critical thinking, Chapter 11 demonstrates how to evaluate and refine your thinking about problems, and Chapters 12 and 13 explain the evaluation and refinement of issues.

10

The Role of Criticism

In the first chapter of this book, you learned that there are two phases to thinking: the *creative* phase, in which ideas are produced, and the *critical* phase, in which they are evaluated. Since then we have discussed the creative phase in detail. Now we turn our attention to the critical phase.

This chapter explains why critical thinking is necessary and gives you an overview of how critical thinking strategies are applied to problems and issues.

G. K. Chesterton once described a poet as a person with his head in the clouds and his feet on the ground. That description also fits good thinkers. They are able to entertain the boldest ideas, the undreamed-of solutions to problems— yet they are also able to fit their ideas to the exacting demands of reality. They are not only imaginative but practical as well. We have examined the former, creative phase of thinking. Now we will examine the latter, critical phase.

Critical thinking, as we define it here, means reviewing the ideas we have produced, making a tentative decision about what action will best solve the problem or what belief about the issue is most reasonable, and then evaluating and refining that solution or belief.

WHY CRITICISM IS NECESSARY

The role of criticism in problem solving is important for two reasons. First, no solution is ever perfect. However creative it may be, there is always room for improvement. Even the best ideas seldom occur in refined form. Like fine gems, they must be cleaned and polished before their potential worth is realized. Second, in many cases solutions cannot just be put into effect; they must first be approved by others. Ideas for the improvement of the office or factory, for example, may require the approval of an employer or supervisor. Ideas about overcoming difficulties in family relationships may depend on the cooperation of other family members. And creative solutions to social problems often require the support of government leaders or the endorsement of the voters. In such cases, the best idea in the world is of little value until others are persuaded of its worth.

Criticism is equally important in resolving issues. A viewpoint may seem eminently reasonable, the ideal ground for compromise between opposing views, yet contain subtle flaws. Sometimes these become evident only when the idea is translated into a course of action.

In the early 1970s, for example, in response to the issue of fairness in divorce settlements, the idea of "no-fault" divorce became law in California, and in subsequent years, in most other states. It was considered at the time an ingenious way to permit a marriage to be dissolved easily and fairly, without squabbling and bitter accusations. Later, many critics identified an effect of no-fault divorce that no one anticipated when it was instituted: the impoverishment of divorced women and their children.[1]

Although there can never be a guarantee that even the most thorough criticism will reveal every flaw in an idea, your responses to issues are more likely to be reasonable if you subject your ideas to rigorous evaluation before reaching a judgment. Critical thinking reduces your chance of error.

FOCUS ON *YOUR* IDEAS

The focus of this and the following chapters is not on criticism of other people's solutions. It is rather on a much more difficult, even painful, criticism: that of *your own* solutions. Like everyone else, you are vulnerable to a variety of errors. You may receive inaccurate reports from others, including the media. In addition, you may misunderstand accurate reports, fall prey to rumor and hearsay, let emotion color your judgment, and suffer lapses in logic. For these reasons, the ideas you produce need criticism.

Ironically, though you are undoubtedly ready to criticize others' ideas freely, like most people you are probably blind to the need for criticism of your own thinking. There are several reasons for this. First, your ego is inclined against self-criticism. Once you have settled on an idea, you feel a proprietary interest in it. "It is mine," you tell yourself, "so it must be good." And once in that frame of mind, you are ready to defend the idea against all attack, even the attack that your own good judgment might mount against it. The situation is something like that of a dog with a bone. The dog will cling to it tenaciously and growl and snarl when anyone approaches, not because the bone is worth anything (it may long since have been chewed out), but simply because it is the dog's possession.

Another reason you will be reluctant to evaluate your own ideas is that their familiarity makes it difficult to see flaws in them. The longer you work on a problem or an issue, the more accustomed you become to its details. And once your effort yields a solution, you have usually got so close to the problem that it is difficult to distance yourself from it, to step back mentally from your solution and see it objectively.

OVERCOMING OBSTACLES TO CRITICAL THINKING

This blindness toward imperfections in your ideas will make it tempting to approach criticism of your ideas with, at best, mock analysis followed by a vigorous nod of approval. There are two ways you can safeguard against this mistake. The first is to say to yourself, before you begin to take a critical look at any idea, "I know this idea is going to look good to me and that I am going to feel it's pointless to look for flaws. That's natural. I thought of it, so I want it to be perfect. *But I'm going to disregard this reaction and force myself to examine it critically.*"

The second safeguard is to use your ego to advantage. Whenever you find yourself ready to stop evaluating your idea before you really should, reflect for a moment on how it would feel to have a serious flaw pointed out by someone else, particularly by someone you don't much care for. Visualize the situation; imagine yourself squirming with embarrassment and awkwardly offering face-saving excuses. Such a mental picture ought to motivate you to continue evaluating your idea.

APPLYING CURIOSITY

We have seen how curiosity increases awareness of problems and issues, enabling you to feel dissatisfactions and annoyances more consciously and to regard them more productively as challenges and opportunities. We have seen, too, that curiosity keeps your mind dynamic and contributes to the playfulness Einstein regarded as "the essential feature of productive thought." That same curiosity is also a valuable aid to critical thinking.

Perhaps you've had the experience of adding up a column of figures and getting the same answer—the *wrong* answer—again and again. Psychologists have long recognized that when we travel a particular mental route a second or third time, we often follow our earlier footsteps without realizing that we are doing so. That's what happened when you added up those figures. You had the impression that each new total was fresh and independent. In reality, though, you were trapped by your initial miscalculation.

That same kind of mistake can occur when you examine your ideas critically. You can look at an idea again and again and still not see its flaws. To be effective, you need to examine the idea from different perspectives. That's where curiosity comes in. By approaching criticism inquisitively—asking "How will my idea work when it is applied?" and "How will others react to it?"—you will increase your chances of finding the imperfections and complications that need to be addressed.

■
————————————————————

AVOIDING ASSUMPTIONS

To assume is to take something for granted, to expect that things will be a certain way because they have been that way in the past or because you want them to be that way. It's natural to make assumptions. Everyone makes them continually. You assume, for example, that your professor will be in class when class is scheduled, that the cafeteria will not serve lunch two hours early, that your car is safe from vandalism in the college parking lot, that the bank that has always cashed your checks will continue to do so, and that the elevator is really going up when the indicator says it is. Making such assumptions is reasonable, even if on occasion they prove to be incorrect.

Nevertheless, it is important to be careful about what you assume. And when you are evaluating and refining your ideas, you should make a special effort to identify assumptions you may not have detected previously. The reason is not only that unexpected outcomes can cause you embarrassment but also, and more important, that *what you take for granted you will not examine critically.* Assumptions obstruct the evaluation process.

It would be impossible to list all the assumptions it is possible to make. However, the following assumptions occur often enough, and interfere with critical thinking seriously enough, to warrant special mention.

1. *The assumption that others familiar with the problem or issue will share your enthusiasm for your ideas.* Although this might seem to be a reasonable expectation, it seldom is. The more familiar people are with a problem or issue, the more likely they are to have their own ideas.

2. *The assumption that small imperfections in your idea will not affect people's acceptance of it.* When other people's ideas differ from yours, they are likely to magnify flaws in your ideas without even realizing it because, subconsciously, they are looking for an excuse to reject your ideas. Small imperfections may provide that excuse.

3. *The assumption that if your idea is clear to you, it will be clear to others.* If you've ever sat in a classroom and heard a teacher offer an explanation that didn't make the slightest sense to you, you should appreciate the confusion this assumption can cause. *Your* understanding of what you are expressing does not constitute clarity. If you want the solution and its presentation to be clear, you must *construct* it to be so and not just assume that it is.

4. *The assumption that the people who stand to benefit most from your idea will accept it automatically without any persuasion on your part.* This assumption has caused creative people incalculable grief. For example, when Elias Howe invented the sewing machine, he knew it would be a boon to the garment industry by revolutionizing garment construction and making the clothing business much more profitable. He may very well

have assumed that the mere unveiling of his invention would be sufficient to have the leaders of that industry praise it and him. But reality didn't match that assumption. Howe couldn't get a single American firm interested enough to buy the machine. He was forced to go to England to find a favorable reception. To spare yourself disappointment, never assume that the value of your ideas will be universally recognized. Expect to have to persuade other people.

REFINING YOUR SOLUTIONS TO PROBLEMS

Refining your solutions means making good ideas even better—that is, making the results of your creative thinking more effective, more workable, more attractive. Although much of what you will be doing in this stage is finding flaws and complications, the emphasis is not negative but positive. Your aim is to *improve* your ideas.

Not every idea, of course, requires refinement. With the problem of the string that slips out of your sweatpants, for example, there is little or no need for refinement and no need to present the solution for others' approval. Once you have decided on a solution, you can just implement it. Most of the important problems and issues you will encounter, however, are more demanding.

Later chapters will develop the refinement and presentation of ideas more fully. The basic approach that follows will enable you to begin using these steps and developing skill in applying them even while you are studying each in greater depth. The approach consists of asking and answering these four questions.

1. How exactly will your solution be applied? List all steps and all important details.

2. What difficulties could arise in its implementation, and how would these best be overcome?

3. What reasons might others find for opposing this solution? What modifications could you make to overcome their opposition?

4. Who, specifically, will have to be persuaded of the merit of your solution? What kind of presentation would be most likely to persuade them?

A SAMPLE PROBLEM

The following problem was included in Chapter 9's applications.

You are the editor of the college newspaper. Your staff consists of two other people who limit their work to a few hours a week. To get the paper out each week, you've had to spend many more hours than your course load permits. On several occasions, you've stayed up all night and slept through the next morning's classes. You've tried putting ads in the paper to get more staff members, but no one answers them.

Let's say you identified the problem as "How to reward students for joining the staff." (This is one good expression of the problem, though not, of course, the only one.) Let's say further that after investigating the problem and producing a number of possible solutions, you chose *giving college credit to those who work on the paper* as the best one. You'd apply the critical approach as follows.

1. How exactly will your solution be applied?

   Here you'd have to decide and list the requirements for obtaining credit for the work. You'd also have to decide which department would grant credit, how much credit would be granted, and whether it would be elective credit or would fulfill some course requirement.

2. What difficulties could arise in its implementation, and how would these best be overcome?

   The most obvious difficulty would involve course requirements and the evaluation of student performance. Who would teach the course? Where? (In a classroom? In the newspaper office?) How could one, two, or three time periods per week satisfy the demands of producing the paper? How would the instructor evaluate performance? Would the editor have to meet a different standard than a reporter or a layout person? If so, how would the registrar clarify on each student's transcript what standard was met? These and other questions would have to be raised and answered satisfactorily.

3. Why might others resist this solution? What modifications could you make to overcome this resistance?

   Here you'd consider such reasons as the inappropriateness of the new course to any curriculum on campus (if the campus did not offer a journalism major), the lack of journalistic expertise among campus faculty, and the possible course overload the solution would represent for faculty.

4. Whom would you have to persuade of the solution's value? What kind of presentation would be most likely to persuade them?

   You'd surely have to persuade the college administration and the faculty, particularly the faculty of the department you are suggesting should teach the course.

REFINING YOUR POSITIONS ON ISSUES

We noted earlier that though the terms *problem* and *issue* both refer to disagreeable situations that challenge our ingenuity, an issue also tends to divide people into opposing camps, each sure that it is right and the opposition wrong. We noted, too, that whereas the aim of problem solving is to find the best course of action, the aim of issue resolving is to find the most reasonable belief, and so we express problems and issues differently and produce different kinds of ideas for each.

Now we will consider another difference. Your approach to refining your positions on issues is to decide not whether the idea works but whether it meets the tests of logic. Thus you must take the following steps.

1. State your argument. That is, state the belief you have decided to be most reasonable concerning the issue, and give your reasons for so deciding.

2. Examine your evidence for relevance, comprehensiveness, and reliability.

3. Examine your argument for flaws in reasoning—for example, errors of narrow perspective, confusion, or carelessness.

In cases where your aim is solely to form a reasonable belief and not to take any action about it, this approach will constitute refinement of the issue. However, in cases in which you wish not only to establish what belief is most reasonable but also to take action on that belief, you will next answer questions quite similar to those used for refining solutions to problems, questions designed to plan a course of action and then to evaluate it critically. Here are those questions.

What action do you recommend be taken, and how exactly will it be taken? List all steps and important details.

What difficulties could arise in taking this action, and how would they best be overcome?

To see how this approach works, let's consider a sample issue.

■─────────────────────

A SAMPLE ISSUE

Let's say that you are addressing the matter of the United States giving monetary aid to foreign governments that victimize their citizens and deny them their human rights and that you have expressed the main issue as "Is it morally right for the U.S. government to provide such aid?" (Note: In Chapter 8, you addressed the larger issue of which this is a part.) Let's also say that your argument is as follows.

It is morally wrong for the U.S. government to provide monetary aid to foreign governments that victimize their citizens and deny them their human rights because the United States is a democracy and holds that government exists for the good of the people and that the people are "endowed with certain unalienable rights." To support tyranny in this way, while preaching human rights, is hypocritical.

Next, you examine your argument for reasonableness and find only one serious flaw: the unwarranted assumption that giving monetary aid to such countries is *necessarily* supporting tyranny and therefore is hypocritical. On reflection, you decide that if the money actually assists needy people, giving it would represent the lesser of two evils and therefore a moral course of action. You modify your argument, replacing the last sentence with this one: "Giving monetary aid in such circumstances is justifiable only if the people would be worse off without it and no other effective way to help them can be found."

Taking Action on the Issue

Recognizing that your argument is a challenge to find a better approach than giving money to corrupt governments, you proceed with your critical thinking as follows:

What action do you recommend be taken, and how exactly will it be taken?

> Let's say that the action you choose is to give aid in the form of technological education and employment opportunities, with the stipulation that the governments end all victimization of the people. You would then detail the kinds of technological education and employment opportunities you have in mind. You would also decide whether the teachers and employers will be sponsored by our government, by private enterprise, or by a combination of the two. Finally, you'd detail any special employment conditions, including wages and benefits.

What difficulties could arise in taking this action, and how would they best be overcome?

> The most obvious difficulty would be policing the country's government—deciding how to ensure that it would end human rights violations. (This problem could be overcome by having a UN task force monitor the situation.) Another difficulty would be preventing the corrupt officials from using your plan in a manner you do not intend, such as by taking advantage of the new cheap labor for their own financial gain. (This difficulty could be overcome by the establishment of profit-sharing plans and cooperatives so that the people would enjoy the fruits of their labor.)

One final suggestion: If you ever become discouraged about imperfections and complications in your work—if you are inclined to say, "How can I ever be expected to work out all the flaws I discover? It's an impossible task!"—try this approach: Treat each significant imperfection or complication as a miniature problem, first finding the best expression, investigating it if necessary, and generating as many possible solutions as you can. Not every issue warrants such meticulous attention, but the more important ones will. And by using a familiar process to address them, you bolster your confidence, overcome discouragement, and stimulate your imagination.

WARM-UP EXERCISES

10.1 Old dishwashing liquid containers (the plastic ones that Dawn, Joy, and Ivory liquid come in) are usually discarded when empty. But perhaps they could be put to some use. Think of as many uses for them as you can.

10.2 A law student hired a tutor to help him with his law studies. He promised to pay for the tutor's services as soon as he passed his bar exam, set up practice, and won his first case. He subsequently passed the exam and set up practice, but a year passed and he still had not won a case. The tutor grew tired of waiting and sued him for payment. The young lawyer then wrote the tutor a letter and said, "If your suit against me goes to court and I win it, I won't have to pay you. And if I lose it, I still won't have to pay you, because the terms of our agreement (my winning my first case) will not have been met."[2] Do you agree with the young lawyer's reasoning? Explain thoroughly.

10.3 In the following dialogue, Lily admits she is confused. Perhaps Daisy is, too. Clear up the confusion for them.

> DAISY: What is the meaning of life?
>
> LILY: There is no one meaning.
>
> DAISY: There's got to be. Otherwise, everyone makes his or her own, and that would create chaos.
>
> LILY: No, everyone *decides* his or her own. Whatever a person says, that's it.
>
> DAISY: Do you mean if I say the meaning of life is "Eat, drink, and be merry, for tomorrow we die," that *is* the meaning of life?
>
> LILY: Yes, for *you* it is, though maybe not for me.
>
> DAISY: That would mean that no one can be wrong in his or her view. And if that's the case, why is everyone so concerned about finding the meaning of life?
>
> LILY: I don't know. That's always puzzled me.

 APPLICATIONS

10.1 In Application 7.5 you applied your creativity to a question concerning the view of romantic love many people have when they enter marriage (see page 137). Refine your best solution to that application, using the approach explained in this chapter.

10.2 In Application 9.3, you applied your creativity to a question concerning the elderly in this country (see page 178). Refine your best solution, using the approach explained in this chapter.

10.3 Since you graduated from high school, you've been wondering what single improvement could be made in your school system between kindergarten and twelfth grade that would have the best and most lasting impact on students. Now you've come up with the answer: have the students be taught *how to think,* directly and systematically. Now take that idea and refine it.

10.4 You are a Hollywood film producer. You have just been tried in federal court for agreeing to buy five ounces of cocaine. The judge deferred final judgment of your case for a year but put you on probation and offered you this challenge: "If you put your talents to work fighting drug abuse by children, I will wipe your record clean." You feel remorse for your own drug use and resolve to meet the challenge. Identify and solve this problem; then refine your best solution.

10.5 Michael is very excited. He has just got his first job, delivering newspapers in a residential neighborhood. The only problem is that he has to pass several large dogs on his route, and he has been afraid of dogs for as long as he can remember. Identify and solve Michael's problem; then refine your best solution.

10.6 Millions of American adults are functionally illiterate. These people cannot decipher a bus, train, or airline schedule; write a letter; or fill out a job application. Such illiteracy is estimated to cost the United States billions of dollars annually in welfare and unemployment payments. With the federal government decreasing its aid to education, that cost is likely to increase. Apply your creative and critical thinking to this problem as you did in previous applications.

■———————————————

ISSUE FOR EXTENDED ANALYSIS

Following is a more comprehensive thinking challenge than the others in the chapter. Analyze and respond to it, following the instructions for extended analysis at the end of Chapter 1. Also, review "The Basis of Moral Judgment" and "Dealing with Dilemmas" in Chapter 2.

THE ISSUE: RELIGION IN SCHOOLS AND PUBLIC PLACES

Hardly a week goes by without some conflict about religion in schools being reported in the news. Many people believe that there is no reason to bar expressions or symbols of religion from public schools. Many others think such expressions and symbols are unconstitutional. Even the U.S. Supreme Court is divided on the issue, so it is understandable that many other Americans aren't sure what to think.

THE ESSAYS

Welcome Religion in Public Schools
By Bernard Hoffman

It's astounding that the same liberal establishment that is forever chanting odes to multiculturalism, diversity, tolerance, and inclusion is fanatical about banning any hint of religion from the public schools. Any hint of traditional Jewish or Christian religion, that is. (Buddhism, Wicca, and Santeria would probably pass muster.)

Liberals believe it is acceptable for students to dress in the costumes, sample the food, and even perform the various rituals of distant cultures but unacceptable for them to practice their own beliefs. Similarly, that it's fine for students to master the art of putting a condom on a cucumber and to memorize every last position specified in the Kama Sutra but not to learn the biblical perspective on sexuality. There's a word for such folderol: *insanity.*

One argument against the mention of religion in schools is that it is a divisive subject. That's phoney. There are dramatic differences of viewpoint in sociology, psychology, economics, history, and many other subjects, but we don't call those subjects divisive and we don't ban them from the schoolhouse. Besides, as attorney Jay Sekulow points out, federal courts begin the day with the words "God save the United States and this Honorable Court," the Ten Commandments are displayed in U.S. Supreme Court, and the world hasn't ended as a result.

Another argument is that every religion has its own scriptures and no one should be given preference over the others. OK, so don't single out any one—let *all* be represented. Post the

Keep Religion Out of School
By Lisa Stepanowsky

The most sensible position on the issue of religion and public schools is to keep it out. That means no prayers, no Bible readings, no devotions, no after-school religious clubs. Not even a "moment of silence" at the beginning of the day—that is, after all, just religious exercise in disguise. Permitting it is like letting the proverbial camel's nose into the tent—before you know it, the whole camel is in.

Why is this the most sensible position on the issue? First, government and religion don't mix. That is why the Constitution forbids the "establishment" of religion. Second, religion causes dissension. Religious people can't even agree among themselves about who or what God is or the right way to worship. Back in the days when the "Our Father" was still being read in schools, Catholics and Protestants were at war over whose version should be used, and Jews were offended by both versions.

Finally, having religion in the schools is stressful for nonbelieving students. Conservative Christians argue that nonbelievers can simply stand or sit silently while others are praying, but this reasoning is specious. When school authorities permit religious expression, they are in effect endorsing it and leaving nonbelieving students with the uncomfortable choice of denying their consciences or risking the displeasure of school authorities and the rejection of their peers. That rejection can take the form of ostracism, insults, threats, and even bodily injury.

Ten Commandments alongside the Code of Hammurabi and whatever others there are. Display the Hebrew Scriptures, the New Testament, *and* the Koran. Problem solved.

To ask students to leave their religious beliefs at the schoolhouse door is like asking them to leave their minds and hearts there. That is a violation of common sense *and* their constitutional rights.

An atheist pointed out to me recently that even Jesus was against religion in the schools. He cited Matthew 6:5–6, and he was correct. In that passage Jesus tells his disciples not to pray in public but to do so in secret, in the privacy of their homes. Christians would do well to heed Jesus' words and keep their religion to themselves.

CLASS DISCUSSION

ED: It seems to me that students should be encouraged to express their deepest and most important thoughts, including their religious beliefs.

NORMAN: The problem is that students express their religious beliefs in a sectarian way. And the schools have to be *non*sectarian.

ED: When students express their views about UFOs, the Iraq War, the campus dress code, or any other controversial matter, they are being sectarian—that is, *partisan*. So why should they be held to a nonpartisan standard when they speak about religion?

NORMAN: Because religion is about faith rather than reason.

ED: The faith/reason distinction is bogus. Reasoning is involved in matters of faith—theological research depends no less on reasoning than does any other research. By the same token, faith is involved in reason—every act of reasoning involves the assumption that careful, logical thinking makes a difference.

NORMAN: For me, Stepanowsky's reference to Jesus' admonition to pray in secret is the most telling argument against religion in the schools. A related fact is that whenever the Gospels mention Jesus praying, they say he went off by himself. In other words, he opposed public prayer by his words and his personal example.

ED: That Scripture quote was taken out of context. Jesus was just admonishing his followers not to be hypocrites and make a big show of their piety. And the fact that he is described as praying in private tells us nothing about whether he also prayed in public.

11

Refine Your Solution to the Problem

This chapter takes a closer look at the application of critical thinking to *solving problems*. (Issues are treated in Chapter 12.) In this chapter you will learn how to work out the details of your solution, how to find imperfections and complications, and how to improve the solution so that it can withstand other people's criticism.

How might the human voice be carried over distances beyond the normal range of hearing? That was the problem facing Alexander Graham Bell. The solution, as we all know, was the telephone. But how did Bell actually invent it? Most of us probably have the vague notion that once he got his creative idea, he merely retired to his workshop, built a model of the machine, sold it, and became rich and famous. In fact, it wasn't that simple. Although Bell was an expert in sound, he knew virtually nothing about electricity. Before he was able to make his idea a reality, he had to learn all about electricity and then put his knowledge to work and solve the technical problems.

The refinement of solutions to problems does not always demand learning an entirely new field, but it is seldom the easy matter many people assume. As Eliot Hutchinson explains:

> There is nothing trifling, incidental or dilettantish about this business of [refining solutions]. It is work, days and nights of it, months and years of it, the perspiration that is nine-tenths genius. And it tires, discourages, exhausts . . . . The history both of art and of science is largely the history of man's personal endurance, his acceptance of labor as the price of success. To be sure, some men dash off a brilliant piece of work, spread themselves for a time. But 90 percent of reputable authors, no matter how sure their technique, and well-nigh all reputable scientists

revamp their work until what was given in insight is so overlaid with secondary material that it is hardly to be recognized. Elaboration is for the mature only; it is for the rigorous, the exacting, the profound.[1]

■───────────────────────

THREE STEPS IN REFINING

Because refinement can spell the difference between success and failure, you should approach it very seriously. Yet there is no reason to be frightened by the task. It usually requires no special gift or talent. Rather, it is achievable by anyone who is willing to work hard and patiently. Three steps are involved: working out the details of the solution, finding imperfections and complications, and making improvements.

Step 1: Working Out the Details

The first step means determining exactly how your solution will be applied. It's easy to overlook this step or to ignore its significance. After all, most of the things we use every day and take for granted—the concepts, the processes and systems, the products and services—appear to us in refined form. We seldom have occasion even to imagine how they appeared in rough form or to appreciate the difficult challenges their refinement posed for their creators.

Consider the ballpoint pen. It was first conceived of in the United States in 1888 by John Loud. He even obtained a patent for his idea of using a rotating ball to deliver the ink to the paper. Yet he never was able to refine the pen enough to make it write cleanly. In 1919, Laszlo Biro of Hungary reinvented this pen, but he was unable to complete his design and market his idea until 1943—and even then the ink came out in splotches. Finally, Franz Seech of Austria worked out the basic difficulties in 1949 (the key to his pen's performance was fast-drying ink) and marketed his pen successfully. Thus, *61 years* elapsed from conception to refinement.[2]

When William Addis, a prisoner in a British jail, got the idea for the first toothbrush in 1870, he faced a number of challenges to his ingenuity. (In case you didn't know, before 1870 people cleaned their teeth by rubbing them with a rag.) What would be the right size for the invention? What shape would be best? What should it be made of? What kind of bristles would work best? How should they be held together? What could be used to contain the bristles? Addis saved a bone from his supper; bored tiny holes in it; obtained some bristles from his prison guard; cut, tied, and glued them together; and inserted them into the bone. When he was released from prison, he marketed his invention and became a business success.[3]

The refinement of the typewriter posed even greater challenges. How to place the keys, how to arrange the keyboard, how to make the keys strike, how to hold the paper, how to make the carriage move so that the keys wouldn't strike the same place over and over, how to move from line to line without turning the carriage by hand, how to ink the keys—these were just some of the details that had to be worked out. In light of such numerous and complex problems, it is perhaps not surprising that before Christopher Sholes and Samuel Soulé completed their first working model in 1867, *51 other inventors* had tried and failed.[4]

We could cite many other examples of the refinement difficulties facing the originators of most new ideas. The point is that even the most creative idea does not become useful until the details of its application are worked out. The following approach will help you work out the details of your solutions more effectively:

If your solution involves *doing* something (as, for example, in a new process), answer these questions.

- How exactly is it to be done, step-by-step?
- By whom is it to be done?
- When is it to be done? (According to what timetable?)
- Where is it to be done?
- Who will finance it?
- What tools or materials, if any, are to be used?
- From what source will they be obtained?
- How and by whom will they be transported?
- Where will they be stored?
- What special conditions, if any, will be required for the solution to be carried out?

If your solution involves *making* something (as in a new product), answer these questions.

- How will it work? Explain thoroughly.
- What will it look like? Be specific as to size, shape, color, texture, and any other relevant descriptive details.
- What material will it be made of?
- What will the product cost to make?
- Who will pay for it?
- How exactly will it be used?
- Who will use it? When? Where?
- How will it be packaged?
- How will it be delivered?
- How will it be stored?

Step 2: Finding Imperfections and Complications

After you have worked out the details of your solution, your next step is to examine those details for imperfections. Remember that despite the normal tendency to regard your solution as perfect and to view this step as unnecessary, it is almost certain that your solution, like any other, contains at least minor flaws. Remember, too, that your success in persuading others of your solution's value will depend in no small part on your willingness to improve your idea in any way you can.

Until you are experienced in examining solutions critically, the biggest difficulty you are likely to encounter is knowing what kinds of imperfections and complications to look for and how to go about looking for them. The following four approaches will prove helpful both in overcoming that initial difficulty and in ensuring that your analysis will be comprehensive.

1. *Check for common kinds of imperfections.* The following areas are the ones in which imperfections most commonly occur. (Not every one, of course, will apply to every type of solution.) Although the list is not exhaustive, and therefore you should not limit yourself to it, it is an excellent starting point for examining most solutions.

   - *Clarity:* Is the solution difficult to understand?
   - *Safety:* Does the solution create any danger for those who use it or those for whom it is used?
   - *Convenience:* Is the solution awkward to use or implement?
   - *Efficiency:* Does using the solution involve significant delays?
   - *Economy:* Is the solution too costly to build or implement?
   - *Simplicity:* Is the solution unnecessarily complex in design or format?
   - *Comfort:* Is the solution uncomfortable to use?
   - *Durability:* Is the solution likely to break or malfunction?
   - *Beauty:* Will most people find the solution ugly or unappealing?
   - *Compatibility:* Does the solution clash with any other product or process it should harmonize with?

2. *Compare the solution with competing ones.* Examine the existing product or process your solution is designed to replace, or study another proposed solution competitive with yours. Determine how the existing product, process, or competing solution is superior to yours. (Although your solution should be superior in most major respects, it may be inferior in one or two minor respects. Any such area should be considered an imperfection.)

3. *Consider what changes your solution will cause.* Ask yourself what will occur if your solution is implemented. Don't overlook even minor changes. Decide which of them, if any, will cause complications.

4. *Consider the effects your solution will have on people.* Look among the physical, moral, emotional, intellectual, and financial areas of life to see how any would be affected. Be sure to consider even the remote effects that might occur on any person or group. Most of the changes you list will undoubtedly be beneficial. But those that are in any way undesirable will often signal imperfections or complications in your solution.

Step 3: Making Improvements
The third and final step in refining your solution is to make improvements that will eliminate imperfections. Here, classified according to the types of solutions

they are usually associated with, are the kinds of improvements you will find applicable in most situations.

For a new or revised *concept:*

- Change the terminology—make it simpler, easier to remember, more eye-catching.
- Change the way it is explained—use different illustrations, analogies, and so on.
- Change the application—use it in other situations or in different ways.

For a new or revised *process, system,* or *service:*

- Change the way it is done, the step-by-step approach.
- Change who does it.
- Change the place where it is done.
- Change the tools or materials used.
- Change the source from which the tools or materials are obtained.
- Change the place the tools or materials will be stored.
- Change the conditions required.

For a new or modified *product:*

- Change its size, shape, color, texture, and so on.
- Change its composition (the material it is made of).
- Change the way it is used.
- Change who will use it or when or where it will be used.
- Change the way it is packaged or delivered.
- Change the way it is stored.

Whenever you address an imperfection and are trying to think of ways to improve your solution, be sure to consider using the approaches for producing ideas explained in Chapter 9. Specifically, you should consider *forcing uncommon responses, using free association and analogy, looking for unusual combinations,* and *visualizing the possibilities.* Each imperfection and complication is, after all, a miniproblem in itself and will therefore respond to the creative process much as the larger problem did.

Most important, be sure not to settle for the first improvement that occurs to you. Instead, extend your effort to produce ideas, and withhold judgment of any one idea until you have produced a generous number of possibilities.

Occasionally, you will encounter an imperfection that requires you to return to the second stage of the creative process and investigate the matter more deeply—much as Alexander Graham Bell did when he took time out to master the principles of electricity. In extreme cases, you may even find that your solution is too badly flawed to be workable. At such times, you will feel as if all your efforts were wasted. But they will not really have been wasted. *To find out what does not work is an important step toward determining what does.*

TWO SAMPLE PROBLEMS

The First Problem

Now let's apply this approach to some cases and note how it works. The first case concerns Rocco, the manager of the movie theater. His problem was discussed in Application 7.4: "In recent years, a number of competitors have cut into his business, and cable television and video rental stores have reduced the number of moviegoers still further. Rocco desperately needs to get more people to patronize his theater, particularly since he has begun to hear the owners talk of closing it and dismissing him if box office receipts don't improve."

Let's say that after considering several expressions of this problem, you decide that the best is "how to attract moviegoers away from other theaters to Rocco's, and how to attract people who ordinarily don't go to movie theaters." Let's say, further, that after investigating the problem and producing a number of possible solutions, you decide that three ideas, in combination, are the best solution: *to present interesting displays, to provide live entertainment, and to offer discounts to groups.* Here is how you would refine this solution. (Only a few ideas are provided for each point. You would, of course, consider many more in your analysis.)

Step 1: Working Out the Details   To present interesting displays:

- What displays? Arts and crafts, for example.
- Which artists and craftspeople? There would be no restrictions.
- How would Rocco find people to display their work? He could check with area arts-and-crafts councils.
- Where would the displays be set up? In the lobby.
- What supplies would be needed and how would they be provided? Tables, chairs, and display shelves. Each displayer would provide his or her own.

To provide entertainment:

- What entertainment? Amateur or professional musicians, performing individually or in small groups.
- How would Rocco find them? He could advertise on posters in the lobby or check with area high school music teachers or the local musicians' union.
- How would he pay them? He could let them pass the hat for donations from theater patrons or let them put up a sign listing their phone number, so they could get jobs by word of mouth among theater patrons.

To offer discounts to groups:

- Which groups? Senior citizens' organizations, employees of particular businesses in the area, members of a union (any union).
- How would he let people know of this discount? He could highlight the fact in his usual newspaper advertisements.

Steps 2 and 3: Finding and Overcoming Imperfections and Complications To present interesting displays in the lobby:

- *Complication:* Such displays might block the flow of traffic in and out of the theater and thus create problems of inconvenience and possibly violate the safety code.
- *Improvement:* Limit the number of displays, and put them in an out-of-the-way corner. Change them each week.

To provide entertainment:

- *Complication:* The musicians' union might object to members working for no pay.
- *Improvement:* Limit the entertainment to young amateurs (high school students, for example).
- *Complication:* Amateurs might not want to hire out for other jobs, so advertising their skills might not be an incentive.
- *Improvement:* Pay them in free admissions, one week free for every night of playing.

To offer discounts to groups:

- *Imperfection:* Senior citizens might not want to attend at night because they fear street crime.
- *Improvement:* Offer them discounts for matinees.

The Second Problem

We first encountered the second problem in Application 9.6. It was phrased this way: "Going to the hospital for the first time can be a frightening experience, particularly for small children. Think of as many ways as you can to make the children's ward of a hospital a nonthreatening, cheery place."

Let's say your best solution to this problem was a combination of these ideas: *to have the hospital staff dress in colorful outfits, to have children's music playing, and to decorate the lounge appealingly.* Here is how you would refine this solution. (As in the previous case, only a few ideas are provided for each point. You would consider many more in your analysis.)

Step 1: Working Out the Details To have the staff dress in colorful outfits:

- What would the colors be? Would the uniforms have a design on them? They'd be pastel colors and have pictures of animals, clowns, and nursery rhyme characters.
- Who would wear them? Doctors, nurses, aides, secretaries—anyone who worked on the children's ward.
- What kinds of outfits would they be? Lab coats for the doctors, smocks or aprons for the secretaries, nurses, and aides.

To have children's music playing:

- What kind of music? Nursery songs, songs from children's movies, and so on.
- Where would the music be playing? Throughout the children's ward—in rooms, halls, and the lounge.

To decorate the lounge appealingly:

- What decorating ideas would you use? Special furniture and wallpaper.
- What furniture specifically, and what would be special about it? Child-size heavy plastic furniture—chairs, bookcases, a table for games, perhaps a small seesaw. Each piece would be in a bright color and shaped like an animal. For example, a chair could be shaped like a kangaroo, with the seat where the pouch would be.
- What pattern would you have for the wallpaper? Scenes from Mother Goose.

Steps 2 and 3: Finding and Overcoming Imperfections and Complications   To have colorful outfits:

- *Complication:* Doctors would be unlikely to want to dress in, say, a Pluto coat—people on other wards might think them strange when they made their hospital rounds. Nurses and others would undoubtedly object to such an unprofessional outfit, too, even though they'd undoubtedly be sympathetic to the idea of making the ward cheery.
- *Improvement:* Let the *children* have colorful gowns and even colorful sheets instead.

To have children's music playing:

- *Imperfection:* Children's music at the nurses' station might upset the work being done there. And it would also be inappropriate in some rooms—for example, the rooms with very ill children or those who have just returned from surgery.
- *Improvement:* Have the music piped into the rooms of those who want it. Also, have it playing quietly in the lounge.

To decorate the lounge appealingly:

- *Complication:* The cost of such extensive redecorating and refurnishing might be prohibitive.
- *Improvement:* Appeal to a local service organization (Lions, Kiwanis, or Rotary, for example) to donate funds.

All the improvements presented overcome the imperfections and complications they address without creating new difficulties. Naturally, not all the improvements you think of will do this. Many will create greater imperfections and complications than the ones they correct. For this reason, you should exercise care in working out your improvements.

WARM-UP EXERCISES

11.1   The chain letter is usually associated with dishonesty, superstition, and even illegality. (The mailing of money is illegal in many places.) But it could be used constructively and beneficially. Think of as many such ways as you can to use the chain letter, modifying it in whatever ways you wish.

11.2   Suppose that you are looking at a star—say, Sirius—on a dark night. Astronomers tell us that light waves started to travel from Sirius many years ago. After all that time, they reach Earth, strike your retinas, and cause you to say you are seeing Sirius. But the star that existed at the time the rays began their journey may no longer exist. To say that you see what may no longer exist is absurd. Therefore, whatever you see, it is not Sirius.[5] Is this reasoning sound? Explain your thinking thoroughly.

11.3   Oscar and Felix are having a discussion.

OSCAR: I'll prove to you there's no such thing as a pile of sand.

FELIX: That's ridiculous. You can't do it.

OSCAR: Oh, yeah? Listen carefully. A single grain of sand is not a pile, right?

FELIX: Right. So what?

OSCAR: If we add another grain of sand, that's still not a pile, right?

FELIX: OK, OK. Get on with it.

OSCAR: If we add another grain, and another, up to 10 million and beyond, we'd never reach a point where *no pile of sand* is converted to a *pile of sand*. So there's no such thing as a pile of sand.

What should Felix say next to prove Oscar wrong?

APPLICATIONS

11.1   Many experts claim that children from one-parent homes have more problems (including health problems) than children from two-parent homes.[6] Yet one-parent families have increased dramatically over the last few decades. Identify and solve this problem; then refine your best solution as explained in the chapter.

11.2   College athletes are supposed to be amateurs. That is, they are not allowed to receive money for performing their sport. The National

Collegiate Athletic Association (NCAA) publishes a manual governing the way colleges recruit athletes, the academic requirements athletes must meet to remain eligible for play, and the limitations on financial and other assistance they may receive. But college athletics is big business; national rankings bring lucrative television payments to colleges and help finance costly educational programs, so colleges are tempted to ignore the NCAA rules. Some time ago, Notre Dame's basketball coach publicly stated that at least seven colleges, and probably more, paid their star basketball players $10,000 a year under the table.[7] Identify and solve this problem; then refine your best solution as explained in the chapter.

11.3 You are the parent of two children, an 8-year-old daughter and a 6-year-old son. They love to watch television, but you believe that most programs either are a waste of time or promote harmful attitudes and values. Identify and solve this problem; then refine your best solution as explained in the chapter.

11.4 The Federal Communications Act of 1927 established in law that the airways belong to the public. Radio and television station licenses are supposedly granted only if the station's programming practices serve the public interest. Yet the practice of interrupting programs every 10 minutes with commercials that all too often assault the senses and insult the minds of viewers is, in the judgment of most people, decidedly not a service to the public. Identify and solve this problem; then refine your best solution as explained in the chapter.

11.5 Professor Danielle Murphy teaches literature at a small liberal arts college. She begins every term hoping to do little lecturing and to devote the larger part of each class period to class discussion. Yet she is invariably disappointed with the students' response. No matter what the assigned work of literature, only one or two students will volunteer their comments, and discussion quickly fizzles out. The rest of the class sit and stare at their desks or cast nervous glances at the clock. Identify and solve Professor Murphy's problem; then refine your best solution as explained in the chapter.

ISSUE FOR EXTENDED ANALYSIS

Following is a more comprehensive thinking challenge than the others in the chapter. Analyze and respond to it, following the instructions for extended analysis at the end of Chapter 1. Also, review "The Basis of Moral Judgment" and "Dealing with Dilemmas" in Chapter 2.

THE ISSUE: GAY MARRIAGE

In the Western world, marriage has traditionally been defined as a formal, legal bond between a man and a woman entered into primarily for the purpose of begetting and raising children. Over time, as society became less agrarian, children became less of an asset; in addition, birth control has made having children a matter of choice. As a result, many people regard the main purpose of marriage as mutual love. At the same time, the American Psychiatric Association has changed its definition of homosexuality from a "deviant" emotional "disorder" to an acceptable alternative lifestyle. Accordingly, many in the gay community believe the law should allow them to formalize their love in marriage.

THE ESSAYS

Legalize Gay Marriage
By Andrew Rossowsky

For centuries in America, the law forbade interracial marriage. Such a union was considered unnatural and against divine law. Eventually, that law was recognized to be discriminatory and today interracial marriage is common. Closely paralleling this historic issue is the issue of gay marriage; the only difference is that the discrimination against gay couples has yet to be removed from the law.

Some people oppose gay marriage because the Bible views homosexuality unfavorably. But the Old Testament also set dietary regulations that are no longer followed. Similarly, the New Testament encouraged second-class citizenship for women, and that view is now rejected, as is the biblical tolerance of slavery.

In any case, for Christians, the deciding factor has always been the teachings of Jesus, and it is noteworthy that Jesus never spoke against gay marriage.

Happily, a number of religious leaders—including Episcopalians, Jews, Methodists, Presbyterians, Unitarians,

Keep Marriage Heterosexual
By Victor Ortiz

Gay marriage supporters argue that only through marriage can they achieve the same civil rights enjoyed by heterosexual couples. That is simply not true. Legal and financial procedures already exist to cover health care, taxation, and inheritance rights.

Gay marriage supporters often compare the prohibition of gay marriage with the prohibition of interracial marriage, but there is no comparison. Whereas opposition to interracial marriage was rooted in bigotry, opposition to gay marriage is found in the laws of nature—a man and a woman of different races can produce children; two men or two women cannot.

The argument that the government has no right to restrict who can and cannot marry is also mistaken. The government prohibits marriages between first cousins, between an adult and a child, between people already married to others (bigamy), and among three or more people (polygamy).

Many feel the most impressive argument for gay marriage is that it and Baptists—now support gay marriage. Various organizations do, as well, including People for the American Way, the National Organization for Women, the American Psychological Association, and the American Civil Liberties Union (ACLU). James Esseks, a spokesman for the ACLU, put the case for gay marriage succinctly: "Same-sex couples who commit to each other and build a life together shouldn't be treated as legal strangers."

Gay marriage would not force churches to perform marriage services in violation of their doctrines; it would merely grant gay unions *civil recognition* and guarantee to gay couples the same *civil rights* enjoyed by married couples, notably those concerning the adoption and custody of children, health care decisions, medical benefits, and inheritance. In a word, the case for gay marriage centers on the ideal of FAIRNESS.

will permit gays to adopt children. In fact, that argument is the weakest of all. In adoption, the needs of the child should be paramount. And adoption by gay couples is not in the best interests of any child.

Dr. Timothy J. Dailey of the Family Research Council cites evidence that "children raised in traditional families by a mother and father are happier, healthier, and more successful than children raised in nontraditional environments." Moreover, gay households are less likely to provide a wholesome environment because such households have more violence, more substance abuse, more promiscuity, more mental health problems, a greater danger of incest, a higher rate of suicide, and less stability than heterosexual households.

For all these reasons, marriage should remain an exclusive heterosexual legal institution.

CLASS DISCUSSION

KATHLEEN: I'm sure there is research that challenges Dailey's findings, yet Ortiz never mentions it.

BARBARA: I took the time to read Dailey's article, and it analyzes opposing research. Dailey demonstrates that studies purporting to show that same-sex partners parent as well as traditional partners suffer from fatal flaws, including "inadequate sample size, lack of random sampling, lack of anonymity of research participants, and self-presentation bias."

KATHLEEN: Fairness demands that all people be treated equally under the law. Forbidding gay marriage is a moral outrage.

BARBARA: If the laws were to allow gay marriage, they would logically have to allow bigamy and polygamy. And that would have disastrous effects on society.

KATHLEEN: I have no problem with allowing bigamy and polygamy. It is people who marry each other; the state merely witnesses the contract and therefore should have no say in it.

By the way, fundamentalist Christians are not only mistaken in their crusade against gay marriage; they are also at odds with Jesus, who never condemned it.

BARBARA: The fact that Jesus didn't condemn gay marriage proves nothing. Gay marriage was not an issue or even a working concept in his time. He didn't speak of insider trading or copyright infringement either, and for the same reason.

KATHLEEN: If you won't accept gay marriage out of fairness, you should at least do so because it would provide a way for thousands of children to be adopted into good, loving families. After all, gender doesn't make a family—love does. And same-sex couples are as capable of providing love as heterosexual couples are.

BARBARA: Gay adoption is a separate issue that doesn't depend on the acceptance of gay marriage. But since you raise that issue, let me explain why I'm against it. First, men and women bring very different, equally important attributes to child-rearing, so a child needs a father and a mother. Also, as Dailey has documented, homosexual unions have more numerous and more serious problems than heterosexual unions. To put it simply, gay adoption would create more problems than it would solve.

12

Evaluate Your Argument on the Issue

In this chapter you will learn how to identify and overcome errors in reasoning. This is a special step that applies only to issues because resolving issues involves finding the most *reasonable* belief.

Two broad kinds of errors are examined—errors affecting the truth of your ideas and errors affecting the quality of your reasoning. A step-by-step approach to evaluating arguments is also included.

B ecause your main objective in addressing an issue is not to find the most effective action but to determine the most reasonable belief, your main task in refining an issue is to evaluate your argument to be sure that it is free of error. Two broad kinds of error must be considered. The first affects the *truth* of the argument's premises or assertions. The second affects the argument's *validity*— that is, the legitimacy of the reasoning by which the conclusion was reached. A sound argument is both true and valid.

■ ERRORS AFFECTING TRUTH

Errors affecting truth are found by testing the accuracy of the premises and the conclusion as individual statements. The first and most common error in this category is simple factual inaccuracy. If we have investigated the issue properly and have taken care to verify our evidence whenever possible, such errors should not be present. We will therefore limit our consideration to the more subtle and common errors:

- Either/or thinking
- Avoiding the issue
- Overgeneralizing

- Oversimplifying
- Double standard
- Shifting the burden of proof
- Irrational appeal

Either/Or Thinking

This error consists of believing that only two choices are possible in situations in which there are more than two choices. A common example of either/or thinking occurs in the creationism-versus-evolution debate. Both sides are often guilty of the error. "The biblical story of creation and scientific evolution cannot both be right," they say. "It must be either one or the other." They are mistaken. There is a third possibility: that there is a God who created everything but did so through evolution. Whether this position is the best one may, of course, be disputed. But it is an error to ignore its existence.

Either/or thinking undoubtedly occurs because, in controversy, the spotlight is usually on the most obvious positions, those most clearly in conflict. Any other position, especially a subtle one, is ignored. Such thinking is best overcome by conscientiously searching out all possible views before choosing one. If you find either/or thinking in your position on an issue, ask yourself, "Why must it be one view or the other? Why not both or neither?"

Avoiding the Issue

The attorney was just beginning to try the case in court when her associate learned that their key witness had changed his mind about testifying. The associate handed the attorney this note: "Have no case. Abuse the other side." That is the form avoiding the issue often takes: deliberately attacking the person with the opposing view in the hope that the issue itself will be forgotten. It happens with lamentable frequency in politics. The issue being debated may be, for example, a particular proposal for tax reform. One candidate will say, "The reason my opponent supports this proposal is clear: it is a popular position to take. His record is filled with examples of jumping on the bandwagon to gain voter approval." And so on. Of course, what the candidate says may be true of the opponent, and if it is, then it would surely be relevant to the issue of whether the opponent deserves to be elected. But it is not relevant to the issue at hand, the tax reform proposal.

Avoiding the issue may not necessarily be motivated by deceit, as the preceding examples are. It may occur because of unintentional misunderstanding or because of an unconscious slip to something irrelevant. But it is still error, regardless of its innocence. To check your reasoning, look closely at each issue, and ask whether your solution really responds to it. If it doesn't, make it do so.

Overgeneralizing

Overgeneralizing means taking a valid idea and extending it beyond the limits of reasonableness. Here are some examples.

- Women who have abortions are poor and unmarried.
- Politicians are corrupt.

- Conservative Christians are intolerant.
- Men have trouble expressing their feelings.

Each of these statements could be true at times. That is, we could find examples of poor, unmarried women who have had abortions; corrupt politicians; and so on. Yet, in each case, we could also find examples that do not fit the assertion. That is what makes these statements overgeneralizations. (The fact that your overgeneralizations do not take the most extreme form—stereotypes, which we discussed in Chapter 3—should not make you complacent about correcting them. They still mar your arguments, usually significantly.)

To find overgeneralizations in your arguments, be alert to any idea in which *all* or *none* is stated or *implied*. (That is the case in each of the preceding four examples.) Occasionally, you will find a situation in which *all* or *none* is justified, but in the great majority of cases, critical evaluation will show that it is not. To correct overgeneralizations, decide what level of generalization is appropriate, and modify your statement accordingly. For example, in the four cases discussed, you would consider these possibilities:

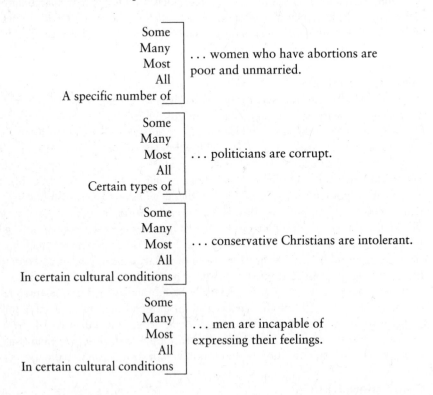

Some
Many
Most
All
A specific number of
   . . . women who have abortions are poor and unmarried.

Some
Many
Most
All
Certain types of
   . . . politicians are corrupt.

Some
Many
Most
All
In certain cultural conditions
   . . . conservative Christians are intolerant.

Some
Many
Most
All
In certain cultural conditions
   . . . men are incapable of expressing their feelings.

Oversimplifying

There is nothing wrong with simplifying a complex reality to understand it better or to communicate it more clearly to others. Teachers simplify all the time, especially in grade school. Simplification is only a problem when it goes too far: when it goes beyond making complex matters clear and begins to distort them. At that point, it ceases to represent reality and misrepresents it. Such oversimplification is often found in reasoning about causes and effects. Here are three examples of this error.

- The cause of the economic recession in the early 1980s was excessive welfare spending.
- The American Nazi Party has a beneficial effect on the intellectual life of the country. It reminds people of the constitutional rights of free speech and assembly.
- A return to public executions, shown on prime-time television, would make crime less glamorous and thus, in time, make us a less brutal, more civilized society.

These statements contain an element of truth (many authorities would say a very small element). Yet they do not fairly or accurately represent the reality described. They focus on one cause or effect as if it were the only one. In fact, there are others, some of them significant.

To find oversimplifications in your arguments, ask what important aspects of the issue your statements ignore. To correct oversimplifications, decide what expression of the matter best reflects the reality without distorting it.

Double Standard

Applying a double standard means judging the same action or point of view differently depending on who performs the action or holds the point of view. It can often be recognized by the use of sharply contrasting terms of description or classification. Thus we may attack a government assistance program as a welfare handout if the money goes to people we don't know or don't identify with but defend it as a necessary subsidy if it goes to our friends. Similarly, if one country crosses another's border with a military force, we may approve the action as a "securing of borders" or condemn it as "naked aggression," depending on our feelings toward the countries involved.

Be careful not to confuse the double standard with the legitimate judgment of cases according to their circumstances. It is never an error to acknowledge real differences. Accordingly, if you find you have judged a particular case differently from other cases of the same kind, look closely at the circumstances. If they warrant different judgments, you have not been guilty of applying a double standard. However, if they do not warrant different judgments—if your reasoning shows partiality toward one side—you have committed the error and should revise your judgment to make it fair.

Shifting the Burden of Proof

This error consists of making an assertion and then demanding that the opposition prove it false. This is an unreasonable demand. The person making the assertion has the burden of supporting it. Though the opposing side may accept the challenge of disproving it, it has no obligation to do so. Suppose, for example, you said to a friend, "Mermaids must exist," your friend disputed you, and you responded, "Unless you can disprove their existence, I am justified in believing in them." You have shifted the burden of proof. Having made the assertion about mermaids, you have the obligation to support it. To overcome this error in your arguments, identify all the assertions you have made but not supported, and provide adequate support for them. If you find you cannot support an assertion, withdraw it.

Irrational Appeal

This error bases your position on an appeal that is unreasonable. The most common forms of irrational appeal are the appeal to *common practice* ("Everyone does it"), the appeal to *tradition* ("We mustn't change what is long established"), the appeal to *fear* ("Awful things could happen"), the appeal to *moderation* ("Let's not offend anyone"), and the appeal to *authority* ("We have no business questioning the experts"). Of course, there is nothing necessarily wrong with defending common practice or tradition, warning about dangers, urging moderation, or supporting the views of experts. It is only when these appeals are used as *a substitute* for careful reasoning—when they aim at an audience's emotions rather than their minds—that they are misused. To correct irrational appeals, refocus your argument on the specific merits of your ideas.

ERRORS AFFECTING VALIDITY

Errors affecting validity do not occur within any individual premise or within the conclusion. They occur instead in the reasoning by which the conclusion is drawn from the premises. Therefore, to determine whether an argument is valid or invalid, we must examine the relationship between the premises and the conclusion. The logical principles governing validity are the substance of *formal logic*, the area of logic concerned with the various forms of argument. Since a detailed treatment of formal logic is beyond the scope of this book,* we will focus on an essential error that commonly occurs in controversial issues: the *illegitimate conclusion*.

An illegitimate conclusion is one that does not follow logically from the premises preceding it. Before examining an illegitimate conclusion, let's first look at a *legitimate* one.

> Anything that shortens people's attention span harms their concentration. Television commercials shorten people's attention span. Therefore, television commercials harm people's concentration.

---

*For a brief introduction to the basic principles of formal logic, see the appendix, "The Fundamentals of Logic."

This conclusion is legitimate because if anything that shortens people's attention span harms concentration, and if television commercials do shorten that span, they therefore must harm people's concentration. Commercials, after all, are a thing, so they fit in the *anything* specified in the first premise. When we are checking for the validity of the reasoning, remember, we are not checking for the truth of the premises or conclusion. That concern is a separate matter. Thus even a ludicrous argument could be technically valid. Here is an example.

> Anything that gives people indigestion harms their concentration. Television commercials give people indigestion. Therefore, television commercials harm people's concentration.

> Let's now look at some *illegitimate* conclusions and see what makes them so.

> All people who take courses significantly above their level of competency will surely fail. Samantha is taking a course well within her level of competency. Therefore, Samantha will surely pass.

Even if it were true that all people who take courses well above their competency level necessarily fail, this would not eliminate the possibility of other reasons for failure, reasons that apply to the competent as well as the incompetent. In other words, the first premise does not imply that *only* the incompetent will fail. Samantha may be extraordinarily proficient and still fail because she cuts classes and does not submit the required work.

Here is another example of an illegitimate conclusion.

> People who care about the environment will support the clean air bill now before Congress. Senator Boychik supports the clean air bill. Therefore, Senator Boychik cares about the environment.

The first premise of this argument says that people—all people**—who care about the environment will support the bill. However, it does not say that no one else will support the bill. Thus it leaves open the possibility that some who do not care will support it, perhaps for political reasons. Which group Boychik belongs to is unclear. Therefore, the conclusion is illegitimate.

Illegitimate conclusions also occur in hypothetical (if-then) reasoning. Of course, not all hypothetical reasoning is faulty. Here is an example of a *valid* hypothetical argument:

> *If* a person uses a gun in the commission of a crime, *then* he should be given an additional penalty. Simon used a gun in the commission of a crime. *Therefore,* Simon should be given an additional penalty.

**Though the premise says *people*, rather than *all people*, the sense of *all* is clearly conveyed. Usually, when no qualifying word or phrase—such as *some, many, the citizens of Peoria*—is present, we presume that the universal *all* is intended.

The first premise sets forth the conditions under which the additional penalty should be applied. The second presents a case that fits those conditions. The conclusion that the penalty should apply in that case is legitimate.

Here, in contrast, is an *illegitimate* conclusion.

> *If* a person uses a gun in the commission of a crime, *then* he should be given an additional penalty. Simon was given an additional penalty for his crime. *Therefore*, Simon used a gun in the commission of the crime.

Here the first premise sets forth one condition for an additional penalty. It does not exclude the possibility of *other* conditions carrying additional penalties. For this reason, we have no way of knowing whether Simon's additional penalty was for using a gun or for some other reason.

The following is another example of an *illegitimate* conclusion.

> *If* a person has great wealth, *then* he can get elected. Governor Mindless got elected. Therefore, Governor Mindless has great wealth.

The first premise of this argument specifies one way of getting elected. There may be others, including endorsements from influential groups and skill in telling people what they want to hear. Did Governor Mindless get elected in this or in some other way? We can't be sure from the information given, so the conclusion is illegitimate.

Occasionally, an illegitimate conclusion in hypothetical arguments takes a slightly different form: the reversal of conditions. The following argument illustrates this.

> *If* the death penalty is reinstated, *then* the crime rate will drop. *Therefore*, if the rate of crime is reduced, the death penalty will be reinstated.

The error here is reversing what is not necessarily reversible. The clear implication in the first premise is that there is a cause-and-effect relationship between the reinstatement of the death penalty and a drop in the crime rate. To reverse that relationship makes the effect the cause, and vice versa. Such a reversal does not logically follow.

A SPECIAL PROBLEM: THE HIDDEN PREMISE

The expression of an argument in ordinary discussion or writing is not always as precise as our examples. The sentence order may vary; the conclusion, for example, may come first. In place of the word *therefore*, a variety of signal words may be used. *So* and *it follows that* are two common substitutes. Sometimes, no signal word is used. These variations make the evaluation of an argument a little more time-consuming, but they pose no real difficulty. There is, however, a variation that can cause real difficulty: the *hidden premise*. A hidden premise is a premise implied but not stated. Here is an example of an argument with a hidden premise. (Such an argument is known in logic as an enthymeme.)

Argument with Premise Hidden	Same Argument, Premise Expressed
Liberty means responsibility.	Liberty means responsibility.
That is why most men dread it.	Most men dread responsibility.
	Therefore, most men dread liberty.

There is nothing necessarily wrong with having a hidden premise. It is not an error. In the preceding case, the hidden-premise argument is from the writing of George Bernard Shaw. In either of the forms shown, the argument is perfectly valid. The only problem with hidden premises is that they obscure the reasoning behind the argument and make evaluation difficult. Accordingly, whenever a premise is hidden, it should be identified and expressed before the argument is evaluated.

Here are several more examples of hidden-premise arguments. Note how much easier it is to grasp the reasoning when the hidden premise is expressed.

Premise Hidden	Premise Expressed
Prostitution is immoral, so it should be illegal.	Everything immoral should be illegal. Prostitution is immoral. Therefore, it should be illegal.
Newspapers are a threat to democracy because they have too much power.	All agencies that have too much power are a threat to democracy. Newspapers have too much power. Therefore, newspapers are a threat to democracy.
If Brewster Bland is a good family man, he'll make a good senator.	If a person is a good family man, he'll make a good senator. Brewster Bland is a good family man. Therefore, Brewster Bland will make a good senator.
AIDS is a costly and, at this time, terminal disease. Therefore, health insurance companies should be able to suspend coverage when people contract AIDS.	Insurance companies should not have to provide coverage for costly terminal diseases. AIDS is a costly and, at this time, terminal disease. Therefore, health insurance companies should be able to suspend coverage when people contract AIDS.
Many celebrities believe that a 35,000-year-old spirit entity known as Ramtha speaks through channeler J. Z. Knight. Therefore, this belief is worthy of respect.	If many celebrities believe something, it is by that fact worthy of respect. Many celebrities believe that a 35,000-year-old spirit entity known as Ramtha speaks through channeler J. Z. Knight. Therefore, this belief is worthy of respect.

RECOGNIZING COMPLEX ARGUMENTS

Not all arguments can be expressed in two premises and one conclusion. Many are complex, involving a network of premises and conclusions. Moreover, some of these premises and conclusions may, like the hidden premises we have discussed, be unexpressed. Consider, for example, this argument.

> The communications and entertainment media have more influence on young people than parents and teachers do, so the media are more responsible for teenage pregnancy, drug and alcohol abuse, violence, and academic deficiency.

At first glance, only one premise may seem to be missing from this argument. Actually, it is a complex argument, and more is missing. Here is how it would be expressed if nothing were omitted.

> The agency that has the greatest influence on young people's attitudes and values bears the greatest responsibility for the behavior caused by those attitudes and values. Although parents and teachers used to have the greatest influence on young people's attitudes and values, the media now have a greater influence. In addition, the messages disseminated by the media generally oppose the lessons of home and school. Typical media messages—that each person creates his or her own morality, that self is more important than others, that restraint of one's urges is harmful, and that feelings are a more reliable guide than thought—tend to lead to impulsiveness and the demand for instant gratification and to create or aggravate such problems as teenage pregnancy, drug and alcohol abuse, violence, and academic deficiency. Therefore, the communications and entertainment media bear the greatest responsibility for these problems.

Here are two more examples of complex arguments. In each case, the argument is first expressed in the abbreviated form often used in everyday conversation and then in its complete logical form.

1. *Abbreviated:* The government wastes billions of tax dollars, so I'm not obligated to report all my income.
   Complete: The government wastes billions of tax dollars. Wasting tax dollars increases every individual's tax burden unnecessarily. I am a taxpayer, so the government is increasing my tax burden unnecessarily. Furthermore, when the government increases the taxpayers' tax burden unnecessarily, the taxpayers are not obligated to report all their income. Therefore, I'm not obligated to report all my income.

2. *Abbreviated:* People who lack control over their sexual urges are a threat to society, so homosexuals should be banned from the teaching profession.
   Complete: People who lack control over their sexual urges are a threat to society. Homosexuals lack control over their sexual urges. Therefore,

homosexuals are a threat to society. Furthermore, people who are a threat to society should be banned from the teaching profession. Therefore, homosexuals should be banned from the teaching profession.

Recognizing that an argument is complex and, where necessary, expressing it more completely is a necessary step in argument analysis. But such recognition and expression do not complete the analysis. In other words, in each of our three examples, we now know what the complete argument is, but we do not yet know whether it is sound—that is, whether its premises are true and the reasoning from premises to conclusion is valid.

STEPS IN EVALUATING AN ARGUMENT

The following four steps are an efficient way to apply what you learned in this chapter—in other words, to evaluate your argument and overcome any errors in validity or truth that it may contain.

1. State your argument fully, as clearly as you can. Be sure to identify any hidden premises and, if the argument is complex, to express all parts of it.

2. Examine each part of your argument for errors affecting truth. (To be sure this examination is not perfunctory, play devil's advocate and *challenge* the argument, asking pointed questions about it, taking nothing for granted.) Note any instances of either/or thinking, avoiding the issue, overgeneralizing, oversimplifying, double standard, shifting the burden of proof, or irrational appeal. In addition, check to be sure that the argument reflects the pro and con arguments and is relevant to the scenarios you produced earlier. (See Chapter 9.)

3. Examine your argument for validity errors; that is, consider the reasoning that links conclusions to premises. Determine whether your conclusion is legitimate or illegitimate.

4. If you find one or more errors, revise your argument to eliminate them. The changes you will have to make in your argument will depend on the kinds of errors you find. Sometimes, only minor revision is called for—the adding of a simple qualification, for example, or the substitution of a rational appeal for an irrational one. Occasionally, however, the change required is more dramatic. You may, for example, find your argument so flawed that the only appropriate action is to abandon it altogether and embrace a different argument. On those occasions, you may be tempted to *pretend* your argument is sound and hope no one will notice the errors. Resist that hope. It is foolish as well as dishonest to invest time in refining a view that you know is unsound.

To illustrate how you would follow these steps, we will now examine two issues.

THE CASE OF PARENTS PROTESTING TV PROGRAMS

You have read a number of articles lately about protests over television commercials and programming. The protesters are mostly parents of school-aged children. They have spoken out either individually or through organizations they belong to, expressing concern that the values taught by school and home are being undermined by television. Specific complaints include the emphasis on sex and violence in television programming, the appeal to self-indulgence and instant gratification in commercials, and the promotion of "if it feels good, do it" in both programming and commercials. The protestors are urging concerned citizens to write to the companies that sponsor programs and threaten to boycott their products unless these offenses are eliminated.

Let's say you identify the main issue here as "Are parents justified in making such demands on companies?" After considering the matter and producing a number of ideas, you decide that the best answer is "No, they are not justified" and state your argument as follows:

> Only those who pay for television programming and advertisements are entitled to have a say about them. The companies alone pay. Therefore, the companies alone are entitled to have a say.

You examine your argument for validity errors and find that it contains none. Then you examine it for errors of truth or relevance. Playing devil's advocate, you ask, "*Do* the companies alone pay?" "How exactly is payment handled?" Not being sure, you ask a professor of business and learn that the sponsorship of television programs and other advertising are part of the overall product budget. You also learn that these costs, along with other costs of raw materials, manufacturing, packaging, warehousing, and delivery, are reflected in the price of the product.

"Wait a minute," you reason. "If programming and other advertising costs are reflected in the price of the product, that means consumers are paying for every television show and every commercial. And if that's the case, parents (and other consumers) *are* entitled to have a say, make demands, and threaten boycotts." And so you revise your argument accordingly:

> Those who pay for television programming and commercials are entitled to have a say about them. Consumers pay. Therefore, consumers are entitled to have a say.[†]

In elaborating this argument you would, of course, address the important questions that flow from it, including this one: What guidelines does fairness suggest consumers follow in making such requests? Your answers to this and related questions should also be evaluated for reasonableness.

[†]Such a formal, logical ($a + b = c$) statement of your argument is essential when you are evaluating your reasoning. However, it is seldom appropriate for a central-idea statement in a piece of writing. In this case, your central-idea statement might be "Because consumers pay for television programming and commercials, they are entitled to make demands and threaten boycotts."

THE CASE OF THE MENTALLY IMPAIRED GIRLS

This case is one we encountered earlier, in Application 2.6c. The parents of three girls with severe mental impairments, you may remember, brought court action seeking the legal right to make the decision to sterilize the girls. The larger issue here continues to be controversial. Let's say you express it as follows: "Should anyone have the right to make such a significant decision for another person?" After investigating the issue and producing a number of ideas, including the major pro and con arguments and several relevant scenarios, you state your argument thus:

> Those who have the child's interest at heart can be expected to judge wisely if they are properly informed. Most parents or guardians have the child's interest at heart. Therefore, most parents or guardians can be expected to judge wisely if they are properly informed. Furthermore, knowing whether the child will ever be able to meet the responsibilities of parenthood constitutes being properly informed. A qualified doctor can tell parents or guardians whether the child will ever be able to meet the responsibilities of parenthood. Therefore, a qualified doctor can properly inform parents.

You examine your argument (a complex one that cannot be expressed adequately in two premises and a conclusion) and decide that though it is valid and essentially true, it raises a serious question that should not be ignored. That question is "Would such a system provide sufficient protection for the child?" You address it by imagining a variety of situations that might easily arise, notably the following ones:

1. The parents are obsessed with the fear that their child will bring shame on them. They pressure the doctor to certify that their child will never be able to fulfill parental responsibilities even though that is not really the case. The doctor, though qualified to make an appropriate diagnosis, is unscrupulous and therefore willing to certify anything for a fee.

2. The parents are responsible and the doctor is not only qualified but above reproach morally. The decision is made to sterilize the child at age four. Several years later, medical science finds a way to overcome the child's mental impairment. The child becomes normal, but the sterilization cannot be reversed.

To prevent the first situation from occurring, you revise your argument to specify that certification be made by a board of physicians rather than a single physician. You might also decide the composition of the board. (All surgeons? One or more psychologists? An authority on mental retardation?) Unfortunately, there is no way to ensure that the second situation will not occur, but you decide there is a way to lessen the risk considerably. To that end you add to your argument the stipulation that no sterilization should be permitted before the onset of puberty.

Both this case and the case of parents protesting TV programming are offered to illustrate the *process* of evaluating your positions on issues rather than to promote the arguments contained in them. What is important is not that you agree with these arguments but that you recognize the value of evaluating your own.

WARM-UP EXERCISES

12.1 Willy Joe and Joe Willy are having a conversation of sorts:

WILLY JOE: There's no such thing as reality, man.

JOE WILLY: No way . . . like, I mean . . . it makes no sense that way. No, there's no way.

WILLY JOE: ÒK, man, you say there's a reality. So describe it to me.

JOE WILLY: Um . . . ah . . . uh . . .

WILLY JOE: You can't describe it, so it can't exist. Case closed.

How would you answer Willy Joe? Explain your thinking carefully.

12.2 One thing, at least, is indisputable about rock music: it produces groups with very creative names. But perhaps you can do even better. Think of as many creative names as you can for a rock group, names you've never heard before.

12.3 In Strangeville it was decided that the local barber should shave all those, and only those, who did not shave themselves. Did the barber shave himself? Explain your thinking thoroughly.

APPLICATIONS

12.1 Evaluate the three arguments presented in the section of this chapter entitled "Recognizing Complex Arguments"—that is, the arguments about media influence on young people, reporting income for tax purposes, and homosexuals in education. Decide whether each argument is sound, and explain your judgment.

12.2 Check each of the following arguments to be sure that it contains no hidden premises and, if it is a complex argument, that all parts are expressed. Revise each, as necessary, to make the expression complete. Then evaluate the argument and decide whether it is sound. Explain your judgment.

a. Having great wealth is a worthy goal because it is difficult to attain and many famous people have pursued it.

b. Low grades on a college transcript are a handicap in the job market, so teachers who grade harshly are doing students a disservice.

c. The Bible can't be relevant to today's problems; it was written many centuries ago and is filled with archaic phrasing.

d. It is dishonest to pretend to have knowledge one does not have, so plagiarism is more virtue than vice.

e. The credit card habit promotes careless spending, particularly among young people. Therefore, credit card companies should not be permitted to issue credit cards to anyone under age 21.

f. No one who ever attended this college achieved distinction after graduation. Marvin attends this college. Therefore, Marvin will not achieve distinction after graduation.

g. Drug dealing should not be a crime because it does not directly harm others or force them to harm themselves.

h. A mature person is self-directing, so parents who make all their children's decisions for them are doing their offspring a disservice.

i. There's no point in attending Professor Drone's class; all he does is lecture in a boring monotone.

j. Power must be evil because it can corrupt people.

k. If the theory of evolution is true, as scientific evidence overwhelmingly suggests, a human being is nothing more than an ape.

l. Rock musicians are contributing to the decline of language by singing in a slurred, mumbling manner.

m. If emphasis on error paralyzes effort, this college is paying my English professor to make it impossible for me to learn English.

n. Nuclear power is a threat to world peace. Nuclear energy stations generate nuclear power. So nuclear energy stations are a threat to world peace.

o. Lew Fairman is the best candidate for governor because he is in favor of the death penalty.

p. All religious authorities are concerned about the dangers of nuclear war. All politicians are concerned about the dangers of nuclear war. Therefore, all politicians are religious authorities.

q. The government should undertake a comprehensive censorship program because censorship eliminates undesirable books and films from the market.

r. If the Social Security system is further weakened, the elderly will have to fear poverty. Therefore, if the Social Security system is not further weakened, the elderly will not have to fear poverty.

s. Challenging other people's opinions is a sign of intolerance, so debating courses have no place on a college campus.

    t. It's ridiculous to think that there will be fewer deaths if we ban handguns. Handguns don't kill people; *people* kill people.

    u. The antiabortionists say that the fetus is human, but they have not proved it. Therefore, they have no reasonable basis for opposing abortion.

    v. We must either defeat communism or be defeated by it. To be defeated by communism is unthinkable. Therefore, we must defeat communism.

    w. There is no way that anyone can ever deserve to live better than her or his neighbors, so capitalism is an immoral economic system.

    x. If an expectant mother drinks, smokes, takes drugs, or fails to get proper rest, she may damage her unborn child. Therefore, if an expectant mother does these things and her child is born with a defect or ailment that can be traced to them, the mother should face criminal charges.

    y. Custom is a form of folk wisdom. In some parts of the world, it is customary for "bride buyers" to buy (or sometimes kidnap) young women from their parents and sell them to men looking for wives. Even though we might find this practice distasteful, it would be morally wrong for us to object to others' practicing it.

12.3 Identify, investigate (as necessary), and resolve each of the following issues. Be sure you do not just accept your reasoning uncritically. Evaluate it by using the approach explained on page 219. Then modify your argument as necessary and decide how you could most effectively demonstrate its soundness.

    a. Radar detectors give speeders a warning so that they can slow down in time to avoid getting a ticket. Some people believe the detectors should be banned because they help people break the law. Others disagree, arguing that they should be able to protect themselves from the sneaky practices of highway patrols.

    b. One proposal for combating the drug problem is government seizure of the property (cars, homes, etc.) of convicted drug dealers. One objection to this proposal is that such seizure could violate the rights of innocent parties, such as spouses and children.

    c. Since smoking is not permitted at one's desk in many companies, significant time is presumably lost in unauthorized smoking breaks in restrooms or outside of buildings. A company could save itself that time, and the money it represents, by establishing a policy of hiring only nonsmokers. Predictably, of course, some people would consider such a policy discriminatory.

ISSUE FOR EXTENDED ANALYSIS

Following is a more comprehensive thinking challenge than the others in the chapter. Analyze and respond to it, following the instructions for extended analysis at the end of Chapter 1. Also, review "The Basis of Moral Judgment" and "Dealing with Dilemmas" in Chapter 2.

THE ISSUE: RACIAL/ETHNIC PROFILING

Racial/ethnic profiling operates on the premise that statistical analysis can identify, with considerable accuracy, individuals that are more likely than others to engage in criminal behavior. The controversy centers on whether that premise is true or false. Proponents say it is true; opponents say it is false and therefore that such profiling amounts to little more than stereotyping.

THE ESSAYS

Racial Profiling Is an Outrage
By Brian Costello

However well most white people understand racial profiling as an abstract category, they haven't a clue about racial profiling as a concrete reality. Consider these brief but typical scenarios.

- It's Saturday morning and a black executive dons a sweatsuit and drives off to the gym in his Lexus. A mile later he is stopped by a white policeman, who asks to see his license and the car's registration and then radios in to see if the vehicle has been stolen. (African-Americans refer to this "offense" as DWB: driving while black.)
- A 25-year-old Latino college student dressed in jeans and a leather jacket is walking to campus when he is stopped by detectives and "frisked." When they find nothing incriminating in his possession, they say, "We know you're dealing in drugs, and we'll be watching you."

Politically Correct Nonsense
By Joshua Levy

Some years ago in the Southwest, the FBI were in pursuit of a serial killer described by one near-victim as a short Hispanic male in his late twenties or early thirties. When an FBI spokesperson mentioned this description at a news conference, a reporter asked, "What would you say to Hispanics who take offense at your racial profiling?" The FBI agent, who happened to be black, gave the reporter a withering look and responded, "I'd say we're following the description we were given." Soon thereafter, the serial killer was found, and, not surprisingly, he fit that description.

That incident reveals how ridiculous all the politically correct blather about racial profiling really is. If a killer is described as Hispanic, should the police include black, white, and Asian males *and even females* in their search? Political correctness says yes; common sense says no.

Political correctness is also at work in airport security. In order to

• While shopping in a department store, two black teenagers are watched closely by the salespeople. As they pass from the cosmetics department to housewares and then to clothing, the teens are "stalked" by new observers. Clearly they are suspected of being shoplifters.

These situations, and their many variations, show racial profiling for what it really is—active discrimination against members of one race, culture, or ethnic group. Such profiling is rooted in negative stereotypes. In the first example, "black people are lower class and shouldn't be driving expensive cars"; in the second, "all Latinos are drug merchants"; and in the third, "black young people are more likely than whites to engage in shoplifting."

In America, we are supposed to be judged by our actions, not by the color of our skin or the style of our clothing, and certainly not by someone's delusion about our inherent badness. Racial profiling makes a mockery of this standard. It is un-American and should be abolished.

avoid offending the sensibility of people of Middle Eastern origin, random selection is used. For example, every tenth person passing through security is subjected to special screening. The people so selected may include elderly Americans and small children; meanwhile, a dozen Saudis and Iraqis and Palestinians will be allowed to pass without special screening.

Is it possible to misuse racial and ethnic profiling? Of course. But the solution to that problem is to punish misuse, not to abolish profiling. The latter response, which all too many people advocate, is an absurd overreaction that compromises both the ability of the police agencies to maintain law and order and the ability of security agencies to keep our nation secure.

Properly used, racial profiling is an invaluable tool for law enforcement and other security uses.

CLASS DISCUSSION

REBECCA: Singling out people for suspicion just because they belong to a certain race or ethnic group is abhorrent.

NIGEL: What about situations like the ones described by Joshua Levy—situations in which the police have been given a description of a suspect? Is it wrong to limit their search to people who fit the description?

REBECCA: I suppose that wouldn't be wrong.

NIGEL: What would you say about situations in which specific descriptions are unavailable but statistical probability is high. For example, if a certain highway corridor is known to be a drug transport route and Hispanic gang members are known to be involved in the transport, would you

approve stops and searches of vehicles driven by
Hispanics?

REBECCA: I'd need to know more about the basis of the statistics.
Consider this possibility: a variety of people have been
involved in past trafficking, including blacks, whites, Asians,
and Hispanics, but only Hispanics have been searched. In
that case, the statistics would erroneously point only to
Hispanics. My point is that statistics are sometimes biased
and therefore an unacceptable basis of profiling.

NIGEL: That's an interesting but highly unlikely scenario.

REBECCA: You have no way of knowing that. Take, for example,
the statistical fact that a disproportionately large number
of prison inmates in this country are African-American.
That *could* mean that a higher percentage of African-
Americans are criminals. But it could just as easily mean
that the police are prejudiced against African-Americans
and therefore are more eager to arrest and prosecute
them. Unless we can be sure which is the case, we should
avoid using statistics as a basis for profiling.

NIGEL: I'm sure the people who use the statistics take such matters into consideration and use only valid statistics.

REBECCA: Sounds a lot like wishful thinking to me.

13

Refine Your Resolution of the Issue

Chapter 11 demonstrated how critical thinking is used to refine the solution to a problem. This chapter makes a similar demonstration with issues. You will learn how to decide what action should be taken about your resolution of the issue and how to recognize and overcome whatever difficulties may arise.

Not all issues require the treatment described in this chapter. In many cases, your analysis of an issue will be complete when you evaluate your argument on the issue and, if necessary, revise it to overcome deficiencies. For example, the issue may concern whether General Dwight Eisenhower, as supreme commander of the Allied Forces in Europe during World War II, made a tactical error in waiting for the Soviet Army before advancing into Berlin. Once you have found the answer that is most reasonable in light of the evidence, nothing more need be done.

On the other hand, in many other cases, you will not be content with deciding what belief is most reasonable; you will wish to consider what action should be taken on that belief. If you were to decide, for example, that television programming and commercials have a seriously negative effect on young people's intellectual development, you would probably consider what should be done to eliminate or counteract that effect. And if you came to believe that handgun control would significantly reduce the number of lives lost in accidents, you might devise a plan to get tougher handgun legislation passed in Congress.

This chapter concerns the latter kinds of cases, those in which your positions on the issues prompt you to recommend further action. In such cases, you must decide what exactly should be done, what difficulties might arise in doing it, and how those difficulties could best be overcome, in much the same manner as you would proceed in refining your solutions to problems. To appreciate the importance of these decisions, you need only reflect on the fact that an ill-considered plan of implementation can make even the most reasonable belief appear deficient.

STEP 1: DECIDING WHAT ACTION SHOULD BE TAKEN

This step consists of asking and answering appropriate questions. Though not all of the following questions will apply in every case, most of them will apply in the majority of cases.

- What exactly is to be done?
- How is it to be done? If, for example, it is to be done in stages, specify the stages. If a special procedure is needed, detail that procedure.
- By whom is it to be done?
- Will those doing it volunteer for the job or be assigned to it? If the latter, how will the assignment be accomplished?
- Will these individuals need to be trained? If so, what will the training consist of? How, when, and by whom will the training be given?
- When is the action to take place? According to what timetable?
- How will this action be financed? Publicized?

STEP 2: RECOGNIZING AND OVERCOMING DIFFICULTIES

At first consideration, you may be tempted to regard your plan of action as foolproof. That view is unwise because no matter how carefully a plan has been conceived, it is likely to encounter difficulties. By acknowledging this fact and making an effort to identify those difficulties in advance, you increase the chances of successful implementation. Following are four approaches to identifying potential difficulties.

1. Check for common kinds of imperfections, such as these.

   Safety: Does your plan create any danger for those who use it or those for whom it is used?
   Convenience: Will the plan be awkward to implement?
   Efficiency: Will the plan involve significant delays?
   Economy: Is the plan too expensive to implement?
   Simplicity: Is the plan unnecessarily complicated?
   Compatibility: Will the plan clash with any other procedure it should harmonize with?

Legality: Does the plan conform to the law or at least include provision for changing a law with which it conflicts?

Morality: Does any aspect of the plan violate one or more ethical principles? (See Chapter 2.)

2. Compare your plan of action with competing ones, if any exist. Determine whether those plans have any worthwhile features yours lacks.

3. Consider what changes your plan will produce in the existing situation. List all the changes that would occur if your plan were implemented, taking care not to overlook any significant ones. Note any undesirable changes.

4. Consider the effects your plan will have on people, including not only physical effects but also moral, emotional, intellectual, and financial effects. Be sure to consider eventual effects as well as immediate ones and subtle as well as obvious ones.

After you have used these four approaches and identified the difficulties that might arise in implementing your plan, consider how the difficulties might best be overcome. As with all idea production, defer judgment and extend your effort to produce a variety of ideas for overcoming each difficulty. Then select the best ideas and modify your plan accordingly.

To see how these steps would be applied in actual cases, let's examine two sample issues.

SHOULD CHILDREN PLEDGE ALLEGIANCE?

From time to time, the issue of pledging allegiance to the flag is revived, and debate rages around the United States. The issue may be expressed as follows: "Should public school students be required to recite the pledge of allegiance in unison at the start of each day?" Let's assume that after careful analysis and some revision of your initial view, you reasoned as follows.

A system of government built on respect for the essential dignity and the corresponding rights of every human being deserves the allegiance of its citizens. Whatever its lapses of application may be, the United States is built on respect for the essential dignity and the corresponding rights of every human being. Therefore, the United States deserves the allegiance of its citizens. Furthermore, any effort to develop in citizens the understanding and appreciation that underlie such allegiance is acceptable as long as it does not violate the dignity of the individual or cause him or her to compromise personal beliefs. Unfortunately, requiring public school students to recite the pledge of allegiance in school does in some cases cause them to compromise their personal beliefs or be subjected to abuse.* Therefore, this requirement is not acceptable.

Because your argument does not merely reject the required pledge but also affirms the value of allegiance and the cultivation of the understanding and appreciation that underlie allegiance, you would probably feel it was appropriate to recommend action on the issue. Accordingly, you might decide that school districts should mandate that teachers begin each day with a period of silence for students to reflect on what they owe their country and their fellow citizens for the blessing of living in this country. Further details of your idea could include the provision of statewide guidelines for the conduct of this period of reflection and a dissemination of these guidelines to the public to prevent any misunderstanding.

In examining this plan for imperfections and other difficulties, you might decide that though it would be noncontroversial, it would not accomplish its purpose. Students might use the time to think about their social life, personal problems, and so on. And even if they used it as intended, there would be no way to ensure that their reflection would have helped them grow in understanding and appreciation.

In this case, your examination might well lead you to change your recommendation to one that more closely meets your objectives. For example, you might recommend that one period a week (a homeroom period, perhaps) be set aside for a class discussion of the rights and responsibilities of living in a democracy. You might further specify that the focus of the discussion be on important historical incidents that dramatize those rights and responsibilities or on timely problems and issues.

SHOULD THE MIRANDA RULE BE ABOLISHED?

Judge Harold J. Rothwax of the Supreme Court of the State of New York believes that our criminal justice system is on the verge of collapse. The goal of finding the truth, he argues, has been superseded by concern for the rights of the accused. As a result, police, judges, and jurors are hampered in the performance of their duties. One of several proposals Rothwax offers for correcting the situation is to abandon the *Miranda* ruling.[1] That is the Supreme Court decision that

---

*In the 1930s, hundreds of Jehovah's Witnesses were given the choice of reciting the pledge or being expelled from school. Because their religion holds that it is a form of blasphemy to recite the pledge, they chose expulsion. As a result, most suffered verbal abuse; some also suffered physical abuse. In Richwood, West Virginia, police forced nine Witnesses to swallow large amounts of castor oil after they refused to recite the pledge. Elsewhere, Witnesses were attacked, tarred, and feathered, and, in one instance, castrated. In Kennebunk, Maine, an angry mob of 2,500 pillaged and set fire to the local Kingdom Hall. At first, the Supreme Court upheld the rights of municipalities to require the pledge; then, in 1943, it reversed itself. For more details on these events, see Jerry Bergman, "Jehovah's Witnesses: A Brief History of a Century of Religious-State Conflicts," at http://www.freeminds.org/history/conflicts.htm (accessed 11/20/02).

requires police to read every suspect his or her rights before they conduct an interrogation. If they fail to meet this requirement, any statement a suspect makes, whether involuntarily or in answer to one of their questions, may be suppressed at trial.

For example, let's say the police take a man into custody on suspicion of murder and before they read him his rights, he begins sobbing and confesses, "I murdered that girl, and she wasn't my first victim but my tenth. I'll take you to where I buried them." Let's say, further, that he then takes them to the other nine graves. Because they failed to "Mirandize" him, the prosecuting attorney will very likely be unable to use either the man's confession or the evidence of the other crimes he confessed to.

Suppose that you examined Judge Rothwax's proposal closely, considered the responses of his critics, and after evaluation and some revision of your initial thoughts, framed the following view.

> Whatever prevents the prosecution of criminals obstructs justice and threatens the safety of law-abiding citizens. The suppression of relevant evidence in the courtroom prevents the prosecution of criminals. Therefore, the suppression of relevant evidence in the courtroom obstructs justice and threatens the safety of law-abiding citizens. However, assault is a crime. Police coercion, intimidation, and threats of violence are forms of assault. Therefore, police coercion, intimidation, and threats of violence are crimes.

Because your argument acknowledges valid points on both sides of the issue, it raises the question "What, then, should be done? Should the Miranda rule be abolished or retained? Should police abuse of suspects, when it occurs, be ignored or punished?" This creates the burden of recommending a course of action and addressing the difficulties involved in implementing it. Out of the many possible responses to this challenge, you might adopt the following:

1. The Miranda rule should be suspended and all relevant evidence be allowed at trial, regardless of how it is obtained. The present system punishes society for the mistakes of police and serves to encourage and embolden criminals. The sole purpose of the criminal trial should be to determine whether the accused is guilty and, if so, whether any mitigating circumstances were present.

2. Emotional or physical abuse perpetrated on the suspect by the police should be treated as a crime. Offenders should face appropriate criminal penalties, as well as possible dismissal from the force. Victims should be allowed to bring civil action against the officer(s) involved and the municipality that employs them.

A final note about refining your resolution of issues: Critical examination of a plan you are enthusiastic about requires real self-discipline. That self-discipline is one of the qualities that distinguishes outstanding thinkers. Moreover, it is one of the principal reasons for their effectiveness in persuading others to endorse their views.

WARM-UP EXERCISES

13.1   Decide whether the following argument is sound. Explain your judgment thoroughly.

> Unicorns must exist because no one has ever been able to prove that they don't.

13.2   Decide whether the following argument is sound. Explain your judgment thoroughly.

> It is wrong to blame people for being born with a disease. Criminality is a disease some people are born with. Therefore, it is wrong to blame people for committing crimes.

13.3   A logician died and left this will: "I leave $1000 to be divided among my four daughters. Some of the money is to go to Annabel or Beatrice. I know that Beatrice and Clarissa are under Deirdre's thumb, so if any of the money goes to either of them, she is to have none. I want Beatrice and Clarissa treated alike—in fact, all four, or as many as possible, are to receive equal treatment." Who was the logician's favorite daughter, and what was the size of her legacy?[2] Explain your reasoning fully.

APPLICATIONS

Apply your creative and critical thinking to the following issues. After resolving each issue, decide whether it would be appropriate to take action on your belief. (In most cases, it would be appropriate.) Where action is called for, apply the two steps explained in this chapter.

13.1   Carelessly used, fireworks can cause severe burns or blindness. That's why many states have outlawed their purchase by the general public. (In those states, fireworks displays on holidays are managed by professionals.) Some people believe that it is not a proper function of government to protect people from their own negligence nor to forbid anyone from buying what a relative few will misuse.

13.2   Many environmentalists believe that the government has an obligation to protect plants and animals threatened with extinction. Others believe that if individuals want to take up that cause, that is their right but that it is not the government's business.

13.3   Some people believe that religious proselytizing (attempting to convert other people to one's religion) is not only morally justifiable but a moral obligation. Others believe that it is morally wrong.

13.4   For years, a controversy has raged over pornography. Some people believe that it affronts human decency and should be outlawed. Others regard it as quite harmless. Still others claim it is beneficial, that it helps people overcome their inhibitions and provides a means to ventilate strong sexual urges.

13.5   Controversy extends even to such a basic question as the nature of humankind. Are human beings essentially good and noble creatures who are corrupted by society in the course of their development? Or are they inherently violent and savage, their darker tendencies kept in check only by the threat of punishment? (There have been intelligent and educated supporters of each view.)

ISSUE FOR EXTENDED ANALYSIS

Following is a more comprehensive thinking challenge than the others in the chapter. Analyze and respond to it, following the instructions for extended analysis at the end of Chapter 1. Also, review "The Basis of Moral Judgment" and "Dealing with Dilemmas" in Chapter 2.

THE ISSUE: STATUTORY RAPE

Statutory rape is a special category of offense in which the age of the parties is the sole determining factor—in other words, an offense in which the element of consent is irrelevant. If one of the persons engaged in the sexual activity is younger than specified in the statute (18 in many states, 16 or a lower age in others), a crime has been committed. Until fairly recently, men were the usual perpetrators of statutory rape. Today the number of women offenders—in most cases teachers—seems to be increasing. The most publicized cases occurred in Texas, Tennessee, Florida, and California; the one that got the most headlines was that of Mary Kay LeTourneau, a 34-year-old married mother who began having sex with one of her students when he was 12, had two out-of-wedlock children with him, spent seven years in jail for the offense, and then married him when she was released.

THE ESSAYS

An Outmoded Concept
By Salvatore Scuderi

Statutory rape is a very old legal category. It made sense in an age when sexual activity was considered to be proper only in marriage and only between adults. But over the last century, Freud, Kinsey, and other

With Age Comes Responsibility
By Quentin Miller

Society has a right to expect that adults will behave more responsibly than children. The laws about the relationships between adults and children are based on that expectation. That is why there are laws prohibiting researchers have documented that sexual desires and urges are present even in young children, that hormones begin raging at puberty, and that acting on such urges is natural.

To appreciate how illogical statutory rape laws are, we need only consider some hypothetical cases. If two 12-, 13-, or 16-year-olds engage in sex, no crime has occurred. In most states, the same is true of a 12-year-old and a 16-year-old (a four-year difference in ages). But in some states, if an 18-year-old has sex with a 17-year-old (a *one-year* difference in ages), statutory rape has occurred.

The supporters of such laws claim that teenagers don't know their own minds and therefore aren't in a position to make a decision about sex. In reality, many preteens are as capable of such decisions as the average 20-year old is. If a 14-year-old is sexually attracted to a 30-year-old neighbor or teacher, and that person also feels an attraction, it is natural and proper for them to act on their desires.

It makes no sense to send the older person to jail simply because he or she is older. In any other context than sex, such punishment would constitute age discrimination. It should in a sexual context, as well.

In sum, laws against statutory rape do not fit our current, advanced knowledge of the nature of human sexuality; nor do they square with the sexual choices that young people make in contemporary society. Laws against statutory rape should therefore be repealed.

parents' neglect of children but not the reverse.

The general rule that has evolved over millennia of human history is that the closer an adult's association with children, the more accountable the adult is for his or her behavior. Teachers, school administrators, and playground personnel, youth group directors, and members of the clergy have an obligation to help young people grow in understanding and wisdom and to protect them from harmful influences. Working with young people is a high calling, and it should never be used for personal gain or for the satisfaction of personal desires.

Tradition wisely holds that young people cannot genuinely consent to sex with adults—that to do so requires an adult understanding of the physical, intellectual, and emotional consequences of such a relationship.

However mature minors may be in other respects and however much they may be physically attracted to an adult, it is impossible for them to have that understanding. That is why adult sexual contact with children or teenagers is considered a particularly egregious violation of their trust.

When adults engage in sex with minors, they are taking advantage of the minors' naivete, much in the same way that a sober person might take advantage of an inebriated or mentally incapacitated one. That is the compelling reason for the law having proscribed such activity in the past and for continuing to do so.

CLASS DISCUSSION

SAMANTHA: The only consideration in any sexual relationship should be whether both parties enter into it freely. And that is measured by the couple's feelings, not by the dictates of legislatures.

ALFONSO: That's especially evident when the adult is a woman and the teen is a boy. Boys fantasize about having sex with women authority figures such as teachers, so they naturally have positive feelings when their fantasies become reality.

MEGAN: I'm surprised that neither of you acknowledges that feelings can be deceptive, particularly young people's feelings. Teenagers feel they can drink large amounts of alcohol without getting drunk, drive fast without endangering themselves and others, engage in sex without emotional and physical consequences. Adults know better and should not pretend otherwise.

ALFONSO: You make sex sound dirty and dangerous when it's actually natural and fulfilling.

SAMANTHA: You also make teenagers seem like infants. They know a great deal more than you give them credit for.

MEGAN: I'm not selling teenagers short. I'm simply acknowledging what you are ignoring—the intellectual and emotional differences between adults and minors and the obligation of adults to protect minors from harm. The people who have the deepest love for children—their parents—overwhelmingly oppose adult/child sexuality and support statutory rape laws. You'd both do well to ponder that fact.

PART IV

Communicate Your Ideas

Some students will be surprised to find the subject of communication included in a book on thinking because they assume that the two subjects are unrelated. In reality, they are closely related. To begin with, expressing ideas clarifies them. As Mortimer Adler, an American philosopher, explains: "Thinking tends to express itself in words, spoken or written. The person who says he knows what he thinks but cannot express it usually does not know what he thinks."*

In addition, the kinds of ideas we are concerned with in this book—solutions to problems and issues—are most meaningful when they are communicated to other people. Chapter 14 explains how to present your ideas persuasively. Chapter 15 presents the fundamentals of effective writing and speaking. This chapter order is appropriate for students

---

*Mortimer Adler and Charles Van Doren, *How to Read a Book*, rev. ed. (New York: Simon & Schuster, 1940, 1972), p. 49.

who have already achieved basic proficiency in writing and speaking and therefore need only an occasional review of fundamentals. (Students who lack that proficiency would do well to read Chapter 15 before Chapter 14.)

14

Persuading Others

Some people manage to gain support for their views quite readily, even in controversial matters, whereas others meet strong resistance. What is the reason for this difference? Do persuasive people have a special talent that others lack? Or is their success due, instead, to habits and skills they have developed? Although talent is surely a factor, persuasiveness is for the most part *learned* behavior. This chapter shows you how to evaluate your audience, anticipate their objections, and present your ideas to advantage.

Boris Noodnik is just finishing his presentation to the Parent-Teachers' Association meeting: "To summarize my proposal, ladies and gentlemen, every teacher in our school system should make students write a composition of from one to three paragraphs every day of the school year and make helpful suggestions for improvement on each paper submitted. This is the only sensible way to have our students become proficient in their use of the written word." He pauses while the audience applauds his presentation and then asks, "Are there any questions?"

A woman in the back of the room raises her hand. Boris acknowledges her, and she stands to speak. "Mr. Noodnik," she begins, "I have done some rough calculating while you were making your presentation. Each teacher in our system has, on the average, 27 students in a class. Figuring an average of 7 minutes to correct a composition (a conservative estimate), it will take each teacher an additional 15 hours a week to correct those papers. Teachers already do most of their planning for class in the evenings and on weekends. Just when do you expect them to find the time to correct all those papers?"

Boris's face reddens. "Uh-h-h, well, u-h-h-h, ma'am," he stammers, "ah, let me see . . . . I'll have to check out those figures. I really don't know right this minute." Poor Boris. However viable his idea seemed to him, and perhaps to many in the audience, it is very likely dead now.

Although readers' reactions are less dramatic and less potentially embarrassing than the reaction of a live audience, they are no less real or critical. Readers may not be able to stand up and ask the hard questions in person, but they can and do still *think* them. This is hardly surprising. Persuasive communication asks the audience to replace ideas they know and accept with ideas they have never heard before or ideas they have considered and rejected. In many cases, it also asks that they cooperate in the implementation of the ideas, investing time and money and taking risks.

Persuasion will not occur for you automatically, any more than it did for Boris. And achieving it will take more than thinking proficiency. This does not mean that creative and critical thinking are unimportant; as we noted time and again in previous chapters, they are essential. You must have quality ideas before you are likely to persuade intelligent people. However, producing quality ideas is not enough—you must also assist your audience in *recognizing* the quality of those ideas. To do this, you must

1. Understand why people reject ideas

2. Know the particular audience you wish to persuade

3. Anticipate your audience's objections

4. Present your ideas to advantage

UNDERSTANDING WHY PEOPLE REJECT IDEAS

The more that people's ideas and beliefs are challenged, the stronger their objections are likely to be. That has been the pattern throughout history. For example, when Nicolaus Copernicus presented his original idea that the Sun, rather than Earth, is the center of the solar system, he was not applauded but scorned. Martin Luther responded to the idea by saying, "This fool wishes to reverse the entire scheme of astronomy." And John Calvin said mockingly, "Who will venture to place the authority of Copernicus above that of the Holy Spirit?" Thirty-one years later, Copernicus had the deathbed reward of seeing his ideas published—but even then they were not accepted.

When Galileo took up Copernicus's cause, he fared no better. He was thought to be a madman and would have been executed as a heretic had not good friends in high ecclesiastical offices interceded for him. The price he had to pay for his life to be spared was public renunciation of the idea he knew to be true.

Women scientists of that era—particularly midwives and physicians—faced another peril: being tortured or executed as witches. An estimated 40,000 women were executed for witchcraft during the seventeenth century alone, and the practice continued well into the nineteenth century. For this reason, only the most brilliant women could succeed in the sciences. One example is Maria

Gaetana Agnesi, the gifted eighteenth-century linguist, mathematician, and philanthropist, whose writings were essential to the foundations of integral calculus. Although she was called the "witch of Agnesi" for her mathematical genius, she was fortunate enough not to be persecuted as a witch. To this day, however, her most famous mathematical formula is called the Witch of Agnesi.

Even the most constructive and helpful ideas were rejected at first. When Charles Newbold invented the cast-iron plow, farmers rejected it because they believed it would pollute the soil. When Horace Wells first used gas as an anesthetic to pull teeth, his peers ridiculed him. Joseph Lister's pioneering of antiseptic surgery was dismissed as needless housekeeping. William Harvey's discovery of the blood's circulation was rejected for 20 years and earned him derision, abuse, and the loss of much of his medical practice. Secretary of State William H. Seward's purchase of Alaska from Russia for *two cents an acre* was considered a mistake and dubbed "Seward's Folly." Before Chester Carlson finally found a company that took an interest in his copying machine, known today as the Xerox copier, five years had elapsed and more than 20 companies had rejected his idea. The lesson in all these cases, and thousands of others like them, is that negative reactions to new ideas are predictable.

The reasons that people commonly cite for rejecting ideas are worth remembering because they provide a basis for anticipating future objections:

- The idea is *impractical.*
- The idea is *too expensive.*
- The idea is *illegal.*
- The idea is *immoral.*
- The idea is *inefficient.*
- The idea is *unworkable.*
- The idea will be *disruptive of existing procedures.*
- The idea is *unaesthetic* (that is, ugly or lacking in taste).
- The idea *challenges accepted beliefs.*
- The idea is *unfair* (that is, it favors one side of the dispute at the expense of the other).

KNOWING YOUR AUDIENCE

The purpose of this step is to determine what your audience knows about your subject, what they don't know, and most importantly, what opinions they hold. Their opinions have very likely been shaped by a variety of factors, including age, gender, educational background, religion, income, race, nationality, and business or professional affiliation. You will seldom be able to learn all these details about an audience; but it is worth the effort to learn as many as you can. Even more important, you should consider the variety of views your audience might take of the issue and determine which of those views are most probable. The following questions provide a helpful checklist.

Is Your Audience Likely to Have Been Influenced by Popular Misconceptions?

This question does not suggest that your audience is stupid or uneducated. As we saw in Chapter 1, there is a great deal of confusion today about such matters as free will, truth, knowledge, opinion, and morality. Many intelligent and educated people have fallen victim to ideas and attitudes that cripple their creative and critical faculties. In many cases, your audience will appreciate your insights only if you first help them get beyond their misconceptions.

Is Your Audience's Perspective Likely to Be Narrow?

This question directs you to consider how your audience's tendencies to mine-is-better thinking, face saving, resistance to change, conformity, stereotyping, and self-deception may interfere with their comprehension of your views. A clue to the way those tendencies are likely to influence your audience on a particular problem or issue is the way they have influenced *you* in the past. (The more honest you are with yourself about your own occasional irrationality, the more sensitive you will be to your audience's irrationality.)

Is Your Audience Likely to Be Unobservant About Important Considerations?

We noted in Chapter 6 that most people give up their curiosity at a rather early age and never fully regain it. Chances are your own experience with the Chapter 6 applications and the later applications in this book have made you more aware of the difficulty of developing curiosity, even when you make a conscious and sustained effort to do so. If your audience has not made such an effort, their observation may be careless, and so they may have missed many of the subtleties of the issue you are speaking or writing about. By considering what they are most likely to have missed, you can determine what you need to explain more fully.

Is Your Audience's Understanding of the Problem or Issue Likely to Be as Clear as Yours?

We have seen how many people rush into a problem with only a vague notion of exactly what the problem is. You have learned the value of expressing the problem or issue in a number of ways and then selecting the best and most promising expression of it. Many members of your audience may not have done so. And if they haven't, they won't realize that your view of it is the best one. It may help open them to persuasion if you discuss the various views of the problem or at least explain your view and its advantage over other views.

Is Your Audience Likely to Be Familiar with the Facts You Found in Your Investigation?

It is easy to forget that once you have investigated a problem or issue, particularly a complex one, you have a tremendous advantage over those who have not investigated it. Their ignorance of the facts can be an obstacle to accepting your solution. By learning what facts and interpretations they are likely to be unaware of, you are identifying matters that deserve emphasis in your writing or speaking.

Does Your Audience Appreciate the Various Solutions Possible? Have They Considered Them Critically?

Again, your effort to produce as many solutions as possible to the problem or issue sets you apart from most of your audience. The best way for them to appreciate your solution's soundness is to realize that other solutions are deficient. As long as they remain convinced that some inferior solution will work, they are not likely to be impressed by your solution. But if you show them how the others *don't* work, that their imperfections and complications are too great to overcome easily, you will have helped them to accept yours.

ANTICIPATING YOUR AUDIENCE'S OBJECTIONS

Your aim in anticipating others' reactions is twofold. First, you want to identify the *valid* objections others may raise to your idea so that you can modify the idea and eliminate the objections. Second, you want to identify the *invalid* objections so that you can respond to them in your presentation.

Two techniques are especially useful in anticipating an audience's reaction: *brainstorming* and *imaginary dialogue*.

The Brainstorming Technique

This technique is an adaptation of the third stage of the creative process: the production of ideas. The aim here is to think of as many possible objections to your solution as you can. Here's how to use this technique. Look back at the list of common negative reactions, and use them as a checklist to guide your brainstorming. In other words, first ask whether anyone might find your solution *impractical*, and then list as many possibilities as you can think of; next, ask in what ways people might find your solution *too expensive*, and list the possible ways; and so on, proceeding through all the common reactions.

Caution is in order here. Whenever you use the brainstorming technique, be sure to withhold all judgment so that the flow of ideas isn't interrupted. Keep in mind that extended effort will always reward you: some of the most helpful reactions will not occur to you until you have purged your mind of obvious and familiar ideas. When you've completed brainstorming all 11 common reactions, then you can decide which possibilities are most likely to occur. The better you have gotten to know your audience, the easier this will be.

The Imaginary-Dialogue Technique

As the name implies, this approach consists of imagining yourself discussing your solution with someone who objects to it. For the best results, think of a specific person, preferably someone you know quite well and are sure would disagree with you. Be sure to put aside any feelings of awkwardness or embarrassment while using this technique. If you find yourself thinking, "What would people think of my talking to myself this way?" remember that no one need know and that you are not doing it out of compulsion but as a deliberate strategy to aid your thinking.

Here is an example of how the imaginary-dialogue technique works. You will recall that in Chapter 2 (pages 42–44), we discussed the case of Ralph, the father who befriended the coaches and used that friendship to gain a special advantage for his son Mark over the other players. We decided that Ralph behaved immorally—that though his actions achieved some good (the development of his son's skills), they caused more harm: they deprived other players of the opportunity to develop their basketball skills, probably caused those players to become bitter, and undoubtedly caused Mark to believe that it was acceptable to disregard other people's rights and needs to achieve his own goals.

If you were addressing the larger issue this case raises—the issue of at what point a father's helping his son or daughter athletically slips from morally acceptable into morally unacceptable behavior—and attempting to resolve the issue by offering guidelines for parents to follow, you would want to anticipate negative reactions. And if you wanted to use the imaginary-dialogue technique to help stimulate your speculation, what better person would there be to talk with than Ralph himself? Surely, he would not look on your disposition of his case favorably.

Just how would you conduct the dialogue in your imagination? First, you'd make an assertion expressing your view. Then you'd put yourself in his position, enter his frame of mind, and answer for him. Next, you'd express a second view, construct the answer he'd probably give to it, proceed to a third view, and so on. The resulting dialogue might go this way.

YOU: Your actions were immoral, Ralph.

YOU-AS-RALPH: That's ridiculous. All I did was help my boy.

YOU: But you developed those friendships with the coaches so that you could use them later. That's dishonest.

YOU-AS-RALPH: You mean I have no right to choose my friends, that I have to avoid friendships with coaches if my boy is an athlete?

YOU: Not at all. There's a difference between developing a friendship because you like someone and developing it to use the person for your son's advantage.

YOU-AS-RALPH: It's a rough world out there. A boy needs an advantage to get ahead.

YOU: But you gained that advantage at other people's expense. Look at what you did to the other boys on the team.

YOU-AS-RALPH: I can't be concerned with them as much as I am concerned about my own son. That's unrealistic.

YOU: That's true enough. But we're not talking about your being concerned or not concerned. We're talking about specific actions you took, deliberately, that hurt them.

YOU-AS-RALPH: But they didn't have the interest or the talent my Mark had.

YOU: That was not for you to judge. It was the coaches' decision to make. Besides, if you were so sure of your son's talent, there would have been no need for you to gain an unfair advantage for him. His talent would have given him all the advantage he needed.

> YOU-AS-RALPH: I did it because I love my son. Is it immoral to help your own flesh and blood?
>
> YOU: Is it an act of love to teach your son that the rules of decency and fairness don't apply where his desires are involved, that he can do whatever he wants to because he's special?

The dialogue shows the benefit of this approach to your thinking. Used properly, it not only reveals the negative reactions you are likely to get from others but also helps you develop better responses to shallow or uninformed reactions. In actual practice, however, you needn't detail your own responses while you are conducting the dialogue. It is sufficient to contribute just enough to move the dialogue along, to prod the "other person" to respond. The most important part of the dialogue, after all, is not your views but the other person's thoughts and feelings about them. The more you are able to focus on the other person's reactions, the more you will gain the insights necessary to make an effective presentation.

There is no limit to the number of imaginary dialogues you can conduct. If your audience is complex and you have reason to expect a variety of reactions, you should consider doing numerous dialogues.

One final point: After you become used to the imaginary-dialogue technique and develop your confidence in using it, you will notice that a dialogue will often gather enough momentum to require little conscious direction from you. It will, in a sense, direct itself. When this happens, don't worry. It is a good sign, an indication that you have fully engaged your imagination and given yourself to the intellectual exchange with your imaginary opponent. Let the dialogue continue; what develops will usually be very useful. If it begins to turn away from the important concerns involved, just steer it back again.

PRESENTING YOUR IDEAS TO ADVANTAGE

No doubt you have noticed that the way people are approached in one-on-one situations often influences their reactions, sometimes strongly. For example, "Why did you behave so stupidly?" will get a very different reaction than "What went wrong?" Similarly, a courteous request is more effective than a rude demand, and emotional restraint is more favorably received than a wild outburst. The same principle applies in the presentation of ideas in speaking to a group of people and in writing. The following guidelines will ensure that your presentations invite acceptance rather than rejection of your ideas.

Respect Your Audience

Whenever there is strong disagreement over ideas, particularly controversial ideas, there is also heightened potential for ill will. Once we feel strongly about a point of view, we can easily conclude that those who disagree with us are stupid or villainous or both. That kind of attitude not only poisons debate but also makes persuasion difficult or impossible.

Since people are not likely to be persuaded by someone who shows disrespect for them, respecting your audience is not merely a matter of courtesy or good sportsmanship; it is a psychological imperative. You may be inclined to believe that you don't really have to respect your audience, that you can get by with pretending. But that is a mistake. Your own experience surely demonstrates that respect and disrespect are difficult to hide. Your manner or expression will usually betray strong feelings no matter how you try to hide it. Attitudes tend to show through what you say and the way you say it.

What can you do to make yourself feel respect for people whose views you disagree with? First, you can remember to distinguish between the idea and the person. It is possible for a decent, admirable person to have a foolish idea or for a disreputable person to have a sound one. Second, in the case of a controversial issue, you can remind yourself that disagreement is more likely to reflect the complexity of the issue than any shortcoming in those who differ with you.

Begin with the Familiar

First impressions may not be very reliable, but they are generally quite strong and therefore difficult to overcome. If you begin your presentation on a point your audience is unfamiliar with or opposed to, they will be wary or opposed throughout your presentation. At best, it will be difficult to change their reaction. That is why it makes sense to begin on a point they are familiar with, if possible a point on which they agree with you. This approach puts the psychology of first impressions to work for you instead of against you.

Beginning on a familiar point does not, however, mean that you should be dishonest and hide your disagreement. You are merely preparing your audience for the point of disagreement—helping them to see your solution more objectively than they otherwise would—and not avoiding disagreement. There is nothing deceitful about this approach, nor does it require that you *manufacture* a point of agreement. If you look carefully, you will usually be able to find at least several significant points of agreement, even when your basic views are sharply divergent. As a last resort, if you can't find anything else that you and your audience are likely to agree on, you can begin by stating the significance of the issue and pointing out that it, like all controversial issues, tends to fan emotions more than is helpful for debate.

Select the Most Appropriate Tone

The concept of tone is a subtle one. Tone may be defined as the mood or attitude suggested by a presentation. It is therefore closely related to the idea of respecting your audience. Certain tones are always inappropriate in persuasive writing and speaking. The now-hear-this tone, for example, goes beyond being authoritative to being *authoritarian* and suggests that the presenter is forcing his or her views on the audience. Another inappropriate tone is the only-an-idiot-would-think-as-you-do tone, characterized by mocking and sarcastic remarks. Still another inappropriate tone is the you've-got-to-agree-right-now-because-there's-no-time-left tone. Serious problems and issues demand careful consideration; it is irresponsible to make any important decision impulsively. Demanding an instant decision from your audience, therefore, only makes them suspicious of your motives. "If the writer [or speaker] really has a solid case," they reason, "why doesn't he or she want to give me time to examine it carefully and ponder it?"

The safest and most appropriate tone in persuasive writing and speaking is the calm, objective, courteous tone. This will reflect quiet competency and a sense of balance toward the issue, as well as a proper view of your audience.

Emphasize the Evidence for Your View

Some writers and speakers believe that the most important factor in persuasion is the clear and forceful statement of their viewpoint. They are mistaken. The most important factor is *the evidence on which their viewpoint rests*. The reason is simple. Evidence alone enables the audience to decide whether an idea is deep or shallow, wise or foolish, valid or invalid. To state your viewpoint is to say what you believe; to provide evidence is to *demonstrate* that what you say is worthy of other people's endorsement.

The amount and kind of evidence you need will depend on the particular idea you are defending and the type of investigation you conducted. In one case, the evidence may consist of eyewitness testimony and published or unpublished reports. In another, it may include expert opinion, experiment, statistics, survey, observational study, research review, and your own experience or that of people you know. (For a discussion of each of these, refer back to Chapter 8.) But it is safe to say that for each sentence presenting your judgment or conclusion, you ought to have at least two or three supporting sentences.

In all but the most restricted presentations, in which you are *required* to be brief, you should consider including all the significant results of your investigation of the issue. In addition to presenting those results, explain what they mean and why they are important. Where the data include your experiences and observations, try to re-create the experiences and observations for your audience. Make them see as you saw, feel as you felt. If they have never had similar experiences, this will be difficult, so aim for vividness wherever possible and try to convey a sense of the immediacy and drama of the original event. In addition, make your interpretation clear and reasonable.

Answer All Significant Objections

You may think that if you identify any valid objections to your solution and modify your solution to eliminate them, you have done enough. That view is incorrect. Even invalid objections may act as obstacles. Therefore, you must deal with all objections directly and thoroughly. Do this subtly and smoothly, without reminding your audience that it is their objection and without interrupting the flow of your presentation.

THE IMPORTANCE OF TIMING

There is one additional element in building a persuasive case. It is not, properly speaking, a guideline for preparing your presentation. Nevertheless, it does have a major bearing on your presentation's effectiveness. This element is your *timing* in presenting your case. Many an insight has been defeated by simply being presented at the wrong time. People's attention, interest, and openness to ideas are not constant. At some times they are greater than at others. It is not always possible to appraise an audience's state of mind, particularly when the audience is large and complex. Nevertheless, you should be aware of the most favorable conditions for persuasion and, whenever possible, time your presentation accordingly. Those conditions are as follows:

1. The audience should recognize that the problem or issue exists and be aware of its importance. A controversial issue should be currently in the news or at least have been there recently. If you have reason to believe the audience is not aware of the problem, use the first part of your presentation to create that awareness.

2. The audience should be relatively free to address your idea. That is, they should have no other pressing concerns commanding their attention.

3. The audience should have no commitment to a competing solution. It is not likely they will be interested in considering your solution to a problem or issue if they have endorsed another, competing solution. In such cases, your wisest course of action is to withhold presentation until the competing idea proves unworkable.

 WARM-UP EXERCISES

14.1 You have just heard a friend make the following statement. Decide whether his or her reasoning is sound or unsound. Then write a paragraph or two explaining your judgment.

I would vote this year if I could be reasonably sure any of the candidates would do a good job. But I have no way to be sure, so it's a waste of time to vote.

14.2 Follow the directions for Exercise 14.1.

Physical fitness is very fashionable today. Yet the great philosophers agree that the mind is more important than the body. So the physical fitness movement should be opposed.

14.3 Follow the directions for Exercise 14.1.

No honest lawyer would agree to represent a person accused of a crime because if the person is innocent, he doesn't need defending, and if he is guilty, he doesn't deserve defending.

◼️ APPLICATIONS

14.1 Each of the following cases was presented in an earlier chapter's applications. Turn back to the chapter in each case and reread the application. Then recall the position you took on it. (If you wish, you may rethink the problem now.) State your position on the matter and the reasons supporting your position. Then anticipate the negative reactions you would probably receive, proceeding as explained in this chapter.

a. The case involving the Jewish dietary laws, Application 3.4, page 63.

b. The case of the illiterate high school graduate, Application 3.5, page 63.

c. The alcohol in sports case, Application 3.6, page 63.

d. The case of the government's conflicting views on tobacco, Application 8.6, page 160.

e. The case involving the patenting of living organisms, Application 8.7, page 161.

f. Any of the issues, a through c, in Application 12.3, page 224.

g. The case concerning religious proselytizing, Application 13.3, page 233.

h. The pornography case, Application 13.4, page 234.

ISSUE FOR EXTENDED ANALYSIS

Following is a more comprehensive thinking challenge than the others in the chapter. Analyze and respond to it, following the instructions for extended analysis at the end of Chapter 1. Also, review "The Basis of Moral Judgment" and "Dealing with Dilemmas" in Chapter 2.

THE ISSUE: CAMPUS SPEECH CODES

Campus speech codes became popular in the 1980s and 1990s. Designed to create a positive atmosphere and to ensure civility among diverse student populations, they listed the categories of words and actions that were prohibited, and specified procedures and penalties for code violations. Such speech codes have proved to be highly controversial.

THE ESSAYS

Maintain Civility on Campus
By Stephanie Ross

    Speech codes were first developed in the workplace in order to prevent

Protect Free Speech
By Helen Fisher

    Speech codes derive from the foolish notion that human beings are fragile employees from being harassed, intimidated, or offended. Companies realized that such behavior not only injured the victims but it also diminished their productivity and thus injured the company.

Campus speech codes serve a similar purpose by ensuring an environment conducive to learning.

In at least one sense, speech codes are even more important in college than in the workplace. The central activity in college is the exchange of ideas, and that exchange can be meaningful only in an atmosphere of civility. Insensitive, mocking, or insulting references to race, ethnicity, sexuality, intelligence, age, or disability destroy that atmosphere. Spoken insults are bad enough; written insults, as in campus newspapers, do even more serious harm.

Opponents of campus speech codes usually base their arguments on the constitutional guarantee of free speech. Any restriction of speech, they claim, violates that right. However, the constitution guarantees other rights, as well, notably the broader right to the pursuit of happiness. Essential to this pursuit is self-esteem and a sense of well-being. Speech codes support these values and are therefore beneficial.

Some campuses have developed lengthy lists of forbidden terms, topics, visual depictions, and gestures. This is a laudable approach that helps to ensure civility and sensitivity toward others by making everyone aware of what language and actions are to be avoided.

Speech codes provide another advantage: they make it easier for injured parties to file grievances and

creatures who cannot bear the burden of a discouraging or insulting word. In reality, people aren't fragile, and speech codes do more mischief than good. Consider just a few examples:

- On one campus a Confederate flag was removed from a dorm hallway after a visiting parent complained.
- Officials on another campus shut down an "affirmative action bake sale," in which black students were charged 30 cents, Latinos 35 cents, and white students $1 for the same item. (The sale was staged to illustrate the unfairness of affirmative action.)
- Another college withheld student-activity fee support from organizations that had a "particular ideological, religious, or partisan viewpoint."
- On many campuses students have been harassed for handing out fliers for speakers—even distinguished ones—who espoused politically incorrect views.

The best argument against campus speech codes is that they violate the constitutional guarantee of free speech. The Foundation for Individual Rights in Education (FIRE) makes this argument, as does the American Association of University Professors (AAUP). The latter maintains, "On a campus that is free and open, no idea can be banned or forbidden. No viewpoint or message may be deemed so hateful or disturbing that it may not be expressed." The AAUP urges all administrators, faculty, and student personnel staff to safeguard free speech on their campuses.

In our grandparents' day, children were taught that "sticks and stones may break my bones but names will never hurt me." With no more psychological for appropriate penalties—ranging from simple reprimand to enrollment in special sensitivity classes to expulsion from college—to be meted out to the offenders.

armor than that, they managed to survive the bumps and bruises of life with their egos intact. We should learn from their example and give up the loony idea that we need elaborate speech codes to protect us.

CLASS DISCUSSION

JO: It's hard enough to do well in college without bearing the added burden of humiliation from others.

JUSTIN: Boorishness and rudeness have always existed. Only in a pampered age like ours have people expected protection from such behavior.

EDGAR: If I understand you correctly, Justin, you oppose all protections from unprovoked attacks.

JUSTIN: No. I approve laws against physical attacks. I just don't think we need protection from *verbal* insults and crudity. However unpleasant they may be they are part of life, and we should accept them as such.

JO: Justin, you seem to be unaware of the impact of words on people. Dirty jokes and sexual innuendo make many women feel intimidated. Negative references to people's intelligence—dumb blond jokes, for example—undermine their self-esteem. Disparaging remarks concerning age, race, political affiliation, religion, disability, or sexual orientation are assaults on our constitutional right to the pursuit of happiness.

JUSTIN: Such a standard is too broad and vague to be meaningful. How could we ever know what constitutes an offense and what doesn't? Who would be in a position to make that determination?

EDGAR: The definition of offensive behavior should be whatever causes one or more people to feel offended. Each of us knows his or her feelings, so each of us would decide.

JUSTIN: By that measure, no one could offer criticism about anything. For example, if I said that diversity and multiculturalism have done more harm than good, I'd be guilty of an offense.

JO: You're overgeneralizing. Such statements would be offenses only if they caused people to feel offended.

15

Writing and Speaking Effectively

Have you ever thought while you were reading a well-written book or article, "I wish I could write as effortlessly as this writer, making my ideas as clear and precise, one flowing so smoothly into another"? Well, guess what? Even professional writers treasure their "delete" and "backspace" keys; they need those keys to undo all the vagueness, ambiguity, and incoherence of their first—and sometimes second and third—drafts. The only reason this isn't common knowledge is that we see the finished product and not the activity that went into producing it, just as we see the finished film and not all the bad "takes" that ended on the cutting room floor. A great deal of effort is required to create the illusion of effortlessness. This chapter shows you how to manage and direct that effort in your writing and speaking.

In all the preceding chapters, we were concerned with the production and evaluation of ideas. These thinking processes are often called the prewriting stage of composition or speech preparation. In this chapter, we consider how to *express* your thoughts effectively. The first half of the chapter focuses on writing; the second, on speaking.

CHARACTERISTICS OF EFFECTIVE WRITING

All effective writing, whether in a book, an essay, or a report, displays four characteristics: *unity, coherence, emphasis,* and *development.**

To Achieve* Unity, *Compose a Central Idea, and State It Early.   Without a central idea, you have no basis for making your composition effective. A central idea provides control over what to include in the composition and what to exclude, where to begin and where to end, and what arrangement of thoughts is best. If it is to provide this guidance, the central idea should be clear to you *before you begin writing.* It saves no time to rush headlong into a composition expecting to find an idea somewhere along the way and then, half an hour later, after much head scratching and eyebrow furrowing, to decide that you are hopelessly lost or at a dead end. Never assume you know what you want to say. Put it down in a clear sentence or two; change it several times, if necessary, to be sure it is what you want to say; and refer back to it for direction while you are writing.

To Achieve* Coherence, *Choose a Recognizable Pattern of Organization and Follow It.   Immature writers have the idea that the world is waiting breathlessly to hear from them. Their attitude is "if the readers have trouble figuring out my meaning, let them struggle to do so; my thoughts are worth the effort." That attitude is naive. Readers of your writing will react to incoherence just as you do when you encounter it in others. In other words, they'll think to themselves, "This person is confused; if she couldn't make her meaning clear, I'm not going to waste my valuable time trying to figure it out." Then they'll throw it aside.

To avoid such a reaction and make your writing coherent, you must be sure that the order of your ideas is sensible. Whenever possible, you must also finish one idea before moving on to the next (so that your readers don't have to jump back and forth between ideas unnecessarily) and provide helpful connecting words or phrases to signal significant shifts from one idea to another.

To Achieve* Emphasis, *Give Each of Your Ideas the Degree of Prominence It Deserves.   There may be occasions when every idea in a composition has exactly the same degree of importance as every other. But those occasions are extremely rare. Much more often, the ideas differ significantly in their importance. To determine the relative importance of the ideas in a piece of writing, consider their exact relationship to your central idea. The larger the role they play in communicating that idea, the more important they are. Use these approaches to give greater emphasis to more important ideas.

1. Assign an important idea more space; that is, provide more information about it and develop it further than other ideas.

---

*In a very brief piece of writing—for example, a memorandum—*development* may not be necessary.

2. Whenever possible, give important ideas the positions of greatest emphasis. The end is the most emphatic position, and the beginning is the next most emphatic. Thus, if you had four points or arguments in the body of your composition, you'd put your most important point last, your next most important point first, and the others in the middle.

3. Repeat key words occasionally, or use echo words. The latter are words that do not repeat the key words but whose sense is similar enough to call them to mind. In a composition about love, words like *respect, devotion,* and *affection* would be echo words. One caution, though: both repetition and echo words must be used judiciously or they will make your composition seem inflated.

To Achieve* Development, *Elaborate on Important Ideas.   Not every idea warrants extended treatment. To honor the principle of emphasis, be sensitive to the development necessary to elicit the response you want from your readers, and then provide that development—for example, by using cases in point, descriptions, definitions, explanations, and so on. When your purpose is to *persuade* your readers, many of your ideas may require considerable development.

A STEP-BY-STEP APPROACH TO COMPOSITION

Planning

In this stage, you create a blueprint to follow in the writing stage. It is easier to experiment with different formats when ideas are in rough, abbreviated form than when they are fully developed in sentences and paragraphs. This is no small concern in situations (such as in the applications in this book) in which you are dealing with a large number of complex ideas and a number of different perspectives. These are the steps you should follow in planning your compositions.

1. **Assemble your ideas.** There's no need for complete sentences here or for concern about neatness and correctness. A list of your ideas or a collection of note pages is sufficient. This list is not a draft of your paper, just a gathering of its ingredients—that is, the results of your creative and critical thinking.

2. **Choose the arrangement.** Decide what arrangement of your ideas will be easiest for your readers to follow and most effective in persuading them. The following ways to organize ideas in a persuasive composition are among the most common. (Long or complex compositions often employ two or more of these organizational patterns.)

   Conclusion-to-evidence order, in which the conclusion is presented first, followed by the evidence that supports it. This is easy to follow, saying in effect, "This is what I believe, and here is why I believe it."

   Evidence-to-conclusion order, in which you lead your readers to your conclusion step-by-step. This is the preferred pattern whenever you are disputing a popular and well-entrenched view.

Cause-to-effect order, in which the causes of a phenomenon, such as the Great Depression, are discussed first and then the effects. (The reverse order, effect-to-cause, may also be used.)

Order of importance, in which the supporting arguments are presented in ascending order from the least to the most important. A variation of this is modified order of importance, in which the second most important argument is presented first, and the most important, last. This arrangement is designed to evoke both a good first impression and a good last impression from the readers.

When you have decided how you will arrange your ideas, number them accordingly, so that you can follow your plan easily when drafting the composition.

3. **Choose your introduction and conclusion.** Prepare readers for your central idea and its development. How can you do that best? Here are some effective ways to *introduce* a composition.

   Ask a salient question and discuss possible answers.

   Tell a brief anecdote that will illustrate the problem or issue you are addressing.

   Use a quotation from a respected person, one that leads into your central idea.

   Concede a point to the opposing side of the issue; in other words, cite a point that those who differ with you have made and that you agree with, and use that as a lead-in to your disagreement.

   Here are some effective ways to *conclude* a composition.

   Recommend an action consistent with the argument presented in the body.

   Elaborate on something mentioned in your introduction; in other words, answer a question raised there or comment on an anecdote or a quotation.

   Use another quotation that reinforces your central idea or a main point.

   Present a new anecdote, being sure that it reinforces your central idea *but avoids raising issues not covered earlier.*

   State the benefits that will result if your ideas are implemented or the harmful consequences that are likely if your ideas are not implemented.

   State, briefly and stirringly, why your audience should endorse the argument you have presented.

4. **Note which ideas need support and how you will support them.** Intelligent people are persuaded not by mere statements of opinion but by the quality of the evidence supporting them. If you have examined the issue carefully and fairly, you will know which of your statements are open to question and what evidence is most relevant and compelling. (That evidence will have guided your own judgment.) Check each of your assertions and decide what evidence you have for it; then present the assertion in one or more of the following ways.

Present factual details, such as statistics.

Describe someone or something.

Offer a summary of an article or book.

Quote or paraphrase an authority.

Trace a historical development.

Offer a brief or extended narrative of a real or hypothetical event.

Present a definition, literal or figurative.

Detail a process or procedure.

Compare or contrast, explaining similarities or differences.

Analyze causes or effects.

Evaluate someone's argument, demonstrating its strengths and/or weaknesses.

Drafting

In this stage, you carry out your composition plan and produce a rough draft. Complete the entire draft at a single sitting, with as few interruptions as possible. Choose your words as carefully as you can, write complete sentences, and break your writing into paragraphs. But do not let yourself get bogged down in doing these things. If the right word doesn't come to mind at once, write a similar word that does. If you aren't sure whether a paragraph break is appropriate, make a tentative decision. Never pause during the writing stage to look up the meaning or spelling of a word or to check some rule of usage or grammar. These are important tasks, but the time for them is later. The more carefully you follow this advice, the better the flow of your writing is likely to be.

Revising

Your purpose in this stage is to transform your rough draft into a polished composition. Begin by reading your rough draft critically, preferably aloud, since hearing plus seeing will reveal flaws more readily than will seeing by itself. Ask yourself the following questions, and make marginal notes wherever the need for revision is indicated.

How else might I express my central idea? What part of it needs fuller explanation to be meaningful to my readers?

How can I improve the coherence of my composition? What rearrangement of my sentences and paragraphs would make the progression of thoughts easier to follow? Where might I add transitions (connecting words) to signal the movement from one idea to another?

Which of my ideas deserve more emphasis? Which deserve less emphasis? What is the best way to change the emphasis?

For which ideas have I failed to provide adequate support? Which techniques will best provide that support?

Editing

Your purpose in this stage is to find and correct lapses in grammar, usage, diction, spelling, punctuation, and paragraphing. For best results, proofread your composition not once but a number of times: one reading for errors in general, followed by separate readings for each of the errors that tend to recur in your writing. Consult a dictionary and a composition handbook, as necessary. Write your final draft.

DEVELOPING A READABLE STYLE

As a literate person, a college student, you have done considerable reading. You have encountered a variety of prose styles, some of them so awkward and difficult to follow that you have almost wished you'd never learned to read, and others that have delighted you and made you sorry to come to the end of the work. Perhaps you've concluded that writing style must be a matter of genetic endowment. There's probably some truth to the idea; after all, some people do seem to have a special talent for verbal expression, just as some have a mechanical aptitude. But writing is essentially a learned activity, so habit is more significant than heredity. If the habits you have acquired through trial and error or imitation are bad habits, you will be a poor writer. If they are good habits, you will be a good writer. Observing the following guidelines can help you build better habits.

1. **Make your writing sound natural.** Many people who write poorly speak fairly well. In fact, some are lively and interesting conversationalists. If you are such a person, you can improve your writing by making it reflect your speech. This doesn't mean, of course, all the little flaws of speaking—the *um*-ing, *ah*-ing, pausing, and repeating yourself. It means the rhythm of your speaking voice. To accomplish this, read your rough draft aloud and note passages that don't sound natural. Revise them so that you feel comfortable saying them aloud.

2. **Strive for brevity.** The idea of brevity may seem inconsistent with writing longer papers and developing your ideas. But it is not inconsistent at all. A paper may be long because it has a lot of unnecessary words in it or because it is filled with ideas. You can develop your thoughts fully and still have your writing be a model of brevity. Simply express each idea in as few words as you can, consistent with conveying the meaning and creating the understanding you intend.

3. **Express your ideas in simple language.** This doesn't mean to avoid all big words, just the ones that are *unnecessarily* big. George Orwell said it best: "Never use a long word where a short word will do."

4. **Put some variety into your sentences.** What is the most boring quality in a speaker? Most people would say speaking in a monotone. A monotone is

the use of a single, unvaried tone of voice. The word is derived from the same Greek word that gives us *monotonous*. Monotones are monotonous. The equivalent of monotone in writing is sentences that begin the same way, have the same structure, and are the same length. They are perfectly predictable; that's why they put readers to sleep. To get the monotony out of your writing, begin some of your sentences differently, vary their structure, and include an occasional short sentence among a series of longer ones (or vice versa).

5. **Paraphrase more often than you quote.** Quotations are valuable, but used too often, they shift the focus from your style to someone else's. Whenever it is possible to paraphrase (to express the other writer's idea in *your* words) without making the idea suffer in the process, do so. You must, of course, give the same credit for paraphrased ideas as you do for quoted ideas—that is, by mentioning the person informally in your sentence or by including a formal footnote.

6. **Be lively.** Purge your writing of bland, mechanical expression. Try to express your ideas colorfully and imaginatively. Your writing will take on a new vitality when you do. Here are two brief examples of lively, imaginative expression.

   a. As you turn the pages of that American history book, the story gets more and more polluted. The pilgrim lands in the New World and discovers a land that is already occupied. How do you find something that somebody else has and claim you discovered it? And we talk about crime in the streets!

   That is like my wife and I walking down the street and seeing you and your wife sitting in your brand-new automobile. Suppose my wife says to me, "Gee, I'd like to have a car like that." And I answer, "Let's discover it." So I walk over to you and your wife and say, "Get out of that damned car. My wife and I just discovered it." The shock and surprise you would naturally feel gives you some idea of how the Indians must have felt.[1]

   b. Only a very soft-headed, sentimental, and rather servile generation of men could possibly be affected by advertisements at all. People who are a little more hard-headed, humorous, and intellectually independent see the rather simple joke and are not impressed by this or any other form of self-praise. If you had said to a man in the Stone Age, "Ugg says Ugg makes the best stone hatchets," he would have perceived a lack of detachment and disinterestedness in the testimonial. If you had said to a medieval peasant, "Robert the Bowyer proclaims, with three blasts of a horn, that he makes good bows," the peasant would have said, "Well, of course he does," and thought about something more important. It is only among people whose minds have been weakened by a sort of mesmerism that so transparent a trick as that of advertisement could ever have been tried at all.[2]

A SAMPLE COMPOSITION

The following analytical paper illustrates how your responses to the end-of-chapter applications can be presented in traditional composition form, observing the principles of writing explained in this chapter. The composition is a response to the issue of violence in contemporary films. Specifically, it answers the question "What is the most reasonable reaction to the recent trend toward the graphic portrayal of violent scenes in films?"

Film Violence Should Make Us Sick

I walked out of the movie after half an hour. It was either leave or throw up. The movie was *An American Werewolf in London*. In an early scene, a wolf attacks two young men, killing one and badly slashing the other. Then, while recovering in the hospital, the survivor dreams he is running nude through the forest, spies a deer, pounces on it wolflike, and devours it.

Two more nightmares quickly follow. In one, the survivor's family is brutally assaulted and killed by monsters with hideous faces. In the other, his nurse is similarly attacked. Soon the young man's dead friend visits him in the hospital to warn that he will become a werewolf. The camera lingers on the dead man's disgustingly mutilated face.

In each of these scenes, no gory detail is left to the imagination. Yet somehow, many people around me in the theater found the visual assault enjoyable. They laughed and laughed. I left.

Like that audience, some critics have taken the film lightheartedly. The *Newsweek* critic, for example, titled his review "Cool Ghoul" and termed the film "a nearly perfect specimen of the wise-guy movie" in which the hero turns into a werewolf and "masticates half of Piccadilly before the bloody climax." That kind of critical reaction reflects a casual attitude toward film violence that has become very fashionable in recent years. That attitude rests on four widely accepted ideas, each of them flawed.

The first idea is that any time an audience is made to laugh, the effect is wholesome. This is nonsense. There's a big difference between laughing at someone making a fool of himself or herself or at an ironic development and laughing at someone being raped or torn to shreds. Some things—mental retardation, physical handicaps, and terminal illness, for example—just aren't funny.

The second idea is that films don't affect our attitudes and values. This view ignores the most obvious findings of psychology. Psychologists tell us that most people aren't born sensitive or insensitive, kind or cruel. Rather, they are shaped one way or the other by their experiences, including their vicarious experiences on the larger-than-life movie screen.

Chicago film critic Roger Ebert reports that in viewing another film on two separate occasions, he observed both audiences laughing in scenes showing a woman beaten, raped, and cut up. One respectable-looking man next to him kept murmuring, "That'll teach her. Give it to her." Ebert found that reaction frightening. So should we all. But we shouldn't be surprised by it. Like any powerful emotional experience, film viewing has the capacity to brutalize us, to make us feel enjoyment where our humanity demands we feel revulsion.

The third popular notion is that films don't affect people's behavior. This idea is questionable at best. Consider the case of the 24-year-old Brockton, Massachusetts, man who, believing himself to be a vampire, killed his grandmother and drank her blood. Or the case of the Cincinnati publisher who marketed the Cat Hater's Calendar, featuring color photos of cats being hanged and wrapped in foil on a grill. No particular film may be responsible for inciting such actions, but surely the climate of violence generated by horror films contributed to them, at least by stimulating the person's imagination.

Finally, it is widely believed that the idea of democracy forbids any restriction on artistic expression, including that of filmmakers. To approve of even the most general guidelines is considered an attack on the U.S. Constitution. This belief is too extreme to be reasonable. Individual rights should not be allowed to take precedence over public rights. No one, for example, should be permitted to poison the air the rest of us breathe. And neither should a filmmaker have the right to poison the social climate.

This is not to say that the movie industry should be forbidden to explore the unpleasant side of reality. On the contrary, no subject should be forbidden to filmmakers because no subject is good or bad in itself. It is the *treatment* that makes the difference. In the hands of a genuine artist, even the most unspeakable violence can be handled inoffensively. Alfred Hitchcock's *Psycho* generated incomparable suspense without the knife once touching the victim on camera.

Not only is there no good reason to approve the kind and amount of film violence we have been subjected to in recent years; there is compelling reason to reject it. Across this country, from small communities to great cities, crime and violence are a daily threat to millions of people. If we are ever to conquer that threat, we must retain our capacity to be outraged by it. But it is precisely that capacity that is diminished every time we suppress revulsion and watch a succession of violent acts on the movie screen.

THE CHALLENGE OF EFFECTIVE SPEAKING

The speaking we are concerned with in this chapter is formal speaking—that is, presenting your ideas to an audience, as opposed to participating in discussion (which is discussed in Chapter 1). Effective speaking has the same characteristics as effective writing—*unity, coherence, emphasis,* and *development*—yet speaking poses special challenges not present in writing. Mortimer Adler observes that writers, like painters and sculptors, can change their work as they are creating it. Speakers, on the other hand, like actors, musicians, or dancers, can never change a particular performance because the audience sees and/or hears it as it is being presented. The best that speakers can do is to make improvements *the next time* they speak.

Adler also notes that the spoken word, unlike the written word, lacks permanence. Once uttered, it is gone. Thus the audience cannot stop and ponder a spoken sentence the way they can a written one.[3] Of course, a tape recorder enables people to hear a speech again and even permits rewinding and replaying. But these actions are more clumsy and less natural than pausing and pondering a written page.

Accordingly, the speaker must take care not only in preparing the speech but also in delivering it.

TYPES OF SPEECHES

Formal speeches are classified as follows: *memorized* (delivered without notes), *manuscript* (read verbatim), *extemporaneous* (delivered from notes), and *impromptu* (unprepared, completely spontaneous). Impromptu speeches are the most difficult to give because the potential is greatest for rambling and incoherence. Memorized speeches can be effective, but if you forget or lose the sequence of the ideas, you'll be left standing in embarrassing silence. Experienced speakers are often able to read manuscript speeches enthusiastically and animatedly without sacrificing eye contact; amateurs, on the other hand, almost always stare at the page, speak in a monotone, and bore the audience. The best choice for the majority of speakers, particularly the inexperienced, is the extemporaneous speech. It provides the security of notes without the temptation of fully written-out sentences.

ORGANIZING YOUR MATERIAL

A formal speech has three divisions: the *introduction,* the *body,* and the *conclusion.*

The Introduction. A successful introduction serves both to focus the audience's attention and to arouse their interest in what you are going to say. Effective techniques for doing so include making a startling statement, asking a question, recounting an anecdote, and reciting a quotation. (If the relevance of your introduction to your central idea is not self-evident, explain it.) Keep your introduction appropriately brief, generally no more than 10 or 15 percent of the overall presentation.

The Body.   The body of a speech consists of the statement and support of your central idea. Unless you have a good reason for withholding your central idea until later in the speech, state it immediately after the introduction. Then present your evidence. Your goal is to have your audience remember your main points and understand how they support your central idea. Listening, of course, is more difficult than reading; even a brief lapse in attention will result in lost information because there is no looking back as in reading. (Remember: If the audience gets lost, they will usually blame you rather than themselves.) Accordingly, you will need to limit your main points. From three to five is standard; more than five is seldom effective.

In addition, use a clear and straightforward pattern of organization. For example, use time order when your evidence consists of a sequence of events, order of importance for a series of reasons, and cause-to-effect order when explaining how a phenomenon occurs. Don't make the mistake of reasoning, "My argument is complex, so the audience will just have to work to grasp it." The more complex the argument, the harder the *speaker* should work to present it clearly.

Following are three proven ways to make your speech even more accessible to your audience.

1. Use large, legible visual aids (charts, graphs, transparencies, and/or videos) whenever possible, making sure that they reinforce rather than substitute for your talk, that you continue to maintain eye contact with your audience while presenting them, and that you allow sufficient time for your audience to absorb each visual aid before putting it aside.

2. Use signal words and phrases to help your audience make connections among the parts of your speech, saying, for example, "One reason for . . . ," "A second reason for . . . ," and so on.

3. Summarize your main points just before the conclusion.

The Conclusion.   In a persuasive speech, an effective conclusion underlines the central idea and reinforces the appeal to understanding and/or action. Among the most effective ways to conclude a speech are these.

1. Recommend an action consistent with the argument presented in the speech.

2. Elaborate on something mentioned in your introduction; in other words, answer a question raised there or comment on an anecdote or a quotation.

3. Present a new anecdote, making sure that it reinforces your central idea but avoids raising issues not covered in your speech.

4. Use another quotation.

5. State the benefits that will result if your ideas are implemented or the harmful consequences that are likely if your ideas are not implemented.

6. State, briefly and stirringly, why the audience should endorse the argument you have presented.

SAMPLE OUTLINE AND SPEECH

You will speak more confidently and effectively if you plan your speech carefully, using an outline. Following are a sample outline and speech:

The Outline

INTRODUCTION	When your children watch a 15-second television commercial, they may be forced to shift their attention as many as 50 times.
BODY	
Central Idea	For the sake of our children and our country's future, the design and format of commercials must be regulated.
1st Main Point	Attention span is an essential factor in all learning.
2nd Main Point	A mature attention span is an asset in everyday adult life.
3rd Main Point	A highly developed attention span is indispensable in most careers.
4th Main Point	The solution is to reduce the number of attention shifts in commercials and to cluster commercials at the end of each program.
5th Main Point	Business leaders should take the initiative to implement this solution.
Summary	To summarize, if America's children are to meet the challenges of learning, everyday living, and careers . . . .
Conclusion	Parents and teachers could and should do a better job of educating young people. But they can hardly be expected to do so effectively as long as . . . .

The Speech

When your children watch a 15-second television commercial, they may be forced to shift their attention as many as 50 times. The camera will quickly cut from one scene or angle to another and then another, artificially creating excitement by multiplying images and accelerating the pace of change. Since there are 11 minutes of commercials in every viewing hour, if children watch three hours of television a day, they may shift their attention well over 6,000 times. No one should be surprised that children find it difficult to concentrate on schoolwork.

For the sake of our children and our country's future, the design and format of commercials must be regulated. There is nothing radical or unprecedented about regulation. The Federal Communications

Commission has always had the authority to set standards. In the early days of television, the standard length of a commercial was a full minute. Over the next few decades, the commission first approved 30-second commercials and then 15-second commercials. Meanwhile, advertisers were building in more and more attention shifts. Why is more stringent regulation desirable now? Because a short attention span is a serious handicap in every area of life.

To begin with, attention span is an essential factor in all learning. The more attentive the grade-school child, the more that child will delight in hearing Dr. Seuss's books read and the more quickly he or she will master the fundamentals of reading, writing, and arithmetic. And the longer the child's attention span grows, the more adept he or she will become in reading complex material, struggling with difficult concepts, persevering in investigation and analysis, and engaging in thoughtful dialogue with others.

Second, a mature attention span is an asset in everyday adult life. Successful relationships with other people are not possible without communication skills. That means not only expressing ideas but also listening carefully to what others say and interpreting their nonverbal clues to meaning. It means being observant and reflective not just when the spirit moves us but also when the occasion demands. In short, it means exercising sufficient self-control to maintain concentration even in the midst of distractions. Individuals who have never learned how to focus their attention for more than a few minutes at a time can never engage in meaningful discussions with friends and family and thus can never solve the problems that divide them or strengthen the bonds that unite them.

Third, a highly developed attention span is indispensable in most careers. Any rewarding job poses challenges to one's ingenuity, challenges that cannot be instantly overcome but require extended periods of concentration on small and unexciting details. In such instances, competency as well as excellence depends on painstaking effort. The lawyer labors over the brief, the accountant pores over the tax data, the doctor focuses, sometimes for hours, on the intricacies of the surgical procedure. People whose habits of mind have been shaped by kaleidoscopic commercials are doomed to mediocrity if not inadequacy in their careers. And their shortcomings deprive all who depend on them.

The solution to the problem is to reduce the number of attention shifts in commercials and to cluster commercials at the end of each program. The Federal Communications Commission has already outlawed subliminal messages—those that appear on the screen so briefly that viewers are not conscious of them. They should extend this regulation and limit the number of shifts of scene or camera angle per commercial and perhaps return to the original one-minute commercial. Moreover, the commission should do as many European countries do and eliminate interruptions within programs by moving all commercials to the end of the hour or half hour.

Business leaders should take the initiative to implement this solution because they alone have the necessary power and influence to do so. The advertising industry is often considered responsible for the commercials that are shown on television. Yet the final approval for commercials rests with the corporations that pay for them. If corporate executives were to say, "Here are our new guidelines—follow them," the advertising industry would comply. And corporations have every reason to issue such directives. The attention span of their employees affects their business; the attention span of their fellow citizens affects the strength of the nation.

To summarize, if America's children are to meet the challenges of learning, everyday living, and careers, television commercials must be prevented from retarding attention spans.

Many business leaders and representatives of the media criticize parents and teachers for failing to educate young people. The criticism may be justified in some cases, but the critics must not ignore their own responsibility to foster the development of a mature attention span in America's children.

If the preceding speech were delivered extemporaneously, the speaker would not take the entire text to the podium, only note cards containing key words or phrases, perhaps one or two for each paragraph.

PRACTICING THE DELIVERY

When you hear an accomplished public speaker make a formal presentation, you may be impressed by his or her apparent spontaneity and envy the person's ability to choose the exact words to express thoughts and to connect ideas so clearly and logically. But in most cases, that seeming effortlessness is actually the result of effort. Effective speaking, like effective writing, occurs less by chance than by diligence. That means rehearsing over and over, until your delivery is flawless. Keep the following points in mind when you rehearse and when you deliver the speech.

1. From the moment you rise and walk to the podium until you return to your seat, your audience will be forming impressions of you. Walk (and stand) straight; gesture freely and naturally, but not frenetically or distractingly.

2. People tend to distrust anyone who doesn't look them in the eye. As you look out at your audience, aim for their eyes and not for the back wall or the ceiling. To be sure that everyone gets the impression you are speaking to him or her, shift your gaze from side to side and front to back of the room, pausing for a second or two after each movement. If you look down at your notes, do so briefly, and then quickly reestablish eye contact with your audience.

3. Be sure you speak loudly enough so that everyone in the room can hear you. Enunciate clearly. Keep your tone warm and friendly, and don't be afraid to

smile. If you have identified any bad vocal habits, such as the tendency to slur your words or to let the ends of your sentences trail off into a whisper, make a special effort to avoid them.

4. Remember that almost everyone is nervous when speaking in public, even the most accomplished professionals. The best way to overcome nervousness is to forget about yourself; think instead about the importance of what you are going to say and your audience's desire for you to succeed. (No audience wants to have a speaker punish them with a poor presentation. They want the speaker to do well.) Instead of trying to calm yourself, channel your energy into enthusiasm and dynamism.

WARM-UP EXERCISES

15.1 Decide whether the reasoning in the following statement is sound or unsound. Then write a paragraph or two explaining your judgment.

> If Sarah were a real friend, she'd agree with me whether I was right or wrong in my idea. Even a stranger would agree when I was right. Friendship demands doing more than strangers do.

15.2 Three girls and three jealous boyfriends went to a distant movie theater on a motorcycle that would hold only two. How did they all get there without any girl being left in the company of a boy other than her boyfriend unless her boyfriend was also present?[4]

15.3 Zane is sprawled on the dormitory lounge, holding forth on various matters of philosophic import. As you approach, he says the following.

> One of the biggest problems in the criminal justice system today is the backlog of cases in the courts. And that backlog gets bigger every day. There's no hope of adding more judges with the economy in the shape that it's in. But there is an answer. It's to abolish trials for suspects who freely confess to crimes.

> No one says anything. Zane turns to you and says, "Makes sense, doesn't it?" What do you answer? Be sure to explain your position thoroughly.

 APPLICATIONS

15.1 Application 14.1 directed you to anticipate the negative reactions you would probably receive to your view on each of eight specific cases. Take one of those cases, review your findings on it, and write a persuasive paper, following the approach explained in this chapter.

15.2 Choose one of the following issues. Then apply all the approaches you have learned in this book, and write a persuasive paper in response to it.

a. Should tobacco be outlawed, as marijuana is?

b. Is it wise for the average person to purchase a gun for protection?

c. Should speed limits be abolished on all interstate highways?

d. Is the practice of acupuncture based on superstition? Does it have any therapeutic value?

e. Do Head Start programs increase a child's chance of academic success?

f. Does censorship always undermine democracy?

g. Should colleges have open enrollment policies? (Such policies guarantee that everyone who wants to attend will be allowed to do so, at least in certain programs, regardless of high school performance.)

15.3 One of the most difficult considerations in divorce cases is which parent should be awarded custody of the children. Traditionally, the courts have favored the mother. Today, however, different judges decide differently. Given all the complex factors involved, there is no easy solution to the question of child custody. What guidelines would you follow if you were a family court judge? Apply all the approaches you have learned in this book, and then write a persuasive paper in answer to this question.

15.4 Most people in the United States today regard higher education as a necessity for a secure future. Yet some critics of education believe that the college degree should be abolished. They argue that it has little relation to the world of work, even in the professions. Many jobs that today carry a B.A. or M.A. education requirement, they claim, could be performed satisfactorily by a fairly bright high school graduate. And where further training is required, they believe, it could easily be given on the job. Decide your position on this issue and follow the directions given in previous applications.

15.5 Is it reasonable to believe that unidentified flying objects (UFOs) exist and that they are manned by intelligent beings from outer space? Decide your position on this issue and follow the directions given in previous applications.

15.6 Modern court trials can be long and costly. One way to save money would be to do away with the jury system and let all cases be decided by a judge. Would this be a good idea?

15.7 Some people believe that schools should have a dress code for students—for example, requiring skirts and blouses for girls and slacks for boys. Would such a code be likely to have any salutary effects?

15.8 Most of the assignments given in this book stop short of setting up the problem completely for you in order to give you practice in defining problems yourself. Nevertheless, in the great majority of cases some minor help was given; at the very least, the presentation suggested some possible directions for you to take. These last problems in the book are different. They give not even the slightest suggestion of the nature of the problem or issue or of the direction you should take. They merely present some interesting facts. What you do with them is entirely up to you. If you have learned your lessons well, each item will suggest a number of ideas.

a. The Second Amendment to the U.S. Constitution states, "A well-regulated militia, being necessary to the security of a free State, the right of the people to keep and bear arms, shall not be infringed." The National Rifle Association (NRA) interprets this to mean that people have a constitutional right to own not only rifles and shotguns but pistols and assault weapons as well.

b. Polygamy is at present against the law in this country. This prohibition makes it impossible for some people to act on their religious beliefs. It also, in the view of many people, seems insupportable at a time when numerous nontraditional forms of cohabitation are practiced, including gay marriages and serial monogamy.

c. Public school teachers in New York State may not count attendance in giving grades, according to a decision by the state commissioner of education. The decision prohibits teachers from either giving bonus points for attendance or reducing students' grades for absence from class.[5]

d. A federal government study revealed that more than 80 percent of convicted white-collar criminals spend little or no time behind bars.[6]

ISSUE FOR EXTENDED ANALYSIS

Following is a more comprehensive thinking challenge than the others in the chapter. Analyze and respond to it, following the instructions for extended analysis at the end of Chapter 1. Also, review "The Basis of Moral Judgment" and "Dealing with Dilemmas" in Chapter 2.

THE ISSUE: BORDER CONTROL

Since 1822 the United States has had laws controlling immigration. The laws served various purposes, notably to ensure assimilation, to minimize language differences, and to keep out people deemed inferior. (At various times, the Chinese, the Japanese, and Southern and Central Europeans were so classified.) Today, the laws are less discriminatory; their main purposes are to ensure the nation's safety by preventing entry by terrorists and to spare citizens the burden of providing social benefits to additional millions of people. But both the northern and southern borders (especially the latter) are extremely porous, people's desire to live in the United States is strong, and enforcement is lax.

THE ESSAYS

Welcome the "Tired Masses"
By Regina Fletcher

The inscription on our Statue of Liberty reads: "Give me your tired, your poor, your huddled masses yearning to breathe free." America's finest moments have occurred when they honored that ideal—when we welcomed the Irish after the potato famine, for example, and when people were fleeing Nazi and Communist tyranny. Today we are challenged to do so once again, when desperately poor people are seeking the opportunity to feed their families.

Sadly, some Americans are demanding that the borders be sealed. To this end they propose significant increases in border guards and/or the use of the National Guard. Some, notably the so-called Minute Men, have taken the law into their own hands and conducted their own border operations. Such actions create the image of a police state and bring disgrace on us all.

Opponents of illegal immigration worry about maintaining the rule of law. But the men and women who colonized the country, and whose descendants wrote the immigration laws, were all, in a very real sense, illegal. (Native Americans issued no invitations to those who arrived on their shores.) Besides, the law of charity toward the unfortunate trumps immigration law.

We are a rich nation, not only monetarily, but in the great physical expanse of our land mass and our abundant natural resources. Of all the peoples of the earth, we can most afford to be generous. For that reason, we should not worry whether the

Uphold Immigration Law
By Paul Albergo

It is not at all surprising that many Americans approve illegal immigration. There has long been a tendency among many people to regard immigration laws as an imposition on human rights. But the fact that such an attitude is prevalent doesn't make it reasonable.

Immigration laws are designed to define the concept of citizenship and to protect the rights of citizens. Just as the owners of a house have a right to decide who can visit or live with them, citizens (the "owners" of a country) have a right to decide who may visit or reside in their country and to set appropriate conditions for those who wish to do so. Anyone who enters our country without meeting those conditions violates our laws and disrespects us.

That people who live in poverty or oppression want to escape is understandable, and our present laws provide a compassionate solution to their problem, as well as a fair and orderly process. But there are practical limits as to how many immigrants any one country—even one as large and prosperous as the United States—can accommodate.

Should we encourage people from foreign countries to become students and "guest workers" in the United States, and even to apply for citizenship here? Certainly. Doing so is to our advantage, as well as theirs. However, the process should be conducted within the boundaries of our immigration laws.

When we extend the rights and privileges of citizenship to people who

people seeking to live here are educated or uneducated, have or don't
have special skills, speak English or
some other tongue, are self-sufficient
or require public assistance. We should
welcome all who desire to live here.

are in our country illegally, we not
only mock our own laws but we
reward criminality and insult every
legal applicant. That is a terrible lesson to give our young people and the
rest of the world.

CLASS DISCUSSION

ALONSO: Ms. Fletcher is wrong about the Minute Men. They didn't
take the law into their own hands. They merely observed
the Mexican border, and when they spotted illegal immigrants, they reported them to the authorities. That makes
them good citizens deserving of praise, not condemnation.

VERONIKA: I object to your use of the term "illegal immigrants." It's
much like the term "bastard" that used to be used to
describe children born out of wedlock. It dehumanizes
people. Use the term "undocumented alien."

ALONSO: That's absurd. The term "illegal immigrant" is perfectly
legitimate. A person who migrates here is an immigrant. If
he does so in violation of the law, his immigration is illegal. By the way, the term "bastard" sounds awful to us
only because it is now used as a vulgarism. Originally, it
was an acceptable technical term.

CLAUDE: Those are side issues. The main question is whether people
who enter our country illegally should be welcomed. I say
that all such people lack the very basis of our society and
foundation of our social order—respect for the law—and
therefore should be considered as the criminals they are.

VERONIKA: Claude, you seem to be ignoring the fact that many
American companies are not above using the people you
call criminals to do the difficult work that others won't do.
And they often pay slave wages because undocumented
workers don't dare complain or report them. The farming,
construction, and hotel industries would go out of business
if it weren't for those workers.

CLAUDE: I don't deny that companies hire illegal aliens. I disapprove
of their doing so, and I believe that when they do so know-
ingly, they should be prosecuted.

ALONSO: As I see it, illegal immigration is an insult to all the *legal*
immigrants who obeyed the law, often at great personal
cost. That group includes our parents, grandparents, or
great-grandparents. We owe it to them to enforce our
immigration laws.

Solutions to Sample Problems

THE THREE GLASSES PROBLEM

The key to solving this problem is to use one or more of the glasses as a measuring device. Here's how to proceed.

1. Fill the 3-ounce glass and empty it into the 5-ounce glass. Fill it a second time and empty as much as will fit into the 5-ounce glass. Now the 3-ounce glass will contain 1 ounce of liquid, the 5-ounce glass 5 ounces, and the 8-ounce glass 2 ounces.

2. Empty the 5-ounce glass into the 8-ounce glass. Then empty the 3-ounce glass into the 5-ounce glass. Now the 3-ounce glass will be empty, the 5-ounce glass will contain 1 ounce of liquid, and the 8-ounce glass 7 ounces.

3. Fill the 3-ounce glass from the 8-ounce glass. Then empty the 3-ounce glass into the 5-ounce glass. Now the 3-ounce glass will be empty, and the 5- and 8-ounce glasses will each contain 4 ounces.

THE YOUNG GIRL/OLD WOMAN PROBLEM

The young girl is looking away from you. You can see only the side of her face. The old woman is looking down, her chin touching the top of her chest.

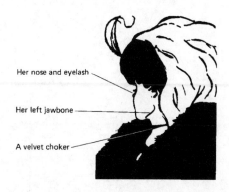

Her nose and eyelash

Her left jawbone

A velvet choker

271

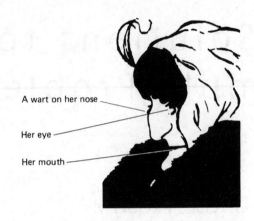

A wart on her nose

Her eye

Her mouth

THE VASE AND FACES PROBLEM

To see the vase, focus on the white object against a background of shadow. To see two faces, imagine a bright light shining through a window and two people standing nose to nose, in silhouette.

Notes

Chapter 1

1. Arthur Koestler, *The Act of Creation* (New York: Macmillan, 1964), p. 173.
2. *Using Your Mind Effectively* (New York: McGraw-Hill, 1951), pp. vi–vii.
3. "Research Synthesis on Right and Left Hemispheres," *Educational Leadership* 40, no. 4 (January 1983): 66–71.
4. William H. Calvin, "Left Brain, Right Brain: Science or the New Phrenology," Chapter 10, of *The Throwing Madonna*, http://universe.com, 2001.
5. Accessed on 11/20/02 @ http://www .nobel.se/medicine/laureates/1981/ sperry-lecture.html.
6. See, for example, Sidney Parnes, *Creative Behavior Guidebook* (New York: Scribner's, 1967), p. 32.
7. *Guiding Creative Talent* (Englewood Cliffs, NJ: Prentice-Hall, 1962), p. 5.
8. Brewster Ghiselin, *The Creative Process: A Symposium* (Berkeley: University of California Press, 1954), p. 115.
9. See, for example, J. Dewey, *Art as Experience* (New York: Milton Balch, 1934), p. 73.
10. Quoted in W. I. B. Beveridge, *The Art of Scientific Investigation* (New York: Norton, 1951), p. 56.
11. Koestler, *Act of Creation*, p. 146.
12. This definition is Henry Hazlitt's, quoted in ibid., pp. 72–73.
13. Benjamin Bloom and Lois J. Broder, *Problem-Solving Processes of College Students* (Chicago: University of Chicago Press, 1950), pp. 25–30.
14. This section copyright © 2002 by MindPower, Inc. Used with permission.
15. *The Art of Thinking* (New York: Simon & Schuster, 1928), pp. 103–104.

Chapter 2

1. According to the CBS news program *60 Minutes*, 17 September 1978, the most popular street names are, first, Park (avenue or street) and, second, Washington. Main is thirty-second on the list, and Broadway is not in the top 50.
2. *Reason and Teaching* (New York: Bobbs-Merrill, 1973).
3. Michael Brenson, "Scholars Re-Examining Rembrandt . . . ," *New York Times*, 25 November 1985, p. 6.
4. John Phin, *The Seven Follies of Science*, 3rd ed. (New York: Van Nostrand, 1912), p. 202.
5. Ibid., p. 208.
6. Robert P. Crawford, *Think for Yourself* (New York: Fraser, 1937), p. 118.
7. Quoted in Harold A. Larrabee, *Reliable Knowledge*, rev. ed. (Boston: Houghton Mifflin, 1964), p. 22.
8. *New York Times*, 6 December 1981, p. 27.
9. "Computer Points to Single Author for Genesis," *New York Times*, 8 November 1981, p. 7.
10. The correct answers are as follows: (1) An English playwright. Although history books have traditionally credited Nathan Hale with the statement, Hale actually said, "It is the duty of every good officer to obey any orders given him by his commander-in-chief." His biographer borrowed the playwright's words. (2) The signal that was used is not known. The poet Henry Wadsworth Longfellow invented the well-known "one if by land and two if by sea" signal. (Both this and the answer to 1 are found in Michael T. Kaufman, "Myths of '76 Revolution Deflated at Yale Parley," *New York Times*, 4 May 1975, pp. 1ff.) (3) Fur. The idea of a glass slipper occurred because the French word for *fur* was incorrectly translated. (4) Siberian squirrel fur. (Both this and the answer to 3 are found in Phin, *Seven Follies*, p. 208.)
11. *New York Times Magazine*, 1 December 1974, p. 31.
12. "The Great Change in Children," *Horizon*, XIII (Winter 1971), p. 4.
13. Walter Lippmann, *Public Opinion* (New York: Harcourt, Brace, 1922), p. 90.

14. *Freedom of the Press* (Indianapolis: Bobbs-Merrill, 1935).

15. *Oneonta* (New York) *Star*, 6 February 1982, p. 3.

16. *The Art of Straight Thinking* (New York: Appleton, 1929), p. 269.

17. Elizabeth Loftus and Katherine Ketcham, *Witness for the Defense: The Accused, the Eyewitness, and the Expert Who Puts Memory on Trial* (New York: St. Martin's Press, 1992), p. 77. See also Elizabeth Loftus, *Eyewitness Testimony* (Boston: Harvard University Press, 1979).

18. Frederick C. Bartlett, *Remembering: A Study in Experimental and Social Psychology* (New York: Cambridge University Press, 1932), pp. 205–207.

19. Columbia Associates in Philosophy, *An Introduction to Reflective Thinking* (Boston: Houghton Mifflin, 1923), p. 189.

20. Larrabee, *Reliable Knowledge*, p. 203.

21. Martin Gardner, *Fads and Fallacies in the Name of Science* (New York: Dover, 1957), p. 123.

22. See, for example, John Altrocchi, *Abnormal Behavior* (New York: Harcourt Brace Jovanovich, 1980), pp. 17ff.

23. Gardner, *Fads and Fallacies*, pp. 155–157.

24. This section is copyrighted © by MindPower, Inc., 2008, and is used with permission.

25. Cited in Robert H. Bork, *Slouching Towards Gomorrah* (NY: ReganBooks, 1996), 144.

26. At first consideration, it might seem that the front driver in each case caused the accident behind him/her. However, the law holds each driver responsible for maintaining sufficient distance to stop and avoid a crash.

27. The story of Raoul Wallenberg is detailed in John Bierman, *Righteous Gentile* (New York: Viking, 1982).

28. "Starving Children Saved by NYC Police," *Oneonta Star*, 13 October 1981, p. 13.

29. Joseph Jastrow, *Effective Thinking* (New York: Simon & Schuster, 1931), p. 121.

30. Warren Hoge, "Machismo 'Absolved' in Notorious Brazilian Trial," *New York Times*, 28 October 1979, p. 24.

31. Quoted in E. L. McKitrick, ed., *Slavery Defended: The Views of the Old South* (Englewood Cliffs, NJ: Prentice-Hall, 1963), p. 53.

32. "Doctor Convicted of Rape Accused of Raping Others," *Oneonta Star*, 19 September 1981, p. 2.

33. "Family Steadfast Despite Girl's Death," *Oneonta Star*, 17 November 1981, p. 2.

34. Diane Henry, "Parents of Three Retarded Girls . . . ," *New York Times*, 2 October 1977, pp. 1ff.

Chapter 3

1. John Godfrey Saxe, quoted in Don Fabun, *Communication: The Transfer of Meaning* (Encino, CA: Glencoe, 1968), p. 13.

2. D. Wallechinsky and I. Wallace, *The People's Almanac*, Vol. 1 (New York: Doubleday, 1975), p. 1089.

3. Ibid.

4. D. S. Hiroto, "Locus of Control and Learned Helplessness," *Journal of Experimental Psychology*, 102 (1974): 187–193. See also C. Diener and C. Dweck, "An Analysis of Learned Helplessness," *Journal of Personality and Social Psychology*, 39 (1980): 5.

5. Maxwell Maltz, *Psycho-Cybernetics* (New York: Pocket Books, 1969), pp. 49ff.

6. The study was done by Children Now and reported in *Better Homes & Gardens*, September, 2002, p. 250. Cited at http://www.med.sc.edu:1081/mediause.htm (accessed 11/21/02).

7. "The Creative Attitude," in *Creativity and Its Cultivation*, ed. Harold H. Anderson (New York: Harper & Brothers, 1959), p. 48.

8. *Clear Thinking* (New York: Longman, Green, 1967), p. 79.

9. Koestler, *Act of Creation*, p. 75.

10. See, for example, May Edel and Abraham Edel, *Anthropology and Ethics* (Springfield, IL: Charles C Thomas, 1959), pp. 88ff.

11. Jepson, *Clear Thinking*, p. 81.

12. Edwin A. Burtt, *Right Thinking*, 3rd ed. (New York: Harper & Brothers, 1946), p. 63.

13. *Clear Thinking*, p. 81.

14. Reprinted in Parnes, *Creative Behavior Guidebook*, p. 19.

15. Wallechinsky and Wallace, *People's Almanac*, Vol. 1, p. 1091.

16. *Toward a Psychology of Being*, 2nd ed. (Princeton, NJ: Van Nostrand, 1968), p. 34.
17. *Public Opinion*, pp. 119–120.
18. William J. Reilly, *The Twelve Rules for Straight Thinking* (New York: Harper & Brothers, 1947), p. 15.
19. Quoted in Ghiselin, *Creative Process*, p. 207.
20. *Art of Straight Thinking*, p. 242.
21. Claudia Wallis, "Going Gentle into That Good Night," *Time*, 8 February 1982, p. 79.
22. Quoted in Jastrow, *Effective Thinking*, pp. 130–131.
23. "Mother to Lose Child over Kosher Food," *Oneonta Star*, 4 February 1982, p. 21.
24. "Graduate Sues for One Million . . . ," *New York Times*, 26 November 1972, p. 41.
25. "Minister Charged in Rooster Rite," *Oneonta Star*, 25 February 1982, p. 2.

Chapter 4

1. Mursell, *Using Your Mind Effectively*, p. 217.
2. James Harvey Robinson, *The Mind in the Making* (New York: Harper & Brothers, 1921), p. 46.
3. Larry Elder, *The Ten Things You Can't Say in America* (New York: St. Martin's Press, 2000), pp. 44–45.
4. Peggy Rosenthal, *Words and Values: Some Leading Words and Where They Lead Us* (New York: Oxford University Press, 1984), p. 21.
5. Ibid., p. 22. Carl Rogers's sentence is as follows: "When the self is free from any threat of attack . . . then it is possible for the self to consider these hitherto rejected perceptions, to make new differentiations, and to reintegrate the self in such a way as to include them."
6. "Photo of Dinosaur Needs Some Help," *Oneonta Star*, 29 December 1981, p. 2.
7. *Time*, 25 January 1982, p. 31.
8. The task of critical evaluation is especially difficult in politics because modern politicians use focus groups to determine what words and phrases will resonate best with voters and what demeanor and speaking style will convey strength, leadership, integrity, and other desirable characteristics. It is therefore difficult to determine whether the message and delivery are genuine, contrived, or some combination of the two.
9. Edward R. Tufte, *The Visual Display of Quantitative Information* (Cheshire, CT: Graphics Press, 1983), unnumbered introduction, 55, 79, 81, respectively.
10. Walter Dill Scott, *The Psychology of Advertising* (Boston: Small, Maynard & Company, 1913), pp. 38, 47, 82.
11. David Cohen, *J. B. Watson: The Founder of Behaviourism* (London: Routledge & Kegan Paul, 1979), 176–80.
12. *New York Times Magazine*, 7 November 1971, p. 30. © 1971 by the New York Times Company. Reprinted by permission.

Chapter 5

1. Paul Smith, ed., *Creativity: An Examination of the Creative Process* (New York: Hastings House, 1959), p. 17.
2. The best source of current works (as well as important older works) is the *Journal of Creative Behavior*.
3. *The Art and Science of Creativity* (New York: Holt, 1965), p. 2.
4. Quoted in Parnes, *Creative Behavior Guidebook*, p. 7.
5. J. W. Getzels and P. W. Jackson, *Creativity and Intelligence* (New York: Wiley, 1962), pp. 21ff. Also Torrance, *Guiding Creative Talent*, pp. 5, 63.
6. *Creative Process*, p. 9.
7. *How to Think Creatively* (Nashville: Abingdon-Cokesbury Press, 1949), p. 79.
8. "Creativity in Perspective," in Anderson, ed., *Creativity and Its Cultivation*, p. 258.
9. Good sources of studies include Getzels and Jackson, *Creativity and Intelligence;* Torrance, *Guiding Creative Talent;* and Parnes, *Creative Behavior Guidebook*.
10. Quoted in C. P. Curtis and F. Greenslet, eds., *The Practical Cogitator* (Boston: Houghton Mifflin, 1945), p. 231.
11. Quoted in William J. J. Gordon, *Synectics: The Development of Creative Capacity* (New York: Harper & Brothers, 1961), p. 116.
12. Joseph Rossman, *The Psychology of the Inventor* (Washington, DC: Inventors' Publishing Company, 1931), pp. 82ff.
13. Gordon, *Synectics*, p. 360.

14. Alex Osborn, *Applied Imagination* (New York: Scribner's, 1957), p. 196.

15. Getzels and Jackson, *Creativity and Intelligence*, p. 53.

16. "Couple Learns Golden Rule . . . ," *Oneonta Star*, 29 August 1981, p. 1.

17. "In Divorce, Kids Get the House," *Oneonta Star*, 20 January 1982, p. 1.

18. *Chronicle of Higher Education*, 12 December 1987, p. A2.

19. http://arbl.cvmbs.colostate.edu/hbooks/ genetics/medgen/dnatesting/, accessed 11/19/02.

20. *Time*, 14 November 1988, p. 22.

21. "Grafitti Gobbler Gets Attention," *Oneonta Star*, 30 November 1981, p. 2.

22. "Crippled Inventor Is Standing Proud," *Oneonta Star*, 6 February 1982, p. 1.

23. "Trouble Sleeping? Call Up the Sandman," *Oneonta Star*, 7 July 1982, p. 1.

24. "Waterbabies," *Time*, 10 May 1982, p. 87.

25. "New Inventions from the Cornfield," *New York Times*, 10 January 1988, sec. 4, p. 36.

26. *U.S. News & World Report*, 7 March 1988, p. 53.

27. J. H. Plumb, "The Great Change in Children," *Horizon*, XIII (Winter, 1971), p. 7.

28. Hutchinson, *How to Think Creatively*, p. 38, for example, lists four stages, but one of them is "verification," which involves the process of solution refinement classified in this text as critical thinking.

29. Henry Hazlitt, *Thinking as a Science* (New York: E. P. Dutton & Co., 1966), p. 17.

Chapter 6

1. Frank Lorimer, *The Growth of Reason* (New York: Harcourt, Brace; London: Kegan Paul, LTD., 1929), pp. 124–126. Reprinted with permission.

2. Parnes, *Creative Behavior Guidebook*, p. 29.

3. Osborn, *Applied Imagination*, p. 130.

4. Interview in *Inc.*, December 1985, pp. 33ff.

5. Beveridge, *Art of Scientific Investigation*, p. 92.

6. Ibid., p. 28.

7. "Man Kills Wife in Spat over Penny," *Oneonta Star*, 16 February 1982, p. 10.

8. Jane E. Brody, "Kinsey Study Shows Deep Predisposition," *New York Times*, 23 August 1981, pp. 1ff.

9. "Shyness Traced to Genetic Base," *Oneonta Star*, 5 January 1982, p. 1.

10. "Tests Said to Predict Criminal Traits," *Oneonta Star*, 8 January 1982, p. 7.

11. "Court Rules Inmate May Starve Himself," *Oneonta Star*, 2 February 1982, p. 2.

12. "Fickle Universe," *Time*, 25 January 1982, p. 61.

13. *Oneonta Star*, 5 February 1982, p. 1.

14. "Motorist Returns License," *Oneonta Star*, 22 January 1982, p. 3.

15. *New York Times*, 28 January 1982, p. 14.

Chapter 7

1. Dan Kaercher, "School Closings: What Can Parents Do?" *Better Homes and Gardens*, August 1982, p. 17.

2. "No Pass, No Drive," *U.S. News & World Report*, 5 June 1989, p. 49.

3. George Iles, *Inventors at Work* (New York: Doubleday, Page, 1906), p. 370.

4. " 'Priestess' Is Convicted as Prostitute," *St. Petersburg Times*, 10 September 1989, p. 7A.

5. Interview on *Good Morning America*, 29 August 1980.

Chapter 8

1. *Logic for the Millions* (New York: Philosophical Library, 1947), p. 55.

2. "Child Abuse a Major Factor in Multiple Personalities," *Oneonta Star*, 31 October 1985, p. 5.

3. Elizabeth Loftus and Katherine Ketcham, *Witness for the Defense: The Accused, the Eyewitness, and the Expert Who Puts Memory on Trial* (New York: St. Martin's Press, 1991), p. 20.

4. Cited in Carole Wade and Carol Tavris, *Psychology*, 5th ed. (New York: Longman, 1998), pp. 656–657.

5. Cited in Wade and Tavris, pp. 672–673.

6. Parnes, *Creative Behavior Guidebook*, p. 40.

7. Koestler, *Act of Creation*, p. 123.

8. "Dolphins May Help Train Retarded Tots," *Binghamton Press*, 28 February 1982, p. 5a.

9. "America's Diet Wars," *U.S. News & World Report*, 20 January 1985, p. 62. See also "Obesity Depends on Genetics," *Oneonta Star*, 23 January 1986, pp. 1ff.
10. This section copyright © 2002 by MindPower, Inc. Used with permission.
11. Marilyn Elias, "Inborn Traits Outweigh Environment," *USA Today*, 9 August 1989, pp. 1Df.
12. "Bank Robber, 10, Back in Trouble," *Oneonta Star*, 13 February 1982, p. 1.
13. "Tot's Testimony Crucial in Murder Trial," *Binghamton Press*, 26 October 1975, p. 2.
14. "A Man Called Jamison," *New York Times*, 26 January 1975, sec. 4, p. 9.
15. "Expert Warns on Testimony . . . ," *New York Times*, 10 January 1982, p. 44.
16. "Fetus Born Alive After . . . ," *Binghamton Press*, 15 November 1981, p. 1a.
17. www.bioethics.iastate.edu, accessed 11/20/02.

Chapter 9

1. This analogy was first made by Zbigniew Pietraskinski, *The Psychology of Efficient Thinking*, trans. B. Jankowski (New York: Pergamon Press, 1969), p. 134.
2. Parnes, *Creative Behavior Guidebook*, p. 57.
3. Quoted in Osborn, *Applied Imagination*, p. 149.
4. Quoted in ibid., p. 151.
5. Parnes, *Creative Behavior Guidebook*, pp. 57–58.
6. Quoted in Beveridge, *Art of Scientific Investigation*, p. 143.
7. Quoted in Clarence D. Tuska, *Inventors and Inventions* (New York: McGraw-Hill, 1957), p. 88.
8. Parnes, *Creative Behavior Guidebook*, pp. 55–56.
9. *The Art of Thought* (New York: Harcourt, Brace, 1926), p. 139.
10. Parnes, *Creative Behavior Guidebook*, p. 57.
11. Max Wertheimer, *Productive Thinking* (New York: Harper & Brothers, 1945), pp. 169–173.
12. Quoted in Koestler, *Act of Creation*, p. 118.
13. See, for example, Hutchinson, *How to Think Creatively*, pp. 35–40.

14. "TV Fights Charges It Undercuts Reading," *Binghamton Press*, 29 November 1981, p. 1a.

Chapter 10

1. See, for example, Lenore Weitzman, *The Divorce Revolution* (New York: Free Press, 1986).
2. Jepson, *Clear Thinking*, p. 194.

Chapter 11

1. Hutchinson, *How to Think Creatively*, pp. 182–183.
2. D. Wallechinsky and I. Wallace, *The People's Almanac*, vol. 2 (New York: Bantam, 1978), p. 817.
3. Wallechinsky and Wallace, *People's Almanac*, vol. 1, pp. 914–915.
4. Wallechinsky and Wallace, *People's Almanac*, vol. 2, p. 821.
5. Max Black, *Critical Thinking* (Englewood Cliffs, NJ: Prentice-Hall, 1952), pp. 156–157.
6. John Leo, "Single Parent, Double Trouble," *Time*, 4 January 1982, p. 81.
7. "Moneyball," *New York Times*, 28 March 1982, sec. 4, p. 22.

Chapter 13

1. Harold J. Rothwax, *Guilty: The Collapse of Criminal Justice* (New York: Random House, 1996).
2. Black, *Critical Thinking*, p. 157.

Chapter 15

1. Dick Gregory, *Write Me In!* (New York: Bantam, 1968), p. 13.
2. G. K. Chesterton, "A Meditation in Broadway," in *The Man Who Was Chesterton*, ed. Raymond T. Bond (Garden City, NY: Doubleday, 1960), p. 150.
3. Mortimer J. Adler, *How to Speak, How to Listen* (New York: Simon & Schuster, 1983), p. 910.
4. Roger W. Holmes, *The Rhyme of Reason* (New York: Appleton-Century, 1939), p. 458.
5. "Teachers Can't Count Attendance in Grades," *Oneonta Star*, 14 May 1985, p. 10.
6. *Oneonta Star*, 17 November 1986, p. 1.

Index

Abbott, Jack Henry, 77
Abortion issue, 129
Abstracting services, 148
Acculturation, 53
Action
    considering, 228
    decisions regarding taking of,
        229
    recognizing and overcoming
        difficulties before, 229–230
    taking, on issue, 192
Active listening, 14
Addis, William, 198
Adler, Mortimer J., 154–155, 237,
    261
Advertisements, 82
Affirmative action, 178–181
Agenda, 13
Agnesi, Maria Gaetana, 240–241
Alcohol, as hindrance to
    creativity, 10, 99
Alexander, Jan, 149
Almanacs, 147
Ambiguity
    of argument, 71–72
    being aware of, in argument,
        71
    of statements, 16
    of terms, 70
Analogy, 166–167
Analysis
    ensuring comprehensive, in
        examining solutions, 199
    of ideas, 171
    if-then, 16
    issue, 5
    necessary step in argument,
        219
Anderson, Harold H., 99
Anecdotes
    in compositions, 255
    in formal speaking, 262
*Anger: The Misunderstood
    Emotion* (Tavris), 152
Appeals, irrational, 214
Appeal to authority, 214
Archimedes, 172
Arguments
    abolishing Miranda rule,
        231–232
    avoiding the issue in, 211
    case of mentally impaired
        girls, 221–222

case of parents protesting TV
    programs, 220
clarity of, 78
complex, recognizing, 218–219
components of sound, 210
constructing pro and con,
    167–168
determining validity of,
    214–216
evaluating, 210–227
finding and correcting overgen-
    eralization in, 212
finding and correcting oversim-
    plifications in, 213
with hidden premises, 216–217
hypothetical, example of
    valid, 215–216
irrational appeals, 214
judging, on merits, 69
negative-effect, 168
pledging allegiance to flag,
    230–231
positive-effect, 168
shifting burden of proof in,
    213–214
steps in evaluating, 219
Aristotle, 69
Asch, Solomon, 143
Assertions
    and burden of proof, 213–214
    in imaginary-dialogue tech-
        nique, 243–245
    key, in critical listening, 81
    overgeneralization in, 212
    presentation for written,
        255–256
    sensitivity to implications of,
        130–131
    thinking of ideas as, 168
Assumptions
    avoiding, 188–189
    based on experiences, 30
    reading for implications and, 17
Attitudes
    of audience, 241–242
    changing habits and, 8
    effect of popular culture on, 53
    evaluating your, 54
    imitating, 51
    individuality and, 53–54
    maintaining critical, during
        problem-solving process, 12
    toward audience, 245–246

Audience
    anticipating objections of,
        243–245
    appeals aimed at emotions of,
        214
    confusion, overcoming, 15
    emphasizing evidence for, 247
    keeping interest of, 262
    knowing, 241–243
    maintaining eye contact with,
        265
    opinions of, 241
    persuading, 239–240
    popular misconceptions of,
        242
    reaction to incoherence, 253
    re-creating experiences and
        observations for, 247
    respecting, 245–246
Authorities. *See also* Expert opin-
    ion/experts
    of differing perspectives, con-
        sulting, 152
    finding, on Internet, 148–151
    interviewing, 152–153
    library as source for, 146
Authority, appeal to, 214
Authors
    bias of, 76
    expressing judgment about,
        75–76
    giving credit to, 154–155
    paraphrasing ideas of,
        155–156

Bacon, Francis, 68
Ballpoint pen, invention of, 198
Banks, Curtis, 143
Beethoven, Ludwig von, 9
Behavior
    avoiding rude and disrespect-
        ful, 14
    control over, 26
    creative, 105
    indicators of, 37
    making observations about,
        117
    onset of criminal, 120
    persuasiveness as learned, 239
Behaviorism, 82
Beliefs
    deciding on most reasonable,
        228

Beliefs (continued)
difference between truth and, 27–28
embracing of, 106
objections to challenged, 240–241
Bell, Alexander Graham, 197, 201
Berson, Lawrence, 29
Bias
of authors, 76
awareness of, through reflection, 74
and construction of arguments, 168
critical listening and, 80
Bible, 28
Biro, Laszlo, 198
Body, for formal speech, 262
Bohemian mystique, 99
Books, accuracy of, 32
Border control, 268–270
Brackets, use of, 154
Brain
-damaged patients, treatment of, 47–49
and mind at work, 6–7
structure of, 6–7
Brainstorming, 243
Brevity, striving for, 257
Burden of proof, shifting, 213–214
Burke, Edmund, 68
Bush, George W., 137

Calvin, John, 240
Calvin, William H., 7
Campus speech codes, 249–251
Capital punishment, 129–130
Carbone, Richard, 29
Carlson, Chester, 241
Causation, 35–39
coincidence and, 35
complexity of, 38–39
defined, 36
force/necessity and, 35–36
free will and, 37–38, 39
Causes, searching for, 119
Cause-to-effect order, 255
Central idea
in composition, 253
in formal speech, 262
Challenges
creative people and, 101
identifying, 131
searching for, 105, 112–126
Change, resistance to, 56–58
Charts, 81
Chesterton, G. K., 185
Childhood, 30–31
concept of, 104
curiosity in, 113–114
suppression of curiosity in, 115

Choice, 26
Chrysler, Walter, 118
Churchill, Winston, 51, 69, 80
Circumstances, moral judgment and, 42
Clarity
aiming for, in discussion, 14
of argument, 78
of thought, 15
Clarke, Edwin L., 32, 60
Classification
of experiences, 30
use of double standard in, 213
Cognitive psychology, 7
Coherence
in effective writing, 253
in formal speech, 261
Coincidence, 35
Columbine High School, 123
Columbus, Christopher, 100
Common practice, appeal to, 214
Communication
persuasive, 68–69
visual, 81
Communication technology revolution, 6
Competition
business, from other countries, 6
comparing plan of action with, 230
comparing solutions with, 200
Complex arguments
examples of, 218–219
recognizing, 218–219
Complexity, 42
Complications, finding, in solutions, 199–200
Composition
achieving emphasis in, 253–254
central idea, 253
coherence in, 253
drafting, 256
editing, 257
effective ways to conclude, 255
introductions for, 255
planning, 254–256
revising, 256
sample, film violence, 259–260
Compulsion, 26
Computer databases, 148
Concentration, 3
thinking and, 11
Concept(s)
childhood as, 104
improving new or revised, 201
inventing or redefining, 104–105
Conclusions
choosing, for composition, 255
evaluating, 76

for formal speeches, 262
illegitimate, 214, 215–216
legitimate, 214–215
reasoning linking premises and, 219
of statements, 16
Conclusion-to-evidence order, 254
Conditioning, 26
Conditions
conducive for thinking, 10
reversal of, 216
Confidence
demonstrating, during discussions, 14
effect of negativity on, 50–52
Conflict
identifying, 77
obligations in, 42
Conflicting testimony, 77
Conformity, 58–59
Confusion, 3, 11
as obstacle to idea production, 171
overcoming, 158
overcoming audience, 15
between taste and judgments, 69–70
Conscience, 41
Consequences, 42, 43
Conservative opinion web sites, 149, 151
Constitution, U.S., 137
Control
over behavior, 26
and thinking, 4
Controversies. *See also* Problems
either/or thinking in, 211
recognizing opportunities in, 120–121
related to human nature, 22–24
Copernicus, Nicolaus, 10, 240
Corpus callosum, 6, 7
Correlation, causation and, 35
Counterarguments, 76
Crawford, Robert P., 112
Creative process, 97–111. *See also* Creativity
brainstorming, 243
expressing problem or issue, 105–106
investigating problem or issue, 106
for making improvements, 200–201
producing ideas, 106
searching for challenges, 105
stages in, 105–106
Creative thinking
counterproductive conditions for, 10

process, 97–111
production phase of mind in, 7
Creativity. *See also* Creative
    process
    applying, to problems and
        issues, 102–105
    characteristics of, 100–101
    counterproductive conditions
        for, 10
    drugs and, 99
    essence of, 105
    as expression of mental
        health, 99
    hindrances to, 99
    IQ and, 98–99
    keeping life in, 158
    key facts about, 98–99
    resistance to change and, 58
Criminal behavior, 120
Critical evaluation, 67–68. *See
    also* Critical reading
    critical listening, 79–81
    critical viewing, 81–82
    defined, 68–69
    making distinctions, 69–73
    sample evaluation and judg-
        ment, 77–79
Critical listening, 79–81
Critical reading, 1, 68, 73–77
    evaluating during, 75–76
    evaluation in, 68
    expressing judgment in, 76–77
    making distinctions in, 69–73
    reflection, 74
    sample evaluation, 77–79
    skimming, 73–74
    strategy for, 73–77
Critical thinking, 7–8, 98, 183
    applying curiosity to, 187
    avoiding assumptions,
        188–189
    defined, 185
    judging opinion by evidence in,
        70
    judgment phase of mind in, 7–8
    overcoming obstacles to, 187
    reduction of error using, 186
    refining positions on issues,
        190–191
    refining resolution of issue,
        228–229
    refining solutions to problems,
        189, 197–209
    sample issue, 191–192
    sample problem, 189–190
Critical viewing, 81–82
Criticism
    of ideas produced, need for,
        186–187
    need for, 185–186
    role of, 185–196

using inquisitive approach to,
    187
Cultural values, 40–41
Curiosity
    applying, to critical thinking,
        187
    connecting dissatisfactions to,
        118–119
    of creative people, 112
    defined, 115
    difficulty of developing, 242
    importance of, 113–114
    loss of, 115
    observations and, 116–117
    recognizing opportunity in
        controversy and, 120–121
    regaining, 115–121
    and searching for causes of
        things, 119
    sense of imperfection and, 118
    sensitivity to implications and,
        120
    suppression of childhood, 115

Daring, as characteristic of cre-
    ative people, 100
Darwin, Charles, 35
Databases, computer, 148
Daydreaming, 4
    slipping in aimless, 166
D.B. Kaplan's, 102
Decision making
    contribution of feelings to, 10
    thinking proficiency and, 5–6
Defense mechanism, 55
Delivery, practicing speech,
    265–266
Details
    alertness to, 171
    factual, as evidence, 69–70
    learning, about audience,
        241–242
    of solutions, examining for
        imperfections, 199–200
    of solutions, working out,
        198–199
Determinism, free will *vs.,* 26
Development
    of composition, 253
    in effective writing, 254
    in formal speech, 261
Dewey decimal system, 102
Diagramming, 16
Dialogue, 16–17
    imaginary-, technique, 243–245
    unstated idea in, 17–18
Dilemmas, 44
Dimnet, Ernest, 15
Discussion, 12–14
    advance preparation for, 13
    atmosphere for productive, 13

avoiding distractions speech
    mannerisms during, 13–14
avoiding rude and disrespect-
    ful behavior, 14
contributing to without domi-
    nating, 13
at its best and worst, 12
judging ideas responsibly, 14
listening actively during, 14
setting reasonable expectations
    for, 13
Dissatisfactions, noting own and
    others', 118–119
Double standard, 213
Drafting, 256
Dramatic presentation, 82
Drug use, as hindrance to creativ-
    ity, 10, 99
Dynamism, as characteristic of
    creative people, 100

Echo words, 254
Edison, Thomas, 10, 51, 100, 101
Editing, 257
Effect-to-cause order, 255
Ego
    disrespect engendered by, 13
    and face saving, 55–56, 100
    and search for truth, 54–55
    threats to, 56
    using, to advantage, 186
Einstein, Albert, 10–11, 171
    early record of, 51–52
    on imagination, 165
    on playfulness, 100, 187
    thinking pattern of, 5
Eisenhower, Dwight, 228
Either/or thinking, 211
Emphasis
    in effective writing, 253–254
    of evidence for view, 247
    in formal speech, 261
Encyclopedias, 147
Enthymeme, 216
Enunciation, 265–266
Errors
    affecting truth, 210–214, 219
    affecting validity, 214–216,
        219
    in logic, evaluating, 76
    made from carelessness, 32
    in news reports, 32
    reducing chance of, with criti-
        cal thinking, 186
Ethical perspectives, 40–44
Evaluation
    of argument, steps in, 219
    of arguments on issues,
        210–219
    in critical listening, 81
    in critical reading, 75–76

.ation (continued)
ɔf experiences, 30
of ideas during critical thinking process, 97
process, of positions on issues, 220–222
of quality of Web sites, 149
questions useful in, 128–130
sample critical, 77–79
of your ideas and attitudes, 54
Evidence, 69–70
in composition, 255–256
conclusion-to-, order, 254
emphasizing, for persuasion, 247
finding most reasonable answer in light of, 229
forms of, 70
judging opinions by, 70
judgments and supporting, 34–35
kinds and quality of, 75, 79
questions to answer relating to, 75–76
to-conclusion order, 254
Experience(s)
memories of, 33
obtaining knowledge by, 30–31
other people's, as information source, 146
personal, as information source, 145
recreating, for audience, 247
Experimental psychology, 33. See also Experiments
Experiments, 32–33, 50–51, 58
categories of, 143
Expert opinion/experts, 142–143
evaluating, 76
Expression
benefits of careful, 131–133
examples of lively, imaginative, 258
refining, 131
of sample issue, 134–135
of sample problem, 133–134
Extemporaneous speeches, 261
Eye contact, maintaining, 265
Eyewitness testimony, 33, 141–142

Face saving, 55–56, 100
effect on thinking of, 56
Facts, 5
defined, 70
determining audience familiarity with, 242
distinction between interpretation and, 70–71
remaining open to, 13
Factual inaccuracy, 210

Failures, 11
False starts, 11
Fashion, behavior and, 37
Fear
appeal to, 214
resistance to change and, 57–58
Feelings, proper relationship of thoughts and, 10–11
Field experiments, 143
Filibusters, 137
Footnotes, 154, 258
Force, causation and, 35–36
Foreign aid, U.S., 161–163
Formal logic, 214
Formal speeches
body, 262
characteristics of effective, 260–261
conclusion, 262
introduction, 261
organizing material for, 261–262
outline for, 263
practicing delivery of, 265–266
sample, 263–265
types of, 261
Foss, Sam Walter, 56–57
Free association, 15, 166, 174
Free will, 25
causation and, 37–38, 39
determinism vs., 26
Freewriting, 15
Fringe thoughts, 169
Fromm, Erich, 53, 99
Frustration, coping with, 11–12

Galileo, 56, 100, 240
Gay marriage, 207–209
General Agreement on Tariffs and Trade (GATT), 6
Generalizations, 59
getting beyond, 42
Genesis, 28
Ghiselin, Brewster, 99
Global economy, 6
Google, 149, 150
Gordon, William, 101
Graffiti, 141
Graham, Martha, 51
Graphs, 81
Greater good, 44
Guilford, J. P., 99
Gutenberg, Johannes, 145, 166

Habit(s)
behavior and, 37
building better writing, 257–258
changing, 8
conformity, 58–59
considerations for work, 9–10

effect of popular culture on, 53
face saving, 55–56
of failure, 51
good thinking as, 8
hindering thinking, 54–61
imitating attitudes and, 51
mine-is-better, 54–55
moving beyond, 131
overcoming bad, 61–62
resistance to change, 56–58
self-deception, 60–61
stereotyping, 59–60
Hamilton, Lee, 103
Haney, Craig, 143
Harvey, William, 241
Hazlitt, Henry, 105
Health information, Web sites for, 151
Herrnstein, Richard, 70
Hidden premise
defined, 216
examples of arguments with, 217
Hilgard, Ernest, 99
Hitler, Adolf, 41, 69, 72
Hoaxes, locating, 149
Homosexuality, cause of, 120
Howe, Elias, 188–189
Human nature, controversy over, 22–24
Hutchinson, Eliot (Dole), 99, 197–198
Hypotheses, testing, 143

Ideals, 42, 43
Idea production, 97, 164–181
aiming for originality, 169
overcoming obstacles to, 170–172
and quality of ideas, 164–165
recognizing and overcoming difficulties, 228–229
sample issue, 175–177
sample problem, 173–175
as stage in creative process, 106
stimulating imagination, 165–169
vagueness and confusion as obstacles to, 171
withholding judgment during, 170
Ideas
assisting audience in recognizing quality of, 240
careful analysis of, 171
central, in composition, 253
central, in formal speech, 262
contribution of, in productive discussions, 13
creativity and production of, 106

criticism of, 186–187
determining relative importance of, in writing, 253–254
distinction between person and, 69
distinction between validity of, and quality of its expression, 72
expressing, in mathematical symbols or pictures, 5
focusing on your, 186–187
giving credit for paraphrased and quoted, 258
need for sensible order of, 253
presenting, to advantage, 245–247, 254–255
producing, 106
quality and production of, 164–165
refinement difficulties facing originators of, 198–199
refocusing argument on merits of, 214
rejection of, understanding, 240–241
and resistance to change, 56–58
responsibly judging, 14
sorting out and evaluating your, 54
support for, 255–256
suppression of, 165
thobbing, 61–62
If-then analysis, 16, 215
Illegitimate conclusions, 214, 215–216
reversal of conditions in, 216
Images
thinking and, 5
Imaginary-dialogue technique, 243–245
example of, 244–245
Imagination
analogy and, 166–167
combining knowledge and, 98
constructing pro and con arguments, 167–168
constructing relevant scenarios, 168–169
forcing uncommon responses and, 166
free association usage and, 166
looking for unusual combinations, 167
and resistance to change, 57–58
stimulating, 165–169
visualizing solution, 167
Imitation, 52
Immigration law, 268–270
Imperfections
checking, in plan of action, 229–230

common kinds of, 200
eliminating, 200–201
finding, in solutions, 199–200
looking for, 118
pointing out, 243
Implications
developing sensitivity to, 120
of questions and assertions, sensitivity to, 130–131
reading for assumptions and, 17
Impromptu speeches, 261
Improvements
creativity and, 104
to solutions, making, 200–201
Inaccurate remembering, 32
Incoherence, 253
Independence
of creative people, 101
and individuality, 53
Indexes, 147–148
subject, 148
Individuality, 50–54
conformity and, 58
key to, 52
steps to achieve, 52–54
Industriousness, as characteristic of creative people, 101
Inflexibility, 172
Influences, causation and, 36, 39
Information
determining headings for, 147
experiences of people you know, 146
experiments, 143
expert opinion, 142–143
eyewitness testimony, 141–142
maintaining questioning perspective, 151–152
most common sources of, 141–146
need for critical evaluation of Internet, 68
observational study, 144
personal experiences, 145
published reports, 142
recording sources of, to avoid plagiarism, 153–154
research review, 144–145
sorting through, 158
statistics, 143–144
survey, 144
unpublished reports, 142
using Internet for, 148–151
using library for, 146–148
Information base, 5–6
Information sources, 76
Insight, 4
achieving, 119
occurrence of, 172–173

sharing, with audience, 242
uncommon responses and, 166
Intellectual insecurity, 14
Intellectual property, 153
Internet
misinformation on, 67
as research tool, using, 148–151
searching on, 13
Internet Service Provider (ISP), 148
Interpretation
defined, 70
differing between irony and literal, 71–72
distinction between fact and, 70–71
of experiences, 30–31
making clear and reasonable, 247
remaining open to, 13
Interruptions, 11
Interviews
managing, 152–153
preparing questions for, 152
telephone, 153
In the Belly of the Beast (Abbott), 77
Introduction
choosing, for composition, 255
for formal speech, 261
Intuition, role in science of, 10–11
Inventions
for classifying books, 102
concepts as, 104–105
creativity and, 103
of new products or services, 103
and overcoming of imperfection, 118
patents for new, 104
refinement of, 197–198
Investigation
audience familiarity with facts found in, 242
in creative process, 105
defined, 140
importance of, 140–141
IQ, 8, 51
scores and creativity, 98–99
tests and inability to measure resourcefulness, 100
Iraq War, 91–93
Ironic statements, distinction between literal statements and, 71–72
Irrational appeals, 214
Issue analysis, 5
Issues
affirmative action, 178–181
applying creativity to problems and, 102–106

s (continued)
avoiding, 211
border control, 268–270
brain-damaged patient treatment, 47–49
campus speech codes, 249–251
controversial, 121
distinguishing problems from, 128
evaluating arguments on, 210–227
expressing, 105–106, 129–130
expressing judgments on controversial, 70
expression of sample, 134–135
gay marriage, 207–209
guidelines for expressing, 131
human nature, 22–24
ideas to seek to produce answers to, 165
importance of criticism in resolving, 186
initial perspectives on, 127
investigating, 140–141
Iraq War, 91–93
judicial activism, 137–139
keeping open lines of thought when addressing, 132–133
outsourcing U.S. jobs, 108–111
pedophilia, 64–66
pledging allegiance to the flag, 230–231
problems becoming, 130–131
problem *vs.*, 102
racial/ethnic profiling, 225–227
refining positions on, 190–191
refining resolution of, 228–236
religion in schools and public places, 194–196
role of criticism in resolving, 186
sample, for idea production, 175–177
sample, for refining positions on, 191–192
school violence, 123–126
statutory rape, 234–236
taking action on, 192
U.S. foreign aid, 161–163
when problems become, 130–131

Jehovah's Witnesses, 231*n*
Jepson, Rowland, 54, 56
Johnson, Samuel, 10, 37
Jones, Jim, 72
Judgment
of arguments, 68–69
basis of moral, 41–44
creativity and, 97
in critical listening, 81
distinction between matters of taste and matters of, 69–70
expressing, in critical reading, 76–77
expressions of, 34–35
of ideas, 14
impairment of, with drug use, 99
phase in thinking, 7–8, 97
responsible, 14
revising, 213
value, 40–41
withholding, during idea production, 170
Judicial activism, 137–139
Just-war theory, 91

Kekulé, Friedrich August von, 172
Kennedy, John F., 80
Kepler, Johannes, 34
Kevorkian, Jack, 120
King, Martin Luther, Jr., 80
Kinsey Institute, 120
Kneller, George F., 98
Knowing. *See also* Knowledge
accurately, 33
difference between thinking we know and, 29–30
experience as means of, 30–31
and inaccurate remembering, 32
quiz, 28–29
that vs. knowing how, 30*n*
through observation, 31
transmitted by reports, 31–32
ways of, 30–32
Knowledge, 1. *See also* Knowing
combining imagination and, 98
creativity and, 98
developing new, 157
expanding, 13
explosion, 5
factual, 5
obtaining, by experience, 30–31
reports as sources of, 31–32
Koestler, Arthur, 11

Laboratory experiments, 143
Language
distinction between reality and, 72–73
expressing ideas in simple, 257
Laziness, resistance to change and, 56
Learning
beginning of, 52
effects of other's attitudes on, 51–52
Left-brain/right-brain theory, 6–7
Legal information, Web sites for, 151

Legitimate conclusion, 214–215
Lesser evil, 44
Lesson, of dramatic presentation, 82
LeTourneau, Mary Kay, 234
Levy, Jerre, 7
Liberal opinion web sites, 151
Librarians, 148
Libraries, 146–148
Library of Congress system, 102
Lincoln, Abraham, 80
Lippmann, Walter, 59
Listening
active, 14
critical, 79–81
difficulty of, 262
Lister, Joseph, 241
Listmaking, 15
Literal statements, distinction between ironic statements and, 71–72
Loftus, Elizabeth, 33, 142
Logic. *See also* Reasoning
ethymeme in, 216–217
evaluating errors in, 76
formal, 214
meeting tests of, 191
suffering lapses in, 186
Loud, John, 198
Luck, 112
Luther, Martin, 240

Magazine articles, accuracy of, 32
Mailer, Norman, 77
Mander, A. E., 141
Manuscript speeches, 261
The Man with the Golden Helmet, 27
Maslow, Abraham, 59, 99
Material events, causation and, 36–37
May, Rollo, 99
Memorized speeches, 261
Memory, 32–34
influences on, 33
Mental blocks, 3, 11
Mental health, creativity as expression of, 99
Mentally impaired girls, sterilization of, 221–222
Message, in critical listening, 80
Metacognition, 62
Mind
and brain at work, 6–8
judgment phase, 7–8, 97
processing of ideas by, 14
production phase, 7, 97
unconscious, 4
Mine-is-better habit, 54–55
Miranda rule, abolishing, 231–232

Misconceptions, audience, 242
Moderation, appeal to, 214
Monotone, 257–258
Moral, of dramatic presentation, 82
Moral issues
  basis of judgments for, 41–44
  debating, 40–41
  posing dilemmas, 44
  prerequisites for discussing, 26
Mozart, Wolfgang Amadeus, 9
Mursell, James, 6

Nader, Ralph, 119
Nathanson, David, 145
Necessity, causation and, 35–36
Negative-effect arguments, 168
Newbold, Charles, 241
News
  accuracy of stories, 32
  online sources of, 151
Newton, Isaac, 100, 165
Non-material events, causation and, 36–37
North American Free Trade Agreements (NAFTA), 6

Obama, Barack, 80
Objections
  answering significant, 247
  anticipating audience, 243–245
Obligations, 42, 43
Observational study, 144
  conducting, 157
Observations
  connections between past experience and, 145
  formal, 144
  and inaccurate remembering, 32
  obtaining knowledge by, 31
  re-creating, for audience, 247
  as technique for regaining curiosity, 116–117
Opinion(s), 1, 34–35
  of audience, 241
  cause and effect and, 35–39
  covering expressions of taste and judgment, 34–35
  judging, by evidence, 69–70
  Web sites for informed, 149, 151
Opportunities
  in controversies, recognizing, 121
  luck, as sensing of, 112
Order of importance, 255
Organization
  in composition, 253
  of material for formal speeches, 261–262

Originality
  achieving, in thinking, 169
  learning, 8
Orwell, George, 257
Outline, of formal speech, 263
Outsourcing, 108–111
Overgeneralizations, 59
  examples of, 212
Oversimplification, 213
  avoiding, 39
Oxford English Dictionary, 64

Paraphrasing, 154–157, 258
  constructing own ideas to blend with, 157
  converting authors' words to your own, 155–157
  deciding whether to quote or paraphrase, 155
Pasteur, Louis, 119, 141
Pedophilia, 64–66
Perceptions, influences on, 31
Periodicals, nontechnical, 147
Person, distinction between idea and, 69
Personal agendas, 13
Personal experiences, 145
Perspectives
  of audience, 242
  avoiding narrowness of, 127
  broadening, 50–66
  and controversial issues, 120–121
  ethical, 41–44
  maintaining flexibility of, 131–132
  maintaining questioning, 152
  narrow, 50
  seeing problems from many, 7
  truth and, 27–28
Persuasion, 68–69
  answering significant objections, 247
  and anticipating audience reaction, 243–245
  attitudes negatively affecting, 245
  of audience, 245–246
  beginning with familiar, 246
  emphasizing evidence for, 247
  in formal speaking, 262
  idea rejection and, 240–241
  importance of timing to, 247–248
  knowledge of audience and, 241–243
  presenting ideas to advantage, 245–247
Persuasive communication
  and need for critical evaluation, 68–69

  selecting appropriate tone for, 246–247
Peterson, Carl, 32
Pfister, Lester, 101
Places, conducive for thinking, 9–10
Plagiarism
  avoiding, 153–157
  defined, 153
Playfulness, 100, 166
Pledging allegiance, to flag, 230–231
Plumb, J. H., 31, 104–105
Point of view. *See also* Viewpoint
  anticipating differing, 13
Political opinion web sites, 149, 151
Politics, critical listening and, 80
Popular culture
  prominent models for discussion in, 12
  as shaper of attitudes, values, and habits, 53
Population, 144
Porter, Katherine Anne, 60
Positive-effect arguments, 168
Preconceptions, setting aside in critical listening, 80
Prejudgment, 74
Prejudice, 74
  creative people and, 97
  stereotyping and, 59–60
Premises
  expressed, 217
  hidden, 216–217
  reasoning linking conclusions and, 219
  relationship between conclusion and, 214–216
"Present understanding," 28
Probability, of cause, 39
Problems. *See also* Controversies
  applying creativity to, 105–106
  applying creativity to issues and 102-105
  becoming issues, 130–131
  distinguishing issues from, 128
  expressing, 128–129
  expression of sample, 133–134
  guidelines for expressing, 131
  ideas to seek to produce answers to, 165
  initial perspectives on, 127
  investigating, 140–141
  issue *vs.*, 102
  keeping open lines of thought when addressing, 132–133
  refining solutions to, 189, 197–209
  sample, for idea production, 173–175

tems (continued)
sample, for refining solutions to, 189–190
when issues become, 130–131
Problem solving
devising or modifying process or system, 102–103
differences between good and poor, 12
discussion and, 12–14
effect of negative assessments on, 50–52
feelings and, 10–11
finding new uses for existing things, 103–104
frustration and, 11–12
inventing new product or service, 103
inventing or redefining concepts, 104–105
making improvements, 104, 201
refining solutions, 197–209
role of criticism in, 185–186
sample one, 202–203
sample two, 203–204
taking a novel approach, 102
thinking proficiency and, 5–6
Process
devising or modifying, 102–103
improving new or revised, 201
Product
improving new or revised, 201
inventing new, 103
Production phase, of mind, 7, 97
Proof, evidence as, 69–70
Proofreading, 257
Proust, Marcel, 10
Psychological Abstracts, 98
Psychology
cognitive, 7
experimental, 33
Publications, specialized and technical, 147–148
Public places, religion on, 194–196
Published reports, 142

Quality management, advent of, 5
Questions
to answer when refining solutions, 199
to be answered by skimming, 73
before deciding on action, 229
effective forms for expressing issues as, 129–130
effective forms for expressing problems as, 128–129

evaluative, in critical reading, 75–76
informed critics might raise, 78–79
preparing interview, 152
for refining solutions to problems, 127
sensitivity to implications of, 130–131
survey, 144
that analyze, 130
Quotations, 154–157
avoiding overuse of, 258
in compositions, 255
constructing own ideas to blend with, 157
deciding whether to quote or paraphrase, 155
as evidence, 70
in formal speaking, 262
Web sites for, 151

Racial/ethnic profiling, 225–227
Rationalizing, 55
reasoning *vs.,* 55
Readable style, developing, 257–258
Reading
critical. *See* Critical reading
for implications and assumptions, 17–18
steps to follow when, 73–77
Reality
distinction between language and, 72–73
imprecise reflections of, 29, 31
Reasoning. *See also* Logic
appeals as substitute for careful, 214
and critical evaluation, 68
linking conclusions to premises in argument, 219
problem solving and, 12
rationalizing *vs.,* 55
showing partiality in, 213
Reference works, 147–148
Web sites for, 151
Refinement
difficulties faced during process of, 198–199
of issues, 210
of resolution of issue, 228–236
of solutions to problems, 197–209
three steps in, 198–201
Reflection, 74
Religion, in schools and public places, 194–196
Rembrandt, 27
Remembering, 32–34

Repetition, judicious use of, 254
Reports
published, 142
as sources of knowledge, 31–32
unpublished, 142
Representative sample, 144
Rereading, 75
Research
avoiding plagiarism when conducting, 153–157
capability, improvements in, 5–6
conducting, 157
on creativity, 98
Internet, 148–151
library, 146–148
observational study, 157
review, 144–145
sources of information for, 141–146
survey, 157
on thinking, 8
Research record, 154
Resistance to change, 56–58
Resourcefulness, as characteristic of creative people, 100–101
Revision
of arguments, 219
of compositions, 256
Right-to-die issue, 47–49
Rogers, Carl, 73, 99
Romanticism, 22
Rosenthal, Peggy, 73
Rothwax, Harold J., 231
Rousseau, Jean Jacques, 22

Sample, representative, 144
Satire, 71
Scenarios, constructing relevant, 168–169
Scheffler, Israel, 27
Schiavo, Terri, 47–49
Schiller, Friedrich von, 10
Schools
religion in, 194–196
violence in, 123–126
Schopenhauer, Arthur, 1
Scientific American, 100
Scientific study, 76
Scott, Walter Dill, 82
Search engines, 149, 151
Seech, Franz, 198
Seldes, George, 32
Self, varied meanings of, 72–73
Self-deception, 60–61
Self-image, 55
Sense of self, 73
Sentences, putting variety into, 257–258

Service
  improving new or revised, 201
  inventing new, 103
Seward, William H., 241
Shakespeare, William, 27
Shaw, George Bernard, 101, 217
Sholes, Christopher, 199
Shyness, 120
Signal words, 216, 262
Simmons, Thomas, 32
Skimming, 73–74
Smulion, Andy, 175
Society, exposure to, 53
Solutions
  achieving creative, 97–98
  comparing, with competing
    ones, 200
  considering changes and
    effects of, 200
  finding imperfections and
    complications in, 199–200,
    203, 204
  flawed, 201
  gaining audience appreciation
    for soundness of, 242–243
  insight and, 172–173
  making improvements in,
    200–201
  refining, to problems, 189,
    197–209
  using questions to produce
    creative, 128–130
  visualizing, 167
  working out details of,
    198–199, 202, 203–204
Soulé, Samuel, 199
Speaking, formal. *See* Formal
  speeches
Speech mannerisms, avoiding
  distracting, 13–14
Spencer, Herbert, 165
Sperry, Roger W., 7
Split-brain research, 6–7
Statements
  ambiguous, 16
  analysis of, 17
  conclusions of, 16
  distinction between literal and
    ironic, 71–72
Statistical graphics, 81
Statistics, 143–144
  as evidence, 70
Statutory rape, 234–236
Steele, Shelby, 156–157
Stereotypes, 59–60
  most common, 59
Stereotyping, 59–60. *See also*
  Prejudice
Style, developing readable writing,
  257–258

Subject
  determining headings of, 148
  indexes, 147–148
  learning fundamentals of,
    before interview, 152
Suicide, 120
Summarizing
  in critical reading, 75
  main points in formal speech,
    262
Supreme Court, U.S., 194
Surveys, 144
  conducting, 157
Systems
  devising or modifying,
    102–103
  improving new or revised, 201

Taste
  distinction between matters
    of judgment and matters of,
    69–70
  expressions of, 34
Tate, Marsha Ann, 149
Tavris, Carol, 152
Television
  commercials, 82
  parents protesting programs
    on, 220
Testimony
  conflicting, 77
  eyewitness, 33, 141–142
Theories, 28
Thinker's block, 170–171, 173
Thinking
  acknowledging influences that
    have shaped, 53–54
  careful, making a difference
    with, 26
  concentration and, 11
  conditions for, 10
  control and, 4
  creative, 6, 7, 98. *See also*
    Creative thinking
  critical, 6, 7–8, 98. *See also*
    Critical thinking
  defined, 4–5
  developing, 3–24
  effect of face saving on, 56
  efficient and inefficient, 11
  either/or, 211
  erroneous, 27–28
  exercises and response samples,
    17–18
  expressed in words, 237
  flexible, 131–132
  frustration and, 11–12
  good, as habit, 8
  habits that hinder, 54–61
  importance of, 5–6

issue for extended analysis,
  21–24
mental activities involved in, 4
places for, 9–10
process, 1, 97–111
strategies, preliminary, 14–17
thinking about your, 62
time consideration related to, 9
using analogy in, 165, 166–167
Thinking skill/proficiency, 3
  foundation for, 25–30
  phases in, 7–8
  problem solving and, 5–6
Thobbing, 61–62
Thought(s)
  discovering and clarifying, 15
  fringe, 169
  keeping open lines of, 132–133
  proper relationship of feelings
    and, 10–11
  stimulating, 165
Three glasses problem, 18
  solution, 271
Time
  considerations for interviews,
    152, 153
  work habits and, 9
Timing, importance of, 247–248
Tone
  inappropriate, 246
  most appropriate, 246–247
Toothbrush, invention of, 198
Torrance, E. Paul, 8
Tradition
  appeal to, 214
  excessive regard for, 56–57
  resistance to change and, 56–57
Truth, 1
  defined, 27
  difference between belief and,
    27–28
  ego and search for, 55
  errors affecting, 210–214, 219
Tufte, Edward, 81
Tulane University Law School, 102
Typewriter, invention of, 198–199

Unconscious mind, 4
Underlining, 74
United States foreign aid, 161–163
Unity
  in effective writing, 253
  in formal speech, 261
Unpublished reports, 142

Vagueness
  of argument, 77
  as obstacle to idea production,
    171
  of terms, 75

Validity
  errors affecting, 214–216, 219
  logical principles governing,
    214
Value judgments, 40–41
Values, 54
Vases and face problem, 132
  solution, 272
Venice (Italy), 102
Viewing, critical, 81–82
Viewpoint. *See also* Point of view
  evidence for, 247
Violence, school, 123–126
Viruses, locating fake, 149
Visual aids, 18, 262
Visual communication, 81
Visualization, of solutions, 167
Visual rhetoric, 81

Wallas, Graham, 169
Wallenberg, Raoul, 40
Ward, Henshaw, 61
Watson, John, 82
Web. *See* Internet
Web sites, 149
  evaluating quality of, 149
  for finding hoaxes and viruses,
    149

Google, 149, 150
  for health information, 151
  for information on search
    engines, 151
  for informed opinion, 149,
    151
  for legal information, 151
  for news, 151
  for quotations, 151
  for reference material, 151
Weigel, George, 91
Wells, H. G., 28
Wells, Horace, 241
White Guilt (Steele), 156
Whitehead, Alfred North, 98,
    164–165
Will, George, 36
Wilson, James Q., 70
Witch of Agnesi, 241
Words
  avoiding unnecessarily big, 257
  echo, 254
  expression of thinking in, 237
  key, 254
  lack of permanence in spoken,
    261
  signal, 216, 262
  thinking and, 5

Wright brothers, 100
Writing
  developing readable style of,
    257–258
  to discover and clarify
    thoughts, 15
  effective, characteristics of,
    253–254
  freewriting, 15
  persuasive, 68–69
  removing monotony from,
    257–258
  sample, 259–260
  step-by-step approach to,
    254–257
  thinking and, 15

Young girl/old woman problem,
    132
  solution, 271–272

Zimbardo, Philip, 143